DATE DUE

4-22-08

Revolution and Ideology

Revolution and Ideology

Images of the Mexican Revolution
in the United States

John A. Britton

THE UNIVERSITY PRESS OF KENTUCKY

Copyright © 1995 by The University Press of Kentucky

Scholarly publisher for the Commonwealth,
serving Bellarmine College, Berea College, Centre
College of Kentucky, Eastern Kentucky University,
The Filson Club, Georgetown College, Kentucky
Historical Society, Kentucky State University,
Morehead State University, Murray State University,
Northern Kentucky University, Transylvania University,
University of Kentucky, University of Louisville,
and Western Kentucky University

Editorial and Sales Offices: Lexington, Kentucky 40508-4008

Library of Congress Cataloging-in-Publication Data

Britton, John A.
  Revolution and ideology : images of the Mexican Revolution in the
  United States / John A. Britton.
    p.   cm.
  Includes bibliographical references and index.
  ISBN 0-8131-1896-4 (alk. paper)
    1. Mexico—History—Revolution, 1910–1920—Foreign public
  opinion, American—History. 2. Mexico—Politics and
  government—1910–1946—Foreign public opinion, American—
  History. 3. Public opinion—United States—History. 4. Ideology—
  Political aspects—United States. I. Title.
F1234.B855 1995
972.08' 16—dc20   94-46148

This book is printed on acid-free recycled paper meeting
the requirements of the American National Standard
for Permanence of Paper for Printed Library Materials.

Contents

Illustrations follow page 176

Acknowledgments

Researching and writing this book took more than fifteen years (with some interruptions) and owes a great deal to individuals who provided encouragement and stimulation at crucial times. Those who read portions of the manuscript and made valuable commentary include Don Mabry, Mark Gilderhus, Tom Leonard, Helen Delpar, Ken Clements, William O. Walker III, and Richard Chapman. Helpful insights and sage advice through interviews, letters, and informal conversations came from Woodrow Borah, Ted Cart, Susannah Glusker, Richard Greenleaf, Charles Hale, Alicia Hernández Chávez, G. Wayne King, Enrique Krauze, Lester Langley, Townsend Ludington, Eugenia Meyer, Don Olliff, Fred Pike, Richard Salisbury, Josefina Vazquez, Ella Wolfe, Lee Woodward, and Heidi Zogbaum.

Financial support for necessary travel to research collections was provided by the American Philosophical Society, Francis Marion University Foundation, Francis Marion University Faculty Research Committee, Mellon Library Research Grant at Tulane University, National Endowment for the Humanities Travel to Collections Grants to the University of California at Berkeley and the Hoover Institution, and the Southern Regional Education Board.

Members of the James Rogers Library reference staff have been helpful in obtaining interlibrary loans and answering a wide assortment of questions over the years. My gratitude goes to Neal Martin (now director of the Coker College Library), John Summer, Suzanne Singleton, Roger Hux, and Yvette Pierce. Students in History 340 at Francis

Marion responded to my incorporation of large parts of my research into their course work with questions and comments that pulled me back from the tangential and toward the need to identify and explore the main themes in modern Mexican history.

The 1989 appointment of Richard Chapman as head of the History Department at Francis Marion University was a turning point. I am grateful for his insistence that scholarly activity should be a legitimate part of the life of the university—a view not widely accepted at that time. His support in overcoming institutional barriers and bureaucratic infighting was crucial to the completion of this project.

Finally, I relied heavily on my family for support. My wife, Kathy, and our children, Jeannie, Dan, and Maria, were very patient with my work habits and my occasional absences. Their tolerance of this project and their instinctive and humorous ridicule of the world of bureaucracy helped me to see it through to completion.

Introduction

Revolution remains a subject of prime importance in the post–Cold War era. Although Communism in general and Marxist-Leninist theory in particular have lost much of their credibility, the continuation of massive social and economic problems provides an environment in which political unrest and social revolution refuse to disappear. Under these conditions, the Mexican revolution of the 1910–40 period has a new significance because it was one of the last major revolutions before the onset of the Cold War and worldwide fascination with the Marxist-Leninist formula for revolution. Although Mexico had a small but active Communist organization after 1918, the revolution lay just on the edge of the reach of the Comintern and other influences emanating from the Soviet Union. In short, Mexico produced a large-scale revolution in which Marxist-Leninist theory and praxis amounted to only one of the many radical and reformist influences that intermingled in a complex and often contradictory movement. The commentary of U.S. observers on the Mexican revolution—largely free from Cold War–style preoccupations with international Communism—constitutes a body of information and opinion concerning a revolutionary movement that, although peculiar to Mexico in these years, has relevance to an understanding of other non-Communist revolutionary movements.

As a conceptual framework to accommodate these circumstances, this book employs a definition of revolution similar to that of Gordon S. Wood in his study of the radical nature of the American Revolution (with allowances for differences in historical context and

social background). Wood argues that the political-military conflicts of
the Revolutionary War were less important than the social transforma-
tions that unfolded in the decades before and, especially, after the war.[1]
Likewise, the changes that took place in Mexico occurred not only in the
violent years from 1910 to 1920 but over the next two decades in frequent outbursts of popular discontent and spontaneous social change
and in various efforts to make fundamental alterations in the nation's
polity and economy. It was in this context and not the global polemics of
the Cold War that Mexico's Communists played their role in the revolution.[2]

Ideology is a central part of this study primarily because most of
the observers who expressed judgments about the Mexican revolution
couched them in ideological terms. The majority of these observers
were not political theorists and did not organize their thoughts in a
systematic way, but they did make use of the existing "symbols, values,
and beliefs"[3] of their time to explain their perceptions. Those who wrote
about Mexico over an extended period generally followed a pattern of
response and rumination that placed them consistently in one of the
seven ideological categories explained in Chapter 1. This classification
scheme may seem an artificial construct imposed upon reality, but a
close examination of the writing of these observers confirms that such a
framework is necessary to explain the patterns of commentary that
emerged with fairly obvious consistency. The ideological categories are
the products of an inductive analysis based upon the publications (and,
in a few cases, speeches) of these individuals, followed by a sorting
process whereby I placed these evaluations in coherent groupings. I
believe that to minimize or ignore these patterns would be a serious
omission in a study primarily concerned with numerous efforts to
evaluate the Mexican revolution for an English-language readership
that was familiar with the ideologies of the first half of the twentieth
century.

Another reason for the emphasis on ideology is the close connection between revolutionary movements and ideological statements.
Revolutions seem to stimulate ideological responses because these massive upheavals often bring to the forefront of public discourse issues
such as the control of political power, the role of the nation-state, the
redistribution of property, and the relative condition of various social
and ethnic groups. When a nation is debating the nature of its polity,
economy, and society, those who observe and comment on this debate
are likely to employ ideological formulations to explain their version of
these issues.

And now for two brief caveats on the ideological analysis used
here. First, this book attempts to avoid excessively rigid boundaries

between ideological categories in order to allow for those individuals whose Mexican experiences led them to question their own original positions, and for those occasional ideological wanderers who moved from one set of beliefs to another. Second, the seven categories came out of discussions of the Mexican revolution by writers from the United States (and to a lesser extent by Britons and other Europeans who wrote for an audience in the United States) from the 1910s through the 1950s. They may or may not be appropriate for the analysis of responses to other revolutions and are used here within their historically specific circumstances; indeed, changed circumstances during World War II and the early years of the Cold War led to some changes in these ideological categories, as explained in Chapter 13.

Within its topical emphases on ideology and revolution, this book uses a chronological organization. For readers unfamiliar with Mexican history, a brief description of the layout of the book can serve as a rudimentary introduction. Following Chapter 1, which sets up the context of events, Chapter 2 covers the period from 1910 to 1920, in which political disorder, military conflict, and endemic violence dominated Mexico. The effort of a few foreign observers to find the ideological meaning beyond the chaos of the revolution is the chapter's central theme.

Chapters 3–6 deal with the presidencies of Alvaro Obregón (1920–24) and Plutarco Elías Calles (1924–28), during which violence gave way to cultural and political activism as the government established order to a large extent on the promise of basic reforms in the economy and society. Foreign observers began to probe the Mexican economy and society to determine how the peasants and workers lived, what they expected from the government, and what the government was actually doing to implement its commitments in land reform, labor organization, and public education. These four chapters emphasize that the Mexican revolution, after an initially enthusiastic response from most leftist observers, began to stimulate the disagreements that in part led me to develop the ideological categories I use here.

The period 1928 to 1934 is covered in Chapters 7 and 8. Mexico appeared to be moving away from its revolutionary goals and toward a right-wing dictatorship under the control of ex-President Calles. Many observers who had praised—or at least expressed sympathy for—the government's work in the early and middle 1920s became critics of these dictatorial tendencies.

Chapters 9–12 discuss the climax of the revolution during the presidency of Lázaro Cárdenas (1934–40), who, more than any other revolutionary head of state, seemed to respond to the needs of the peasants and workers. Most leftist commentators found much to praise in the Cárdenas administration, which approximated and sometimes went beyond the leftist tendencies in Franklin D. Roosevelt's New Deal of the same period. As might be expected, conservative writers disagreed quite strongly, and, somewhat unexpectedly, a small handful of leftists expressed concerns about the growth of a strong central government under Cárdenas.

Chapters 13 and 14 cover the years from 1940 to 1960 when Mexico turned away from revolutionary ideals and policies and toward the middle of the ideological spectrum. World War II and the Cold War brought a similar ideological shift in the United States. These parallel changes created a setting for retrospective reappraisals of the Mexican history from 1910 to 1940. Commentators who looked back over those years from the perspective of the 1940s and 1950s often found specific changes to have been less radical and the movement in general less revolutionary than had earlier observers. Yet this revolution and the discussions it stimulated among writers and policymakers in the United States provide a useful legacy for the post-Cold War era.

1

Revolution in Context

In 1916 Pancho Villa, a hero of the early Mexican revolution but a controversial and enigmatic figure during the Carranza and Obregón presidencies, came to symbolize mindless violence and rapacious banditry for many in the United States. In the predawn darkness of March 9, a detachment of 485 Villistas crossed the United States border and descended on the small, isolated town of Columbus on the southern edge of New Mexico. Within two hours the Villistas killed eighteen U.S. citizens and left much of the town a burned-out shambles. Although this incident may have been connected to Villa's effort to survive in Mexico's confused revolutionary struggle, the immediate press reaction in the United States attributed no such rational motive to its chief perpetrator. To the nation's political leaders and the general public, the Columbus raid offered evidence only of the barbarity of Mexican politics. The civil strife that had begun with the overthrow of Porfirio Díaz in 1911 had spilled across the border. President Woodrow Wilson claimed that the revolution was out of control and that only U.S. military intervention could stabilize Mexico.[1]

Ten months later a thirty-two-year-old leftist army officer, Franciso J. Múgica, presided over the writing of Article 27 of what was soon to become Mexico's new constitution. Radical in theory but—to Múgica's dissatisfaction—with no provisions for immediate application, Article 27 established the principles that the national government could regulate and even nationalize private property and that foreign owners of Mexican resources were subject to this and other constitutional provisions. Múgica realized that the actual enforcement of Article 27 depended on the will and the ideology of subsequent Mexican presidents, but U.S. businessmen and diplomats saw the new law as a direct threat to their operations in Mexico, especially the recent investment of roughly $500 million in petroleum.[2]

The Columbus raid and Article 27 both disturbed observers in the United States, but in different ways. Pancho Villa was in the American mind the archetypal murderous bandit, devoid of respect for law and human life. Múgica and Article 27, however, posed a challenge to the sanctity of private property and the U.S. presence in the Mexican economy. Villa's dramatic threat inspired an intense, immediate fear along the border, but Article 27—though it contained no danger to American lives—aroused antagonisms on Wall Street and Pennsylvania Avenue that were to continue for a generation. This law established the nation-state as the prime actor in the economy and created the possibility that government would redistribute wealth on a large scale. The United States Army could respond to Villa, but projections of Article 27 suggested the emergence of a socioeconomic system beyond the bounds of private enterprise capitalism and even reform-minded progressivism.

The main purpose of this book is to analyze the responses of observers from the United States to events and trends in Mexico in the half-century from 1910 to 1960. Many of the individuals who wrote about Mexico in these years would qualify as intellectuals by most definitions of that term, but the scope of this investigation is not limited to them. Rather than restricting my focus to a handful of well-known pundits, political commentators, and academics, I include a wide range of journalists, creative writers, politicians, businessmen, ministers, and diplomats.[3] The justification for this broad approach is that the discussion of Mexico in the United States included important statements from individuals in all these groups. For example, in various forums and coalitions, leftist journalists joined an odd assortment of Protestant ministers and bohemian writers to argue against the conservative diplomats, businessmen, and politicians who favored U.S. intervention in Mexico in 1919, again in the mid-1920s, and again in the late 1930s. In 1919 the debate pitted oil entrepreneur Edward Doheny and New Mexico's Senator Albert Fall against Protestant minister Samuel Guy Inman. To exclude any one group would result in a superficial and incomplete analysis of the debate.

Such diverse sources contained contradictions, of course. After 1920, Mexico experienced an increase in tourism from the north and, at the same time, drew frequent and hostile accusations of dangerous radicalism from U.S. businessmen and clerics. Hollywood films ranged from caricatures of vicious bandits to the respectful portrayal of the idealistic, tenacious Benito Juárez. The mass circulation press also featured variety and inconsistency. Newspaper publisher William Randolph Hearst demanded intervention in 1927; eleven years later *Time* magazine lauded left-wing president Lázaro Cárdenas with a flattering cover story. Serious-minded commentators often decried this media melange as unreliable and unfit for public consumption, but many realized that in order to reach the general public they had to work within this influential, constantly shifting, and frequently jumbled set of images.

Students of Mexican affairs often encountered another problem: the persistent prejudice in the United States against Mexico and Mexicans. Originating in the nineteenth century during the period of Anglo-Protestant expansion and Mexican-Catholic retreat in the Southwest, the notion that Mexicans were lazy, intemperate, untrustworthy, and violent took hold in many sectors of U.S. society. Even during the economic growth of the Díaz years, many rationalized their bias against the common people of Mexico by the claim that Don Porfirio and his enlightened elite were the real reasons for prosperity. Their assumption that the unstable mestizos could not participate in progress was belied by the fact that Díaz himself was a mestizo from provincial Oaxaca; nevertheless, the prejudices held firm. Numerous observers fell back on them to explain the disorder and, from their perspective, the irresponsible egalitarian rhetoric that coincided with the outbreak of the revolution.[4]

An International Context

The stream of information and images from Mexico to the United States constitutes an important but generally neglected chapter in what scholars have recently begun to call international history. This approach to the study of relationships among peoples and nations enlarges upon the traditional methods of diplomatic history (which concentrates on intergovernmental relationships usually handled by diplomats) to encompass a wide range of activities and actors: merchants and bankers in the field of business; missionaries, educators, and artists in cultural relations; journalists, academics, and other observers in the areas of communications. I explore these areas with particular emphasis on the flow of messages from Mexico to the United States.

For more than three decades after 1910, several waves of travelers moved across the border to see and to write about the revolution. These trips constituted exciting and often overly romanticized experiences for U.S. writers who used Mexico as a vehicle for expository prose on the drama of internecine combat in the desert, heated political debate in the halls of government, and, at the other extreme, the restoration of the placid and seemingly incorruptible life of a peasant community brutalized by the Díaz dictatorship. In short, Mexico combined tropical exoticism with revolutionary excitement, a mixture that periodically captured the attention of many readers in the United States.

At a deeper level, the response of U.S. observers to the revolution was a central component of a major event in international history: a social revolution in a partially developed nation in the immediate neighborhood of the world's emerging free enterprise power. Visitors to Mexico experienced what no other group of foreign commentators could match: they witnessed the unfolding of a non-Communist social revolution in a country that, even though it was outside the developed Euro-American world, nevertheless shared a 2,000-mile border with the United States. Foreign to the culture and language of the United States, Mexico also had political and economic systems that offered considerable contrasts with those of its neighbor to the north. Yet Mexico had direct ties to the economies of the United States and western Europe through its extractive industries—mining, oil, agriculture—and the investments associated with them. Because of these economic connections and the common border, events in the Mexican revolution often carried a sense of urgency and even alarm for many readers in the United States.

In the relationship between the United States and Mexico, there was a decided power advantage for the farmer. During more than three decades after 1910, the United States exercised an informal imperialism, using military intervention, threats of military intervention, diplomatic pressure, and economic clout to influence and at times to manipulate events in Mexico. Those at the centers of power generally accepted the ethnic prejudices and antirevolutionary assumptions that Michael Hunt has found to be typical of the United States during these years. But as Michael Doyle's study of imperialism suggests, events and trends in the periphery can often have a significant impact on the imperial relationship, and in this case, U.S. observers in Mexico furnished information that often contradicted the ideas of those who held power in Washington and on Wall Street. This information contained messages at variance with what government and business policymakers wanted in the public media.[5]

Emily Rosenberg has called international history "a vast empty plain with undetermined borders and topography that must be sketched by the historian-guide."[6] This study attempts to track the migration of observers from the United States to Mexico and to analyze the returning flow into the U.S. media of their observations on the revolution. Focusing on the interaction of Mexican and United States history within fairly specific boundaries, it concentrates on those persistent observers who wrote for (and in some cases spoke to) audiences north of the border over a period of several years. These observers played important roles in the histories of both nations. They had an impact on Mexican history in that many of them worked with Mexican political leaders and intellectuals, sometimes as professionals (journalists and academics) and sometimes advisers (formal and informal). A few were objects of Mexican government manipulation intended to create a favorable image of Mexico in the U.S. media.

Their larger impact, however, was in the realms of academic discourse, journalistic reportage, political debate, and popular culture. Their evaluations were the main sources of images and information about the Mexican revolution within the communication system of the United States. Yet their messages were often heavily Mexican in content, generally espousing the notion that Mexico and its revolution deserved serious consideration alongside other large-scale social and political phenomena of the Americas, Europe, and Asia. As Helen Delpar has demonstrated, in the 1920s and 1930s Mexico became one of the first non-European nations to gain significant cultural influence in the United States. In the areas of art, anthropology, archaeology, education, and motion pictures and through the work of such varied individuals as Diego Rivera, Manuel Gamio, José Vasconcelos, and Dolores del Rio, Mexico achieved a new level of popular interest and critical respect in the United States.[7]

This work focuses on the movement of images and information through the often shifting drainage basin of various media: news magazines, newspapers, journals of opinion, academic periodicals, and both commercial and scholarly books. Obviously, this flow had many sources and was uneven, changing from one period to another and often reflecting transient concerns with dramatic action (such as the Veracruz intervention of 1914) and virtually disappearing at times (as happened during World War II and the onset of the Cold War). The book attempts, however, to detect deeper currents with long-term implications that were more likely to reflect major changes in the landscape.

Revolution Defined

The subject of revolution had an unfamiliarity in 1910 that is easy to overlook in light of events of the more recent past. The victory of the Sandinistas in Nicaragua in 1979, the rise of Fidel Castro in Cuba two decades earlier, and other upheavals in the years between made revolution a subject of great interest, as the extensive and varied literature on this topic since 1959 indicates.

The conventional definition of the term "revolution" as simply the ouster of one political faction by another does not contain much explanatory value here. The term "social revolution" is more appropriate, because it better conveys the complexity of the subject explored. "Social revolution" can be defined as a broadly based uprising of people from the lower and middle strata of society against a government that is in the hands of a privileged elite. After the government collapses under pressure from the discontented, the revolutionary state that arises draws its leadership from various (often competing) factions representing the interests of some combination of peasants, workers, and the middle class, or perhaps a self-proclaimed leftist faction from the military or the old oligarchy. The state then proceeds to project itself as the primary actor on the revolutionary stage and the progenitor of a drastic socioeconomic restructuring of the nation. In reality, many of the projected goals do not materialize, and the state often has to struggle to maintain a life of its own, sometimes as social engineer, economic planner, or political mobilizer. In other cases, the state, or more precisely, those in command of it may become responsive to the perceived demands of powerful interest groups—especially, aroused labor and peasant organizations.

My main focus is on the consequences of the revolution rather than causes or origins. Many general works such as Crane Brinton's *Anatomy of Revolution* and Barrington Moore's *Injustice: The Social Origins of Obedience and Revolt* emphasize etiology, but the recent collapse or decline of revolutionary governments in the Soviet Union, Cuba, and Nicaragua indicate that what happens after civil strife ends deserves closer attention. Alan Knight has argued that the violent upheavals of the 1910s did not commit Mexico to a single, inexorable path; quite to the contrary, the less obvious but equally significant political and organizational struggles for power were also very much a part of the revolution.[8]

The analysts of revolution have pursued a variety of conceptual approaches, but two themes stand out in much of their more recent writing: (1) the emergence of the revolutionary state to a position of national importance if not dominance, and (2) the interaction of the revolutionary state and the partially mobilized lower and middle strata of society. According to Theda Skocpol, John Dunn, Samuel Huntington, and others who have made comparative studies of social revolutions, the rise of the national state is the most prominent outcome of these movements. In Mexico the consolidation of political and military power by Venustiano Carranza from 1914 to 1920 established a central government that was to extend its authority throughout the next three decades.[9] As for the efforts of the Mexican government to carry out programs benefiting peasants, workers, and the middle class, the rhetoric of revolutionary leaders and the Constitution of 1917 aroused the expectations (and fears) of U.S. observers that the state would remake the economy to favor the disadvantaged at the expense of wealthy landowners and large corporations. In general, most Mexican administrations did not fulfill the revolutionary promises, but observers did find some cases in which a particular regime made a genuinely revolutionary effort. In the late 1930s many commentators insisted that President Lázaro Cárdenas had followed such a course.

This mixed record has led some authorities to label the Mexican revolution as a failure because it did not transfer sufficient wealth and power from the prerevolutionary elite to the peasants and workers.[10] That conclusion may seem valid from the perspective of the troubled 1980s and 1990s; however, the commentary of contemporary observers gave the distinct impression of a social revolution in the making, especially in the consolidation of a state committed in principle to radical goals and in practice to sporadic bursts of partially successful redistribution programs. This pattern resembles the models constructed by Skocpol, Dunn, and Huntington and thoughtfully revised in their application to Mexico by Alan Knight and John Hart (although these two historians have followed distinctive lines of thought). In this complex, shifting paradigm a revolution rarely lives up to its early social and economic goals but seldom fails to expand the authority of the state, which seems most likely to thrive when it responds to the demands periodically raised by peasants, workers, and portions of the middle class.[11]

The Mexican revolution clearly did not trigger the international anxiety inspired by Russia under Lenin and Stalin, nor did it equal the extensive internal changes carried out by the Soviet Union. Land reform proceeded piecemeal until Cárdenas took office, and even he did not complete the process. In contrast the Soviet state accomplished an immense and coercive redistribution of property in rural areas. Property generally remained in private hands in Mexico (except for oil and rail nationalizations and some collective farms), but in the Soviet Union the state controlled not only farms but factories, transportation, and most aspects of material and cultural life. Nevertheless, Mexico experienced enough generalized disorder, labor and peasant activism, ideological-political conflict, shifts in political power, redistribution of resources, and state-controlled programs to justify the conclusion that it underwent an uneven, incomplete, and often confused mass upheaval which, despite its ideological and structural shortcomings, qualifies as a social revolution.

American Observers on Unfamiliar Ground

As U.S. observers followed the Mexican revolution's meandering course and attempted to provide commentary and analysis on an unfamiliar subject, their ideologies often gave them guideposts in their explorations. Michael Hunt, dealing with ideology in the context of U.S. foreign policy, chose to emphasize a broad, cultural explanation. He argues that stress on a single set of motives, particularly economic motives, may be useful in some cases, but that the proponents of different schools of thought in the diplomatic arena operate within complex cultural and institutional frameworks that include a variety of factors. Although only a few of the individuals examined here were directly involved in diplomacy, Hunt's approach seems relevant because, like diplomats, these observers left the familiar ground of domestic affairs to evaluate difficult issues in a foreign land and then attempted to explain this complicated, alien environment to an audience at home.[12]

It seems clear that the appearance of the Mexican revolution created difficulties for those who wanted to explain it, whether their audience was made up of popular magazine readers, politicians and the politically engaged, or small circles of academics. Some (sometimes self-appointed) experts on Mexican affairs experienced what cultural anthropologist Clifford Geertz has called "conceptual confusion" resulting from the absence of "usable models" for explaining what went on. Not only did the revolutionaries dislodge the promoter of economic development, Porfirio Díaz; they also questioned assumptions—such as the nature of the rights of private property ownership—that were axiomatic to most U.S. citizens. This examination of responses to the Mexican revolution in the United States therefore draws upon Geertz's suggestive generalization concerning the causes and consequences of such cognitive dissonance of "strain":

> It is a confluence of sociopsychological strain and an absence of cultural resources by means of which to make sense of the strain, each exacerbating the other, that sets the stage for the rise of systematic (political, moral, or economic) ideologies.
>
> And it is, in turn, the attempt of ideologies to render otherwise incomprehensible social situations meaningful, to so construe them as to make it possible, to act purposefully with them, that accounts both for the ideologies highly figurative nature and for the intensity with which, once accepted, they are held.[13]

Geertz writes of culturewide strain, but I am concerned with a more limited phenomenon. Although the Mexican revolution produced heated debate within a small but significant segment of the culture of the United States, it did not in and of itself generate an entirely original, clearly defined ideological system. Rather, it served as a focal point for the intermittent discussion of the previously ignored subject of revolution that drew mainly from existing ideologies. The result was important, however, because in the five decades between the fall of Díaz and the ascension of Castro, the United States became increasingly entangled in similarly troublesome and ambiguous revolutionary situations not only in Latin America but also in Africa, the Middle East, and Asia. In this sense, commentary on Mexico was a kind of pioneering venture for U.S. observers, their first experience with a revolutionary movement outside the more familiar territory of North America and Europe.

The numerous examinations of social revolutions since 1959 offer a sharp contrast with the dearth of writing on this topic in the late nineteenth century and the early years of the twentieth. Despite the influence of Karl Marx and Friedrich Engels among European intellectuals, writers in the United States avoided the subject. *The Readers Guide to Periodical Literature* from 1905 to 1914 lists only nine articles under the heading of revolution. Perhaps the best-known cultural commentator to approach the subject was Brooks Adams. A gloomy, iconoclastic lawyer and social critic who carried the blessing and burden of a great family name, Adams was deeply disappointed by the defeat of his friend, Theodore Roosevelt, in the presidential election of 1912. In the aftermath Adams concentrated his pessimism on the courts, the legislatures, and the business system of the United States and argued that the collusion of politics, law, and wealth would cement the advantages of the rich and exacerbate the frustrations of the poor. The results would be a social revolution caused by the greed and myopia of the political-business elite. This dramatic and incorrect prediction was not a pro-revolutionary tract but rather a warning intended to alert those in power that they should mend their excessive ways in order to avert a massive uprising. Adams had broached a subject that most members of the intelligentsia chose to ignore.[14]

By contrast with the doleful philosopher Adams, popular writers who mentioned the subject of revolution, especially in connection with Latin America, often relied on comedy, ridicule, and disparagement. William Sydney Porter, who wrote under the pen name O. Henry, published perhaps the prototypical fictional account of a revolution in a "banana republic" in *Cabbages and Kings*. In the fictional Caribbean county of Anchuria he showed local politicians plotting nastily against each other, leading corrupt and ragtag armies, and falling easy prey to clever foreign visitors. O. Henry presented with little sympathy the plight of this small country at the mercy of the "game" played by foreign rivals for control of its resources and politics: "Gentleman adventurers throng the waiting rooms of its rulers with proposals for railway concessions. The little opera-bouffe nations play at government and intrigue until someday a big, silent gunboat glides into the offing and warns them not to break their toys."[15]

One of the first twentieth-century U.S. authors to penetrate the surface of this superficial version of revolution was Paxton Hibben, a young diplomat and literary radical who wrote a little-noticed article on the subject in 1913. Hibben realized that revolution in Latin America was the butt of jokes in the United States: officers in "gold-braided coats" commanded barefooted soldiers in a slapstick performance leading to a grotesque climax in which a group of predatory militarists ousted another group of corrupt politicos. Hibben argued that in fact there was very little comedic content in such events—quite to the contrary. Explaining these changes in government in a social context, Hibben insisted that the coups d'état constituted "one kind of true democracy" in that the governing class either responded to the pressure from the discontented general populace or faced an uprising from the depths of society, led, of course, by disaffected members of the elite. He cautioned his readers not to dismiss Latin American revolutions so lightly, but apparently few writers for major journals of opinion or large publishing houses followed his advice.[16]

The Bolshevik Revolution in Russia four years later, however, fired the imaginations of radicals and the fears of conservatives from Boston to San Francisco, and unwillingness to discuss Marx and Engels suddenly gave way to an obsession with the revolutionary trinity of Marx, Engels, and Lenin. Thereafter social revolution of the Marxist-Leninist variety was never far from the center of the North American consciousness. Many U.S. businessmen, diplomats, and politicians almost immediately perceived a loose analogy between the Russian and Mexican revolutions, but oddly, liberals and radicals made little serious effort to assess similarities and differences. To intellectuals, especially along the East Coast, Mexico remained an unimportant backwater. The leftists among them believed that the future was being made in Moscow and that Mexico was simply a tempestuous and irrelevant sideshow.

The reluctance of most U.S. journalists and academics to compare the Mexican revolution with movements in Europe continued into the 1920s and 1930s, even though successive governments in Mexico City after 1917 challenged the status of the private oil and agricultural holdings of U.S. citizens, and even through the conflict between the aggressive secular state and the Catholic Church and the rise of labor and peasant groups created an image of growing radicalism. To experts on revolution, Mexico did not fit the pattern. In Lyford Edward's pioneering 1927 study, *The Natural History of Revolution*, and Crane Brinton's 1938 *Anatomy of Revolution*, Euro-American examples predominated. Edwards would probably have included Mexico in his generalization that "Balkan and South American 'revolutions' are mere outbreaks of lawlessness which leave the institutions of the countries concerned practically unchanged."[17] Brinton limited his comparative analysis to "four relatively well-studied revolutions": the British of the mid-1600s, the American of the late eighteenth century, the French of 1789–1815, and the Russian of 1917.[18]

Nevertheless, other U.S. scholars, journalists, diplomats, and social critics were earnestly engaged in efforts to explain the Mexican revolution, though their commentary evolved separately from studies of social revolution such as those of Edwards and Brinton. In 1933 Frank Tannenbaum's *Peace by Revolution* seemed to provide a benchmark analysis. Tannenbaum built an impressive case for the outbreak and episodic continuation of a major social revolution in Mexico. His chief protagonists were unnamed peasants who took up machetes and rifles when the national authorities refused to respond to their demands. In concepts not very distant from Paxton Hibben's insights two decades earlier, Tannenbaum argued that the main driving force behind the revolution was unrest at the rural grassroots.[19] His emphasis on the primacy of the peasantry and the absence of a controlling eminence such as Lenin or Robespierre suggested a decided contrast with Brinton's discussion of the Russian and French upheavals, but this contrast unfortunately escaped serious students of revolution in the 1920s and 1930s. The significant and sophisticated attempts of Tannenbaum, Ernest Gruening, Eyler Simpson, and several other writers to explain the Mexican social upheaval flowed in their own separate channels, unconnected to the mainstream studies of revolution.

While most U.S. students of revolution focused on Russia from 1917 to the 1950s, a small but growing group of observers continued to probe the meaning of current events in Mexico. The Mexican experience provided exposure to a situation that was to become increasingly common after World War II: a massive uprising in a less developed nation of strategic and economic importance for the United States. Those later revolutions inspired little comedic satire of the O. Henry type. Instead, unkempt peasants, strident labor leaders, and radical proselytizers called for the dawn of a new day in their homelands in language similar to the words of Múgica and Cárdenas. That several writers and diplomats and a few politicians in the United States during the 1920s and 1930s had been able to understand the demands emanating from Mexico and that the U.S. government had even been able to reconcile itself to the implementation of such radical policies as the nationalization of properties owned by U.S. citizens seemed, unfortunately, to mean virtually nothing by the late 1940s. As the menace of Soviet Russia—real or exaggerated—assumed alarming proportions in the American mind, the Truman Doctrine and the commitment to contain Communism made dispassionate discussion of social revolution almost impossible. Projecting the profile of the Cárdenas administration into this period would have brought cries of "Communist conspiracy" and "red foothold in the Americas"—phrases that appeared in U.S. government rationalizations for the overthrow of the Guatemalan government in 1954, ten years after that country set out on a path similar to the one followed by Mexico in the 1920s and 1930s.

The Ideological Context

From an ideological perspective, U.S. commentary on the revolution spread out along a broad spectrum from the far left to the far right, and the commentators were usually strong-willed individuals with deeply-held convictions. They rarely debated their opponents directly in a formal sense, but the cumulative effect of their writing and (in a few cases) speaking left a body of thought that expressed consistently divergent points of view on the nature of the revolution. Hence, the dictates of textual organization require the erection of a consistent framework within which to view their responses. The spectral framework I employ (see the accompanying table) includes three fairly broad categories—leftists, liberal, and conservative—each with subcategories.

Which schools of thought dominated the discussion of the Mexican revolution within the U.S. media? The contest for dominance in this corner of political and ideological debate was a struggle for cultural hegemony on issues that had relevance not only for Mexico and U.S.-Mexican relations but also for later revolutions and the responses to them of American political, intellectual, and business leaders.[20]

Many leftists came to Mexico to witness what they thought would be the sudden emergence of a new socioeconomic system rising out of the ruins of the Porfirian mix of feudalism and capitalism. At the extreme left of the spectrum were the independent leftists, individuals who shared a deep mistrust of large organizations, whether they were political parties, governments, or business corporation. Most earned a modest but adequate living in journalism or academics, usually in positions that gave them the opportunity to express their leftist ideas. These assertive individuals often viewed the world in their own terms, improvising their own ideological refinements from a variety of sources that included anarchism, leftist populism, and Marxism.

To attempt to impose strict ideological unity on this group would be futile, but at least two consistent if controversial themes emerge in their writing. The first, shared with virtually all leftists, was the perceived need for extensive social and economic change to benefit the

Table 1. Ideological Positions and Institutional Affiliations

	Left			Liberal		Business Conservatives	Right
	Independent Leftists	Communists and Fellow Travelers	Socialists	Liberal Statists	Liberal Capitalists		Racists
Socioeconomic recommendations for Mexico	change originating or in harmony with local community	revolutionary activism with Communist Party (CP) as vanguard	large-scale reform of basic structure	state-directed economic and social programs, state regulation of private sector	private sector initiatiave, some governmnet regulation	private sector autonomy with emphasis on foreign investment	tutelage by foreign governments, domination by foreign corporations
Attitude toward central government	suspicion skepticism, at times hostility centralized power	rival of Mexican government	approval of central control of planning and resources	sympathy with national government and institutions	approval of government as coordinator and limited regulator of private sector	skepticism, often opposition to state action in the economy	acceptance of government by Mexican elite, not of Indian-mestizo participation
Institutional affiliation	journalism, academics, or independent writers	CP or affiliated groups, some nonmembers identified with the party	academics, journalism	journalism, academics, government	banking, industry, government, journalism, academics	industry, investments in land and resources	
Representative advocates	Frank Tannenbaum, Carleton Beals	Bertram Wolfe, Joseph Freeman	Eyler Simpson, Nathaniel & Sylvia Weyl	Ernest Gruening, John Dewey, Herbert Croly	Woodrow Wilson, Dwight Morrow, Herbert Priestley	Edward Doheney, William F. Buckley, Sr.	Richard Harding Davis, Jack London

lower classes. This change was to affect all social strata through the transfer of property from wealthy landowners, industrialists, and foreign investors to the poor. The second theme set the independents apart from other leftists. They emphasized the coercive potential of a national government or any large political entity and, simultaneously and interconnectedly, they asserted their confidence in the viability of local communities as authentic representatives of the common people, especially the peasantry. In particular, the social anarchist perspective of Frank Tannenbaum and the left-wing populism of Carleton Beals sharply questioned the role of the nation-state.[21]

Many commentators on the revolution worked or at least wrote for a political or economic institution, an arrangement often reflected in their writing. The Communists were no exception. Although Communist parties on both sides of the border were struggling for their existence during much of this period, U.S. Communists did produce a small but significant body of literature on the revolution, and from 1918 into the early 1930s their main interest in Mexico seemed to be institutional: they devoted most of their energies to building Mexico's fledgling Communist party. Therefore, their view—best exemplified by Bertram Wolfe—offered a partisan, self-serving perspective on the inadequacies of Mexico's government, which they saw in Marxist terms as a falsely revolutionary, essentially bourgeois state. At the same time, Wolfe and his comrades made some perceptive notes on the foibles of Mexican politics and political leaders.

Not far to the right of Wolfe were the fellow travelers who remained close to but on the fringe of the party. Waldo Frank, a well-known literary figure, was a nonconformist party member who seemed to respect its aims but propounded an idiosyncratic ideology expressed through social criticism, philosophical abstraction, and selective Marxism. Like many fellow travelers, Frank strayed far from the Marxist mainline; his analysis of Mexico was usually free of the dogmatism typical of dedicated party members. (Another type of nonconformist, the bohemian, had an even more freewheeling approach that emphasized cultural factors over politics; their role is considered in Chapter 3.) Perhaps the most useful key to understanding the institutional and cultural background of the fellow travelers is that they shared with their orthodox comrades a sense of revulsion regarding the capitalist system but lacked any long-term sense of personal commitment to the party. In Mexico they wrote wide-ranging critiques that were usually more sympathetic to the native radicalism than the harsh criticisms that came from the pens of party members such as Bertram Wolfe.[22]

Immediately to the right of the Communists and the fellow travelers were the socialists. Often admirers if not avid readers of Marx and his interpreters, these individuals, like the fellow travelers, did not commit themselves to party membership. The socialists believed that the creation of a modern, efficient government to carry out a fundamental remaking of the Mexican economy and society was well within the realm of possibility. They advocated a centrally planned economy and outright state control of key resources and industries. This ideology, prominent in Europe and elsewhere in Latin America, had few supporters among U.S. observers in Mexico from 1910 to the early 1930s. In 1936, however, sociologist Eyler Simpson filled this lacuna with his study of agricultural economics, *The Ejido: Mexico's Way Out*, which posited state socialism as a solution to the nation's problems. Simpson was joined by journalists and other academics who seemed to be caught up in the leftward shift in politics and ideas on both sides of the border in the last years of the decade.[23]

To the right of the socialists were the liberals, advocates of moderate change, many of whom rose to prominence in the early twentieth century within the broad boundaries of the progressive movement. Progressivism was at once amorphous and pervasive. It included reform impulses from temperance to antitrust measures and easily overshadowed the dispersed independent leftists, the nascent Communists, and the struggling socialists. Although it declined after World War I, progressivism survived the 1920s to return in many of the policies of the New Deal in the next decade. During the 1920s, individuals such as Herbert Croly and John Dewey kept the vitality of reform alive in their public discussions and writing and, for a while, turned to Mexico as a case study in state-directed social change.

Many of the observers drawn to Mexico were on the left wing of progressivism and, in this book, are termed liberal statists. Ernest Gruening, who was, like Croly, a journalist and political analyst, and Dewey, a philosopher at Columbia University, were typical of this group's institutional affiliations in the print media and higher education. Most liberal statists were located in the urban Northeast, a cultural environment that provided them with opportunities to pursue their inquiries. Unfortunately, their selective exposure to Mexico led them to dwell on abstractions that evolved from Euro-American values more than from authentic Mexican themes.

In most instances, liberal statists agreed with leftists that Mexico's society and economy must undergo a general restructuring, but their proposals advocated a less drastic redistribution of property than did the exhortations of their more radical compatriots. Probably the essential contract was the liberal statist faith in the capacity of the nation-state to devise an efficient bureaucracy that would solve the ills of society and, at the same time, respect the institutions of democracy and private property. To Croly and especially to Dewey, government programs in areas such as education held the keys to unlocking the peasant population's potential for a sweeping but smooth transformation from poverty-plagued, isolated backland settlements to cohesive and productive communities active in national affairs and, eventually, in the modern world of international affairs. In contrast to the liberal statists, the socialists called for more comprehensive state involvement in the economics of land reform and industrialization. The independent leftists disagreed with both; they were too skeptical to accept the central government as the font of social uplift and also rejected the liberal statist assumption that middle-class democracy was the appropriate goal for the Mexican revolution.[24]

To the right of the liberal statists and often at the center of the storms of controversy about Mexico were the liberal capitalists: politicians, diplomats, and bankers who believed that the international system of free trade and the politics of representative government could survive and even prosper through a careful handling of revolutionary nationalism. It may seem strange to use the word "liberal" to describe two distinct ideological positions; however, this vague term has been applied to a wide variety of ideas and policies. Among commentators on Mexico two fairly consistent positions emerged, both involving figures generally regarded as liberals: the previously described Croly-Dewey-Gruening group, and the somewhat more conservative school inspired by Woodrow Wilson and sustained by Thomas Lamont and Cordell Hull. The differences lay in methods more than in goals. Both shared the ideal of a putative middle-class democracy for Mexico, but they saw different ways to reach it. For liberal capitalists the free enterprise economy within the prudent restraints of a regulatory state was the proper avenue; in their view, beneficial social change would flow automatically from this regulated form of capitalism. By contrast, liberal statists upheld the virtues of government-directed reform to the point of treading upon but not uprooting the legal and cultural sanctity of private property.

Liberal capitalists also saw free trade through international law as an appropriate policy for the Mexican government. More intolerant than the liberal statists on matters of law, economics, and politics, the liberal capitalists were also quicker to call for intervention in Mexico's internal affairs to achieve their aims. Direct military interventions were the most obvious methods, but intimidation and manipulation through diplomatic and political devices also had places in their repertoire. Virtually all these methods drew criticism from liberal statists and those further to the left.[25]

Woodrow Wilson exhibited a deep ambivalence between his apparent sympathies with the ultimate purposes of revolution and his rejection of its undisciplined and disruptive nature. Although he did not travel to Mexico, his persistent and influential comments on Mexico necessitate his inclusion in this study. He had an abstract understanding of social revolutions and their commitment to the eradication of injustice. His pedantic lectures (particularly his Mobile speech of 1913), however, revealed a misplaced expectation that the popular uprising would soon adopt republican governmental practices, which would contribute to a resolution of the differences between the two countries. Wilson found it difficult to tolerate the civil strife and radical rhetoric that challenged the Anglo-Saxon priorities of parliamentary procedure and gradual, legalistic change. Nor could he envision international order without free trade.[26]

The 1920s saw a slight modification of the liberal capitalist approach in the statements of banker Thomas Lamont, journalist Walter Lippmann, banker-turned-politician Dwight Morrow, and other members and admirers of the Council on Foreign Relations. They were less prone than Wilson to favor military interventions but no less committed to aggressively expansionist economic policies. Diplomatic historian Robert Schulzinger's depiction of the ideas of the editorial board of *Foreign Affairs*, the council's prestigious publication, also applies to the liberal capitalist attitude toward Mexico: "While the editors saw themselves as the models of impartiality, no reader could be fooled into thinking that the journal was anything other than a plea for a forward United States foreign policy, interested in exploiting the world's natural resources and putting affairs in Washington in the hands of serene, dispassionate experts who, unlike the public at large, knew what they were doing." In short, they "advocated a ferocious form of Wilson's missionary diplomacy."[27]

Much like their colleagues on the Council on Foreign Relations; Lamont, Lippmann, and Morrow operated within the institutional hierarchies of corporate boardrooms and political conferences. In their actions, public statements, and published writing, they emphasized the importance of peaceful solutions arrived at through persuasion and, if necessary, intimidation.[28] In a sense, Lamont, Morrow, and their Mexican collaborators exhibited an international version of what Robert Wiebe has termed bureaucratic thought. They were confident that informed men in positions of power could resolve conflict through calm discussion.[29] Their application of these ideas with the Mexican political elite, however, made them the subject of frequent criticisms from both the left and the far right. Communists, independent leftists, and even liberal statists denounced them for behind-the-scenes deals with devious Mexican officials; rightist critics damned them for sacrificing the strategic, property, and political interests of the United States.

To the right of the spectrum were those who spoke for particular economic and political institutions or social attitudes and—like their enemies on the far left, the Communists—usually had a highly focused and sometimes skewed perception of events in Mexico. The nature of diplomacy and banking led liberal capitalists to include several institutional interests in their calculus, but conservative businessmen typically focused on their specific corporate interests. Petroleum entrepreneurs Edward Doheny and William F. Buckley worked with Senator Albert Fall in his 1919 investigation of conditions in Mexico, expressing disappointment and disdain at what appeared to them to be hopelessly irresponsible disorder around the oil fields. Their implicit and explicit advocacy of military intervention to safeguard the private property of foreign—mainly those from the United States—investors, was based upon sweeping assumptions about the inability of Mexicans to govern themselves and the uncontrollable destructiveness of the revolution. These assumptions exceeded Wilsonian impatience, and those who held them placed little confidence in the outcome of dealings of the type practiced by Lamont and Morrow. Yet unquestionably, Doheny, Buckley, and other conservative business spokesmen represented ideas and values that were shared by many U.S. citizens.[30]

At the far right end of the spectrum were, to use a blunt term, the racists. Sometimes in accord with the liberal capitalists and more frequently in alliance with business conservatives, these opinionated writers condemned Mexico to a fate of foreign domination and exploitation because of the alleged biological inferiority of its Indian and mestizo (mixture of Indian and European) peoples. The racists clung to the nineteenth-century pseudoscientific beliefs that underlay their prejudiced assumptions and were unreceptive to evidence that contradicted these preconceptions. In the early years of the revolution, journalists Richard Harding Davis and Frederick Palmer used racist values as a short, convenient explanation of Mexico's confused political situation. Surprisingly, novelist Jack London adopted the same rationalization.[31]

In some ways the obverse of the left, many conservatives went to Mexico with the expectation of finding a nation on the edge of barbarism. During the first decade of the revolution Davis, Palmer, Buckley, and Doheny found evidence to support that expectation. In the 1920s, as civil strife diminished while government-directed reform programs expanded, most conservative commentators saw only marginal value at best, in these programs; at worst, they decried them as threats to U.S.-owned property and challenges to U.S. foreign policy. If they traveled to Mexico at all, they rarely remained for extended periods. A variety of leftists were drawn to Mexico, but most conservatives seemed to have an aversion to that nation. As a result, they wrote less than the leftists did, and their observations were usually confined to disruptions in national politics, the anticlerical campaigns, and business conditions. These preoccupations were understandable, given the institutional affiliations they brought to Mexico, but limited their grasp of the predicament of a government that faced an aroused peasantry and working class at home and a hostile international environment.

The Uniqueness of Mexican History

While Mexico gave the abstract concept of revolution a forceful but blurred reality, it also offered evidence of the uniqueness of its own history. Any attempt to analyze the consequences of a social revolution must take into account the peculiar circumstances that combined to shape the outcome of such a mass movement. In this regard, two singular aspects of Mexico's history are of special relevance here. First, the Mexican experience was different from other modern social revolutions because of the country's 2,000-mile border with the United States. With a deep mistrust of revolutionary movements in general, the United States was even more sensitive to events in Mexico because of the porousness of that border (which Villa's forces crossed with ease in 1916).[32] By the same token, the presence of a powerful and intrusive neighbor to the north was a critical factor in the policies of every Mexican head of state in this period. The Soviet Union under Lenin and Stalin also knew the hostility of the outside world, but the British-U.S. interventions of 1919 and 1920 had limited impact and were difficult to maintain because of logistics. U.S. military-naval interventions in Mexico (although they took place only twice) were not nearly so difficult to execute. From the point of view of Mexican leaders, such actions were a genuine threat until (and perhaps after) the Good Neighbor Policy changed the tenor of relations between the two nations in the 1930s. Moreover, gunboats, marines, and cavalry were only the most obvious forms of intervention. The reports and accusations of U.S. diplomats, politicians, and businessmen were often made public and had influence in Washington. Mexican leaders were aware of the connection between the moods on Main Street and Wall Street and the pronouncements and policies that emanated from the White House and Congress.

Second, this revolution differed from others in the absence of a dominant elite and a guiding ideology comparable to the cadres and concepts that led the movements in Russia, China, and Cuba. Clearly, the Mexican revolution was not a Marxist-Leninist movement—but then what was it? Visitors to Mexico who managed to look past the simplifying Soviet example often saw political manipulation instead of ideological utopias and investigated the consequences of socioeconomic change rather than the nuances of radical rhetoric. Some Mexicanists romanticized the revolution, but many went beyond the excitement of personal interaction with a perceived revolutionary environment to assess the strengths and weaknesses of what they saw. If there was a set of ideological blinders applied to their work, it came with them in their cultural baggage. That Mexico did not produce a world-shaking vision of a revolutionary millennium may have benefited such visitors. Instead of wrestling with the polemics surrounding the Communist model, these observers, once past the enthusiasms common to highly motivated travelers to foreign lands, began to detect flaws in Mexico's revolutionary process.

2

A Search for Meaning

Journalists and other serious observers who visited Mexico during the first decade of the revolution confronted a broad panorama of military, political, and social conflict that was too complex to be quickly understood. Unable or perhaps unwilling to grasp enough facts to form a comprehensive judgment, most U.S. writers fell back on the attitudes they brought with them to make sense of the revolution. Many turned to familiar stereotypes spawned in America's early contacts with foreign peoples and fully developed in the jingoistic, racist mood of the late 1800s. The Anglo-Saxon proclivity to denigrate anyone with a darker pigmentation or an alien culture put Mexicans into the category of inferiority along with most Latin Americans, Africans, and Asians. The revolution added other negative factors: social unrest and political dispute translated into banditry and demagogy. In this amalgam of prejudices—unfortunately held by a large segment of the U.S. public—the hapless Mexicans were seen as engaged in a hopeless struggle that seemed to validate the widely held rejection of revolution as a legitimate or even tolerable expression of the frustrations and hopes of the aroused downtrodden.[1]

The U.S. media were filled with derogatory depictions of Mexico and its people. Newspaper editorial cartoons often portrayed Mexicans as obstreperous children or bearded beggars in need of discipline by Uncle Sam.[2] The new motion picture industry, discovering a market for stereotypes, emphasized Mexican banditry, and among film outlaws "the Mexican bandits were clearly the most vile. They robbed, murdered, plundered, raped, cheated, gambled, lied and displayed every vice that could be displayed on the screen." When movie cowboy hero Bronco Billy Anderson had to deal with Mexicans, they carried the label "greaser," and by the end of the film they would either meet justice at the business end of a six-gun or experience a remarkable transformation in which they abandoned their villainous "Mexican" ways for the moral uprightness of Anglo-Saxon culture.[3]

At the peak of his revolutionary adventures Pancho Villa attempted to counter this image by making himself into a screen hero in the United States. In 1913 he contracted for a film biography with the Mutual Film Corporation. The result was a photographic record of subjects ranging from primitive battlefield conditions to Villa's rebuilding of mangled rail lines and concluded with a flattering filmic biography of the Chihuahua rebel. After his 1916 raid on Columbus, New Mexico, however, Villa was relegated to the stereotypical category of bloodthirsty bandit and border ruffian, a perception reinforced by William Randolph Hearst's anti-Mexican, anti-Japanese serial, *Patria*. Released in that same year, *Patria* depicted an invasion of the United States across the southern border by the combined forces of Mexico and Japan. When the Wilson administration protested the serial as an insult to the Japanese, Hearst had references to Japan removed from the subtitles, leaving the Mexicans as the villains—even those clad in Japanese uniforms and bearing Japanese facial characteristics.[4]

Prejudice found its way into the courtroom, as well. In 1918, a California judge, Benjamin F. Bledsoe, charged the jury in the espionage trial of the ill-fated anarchist rebel Ricardo Flores Magón (who was convicted on flimsy evidence) in language that evinced bias against Mexicans, as described by historian Dirk Raat: "Injecting a note of chauvinism into his charge, the judge said,'It is the glory of the Anglo-Saxon theory, the glory of American tradition and American vision and American determination, that in this country of ours we have a land and a government of liberty under law.' Then as if to imply that the Mexicans lacked all of these Anglo-Saxon 'virtues,' Bledsoe went on to say that the defendants were 'entitled to have their rights measured just as though instead of being members of another nation they were of our own race.' "[5]

Some observers recognized the injustice of the prevailing attitudes. Toward the end of the decade, probably in 1919, Herbert Ingram Priestley took a trip to Mexico to gather some firsthand impressions of the current scene. A careful reader of newspapers and news magazines, the Berkeley historian was dismayed by the quality of the coverage of events in Mexico and by the distortions created by propaganda campaigns: "It is a widespread, an acute ignorance, caused by our native apathy and indifference to everything international that is not sensational. Under the stress of the current campaign to make Mexico known to us in the terms of self-interested investors there, or in the terms of Mexican government propaganda, we are apt to yield to a sense of bewilderment and impatience which will end with the exclamation: 'The United States will have to go in and clean 'em up someday anyhow, so why not now?' "[6]

"The Trouble Makers in Mexico"

The revolution that originated with Francisco Madero's overthrow of Porfirio Díaz in 1911 took another violent turn in 1913 with the overthrow and assassination of Madero, creating a monumental challenge for U.S. observers in Mexico. Not only did the new president, General Victoriano Huerta, have the image of traitor to Madero and his cause, but he also faced insurrections in the north, led by an uneasy coalition of Venustiano Carranza and Pancho Villa, and in the south, led by Emiliano Zapata. To make matters even more confusing, President Woodrow Wilson decided to send troops into the Caribbean port of Veracruz, ostensibly in response to an incident in Tampico but actually in an effort to block the shipment of arms for Huerta's forces.

This multilayered conflict—involving on the one hand United States-German-British rivalry for influence in the oil-rich sections of Mexico on the eve of World War I and, on the other, the three-cornered civil war among Huerta, Carranza-Villa, and Zapata—was too much for most onlookers to grasp. Hence they fell back on simplistic and erroneous stereotypes. Their position, put in its rawest form, was that Mexico lacked the capacity for self-government because its population was predominantly Indian or a mixture of Indian and European.

Perhaps the leading proponent of this racist view was the well-known leftist and novelist Jack London, whose condemnation of the revolution both confused and appalled many of his fellow radicals. London had entered a conservative middle age which his daughter later described to biographer John Perry as "a tragic sellout, for he had been subsidized, bought body and soul by the kind of life he thought he wanted."[7]

London undercut the legitimate motive force behind the Zapatista and other peasant uprisings with the assertion that the Indian masses neither wanted land reform nor even understood the issue: "There are twelve million peons. They have had four centuries to get interested in the subject [of land reform]. Considering the paucity of the numbers of their masters, they have evidently not considered the matter to any purpose. I doubt, by a count of noses, if one-fourth of one percent of the peons of Mexico are bearing arms for the purpose of gaining free land or of gaining anything else their leaders desire." According to London, red-blooded Anglo-Saxon Americans would have rectified such a situation long before: "It is impossible to conceive of twelve million Americans, gnawed by the land hunger, arming and sending into the field one-fourth of one percent of their number to fight for land. Either the peon is different from the American, or land hunger is one to the one and another thing to the other. Apparently both contentions are true. The American is Anglo-Saxon. The peon is an Indian, and a Mexican Indian at that."[8]

The greatest troublemakers were the mestizos, or, as London called them, "half-breeds": "They are what a mixed breed always is— neither fish, flesh, nor fowl. They are neither white men nor Indians. Like the Eurasian, they possess all of the vices of their various comingled bloods and none of their virtues."[9] London saw the racial causes of Mexico's political instability as beyond remediation. Only a Porfirio Díaz could bring order to the nation, and Díaz was gone. The current disorder, from London's point of view, revealed that "there is no other Porfirio Díaz in sight. There is no strong 'breed' capable of whipping the rest of the disorderly 'breeds' and the country into shape."[10]

Like his friend Jack London, Richard Harding Davis brought his own agenda to Mexico and succeeded in selecting the appropriate facts to reinforce his prejudgments. In his 1896 adventure story, *Three Gringos in Venezuela and Central America*, Davis had made clear his disdain for the Latin-Indian peoples of the region.[11] His adventures in Mexico in 1914 did nothing to change these opinions. He and London had the audacity to attempt to interview Huerta while U.S. forces held Veracruz, and although they never reached the Mexican president, they endured enough unpleasant train rides and imperious interrogations by officials to leap to conclusions: "The difficulty now is that while the American in Mexico considers himself a tourist and entitled to protection, the Mexican regards him as the hated invader and friend of the traitors Villa and Carranza—and that different point of view leads to trouble. If war is finally declared, we can come out squarely as enemies and things will run more smoothly."[12] In short, Davis assumed that enduring the hot, humid climate of Veracruz and the hostility of Mexican officials would all be worthwhile once the fighting started. The United States had no shortage of heroes among the soldiers and sailors in Veracruz, and the Mexicans would supply the villains from their army of swarthy and unkempt peasants. But war did not come; much to Davis's dismay, Wilson turned to diplomacy to resolve the conflict. With no hope of a fight, Davis left, soon to find his war in Europe.[13]

Veteran foreign correspondent Frederick Palmer, who had covered military and civil strife in east Asia and the Balkans, was the frequent companion of Davis and London in the summer of 1914. He was not a member of Davis's daredevil school of journalism, nor did he subscribe to London's ethnocentric extremism. Palmer examined the Mexican point of view, especially on the widespread resentment of Yankee economic penetration, and he also explored Mexican politics in greater depth than either of his colleagues.[14] But in his overview of the Veracruz occupation, Palmer lapsed into the jingoism and racism typical of Davis and London: "It proves that, in a military occupation against the hostile population of another race, the conduct of our soldiers and sailors is working the real American spirit. [In the dangerous street fighting] our bluejackets and marines shot with deadly accuracy. Then, the fighting over, they became gentle, considerate masters. . . . Even Greasers can accommodate themselves to kindness."[15]

Palmer attempted to reflect the attitude of the U.S. soldiers when he repeated the often-made comparison between the Veracruz operation and the suppression of the uprising in the Philippines from 1899 to 1902. According to Palmer, the Mexican peasant turned soldier "will not let us help him until we give him first the proof of strength, as we had to give the Filipinos. . . . A marine officer on a transport before sailing for Veracruz expressed it perfectly: 'We must teach them to respect us,' " he said. "Then we must teach them how to behave."[16]

Other writers too subscribed to the racist view of Mexico. James Creelman was perhaps the most widely read U.S. authority on Mexico in this period because of his laudatory biography of Porfirio Díaz.[17] Yet even Creelman's praise for the mestizo master of Mexico did not signal a modification of his ethnic prejudices. The ouster of Díaz in 1911 and the subsequent political-military struggle prompted Creelman to restate a central thesis of his biography. Díaz was to be measured, in part, by his remarkable achievement of governing a nearly ungovernable people. In his absence Mexico could only flounder in chaos, demonstrating "the racial unfitness of an Orientally derived people [the Mexican Indians] for free institutions won through a thousand years of Anglo-Saxon growth and struggle."[18]

The racist explanation of Mexican character reduced the revolution to a mere series of violent explosions engendered by instinctive urges that had no counterpart in the calm, decent world of Anglo-Saxon legal and constitutional traditions. These assumptions quickly eliminated any need to consider the larger questions that could emerge from the recognition of a transfer of political power from the Porfirian elite to a party or faction or army that claimed to represent the lower strata of the social structure. That an activist, organized state could arise out of the inchoate melee was, from this point of view, impossible; the common people of Mexico simply could not form the basis for any responsible government. And London's cynical dismissal of "land hunger" as irrelevant to the Indians meant that any significant redistribution of agricultural land did not merit serious consideration. The ethnocentric perspective conveniently raised the United States far above the fray to a high moral plain from which it could stoop to "assist" its neighbor, whether the neighbor really wanted help or not.[19]

The Liberal Capitalist Tradition

Woodrow Wilson did not hold such a low opinion of Mexico and its people. His faith in that nation's future, however, grew out of his hope of projecting a liberal capitalist ideology into the Mexican polity and economy. Wilson had a firm confidence in the ability of educated, honest men to win the mandate of the electorate and then establish a responsible reformist state that would coexist with and, at times, regulate and even chastise the operations of privately owned corporations. Nevertheless, these corporations were to remain independent agents in pursuit of profits, both at home and abroad. In Wilson's missionary view, this system of regulated capitalism and representative governments cooperating in the promotion of free trade was to expand throughout the hemisphere and ultimately the world, internationalizing prosperity and democracy.

Wilson's first major statement on Latin America came on October 27, 1913, in Mobile, Alabama. Widely hailed as a disavowal of U.S. intervention in the internal affairs of its neighbors to the south, the statement was more accurately a recognition of the intensifying competition for credit and commerce in Latin America in anticipation of the opening of the Panama Canal. Wilson, who saw politics and commerce as means for the uplift of humankind, couched his ideas in moral terminology. In his version of recent history, unscrupulous European bankers had forced on the insolvent Latin American states much-needed loans at exorbitant rates of interest. But Wilson saw a brighter day dawning: "I rejoice in nothing so much as in the prospect that they [Latin American nations] will not be emancipated from these conditions, as we [government and bankers] ought to be the first to take part in assisting in that emancipation."[20]

As for Mexico, the persistent crises, particularly the presence of the dictator Huerta in the presidency, led Wilson to make a public statement. Interviewed by journalist Samuel G. Blythe of the *Saturday Evening Post* on April 27, 1914, Wilson expounded upon his subject in the style of a forceful, righteous pedagogue. According to Blythe:

> The President closed his fingers into a sinewy fist. He leaned
> forward in his chair—leaned forward as a man leans forward
> who is about to start on a race, his body taut, his muscles tense.

> I could see the cords stand out in the back of his neck. His eyes
> were narrowed, . . . his vigor and earnestness impressive.
>
>   Bang! He hit the desk with that clenched fist. . . .
>
>   "I challenge you," he said, "to cite me an instance in all the
> history of the world where liberty was handed down from
> above! Liberty always is attained by the forces working from
> below, underneath, by the great movement of the people."[21]

Evidently Blythe could not think of a counterexample. Instead,
the journalist dashed down notes as the president took verbal flight to
establish himself as a friend, at least on paper, of popular uprisings. In
Mexico, according to Wilson, "the old order is dead" and a new order on
the rise. The chief executive showed no inhibitions in outlining the
shape that the new state should take. Excluded from that future was
Victoriano Huerta, whose usurpation of authority violated Wilson's
notion of representative government. The president was adamant "that
those in de facto control of the Government must be relieved of that
control before Mexico can realize her manifest destiny." The expression
"manifest destiny" was provocative and inflammatory for Mexicans
because it recalled the aggressive acts of the United States in the war of
1846–48 and the Treaty of Guadalupe Hidalgo, whereby Mexico lost
almost half its national territory. Wilson's apparent intent, however, was
not to revive those painful memories but to point out the direction
Mexico should follow in erecting its institutions of the new order—specifically, the direction already taken by the United States. The manifest
destiny of the two nations would then coincide through the emergence
in Mexico of a political system that would evolve toward the U.S.
model. Wilson responded to his conservative critics on this question:

> They say that the Mexicans are not fitted for self-government,
> and to this I reply that, when properly directed, there is no
> people not fitted for self-government. The very fact that the
> extension of the school system by Díaz brought about a certain
> degree of understanding among some of the people which
> caused them to awaken to their wrongs and to strive intelli-
> gently for their rights makes that contention absurd. I do not
> hold that the Mexican peons are at present as capable of self-
> government as other people—ours, for example; but I do hold
> that the widespread sentiment that they never will be and never
> can be made to be capable of self-government is as wickedly
> false as it is palpably absurd.[22]

The president's awkward explanation of Mexico's being "made
to be capable of self-government" reeked with Anglo-Saxon paternalism, yet it exemplified the president's devotion to abstract idealism. He
used the same sort of reasoning in his analysis of inequities in land
ownership: "Farm after farm passed into the control of the big land-

owners and there was no recourse for the former owners or their families but to work at dictated terms and practically as slaves on the land that had formerly been theirs."[23]

Wilson championed justice for the unfairly dispossessed, but his conversation with Blythe indicated that he did not have the most basic understanding of how justice was to be meted out in rural Mexico. His most specified statement to Blythe on this issue provided for a "settlement of the agrarian question by constitutional means—such as that followed by New Zealand, for example." Beyond this loose comparison (British legal and agricultural practices in the Pacific seemed to have little relevance to Mexico), Wilson simply did not address the agrarian question.

The president and his advisers apparently gave even less attention to labor unrest and the small but growing industrial working class in Mexico. This omission, at a time when his own nation was preoccupied with a similar situation in Ludlow, Colorado, was an especially telling aspect of Wilson's attitude toward Mexico. Engrossed in diplomacy and international rivalry in the Caribbean and devoted to his ideal of a world of representative governments committed to the untrammeled expansion of commerce, he placed Mexico's fundamental social and economic issues on the periphery of this perception of the revolution. Yet the connection between Mexico's foreign relations and its internal agrarian and labor movements was too intimate to be denied for long. Wilson had opened the Blythe interview with the assertion that "Liberty always is attained by the forces working from below," but he revealed little understanding of the nature and expectations of these forces in Mexico.[24]

Wilson ordered two interventions in Mexico: the occupation of Veracruz in 1914, and the Pershing expedition against Pancho Villa in 1916. Both were products of political and strategic considerations in the United States rather than of any effort to achieve direct seizure of territory. Their results, however, were ambiguous at best for Wilson: Huerta fell from the presidency in July of 1914, but not because of Wilson's intervention in Veracruz; and Villa eluded Pershing. The most obvious results were two successive waves of anti–United States sentiment that swept much of Mexico. With Blythe, Wilson had attempted to speak as the ally of the revolutionaries, but in Mexico the leaders of the movement came to see him as their enemy.[25]

In early 1917, the intervention issue diminished with the departure of Pershing's troops while Carranza tightened his grasp on the government. The issues of land reform and labor activism vaulted to the forefront with the completion of the constitutional convention in Querétaro. The new document's Article 123 provided the legal basis for an advanced labor code that would eventually pose problems for U.S. corporations operating in Mexico. Of more immediate concern, however, was Article 27, which not only set up the legal basis for land reform but also invested the government with the power to regulate, to tax, and to expropriate foreign-owned oil properties. Wilson's vision of the free flow of capital and profits collided head on with this constitutional formula for the assertion of the nation's economic self-interest. As Mark Gilderhus, a careful analyst of Wilson's ideas and policies, has observed, Article 27 "defied Wilson's liberal-capitalist proclivities and the entire body of assumptions implicit in America's policies toward Latin America."[26]

Through the constitution a new generation of Mexican political leaders expressed to Wilson and the world their intention of making the state a primary component in their restructuring of their nation's economy and society. Wilson sympathized with the need for land reform and seemed committed to a broader distribution of wealth, but he did not explain the means by which Mexico might achieve these ends. He voiced his confidence in the ability of the Mexican people to develop representative political institutions, but he did not anticipate the assertive nationalism of Article 27. He accepted revolution as a struggle for human liberty "always ... attained by forces working from below."[27] Yet this manifestation of a movement that was broadly based (if not the will of the majority) threw him off balance because it clashed with another of his cherished assumptions: the need to protect private property. According to Gilderhus this conflict, along with German overtures to Mexico during World War I, confounded Wilson:

> After April 1917 Wilson lost all sense of common purpose with Carranza and the Constitutionalists. Article 27 menaced important economic interests in ways compounded by the possibility of an alignment between Germany and Mexico. Paradoxically, imperialism and revolution threatened to unite in common opposition to liberal capitalism on the Mexican front. The breakdown of Wilson's position resulted in part from the intransigence of Carranza's nationalism. Lacking justification derived from a sense of ideological affinity with the Constitutionalists, Wilson could not bludgeon Mexico into line through the use of military force. ... The internal coherence of his position collapsed with the divergence of ideological and material components in his thinking. As his commitment to human liberty became even more incompatible with the need to safeguard material interests in Mexico, the president experienced a kind of mental paralysis. He needed to act yet he could not justify the kind of measures wanted by vested interest groups.[28]

Wilson's "mental paralysis" led to an indecisive Mexican policy from 1917 to 1921. He resisted pressures from the oil interests and his own State Department to employ military intervention again, but beyond this refusal his relations with Mexico merely drifted.[29]

Wilson's vision of hemispheric harmony based on free trade and civic virtue did not end with his administration, however. Loudly and awkwardly supported by the idiosyncratic John Barrett, director general of the Pan American Union from 1907 to 1920, and quietly championed by diplomat-banker Henry Bruére, the Wilsonian liberal capitalist ideal survived and, at times, even flourished in the next two decades.[30] Perhaps its most successful advocates were banker and unofficial diplomat Thomas Lamont, banker-diplomat-politician Dwight Morrow, and the soon-to-be secretary of state, Cordell Hull. Lamont, a partner in the Morgan bank, set up a committee of financiers to coordinate the efforts of several lending institutions and the State Department, and he was one of the founders of the prestigious Council on Foreign Relations.[31] Hull would become deeply involved in the 1930s Good Neighbor Policy.[32]

The Liberal Statist Perspective on Social and Economic Change

Like the liberal capitalists, the liberal statists relied on ideas evolved in other settings. Lincoln Steffens was the best known muckraking journalist to visit Mexico in the revolutionary years. His flamboyant life-style contrasted sharply with the demeanor of two Protestant ministers whose devotion to the social gospel nevertheless brought them alongside Steffens on the Mexican issue. Alexander McKelway and Samuel Guy Inman premised their theology on the ideals of social and economic justice for the lowly, which gave the revolution's potential for massive redistributive uplift a special appeal. Steffens, with a reputation for the exposure of corruption in high places, seemed more concerned about the quality of Mexico's leadership. But the muckraker and the ministers agreed that Mexico was an exciting arena for the rapid enactment of reform in comparison with the slow-moving mechanisms of U.S. politics.

Perhaps the first U.S. writer to grasp the revolution's socioeconomic dimensions, McKelway was a North Carolina Presbyterian minister who wrote under the pseudonym McGregor—probably to conceal his identity from President Wilson, whom he served as an adviser on child labor.[33] As early as December 1913, McKelway identified Emiliano Zapata less as a guerrilla than as an innovative leader in the process of land reform. In Zapata's home state of Morelos, land reform moved rapidly but within a legal framework. Crucial evidence was Zapata's "Plan of Ayala." According to McKelway: "Land not in use has to be divided and cultivated [by peasants]. The big landlords of Morelos have fled the country and the people are working for themselves and not the landlords. And the Plan of Ayala rests upon the fundamental law of Mexico adopted in 1857, maintained by Juárez in his contest with Napoleon III and Maximilian, and overthrown by Porfirio Díaz in his infamous despoiling of the people to satisfy his favorites."[34]

More sensitive to peasant needs and the possibilities of social experimentation than liberal capitalist Wilson, McKelway's discussion was a basically liberal statist tract that made clear its author's faith in orderly social change. According to Zapata biographer John Womack, the Plan of Ayala was an original, amorphous, militant document that drew more from the frustrations of the Morelos peasantry and the ambience of the early revolution than from the Constitution of 1857.[35] McKelway, however, conscious of his Yankee readers and particularly the president, knew that a land reform program based on accepted constitutional forms would be more acceptable in the White House.

The Texas-born Inman sustained the thrust of McKelway's argument during the last years of the decade. He looked with favor on the rise of Venustiano Carranza to a position of dominance (at times slipping to near-dominance) in the six years after 1914 and had ready praise for Mexico's "First Chief:" "I never saw a man enter into the hard task of bettering labor conditions, equalizing taxation, and extending the educational work of his State [Carranza had been governor of Coahuila] with more enthusiasm and apparently with a greater desire to serve his people."[36]

When Steffens went to Mexico in 1914 he seemed to be in a transitional phase between his muckraking ventures in Cleveland and St. Louis and his later voyage of ideological discovery to Soviet Russia.[37] He saw Porfirio Díaz as the "great boss" of Mexican politics who fell before the onrush of those who sought, with justification, improved conditions for the masses.[38] By the time Steffens arrived, Carranza had taken on the responsibility of national leadership. Steffens expressed his estimate of the Carrancistas' intentions in terms familiar to progressive readers: "Their theory is that the problem of civilized society is not poverty, but riches; that the solution of it is not to cure or nurse the poor; but to prevent the accumulation of enormous individual wealth, and so their policy is to find out and close up holes through which some of the products of labor leak through the workers, intellectual and physical, into the possession of philanthropists. Thus it is economic, not political, democracy they are working for."[39]

Steffens, like Inman, identified Carranza as the man who could implement these theories. Both the pundit and the preacher had faith in the First Chief's personal honesty and strength of character.[40] As later events would show, both overestimated Carranza's ability to produce sweeping social change, but their views of his tenacity were not far from the mark.[41]

Harry Stein's perceptive assessment of Steffens's journalistic effort in Mexico applies to Inman and other liberal statists as well as to its central character:[42]

> Almost invariably, then, Steffens understood and interpreted Mexico in terms brought from home, stereotypes included. His press release for a 1914 lecture tour baldly promised that he would speak "on Mexico in terms of the United States"; he did exactly that. He viewed Mexico and its revolution in 1914 and thereafter through lenses which reflected long-time opposition to business Privilege subverting [American] society and a more recent liking for radical change as alone promising complete destruction of Privilege. The lenses also reflected his exaggerated faith in powerful leaders, similarly expressed in his former muckraking. The lenses highlighted certain observations, such as Carranza's unyielding nationalism, and obscured others, including Carranza's acute distaste for radical change. Such lenses were hardly unique to Steffens. The meanings imposed would guarantee large, receptive audiences in the United States; the actions prompted by his views would earn continuing aid from anti-interventionists at home.[43]

Discord on the Left

The liberal statists saw merely the surface of the revolutionary potential in Mexico. Two radicals, John Reed and John Kenneth Turner, stood out among visitors to Mexico during the first half of the decade not only because their books became *de rigueur* among sympathizers of the revolutionary causes but also because they created an aura of excitement by becoming virtual participants in the movement itself. Turner traveled across Porfirian Mexico in disguise in order to expose the brutal working conditions on Yucatecan and Oaxacan plantations; Reed rode with Pancho Villa during the battle for Torreón in 1913. Yet despite their authentic revolutionary baptisms and their favorable attitudes toward the movement, in the last analysis they did not agree on its nature or purposes.

These differences arose, to some extent, because of their divergent backgrounds and ambitions. An Oregonian, Reed was a tall, handsome, curly-haired idealist whose radicalism was molded by his education at Harvard, his experiences with workers in industrial New Jersey, and his desire to be a successful writer. While faithful to a romantic vision of what a revolution should be, Reed adjusted his depiction of the struggle in northern Mexico to suite the literary needs of a good story.

Turner's rangy physique and dark visage conveyed an air of

seriousness that was reflected in his writing. If he did not quite equal Reed's polish and volubility, he matched the Ivy Leaguer's unwavering determination. Also a native of Oregon, he spent his youth as a printer's apprentice and in 1896, at the age of seventeen, moved into journalism in Stockton, California. A headstrong activist more than a self-conscious writer, Turner was more concerned with specific economic and social circumstances in Mexico than with a literary version of events.

As a result of their contrasting approaches, Reed and Turner provided fundamentally different versions of what was happening in Mexico. John Reed's legendary stature in the history of the international left would result primarily from his *Ten Days That Shook the World*, a dramatic first-person account of the Bolshevik victory in Russia in 1917. His 1914 book on Mexico, *Insurgent Mexico*, did not achieve the apocalyptic appeal of his later Russian adventure, but it did attract much attention among U.S. readers interested in Mexico. Reed accented the excitement of peasant revolution with a highly favorable view of Pancho Villa. One Reed biographer, Robert Rosenstone, claims that his Mexican journey was "a rare experience that served to fuse self fulfillment and social concerns." Through his evocative glimpses of the Mexican people rising against oppression, Reed found a channel for personal expression that he hoped would elevate both the revolution and himself to public prominence in the United States.[44] He succeeded in the second but not the first. There is little doubt that his descriptive, discursive style was effective as literature, but historian Diane Christopulos concludes that "Reed contributed relatively little to the North American discussion of Mexico."[45] Rosenstone agrees to the extent that "the revolutionary impulse in John Reed was deeply rooted in premises he never clearly articulated."[46]

Reed seemed lost in the details of atmosphere and personality at the expense of perspective. *Insurgent Mexico* explained two aspects of the revolution—the motives and the fighting—but left out the final stage: the kind of society and economy to be created by the revolutionaries. Critic Jim Tuck's analysis notes Reed's portrait of Villa's ally, Tomás Urbina, as a violence-prone brute but faults the author for his failure pass some judgment on the brutality.[48] The acts of such a grotesque personality and the bloody battle of Torreón might have found some rationalization in a vision of the revolutionary future, but Reed did not present this vision. As Tuck, Rosenstone, and Christopulos point out, ideology was not Reed's strength. On at least five occasions his text mentioned peasant demands for land reform, yet he did not explore the issue in an ideological dimension.[49]

Turner, by contrast, did identify revolutionary ideals. His knowledge of Mexico was deeper than Reed's, and his understanding of the origins and goals of the revolution reflected his grasp not only of the present but also of the recent past. Turner twice ventured into Porfirian Mexico in order to see the cruel working conditions of the agricultural "slaves" or, more accurately, those field workers tied to their jobs by debt peonage. Turner's exposé of worker exploitation elicited praise from U.S. leftists and, simultaneously, a hostile response from the Díaz regime, which for many years had received nothing but kind words from writers such as James Creelman.

Turner did not limit his attacks on Díaz to the printed word. He joined the forces of Ricardo Flores Magón in California and transported guns and ammunition across the border to Baja California in the revolt of 1910–11, which ultimately failed.[50] Disappointed but undaunted, Turner returned to journalism in 1913 and discovered two promising revolutionary movements in Mexico. More than Reed, Turner revealed an awareness of the issues that had aroused the peasants and a clearer perception of their immediate goals. For example, his 1913 article on Emiliano Zapata insisted that the rebel leader of Morelos and his followers were bandits only in the sense that they sought a basic redistribution of property from the rich to the poor. They were "fighting for liberty—not some chimerical or ideal liberty that is of the mind and far away, nor even for a liberty so immaterial, though universally demanded, as political liberty, but for a concrete, tangible thing that means to them not only the broader liberties of the mind but the more pressing needs of the body. The [so-called] bandits of Mexico are fighting for land to stand on."[51]

Two years later Turner visited Monterrey, the capital of the state of Nuevo León, where his old friend and ex-Magonista Antonio Villareal was in the midst of his vigorous gubernatorial reform program. Turner praised Villareal's abolition of debt peonage and his support of striking streetcar workers against a private corporation. In general, Turner saw an admirable program "inspired by socialist ideals."

Villareal employed an eclectic set of policies that included socialist methods in land reform and state-run corporations, but he also had the support of the anarchism-inclined Casa del Obrero Mundial, Mexico's link with the Industrial Workers of the World (IWW).[52] Like his observations on Zapata, Turner's view of Nuevo León under Villareal stressed specific programs with the potential for substantive socioeconomic change.

The contrast between Turner's political-ideological perception of the revolution and Reed's more impressionistic view became readily apparent in their colorfully drawn, highly imaginative depictions of Pancho Villa—which revealed more about the authors than about their subject. Reed was impressed by Villa's instinctive prowess as a military leader but also emphasized his generous concern for the poor: "In times of famine he [Villa] fed whole districts, and took care of entire villages evicted by the soldiers under Porfirio Díaz's outrageous land law. Everywhere he was known as The Friend of the Poor. He was the Mexican Robin Hood."[53] Turner saw none of Robin Hood in Villa. Instead, he held the Chihuahua rebel in contempt as a brutal, mindless tool of reactionary forces in the United States. In Turner's view, Villa "was a scoundrel who could be corrupted" by Wall Street investors, the Wilson administration, and William Randolph Hearst; the Columbus raid was a prearranged provocation leading to a U.S. intervention that satisfied these powerful interests.[54]

The two radical writers seldom met, but they had a brief conversation soon after Villa's attack on Columbus. Reed told Turner, "I don't care if he is a bandit. I like him just the same."[55] Turner's response went unrecorded, but he expressed his opinion unequivocally in print.

Neither Turner nor Reed has a clear understanding of Villa,[56] but their contrasting views reveal much about what they looked for in Mexico. Reed saw a leader with special qualities of near-mythic proportions (the "Mexican Robin Hood"). Turner, who regarded the revolution as a struggle that pitted an alliance of feudalistic landlords and capitalistic money lords against the grassroots protagonists of socialism, saw Villa as a man in league with the former group, part of the conspiracy behind the headlines. For Reed, the revolution was a classic tale full of heroic and literary potential. For Turner, it was a class struggle full of nastiness but with the potential for change to benefit the masses.

Venustiano Carranza provided the two authors with another subject on which to practice their varied approaches. Reed attempted to interview Carranza and presented some questions to him—including the matter of land reform—but found the First Chief distant and unreceptive behind a coterie of advisers. Finally, Carranza appeared and delivered a rambling diatribe against U.S. intervention, after which Reed wrote the following word picture of a passive, aloof politician: "We saw the gigantic, khaki-clad figure of Don Venustiano Carranza sitting in a big chair [in the dark room]. There was something strange in the way he sat there, with his hands on the arms of the chair, as if he had been placed in it and told not to move. He did not seem to be thinking, nor to have been working—you couldn't imagine him at that table. You got the impression of a vast inert body—a statue."[57]

Turner was less concerned about Carranza's physical appearance than about his plans for reform once the fighting ceased. At first he believed that the First Chief was committed to socialism, but after a written interview Turner realized that this impression was mistaken. He saw Carranza as a gradualist who took an uncompromising stand on economic nationalism but had little taste for the sudden, sweeping changes that Zapata and Villareal wanted. Turner was disappointed but seemed to believe that Carranza's partially revolutionary, partially bourgeois platform was the best that Mexico could expect under the pressures of internal disorder and external intervention.[58]

Turner outdistanced Reed in presenting an ideological view of the revolution, but his view lacked consistency. He first committed to Flores Magón's anarchism of the 1906 to 1911 period, but in 1915 he also was supportive of Villareal's socialism; in between he espoused Zapata's community-based land reform, which was probably closer to an agrarian version of anarchism than to the socialism of Nuevo León.[59] In short, Turner did not propagate a single or unified ideological position but accepted virtually any ideas or programs that emphasized the breakup of the Díaz amalgam of hacienda agriculture and Wall Street capitalism by extensive land reform and other redistributive devices. He did not formulate a clear conception of the revolutionary state, the form of government that would best suit the needs of the nation once the movement shifted from the battlefields to the legislature, presidential palace, state assemblies, and village councils. He accepted the imperative for a remaking of Mexican society but could not find a formula for its institutionalization.

The Shadow of Bolshevism

Russia's Bolshevik Revolution drew the attention of Reed, Steffens, and many other commentators away from Mexico. If the Mexican Constitution of 1917 contained the potential for a fiscally weak but diplomatically adroit nation-state to project a menacing but amorphous specter of revolutionary change, the Bolshevik uprising in Russia later that year created a monster—class conflict joined with subterranean intrigue and Machiavellian politics—that threw its massive shadow not only across war-ravaged Europe but also over U.S. investments from Sonora to Yucatan and, in the minds of some, private property around the world. This new fear added to emotions aroused by President Wilson's declaration of war and its enormous material and psychological commitments. John Reed's combination of journalism and mythmaking in *Ten Days That Shook the World* convinced many radicals and some liberals that the Communist millennium was near; on the very same pages, many conservatives found the death knell of modern civilization.

The Russian Revolution meant that in North America, at least, the word "revolution" now carried a new connotation. Events in Mexico since 1910 had been frustrating and even threatening to U.S. observers, but the Bolshevik victory added a new sense of urgency. Words written about Mexico before 1917 were suddenly more ominous. Two conservative analysts, Edward I. Bell and Clarence Barron, surveyed conditions in Mexico from 1914 to 1917 and found a nation totally lacking in the requirements for self-government and, by implication, highly susceptible to Bolshevism. Bell saw the majority of Indians and mestizos "as children, wholly incapable as yet of exercising a voice in their government."[60] Business reporter Barron saw the Mexican as "the same childlike, dependent, trusting fellow whether at work, play, or revolution."[61] Such naive people, untutored in politics and ideology, would be easy prey for Moscow's agents.

In 1919, Senator Albert Fall of New Mexico chaired a headline-grabbing investigation of Mexican affairs; voluminous testimony on the disorder and violence in Mexico included claims that Bolshevism was on the rise. The testimony of oil entrepreneurs William F. Buckley and Edward L. Doheny added to this impression. Two strong-willed businessmen who accumulated much of their wealth in the ruggedly competitive petroleum fields of Mexico in the first two decades of the twentieth century, this pair complained loudly about the peril to private property. Again, Article 27 and Carranza were the targets as Buckley lamented that "Carranza [had] accomplished three of the great bolshevist objectives of the revolution—the abolition of private property, the crippling of the church, and the expulsion of the foreigner."[62]

Fall, Buckley and Doheny were leaders of the Murray Hill group, an informal cluster of businessmen and politicians who used the forum offered by the Senate investigation as a means of building public pressure on the Wilson administration to take decisive action to restrain Carranza. The Murray Hill group supplied the subcommittee with willing witnesses against the Mexican government and employed a publicity agent to furnish news releases to the national press. Fall joined Buckley and Doheny in the claim that Bolshevism was spreading into the United States through the work of Mexican consular and diplomatic officials.[63]

Another member of the Murray Hill group was Thomas E. Gibbon, a California attorney who was among the first to claim that there was a similarity between the two revolutions. Employed by the Richardson Construction Company of Sonora (which felt the brunt of attacks by the Yaqui Indians), Gibbon saw in the Mexicans under Carranza: "a striking parallel to the Russians at the hands of the Bolsheviki. In every country there exists a predatory element whose chief ambition is to secure control of the machinery of government by violence and then to use it in depriving industrious, frugal people of the property they have accumulated, and dividing it among themselves. This element is represented in Mexico by the Bolsheviki, and in the United States by the IWW."[64]

Gibbon, Fall, Doheny, and Buckley generated considerable media coverage, and they received reinforcement from an unexpected source. The most strident warnings about Bolshevism south of the border came from Jorge Vera Estañol, an expatriate Mexican living in California and a former minister of education under Huerta. As the author of an ambitious but short-lived program of rural education, he was hardly a narrow-minded conservative, but his diatribe against the Carranza government was far from a model of objectivity. Vera Estañol claimed that Carranza had created a Communist dictatorship. In the Red Scare year of 1920 he asserted that Bolshevism was the prime force in the government and repeatedly used this fear-inspiring term: "Bolshevism is the absolutism of the one-time proletariat-in-arms over the rest of society. The Carrancistas now aim to perfect the Bolshevism of the Constitution [of 1917]."[65]

Article 27 and other parts of the constitution that dealt with state authority over private property were, in Vera Estañol's view, based on the most vulgar of human motives: "The spirit which animates such law is more Bolshevik still [than the law itself]. . . . It is inspired not by love of justice, but by hatred of all non-proletarian classes, particularly the wealthy; and it is dominated by a lust for wealth."[66]

If the North American readers of Vera Estañol and the Murray Hill group had possessed sufficient information and had taken the time to analyze these alarmist theses, they would have found at least three major gaps in the argument. First, although the alarmists proclaimed that the Carranza government was determined to enforce the new constitution, they seemed unaware that the president had been a hesitant supporter of its more radical provisions. Though indisputably a nationalist, Carranza was hardly at the far left of Mexico's political spectrum and certainly not a Bolshevik.[67] Second, the alarmists gave very little attention to Carranza's struggle for a power base among peasants and, third, did not explain the political connection they claimed to see between the allegedly radical movement in Mexico and the government in Russia. By use of the emotion-laden term "Bolshevism," they clouded the issue enough to obscure these points.

The anti-Bolshevik conservatives were convinced that Moscow had established a beachhead in Mexico, but they were apparently unable to name its leaders or to describe its organization. At least Fall, his colleagues, and Vera Estañol did not publish any such information. Yet ironically, their charges though more supposition than substance, had some basis in fact: the Communist International did establish itself in Mexico City in 1918. It was not the threat that U.S. anti-Bolsheviks believed it to be, however: at most, numbering a few dozen members, and, at best, clutching for some rudimentary institutional structure, the early Communist Party in Mexico barely survived the years from 1918 to 1921. It apparently had no Mexicans in positions of leadership, had virtually no impact on the labor and agrarian movements, and was torn by deep internal squabbles. In short, the alarmist conservatives gave Communists far too much credit for effective intrigue and attributed far too much importance to the influence of Marxist ideas in Mexico.

Nevertheless, at least two U.S. Communists worked to determine the role of international Communism in a largely rural, unindustrialized nation undergoing its own revolution. Should Communists support the native revolutionary movement, or should they attempt to control it for the benefit of the worldwide movement? Len Gale held to the first assumption. He tried to pull together the fractious left-wing groups around the banner of Communism in Mexico; at the same time, he collaborated with the Carranza government (as a publicity agent) and, later, with labor leader Luis Morones. Gale also published his own magazine, *Gale's Review*, in which he explored these and other issues.[68]

Gale's ideas were inconsistent and often self-serving, in part because he was uncertain of his status in Mexico as a draft evader from New York and in part because he was experimenting with the implications of Marxism-Leninism in the context of a mass uprising with its own historical roots.[69] Still, he achieved an interesting insight in justifying his work for the Carranza government, as historian Diana Christopulos explains:

> Gale's main point ... involved "the importance of supporting the national claims of 'backward' nations as a tactical weapon in the struggle for Communism." He quoted from Lenin and Karl Radek to show that nationalism was a progressive force in backward or colonial areas which could help to undermine the power of major capitalist nations. Gale stated the core of his own defense [as follows]:
> I believed that an independent nationalist Mexico ... might be utilized as counter artillery with which to weaken the position of capitalism of other nations, especially American capitalism. For this reason I wanted to see Carranza and was willing to make certain compromises.[70]

Luis Fraina disagreed with Gale. The son of Italian immigrants who had come to New York City in the 1890s, Fraina converted to radicalism as a teenager. He soon developed the conviction that capitalism was an unjust and doomed system, and acquired a profound distrust of large organizations, including governments and political parties as well as corporations.[71] After an impressive early career in radical circles in New York, his mission to Mexico proved to be a fiasco. Under orders from the Comintern to work with Mexican nationalist Carranza, Fraina chafed, balked, and eventually gave up. The very course that

Gale championed, Fraina saw as futile. He believed that Carranza wanted a liberal capitalist state, nationalistic only in the sense that it would preserve Mexican resources and protect Mexican enterprises. In his view, this same system would betray the workers and peasant, leaving them in poverty and political irrelevance.[72]

Neither Gale nor Fraina gained access to the inner workings of the revolution. Gale eventually penetrated the fringes of Mexican politics but, for his labors, was deported to Guatemala and ultimately sentenced to prison in the United States for draft dodging.[73] Fraina broke with what he saw as the overly arbitrary and impractical Communist Party.[74] In their disagreement on the tactics necessary to deal with indigenous, non-Communist revolutions, these two men exemplified in theory and practice one of the dilemmas that troubled U.S. Communists in their relationship with the Mexican revolution for the next two decades.

The frustrated Friana was apparently isolated from Mexico City's cosmopolitan radical community, but not so Len Gale. In pursuit of his goal of melding Bolshevism with the Mexican movement, Gale was active in that left-wing polyglot. His acquaintances and eventual rivals included Michael Borodin, Manbendranath Roy, and Manuel Gómez. Borodin, the forceful Russian Communist agent, and Roy, the "deadly serious" Indian nationalist who had served the Kaiser's Germany as an anti-British operative in Mexico, made an odd couple, but with the peripatetic Gómez they gained the much-coveted recognition of the Comintern and thereby pushed Gale toward an alliance with the Mexican government.[75]

Carleton Beals, a young and not yet published writer with leftist inclinations, knew the main actors in this drama and, from the point of view of a bemused member of a small audience, recorded some humorous and belittling observations twenty years later. Beals saw Roy as "a conservative Hindu nationalist [who] suddenly joined the Mexican Socialist party." Teamed with Borodin against "the red-bearded American" Gale, Roy achieved a victory that had few lasting consequences.[76] Roy and Borodin as well as Gale and Fraina soon left Mexico to Beals and the radicals who had begun to drift into Mexico City during World War I. Some, like Gale, were seeking refuge from the draft. Others, like Beals, seemed drawn to Mexico by a vague desire to experience what they thought was a revolution in the making.

Breaking Predispositions

Although the Mexican melee seemed to stir the thought processes of most U.S. visitors in narrow, familiar, and sectarian ways, there were exceptions. Herbert I. Priestley and William Gates, despite their ideological predispositions, managed to grasp some of the fundamental issues in the revolution in a depth that was rare among Bolshevik-sensitive visitors from the north.

Priestley was a professional historian trained at the doctoral level under the watchful Herbert Eugene Bolton of the University of California. After more than a decade of teaching and administrative experience in elementary and high schools, Priestley had entered graduate school in 1912 and five years later, at the age of forty-two, completed his doctorate in Latin American history. He secured a position in Mexican history at Berkeley, where he remained until his death in 1944. He was a typical academic who wore a business suit, spoke in a dignified manner, and was aware of the circumspection and conformity necessary for advancement in higher education. Not surprisingly, he held a liberal capitalist ideology.[77]

Priestley was a careful scholar who took professional standards seriously. His dissertation, which became his first book, was largely an elite-oriented political-administrative narrative of New Spain in the 1760s with only incidental mention of the lower strata of society.[78] His 1921 outline for a course called "Diplomatic Relations of the Untied States with Mexico and the Caribbean Area" was well within the traditions of the time with its stress on U.S.-British-French rivalry and very little indication of the Mexican, Nicaraguan, or Cuban point of view.[79] Priestley seemed typical of this period in the evolution of the history profession, when European culture and ideas dominated the training of historians in the United States. Frederick Jackson Turner's raising of the banner of a unique frontier experience helped to add the American West and the nineteenth century to the realm of professional history, and Bolton's ground-breaking work brought colonial Hispanic America into a small corner of the domain.[80] But in general the discipline of history remained heavily traditional, and Priestley worked within those parameters.

Yet Priestley's scholarly perspective included a penchant for disinterested judgment, a modulated willingness to delve into the condition of all levels of society from the mighty to the meek. Perhaps three years as a primary school teacher in the Philippines had helped to arouse his social consciousness; in any case, his continued reading and writing on Hispanic American history revealed a growing awareness of the harshness of the Spanish Conquest and subsequent subjugation of the Indian peoples through the colonial period.[81]

Priestley usually avoided direct reference to ideological issues in his work, but contemporary Mexico made that form of controversy inescapable. He saw that the purpose of the Constitution of 1917 was the creation of a socialistic state, but he also realized that Carranza had not attempted to implement the document's most radical provisions. The following passage reveals the mind of a liberal capitalist struggling with the consequences of a popular uprising:

> I am not arguing for the Mexican revolutionary program. While I feel reasonably firm in the conviction that if it were honestly carried out, it would result in greater good than the present system of exploitation of Mexico, I feel that it is a dubious scheme, and that its sponsors have faint realization of its bearings, its significance, its possibilities and dangers. I doubt their will, courage, and unselfish purpose to see it through. But the point at issue is that if this program is the will of the Mexican people as shown by their government the American people have no colorable right to intervene in their carrying out of its provisions until it is manifest that injustice is to result to Americans, injustice that cannot be remedied by legal means.[82]

Priestley's 1922 review of Wallace Thompson's three books on Mexico testified to the Berkeley historian's efforts to grasp the meaning of the revolution: "The new system may be a grotesque conception evolved with a bizarre idealism, as the revolutionary socialism of Mexico has been, and it may be malformed in the executive by private and public thievery, graft, persecution, and horror, as the Mexican revolution has been, but somewhere there is a real and sufficient cause if unrest is general and widespread, and somewhere there is a real and sufficient cure, if a true analysis is made and the suitable remedy applied."[83] Priestley's 1923 textbook expressed similar concerns. Madero, the inept politician, had unleashed forces he did not understand and could not control. His "movement was an explosion of pent-up hatreds of the lowly against the better-bred. It was not a movement for a better government in essence, but a movement for the reversal of the relative positions of the social classes in the political and economic scheme of things.[84]

The current discontent in Mexico could not be denied, but neither could the burden of the nation's past. Priestley warned that an elite—albeit a new one—was still in charge.[85] The viceregal system, the Bourbon reforms, the tumult of the early and middle nineteenth century, and the Díaz era all revealed a deeply embedded tendency toward oligarchic government. Priestley chastized Carranza's critics because "they forgot that from the time of old Spain's conquest to that moment [Carranza's rise to power] there had never been a successful government in Mexico which had not been a dictatorship."[86]

Bringing to bear a thorough knowledge of the past and a perceptive awareness of the present, Priestley carefully explored the revolution from railroad car and library. But William Gates, an amateur

enthusiast rather than a professional scholar, plunged into the backlands in search of archaeological sites, rare books, and revolutionaries.
He found many of the first two, but his most remarkable encounter in
the third category was with Emiliano Zapata, the rebel chief of Morelos.
Gates was a beneficiary and defender of free enterprise capitalism and
an opponent of what he believed to be Bolshevism in Mexico, especially
in Salvador Alvarado's Yucatán. He had neither Priestley's scholarly
reserve nor his progressive inclinations. In view of this conservative
mindset, Gate's sympathy for Zapata's revolutionary program was all
the more remarkable.

Unlike Priestley's academic preparation, Gate's learning was
largely impromptu and self-instilled. With a comfortable income from a
printing business, he had the time and the wherewithal to travel. He
chose Mexico because of its untapped archaeological riches and, despite
a prickly personality and an idiosyncratic intelligence, built artifact and
book collections that formed the basis for Tulane University's movement into Latin American research in the 1920s.[87]

Gates traveled widely in the states of Yucatán, Oaxaca, and
Morelos in 1918 and found what he believed was the key to understanding the insurrection in Mexico: the movement led by Zapata. At a
dinner hosted by Manuel Palafox, one of the movement's main ideolo-
gists, Gates listened to an extensive and unexpected monologue on
plans for land redistribution, credit, and irrigation: "The dinner got cold
while he [Palafox] talked," Gates recalled. By contrast, Zapata's speech
was slow and labored. Gates was impressed by the rebel chieftain's
ideas but frustrated by his difficulty in articulation: "Zapata is like a
man whose ideas and purposes are limpid in their simplicity, but to
whom language is a difficult and puzzling area, yet his self-consciousness is so clear that this fact does not abash him."[88]

After conversations with Zapata, Palofox, Antonio Díaz Soto y
Gama (a lawyer and national political figure), and other Zapatistas,
Gates attempted to sum up the promise and predicament of these
agrarian revolutionaries. Mexico had to be "rebuilt economically from
the bottom up" but lacked the necessary resources. His conclusion
contained the lingering doubts of a conservative who had come to
accept the legitimacy of the Zapatista's efforts but could not abandon
his commitment to a kind of paternalistic interventionism: "The Revolutionists and actual honest people of Mexico, who are struggling to
save her, have the right to prove that they can do so. (And then came the
clause that was hard:) But if they cannot, still Mexico must not go on in
self-destruction."[89].

With a mixture of regret and trepidation, Gates presented his

conclusions directly to Zapata, including a phrase at the bottom of the
list that contained the possibility of foreign intervention:

> As I read the sentences that Mexico's patriots still have the right
> to prove their ability to rebuild her, I began to fold the bottom of
> the paper across. Then at the first words saying that it must still
> be done anyhow, Zapata broke in, not antagonizing me yet
> absolutely himself: "No quiero ni aun oirlo, I do not wish even
> to hear it." As he began to speak I rose, tearing off the alterna-
> tive, and leaving the statement of facts at the end with the right
> of the Revolutionists to overthrow Carranza themselves as
> Mexicans; and as he finished I tore the alternative to bits and
> strewed them on the floor, looking at him. I felt rather than saw
> Soto y Gama's smile. And to Zapata I answered: "Good; it is
> exactly what I wanted to hear you say. The responsibility in this
> cause lies already on your shoulders, and of other Mexican
> revolutionists, and to avert what will never come if President
> Wilson can prevent it, and shall not come if I can tell the story of
> what I have seen in Mexico well enough to do something to
> forestall the approach. You need no urging: but I say it: See that
> Mexico does not make intervention necessary, for her own sal-
> vation." As I spoke, a little fugitive and gratifyingly comfortable
> smile broke on the corners of his mouth.[90]

Gates respected Zapata's rejection of foreign control of Mexican
affairs, but upon his return to the United States he expressed in print his
belief that such intervention was likely. Mexico had to be saved from
itself; in particular, according to Gates, it had to be saved from Carranza's anti–United States Pan-Latinism, which challenged U.S. interests throughout the hemisphere. Gates argued that the expansion of
U.S. corporations in Latin America had to continue and that the Constitution of 1917 was an impediment to that process. Gate's fundamental
attachment to the free enterprise system had loosened enough to accommodate the Zapata land reform scheme, but that was his limit.[91]

Like other commentators on Mexico, both Gates and Priestley
carried with them certain ideological commitments. Gate's opposition
to Bolshevism (or perceived Bolshevism) in Yucatán would have
pleased Fall and Doheny, but his acceptance of Zapata's case for a
massive redistribution of private property by government intervention
would have enraged them. Priestley's liberal capitalism was more consistent internally and more restrained polemically, but when confronted
with indisputable evidence of widespread peasant and worker unrest,
the historian recognized that the actions and hopes of these people—
however "dubious" and "bizarre"—could not be dismissed as irrelevant. Both men were willing to analyze conditions that challenged their
ideological predispositions—a rare quality among visitors to Mexico in

those years. In their own ways, both expressed judgments that there was under way in Mexico a revolutionary movement that did not fit conveniently into the ideological and political categories north of the Rio Grande.

3

Revolutionary
Enthusiasm

It was a "wild party"—not unlike raucous gatherings in New York and Paris in the 1920s. Alcohol flowed freely, conversation was uninhibited, and the air contained a smoky haze of tobacco and perhaps marijuana. The hosts of this boisterous bohemian event at a rented house near Chapultepec Park in Mexico City in early December 1925 were photographer Edward Weston and erstwhile film actress turned model Tina Modotti. The guest of honor was Mercedes, Tina's sister. In attendance was a collection of artists, art critics, and writers dominated by Diego Rivera, the mountainous, free-willed Marxist muralist, with his strikingly beautiful, unpredictably assertive wife, Lupe. Rivera loomed over the group not only by his artistic eminence but also by his imposing six-foot, three-hundred-pound frame. Three of his admirers (at least in the 1920s) were there: Jean Charlot, a sensitive young artist enamored of Mexican themes; Carleton Beals, a loquacious journalist with a misdirected inclination toward poetry; and Anita Brenner, a precocious Mexican-born writer and art critic. All of them were lively conversationalists with literary ambitions. Manuel Hernández Galván, a radical Mexican politician with a talent for playing the guitar and singing, performed for the group. Frances Toor was not as garrulous as the others, but her rejection of bourgeois values and dedication to Indian culture gave her acceptance among the bohemians.[1]

In comparison with wild parties in the United States and Europe, this Mexico City affair offered a cosmopolitanism that mixed typically rebellious writers and artists seeking refuge from the mercenary, middlebrow Main Street of the United States with a distinctively Mexican component: the self-proclaimed revolutionaries who believed that somehow they could remake their nation. Rivera, Brenner, and other Mexican leftists advocated an unprecedented but ambiguous thrust for social change to benefit the Indian-mestizo peasants and, in apparent contradiction, a program that would preserve and enhance their traditional values. Mexico's radical artists and writers led by Rivera found prominent positions in the rapidly shifting matrix of politics and culture in Mexico City. The visitors from the United States were fascinated by this prospect of the creation of a new world in old Mexico by means of processes that operated outside the realm of bourgeois values.

But political ambiguity would soon rival cultural innovation on the Mexican scene. Like most outbursts of high idealism, the visitors' enthusiasm for revolutionary Mexico was transient. They relished this momentary blaze of revolutionary culture, but soon the cold realities of political infighting and the return of violent revolt dashed much of their sincere but fragile optimism.

Beals, Toor, and Weston were part of a small but growing number of U.S. writers and artists who visited Mexico in the 1920s. As the disruptions of civil strife diminished in the early years of the presidency of Alvaro Obregón (1920–24), readers in the United States became aware of the nonviolent cultural ferment under way in Mexico. In the pages of the *Nation*, Helen Bowyer exhibited the typical excitement of a first-time visitor to Mexico. In 1922 she enrolled as a student in the Mexican National University's summer school. Based in Mexico City, the National University provided for visitors a curriculum that included archaeology, art, botany, zoology, ethnology and Spanish—all greatly enhanced by field trips to ancient pyramids, verdant jungles, and rustic Indian villages. Bowyer's prose was laced with such phrases as "the delight of a summer at the Mexican university" and "the indescribable blue of the moonlight" over the Zócalo. The first contingent of 150 students in 1921 went home with such "a glow of enthusiasm" that many of them returned with compatriots to form an enrollment of 500 students the next summer.[2] Bowyer's essay was indicative of a widening interest in Mexico that sustained an academic and lay readership in the United States.[3]

Bowyer's suggestions not only enticed teachers and university professors but also captured the attention of independent travelers who did not want the structure of an academic course. Herbert Corey, a travel author, appealed to the latter group as well with three illustrated articles in the *National Geographic* on his venture from the deserts of Baja California to the jungles of the Isthmus of Tehuantepec. Comparing Mexico with distant India, he commented on "the swarming natives in their thin cotton, paddling about barefooted, and ox-carts, donkeys, fine horses, and—if one is interested—alligators in the lagoons, bears in the mountains, and a bad cat the natives call a tiger. All the country needs is a Kipling."[4]

Few visitors, however, followed Corey's footsteps through the deserts and jungles. Even though travel in the early 1920s was not yet simplified by modern highways or regular airline routes, both the academic and the independent traveler—whether bohemian, would-be Kipling, or sales representative—could find a number of reliable ways of getting to Mexico. University of California historian Charles Chapman advised Atlantic coast visitors that Pullman coaches from Matamoros and Nuevo Laredo to Mexico City offered good service, as did the boat connection to Veracruz and its continuation by rail to the capital.[5] Bowyer added that the Ward Line provided special discounts for students and that the Mexican government offered rebates on their rail tickets from the border to Mexico City.[6] In 1922 Edward Weston found the Pacific coast boat trip considerably less arduous than Corey's overland hike.[7]

Yankee Bohemia and Its Fringes

The Mexico City that attracted U.S. visitors had only recently emerged from a decade of intermittent revolutionary convulsions. Alvaro Obregón became president in 1920, six years after establishing himself as the nation's premier general by his defeat of Pancho Villa. Not a radical, Obregón implemented social and economic reforms on a limited scale, including a substantial budget for José Vasconcelos as minister of education. Vasconcelos, in turn, hired Diego Rivera to paint murals on the walls of important government buildings. For travelers, the combined impact of treading in the steps of guerrilla leaders Pancho Villa (assassinated in 1923) and Emiliano Zapata (assassinated in 1919) in the countryside, observing the surge of labor organizations, and witnessing the endeavors of Rivera and other artists in Mexico City provided a sense of being in the midst of a genuine revolution that was pushing upward beneath the inertia of a reluctant national government. Indeed, President Obregón and his successor, Plutarco Elías Calles, found that they could not completely ignore this spontaneous movement.

Mexico City itself seemed to project the excitement of rapid social and cultural change and, at the same time, a return to business expansion. Ernest Gruening, managing editor of the *Nation*, detected "the rising hum of revolutionary fervor, of a people reborn, of hopes rekindled."[8] Carleton Beals, after a three-year sojourn in Europe, saw that in 1923 Mexico City "had more than doubled in size. The suburbs were changing from semi-Indian rural communities to important middle-class residential towns." The horse-drawn carriage of the Porfirian era had given way to the automobile, and the city had taken on the bustle of a fragile prosperity.[9] Weston complained that the ever increasing automobile traffic often spoiled the otherwise pleasant climate of the Valley of Mexico.[10]

Although the second group of bohemians shared some of the leftist attitudes of their predecessors, the new arrivals were more concerned with literature and art than politics and ideology. Two figures who had departed Mexico in the heyday of the Len Gale group and returned to join the new bohemian congregation were Beals and Katherine Anne Porter. Beals preferred the literary and artistic strivings of the second group to the often strident, factionalized disputes of the first.[11] Porter returned to Mexico City in March 1922 to become a leading observer and advocate of the cultural aspects of the revolution.[12]

Porter and Beals eventually became close friends. She observed his psychological distress after the breakup of his first marriage and used these observations in constructing "the journalist" as the central character in her short story "That Tree." The fictional Beals emerged as a frustrated poet whose main aspiration was to lie under a shady tree and compose poetry. Reality and the demands of his soon-to-depart wife drove him to journalism in order to earn some income and a modicum of respectability. Porter's portrait was apparently not far from Beal's actual experience, and, more important, gave an insight into the difficulties of Yankee bohemians who yearned for creative independence but capitulated to economic necessity.[13]

Within a few months after his return from Europe in the spring of 1923, Beals met several of the new arrivals, including Weston and his model-student-paramour, Tina Modotti. In early 1922 the photogenic, voluptuous Modotti had brought several of Weston's photographs for exhibition in Mexico City, where their positive reception spurred Weston to leave the restrictions of his photography business in California for the promise of artistic and personal liberation in Mexico.[14] Beals, Weston, and Modotti soon befriended Frances Toor, a plump, bespectacled graduate of the University of California whose shy manner concealed a likable personality.[15] Beals and Toor soon brought Lesley Simpson into the widening circle. Simpson was on the Spanish faculty at Berkeley and lent his talent with the guitar and his deep interest in Mexican history to many informal gatherings.[16]

Beals, Toor, Simpson, Weston, Modotti, and Porter formed the center of this highly fluid group of expatriates and travelers who in some ways resembled the bohemians of New York's Greenwich Village in the 1912 to 1917 period. For example, Beals, Porter, and Weston shared a sense of alienation from the middle-class materialism that dominated the United States in the 1920s.[17] They had little commitment to traditional institutions such as marriage and sexual restraint. With the exception of Professor Simpson, they survived on low incomes, in part with the help of more fortunate colleagues.[18] Mexico City offered a stimulating cultural environment and a modest cost of living, a combination that the northern visitors found immensely attractive.

The parallel with Greenwich Village is imprecise, however, because the Mexico City group was more widely dispersed throughout the city and in rural areas and probably diminished more often by extended absences. Nevertheless, in one sense the two bohemias shared a common characteristic: both were temporary phenomena. Their importance lay not with the physical edifices and artifacts of the community, nor with their free-floating social relationships, but rather with the intellectual contributions that their members were to make on a larger stage in later years.[19]

For many of the Mexico City group, Anita Brenner personified an ideal of cultural diversity. Brenner was born in 1905 of Jewish parents in Aguascalientes, Mexico, but the family moved to Texas a few years later, where she grew up fluent in both Spanish and English. After an unhappy adolescence among the anti-Mexican, anti-Semitic elements of the Anglo-Saxon community of Texas, the intellectually advanced eighteen-year-old left home to thrive in the bohemian community of Mexico City. In that cosmopolitan atmosphere her multi-ethnic background, alert mind, lively personality, and physical attractiveness made her a prominent figure.[20]

Although the bohemians lived in various parts of Mexico City, their area of concentration was west of the National Palace along or near Avenida Francisco Madero and its continuation, Avenida Juárez, as far as the Paseo de la Reforma. The hotels, restaurants, and apartments for several blocks on both sides of Madero-Juárez were shifting focal points for their afternoon and nocturnal meetings. Brenner and Weston recorded special delight in visiting the *pulquerías* of the city, although the potent alcoholic *pulque* offered there was less attractive to them than the uniquely decorated walls and equally colorful names, such as "The Loves of Cupids," "The Celebrating Monkeys," "Men Wise without Study."[21] Their conversations ranged from innocuous social patter to extended discussions of culture and politics. Brenner recalled a "workshop atmosphere" in which the participants exchanged perceptions and ideas.[22]

All was not harmony, however. Like most collections of talented and determined people, the bohemian community endured moments of rancor and even angry withdrawals. Most of the discord arose from rivalries and jealousies that involved personalities and artistic temperament, but in at least one case politics sparked ill will: a triangular controversy about Mexico's labor unions set Communists Rivera and Bertram Wolfe (a migrant from New York) against government-connected labor organizer Roberto Haberman, while the third and largest group in this dispute held a rather jaundiced view of both factions and preferred to explore the less politicized field of literature and art.[23] Such clashes augured ill for the community's longevity but also testified to the resolve of its individual members.

Porter, Beals, and other writers drew the attention of many U.S. leftists to Mexico, including John Dos Passos. Something of a literary celebrity following the success of his novel *Manhattan Transfer*, Dos Passos came to Mexico in part to find material for a new novel. Although his fluency in Spanish made his movement about the Mexican capital quite easy, he relied on Beals as a guide.[24] Eventually he met "other Americans and numerous Mexican writers, journalists, and painters, many of whom had the stories he wanted to hear." Among the Americans was Gladwin Bland, an ex-member of the Industrial Workers of the World, whose stories of life among the "Wobblies" inspired the character Fenin "Mac" McCreary in Dos Passos's next novel, *The 42nd Parallel*.[25]

While Dos Passos enjoyed these tales, Ernest Gruening cultivated Mexico's presidents, first Alvaro Obregón and later Plutarco Elías Calles. On his arrival in 1922, Gruening was managing editor of the *Nation*, known in the United States and to a lesser extent in Mexico for his criticism of Washington's interventions in the Caribbean. Gruening got acquainted with his fellow journalist Beals[26] and enjoyed dinner with Edward Weston,[27] but he inspired the suspicion of Bertram Wolfe's wife, Ella, who felt that he was too close to the center of power in Mexico and a "fellow traveler" of dubious intentions.[28] Gruening did not mention the Wolfes in his massive study *Mexico and Its Heritage* and alluded only briefly to the Communist Party.[29]

Though a diminutive man of rather unimpressive appearance, Gruening was gregarious and persuasive in conversation, commanding respect if not admiration for his energy and aggressiveness. The only son of a successful New York City physician, he had had the advantages of Hotchkiss and Harvard, and connections in the New York social sphere. His choice of journalism over medicine disappointed his parents, but he did not abandon the highly placed contacts his education and Jewish family brought him.[30] His penchant for striking up good relationships with presidents and other authority figures troubled many of his fellow writers and, a decade later, aroused the distrust of his boss in the New Deal's Department of the Interior, Harold Ickes.[31]

Yet the transparently ambitious Gruening had a defender among the antiestablishment bohemians. Anita Brenner, who worked as his research assistant for nearly two years, found him "honorable, courteous, and cultured." She minimized his aggressiveness, identifying his main character flaw rather as a materialistic value system—not uncommon among Marxists, liberals, and businessmen. Brenner confessed to her diary that "he pivots on facts . . . seeable, tangible, provable facts . .

which is therefore the cause of [his] spiritual poverty."[32] This passage reflects the gap between the literary-artistic group and the generally more prosaic and power-conscious journalists and academics who came to Mexico in greater numbers after the mid-1920s.

Gruening's commitment to his marriage and his three sons left him outside much of the bohemian activity, but he did host frequent dinner parties to which the likes of Beals, Toor, Brenner, and Haberman were invited. Brenner recorded her impression of the conviviality of one such occasion: "Gurening [sic] gave me the place of honor at his right hand . . . telling Frances [Toor] to move, and was very attentive and courteous. Shakes a mean cocktail. Dinner was very good. After [dinner] we danced and sort of loosened up and I liked that. . . . Everybody amiable. Was it the cocktails?"[33]

Though apparently not in attendance at any of Gruening's dinner parties, two academics from Columbia University likewise penetrated the fringes of the bohemian community. The first and better known was philosopher John Dewey. His international reputation, friendly demeanor, espousal of social reform, and, especially, praise for the Mexican government's education program all combined to win him quick acceptance during his brief stay in the summer of 1926.[34]

The second, Frank Tannenbaum, was a former undergraduate student of Dewey and, in the late 1920s, a doctoral candidate at the Brookings Institution. Over the next two decades Tannenbaum became arguably the best known and most widely respected academic authority on contemporary Mexico in the United States. In these early days, nevertheless, he had a tenuous and often distant relationship with his compatriots in Mexico. In Weston's quick evaluation, he displayed "all the petty dogmatisms of the average labor leader."[35] A few years later Porter observed him "still busily 'writing up' in his faithful wooden way, everything he sees, with statistics to back him up, and a thesis to begin with. He can't move a leg without a thesis as a crutch."[36] Brenner—again—has a more tolerant view: "everyone has always said that Frank Tannenbaum is a monstrous egotist, and I have always found him to be quite the reverse. It is the humility of apologia pro mea vida. The fact of [his] being a Jew might have something to do with it."[37]

Tannenbaum was born in Austria in 1893, migrated with his parents to America in 1904, and spent the next two years on a farm in the Berkshires of Massachusetts.[38] That experience may have accounted in part for his lifelong interest in the rural environment and the small communities typical of village life. In contrast to the well-heeled, traditionally schooled Gruening, Tannenbaum cut a large swath through New York City in 1914 as a street agitator and leader of protests against government indifference toward the unemployed. His display of radical temperament landed him in jail but brought him to the attention of a wealthy benefactor, who directed him to Columbia University; there Tannenbaum channeled his energy into more acceptable endeavors. At Columbia and the Brookings Institution he evolved from agitator to academic with an awareness of the nuances of politics in higher education and in Mexico's daedal system. Yet he retained elements of impetuousness, sometimes manifested in the manner of an overbearing scholar. His forceful earnestness and occasional lapses into sociological theorizing irritated many of the bohemians, who preferred subtlety and shadows.[39]

His devotion to the study of Mexico spilled over into some of his early writing. Particularly in "Mexico—a Promise"—a 1924 article for the *Survey Graphic*—he implored his U.S. readers to take the country seriously: "We know more about Albania, about Armenia, about Afghanistan, than we do about Mexico—and yet to know Mexico is almost a moral obligation. To the United States Mexico is more than a neighbor, more than a different country, more than a field of commercial and industrial exploitation. It is the gateway to a continent, not only physically but spiritually, culturally—the gateway to understanding a hundred million people who inhabit the mountains and valleys from the Rio Grande to the Straits of Magellan."[40]

In 1925 a photograph of Tannenbaum in the *Literary Digest* revealed a tousle-haired young man beaming with apparent pride after his transformation from fiery rabble-rouser to respectable academic with a lingering commitment to socialism.[41]

The Discovery of the Mexican Indian

Like their counterparts in New York, the bohemians in Mexico sought experiences among the ethnically exotic. Mexico's Indian population—scattered among the mountains, deserts, and jungles—offered a remarkable variety of languages, cultures, and life-styles that captured the imagination of the bohemians and their compatriots.

The visitors to Mexico in the 1920s were not the first U.S. observers interested in the Indian peoples. Diplomat John Lloyd Stephens and artist Frederick Catherwood had introduced the reading public of the United States to the monumental ruins of Mayan civilization in the 1840s;[42] in the late nineteenth century Adolph Bandelier made archaeological studies of Mexico's Indian past;[43] and in the early 1900s Frederick Starr described the isolated and often forlorn condition of the largely Indian states south and east of the nation's capital.[44] The decade of civil disorder from 1910 to 1920 aroused the Indian population and brought into the nation's cultural and political leadership a new generation that not only accepted the Indian as an important part of Mexican society and polity but also elevated the Indian past to a position of equality with if not superiority to the Spanish. Travelers who arrived in the early 1920s found excitement in this combination of ethnic awareness and cultural ferment that somehow united the dogged idealism of Zapata with the artistic creativity of Rivera.

Porter was one of the first aficionados of Indian art. Along with Minister of Education Vasconcelos, director of the National Preparatory School Vicente Lombardo Toledano, and artists Adolfo Best-Maugard, Xavier Guerrero, and of course, Rivera, Porter arranged for the exhibition of an 80,000-piece collection in Los Angeles in 1922. She wrote a fifty-five-page description of the exhibition to give viewers not only an admiring introduction to Indian art but also a broad and sympathetic portrayal of the native people of Mexico. Her prose radiated enthusiasm. She attacked point-blank the notion that the rise of Indian influence meant that Mexican art "had degenerated into a mere meaningless peasant art." On the contrary, Porter insisted, the European influence of the colonial and early national periods had been stifling and inhibiting. The Indians were reasserting an aesthetic tradition that in its current form: "is filled with a rude and healthful vigor, renewing itself from its own sources. Above all there is no self-consciousness, no sophisticated striving after simplicity. The artists are one with a people as simple as nature is simple; that is to say, direct and savage, beautiful and terrible, divinely gentle, appallingly honest."[45]

Porter's interest ranged from the individual objet d'art to the larger quest for universality of expression. Her descriptions of various pieces in the exhibition indicated an awareness of personal style as well as regional variations. Her central message, however, seems to have been that this florescence of native art provided impressive evidence of the ultimate unity of humanity: "In his terrors the child is primitive man. He fears flood, fire, lightning, the mysterious and awful portents of nature. He creates superstitions about his birth, his emotions, his sex. I submit that these instinctive gropings make all men akin, and that they derive from within the individual. A race in China and a race in Mexico, emerging into the adolescence of civilization, would do similar things because those are the things all the men in the world did in the beginning."[46]

Porter's understanding of the Indian and the revolution also found expression in her fiction, first in the 1922 story "María Concepción." The female protagonist, abandoned by her unfaithful husband while she is pregnant, kills his lover when he returns after the death of her newborn infant. She then finds acceptance in her village. Through this act of primitive revenge, Porter portrayed Indian culture as stronger than the artificially imposed Catholic culture, a point of view that many U.S. writers shared in the early 1920s.[47]

Beals too was caught up in the enthusiasm for the Indians and their art, but he saw another side to the native heritage in the Aztecs' brutal practices of human sacrifice and imperialism. His focus, however, was on the common people, not their elite of emperors and priests. Beals saw in the Indian a mystical sense of beauty sadly lacking among the middle and lower classes of the United States. He found that "the humblest peon is an embryo artist, something that cannot be said for the American office drudge and factory hand. The peon is still close to the artistic handicrafts. Mexico is a land of widely diffused popular artistic culture."[48]

The magazine founded by Frances Toor, *Mexican Folkways*, welcomed the writings of the students of Indian art and culture. In her "Editor's Foreword" to the first issues, Toor stated her motives for establishing the publication: *"Mexican Folkways* is an outgrowth of my great enthusiasm and delight in going among the Indians and studying their customs."[49] Her "enthusiasm and delight" seemed unflagging in the ten years that she kept the magazine in print despite limited subscriptions and financial resources. Her contributors included Rivera, Beals, Modotti, and a young anthropologist from the University of Chicago, Robert Redfield. Redfield's academic orientation, however, though he shared some of Toor's sympathies, led him to find problems and weaknesses in the Indian community as well as strengths.[50]

John Dos Passos had few of Redfield's doubts and much of Toor's optimism, but his was a polemical, left-wing perspective. He made most of his judgments about Mexico in Mexico City, where the paintings of Rivera, Clemente Orozoco, and Guerrero introduced him to the Indian roots not only of contemporary Mexican art but of the revolution itself. Dos Passos was excited by the painters' organization of a labor union, a kind of proletarian coterie of artists, which seemed to him to prove that the initial stages of a genuine social revolution were already under way.[51] With Guerrero he traveled to Indian villages in the mountains not far from Mexico City, where he found what most U.S. leftists found in rural areas—confirmation of the vitality of Indian culture.[52] Dos Passos wrote to a friend that "everything's so Goddammed pictorial it takes my breath away. . . . And everything really is Indian—much more than I had expected."[53]

Brenner's *Idols behind Altars* was probably the culmination of the decade's fascination with the origins of Mexican art. She combined acute observations with a talent for clear prose to produce a lengthy treatise on the contemporary artistic scene in its full ethnic, political, and ideological context. As a small child in Aguascalientes she had witnessed a Villista campaign, and in her twenties she incorporated this experience into her analysis of the revolution as a rising of the masses against injustice and oppression.[54] She gave ample consideration to the guerrilla exploits and defeats of Villa and Zapata and to the ill-fated revolutionary programs of the Yucatecan governor, Felipe Carrillo Puerto, but her conclusion was that "the first and definitive gesture" of the revolution was "artistic."[55] She traced the course of artistic expression in Mexico from the classic Mayan to the superimposition of European forms in the colonial period, to the reassertion of a Mexican spirit in the prints of José Guadalupe Posada in the late 1800s, to the revolutionary explosion of the 1920s. Throughout her exposition she stressed that authentic Mexican art had a strong collective character: pottery shaped first by one pair of hands and then another; pyramids built by generations of workers and architects; and finally the murals of Rivera and Orozco, the results of collaboration between painters and masons.[56]

The prose of Brenner, Porter, and Beals had a sense of urgency that was in part a reaction to the racist indictments of the Indian by Wallace Thompson, Richard Harding Davis, and Frederick Palmer. Yet there was a more profound critic of the cultural potential of the Indian who also aroused the ire of the Indianists. The most formidable critique came not in the blunt clichés of Davis, or Palmer but in the polished language of the English novelist D.H. Lawrence, who visited Mexico in the mid-1920s. Lawrence's much more intricate quest resulted in two serious pieces of literature: a novel, *The Plumed Serpent*, and a book of reflective essays, *Mornings in Mexico*. According to Drewey Wayne Gunn, Lawrence was the most important English-language writer of the period to place the main characters of a major novel in a Mexican setting and involve them in Mexican themes.[57]

Lawrence's depiction of Mexico in *The Plumed Serpent* has been the subject of considerable dispute among literary critics and historians, but his perception of the Indian in both sociological and ethnological terms had an especially sharp impact on the U.S. contingent living in Mexico. Katherine Anne Porter took on the challenge of reviewing *The Plumed Serpent*. She praised Lawrence's talent for descriptive prose, but she regarded as a fatal weakness his inability to surmount his own cultural assumptions in order to penetrate the world view of the Indian. Porter saw this futile quest for understanding personified in the character of Kate Leslie, the Irish woman who vacillates between her European roots and her attraction to the powerful, mysterious manifestation of the ancient Mexican god Quetzalcóatl. According to Porter: "Lawrence identifies her [Kate's] purpose with his own, she represents his effort to touch the darkly burning Indian mystery. It could not happen: he is too involved in preconceptions and simple human prejudice. His artificial Western mysticism came into collision with the truly occult mind of the Indian, and he suffered an extraordinary shock. He turned soothsayer, and began to interpret by formula: the result is a freak myth of the Indian, a deeply emotional conception, but a myth none the less, and a debased one."[58]

Lawrence's intense, seemingly frightened response to the Indian was probably one fruitless culmination of his attempt to find in a non-European "primitive" culture an alternative to the modern world's religious values that, for him and many of his generation, had been discredited or at least cast into doubt. Porter sensed that Lawrence saw the Quetzalcóatl myth as a tentative substitute for the Christian bases of Western civilization. His 1923 novel *Kangaroo* contained evidence of a similar search for a vital religious outlook that would somehow combine the forces of nature and human morality, and in *Studies in Classic American Literature* his deeply ambivalent feelings about probing the primitive world for a solution to the modern world's spiritual crisis surfaced in an outburst of doubt:

> "Try to go back to the savage, and you feel as if your very soul was decomposing inside you. . . .
> We can only do it when we are renegade. The renegade hates life itself. He wants the death of life. So these many "reformers" and "idealists" who glorify the savages in America. They are death-birds, life-haters. Renegades."[59]

His critics plumbed the depths of *The Plumed Serpent* and found Lawrence's view of the Indian deeply flawed. Even in the nonfiction *Mornings in Mexico*, it is possible to see the moody Rosalino as the author's view of the "dumb-bell" Indian—although Rosalino stands out as an individual more than as Lawrence's version of a type. But in one far more insightful assessment he revealed a firmer grasp of both his subject and his own emotions: the chapter "Indians and Entertainment," which explores the nature of the Indian and the predictable response of the white observer, both European and American, to the natives' way of life. Without making any brief for racism, Lawrence called on white people to abandon their excessive and misplaced sentimentality. Even anthropologists fell into this trap, he said, and named Adolph Bandelier as an example. The British novelist issued an ultimatum to his fellow English-language writers: "You've got to de-bunk the Indian, as you've got to de-bunk the Cowboy. When you've de-bunked the Cowboy, there's not much left. But the Indian's bunk is not their invention. It is ours."[61]

Lawrence then proceeded to do some "de-bunking" of his own. In concepts that anticipated the thinking of French social critic Pascal Bruckner a half-century later, he saw the intellectual's propensity to idealize the Indian as a "mental trick," a form of self-deception to avoid the notion that the Indian "way of consciousness" was entirely different from and totally alien to the mind of the whites.[62] Lawrence attempted at least to see across this gulf between Indian and European, and what he saw was apparently the source of much of his fears. His observations of Indian dances and other rituals convinced him that their rhythmic movements and utterances were the outward signs of a mindless communalism that provided an immediate sensual satisfaction but held no answer to the larger questions of existence.[63] The Indian religious beliefs placed divinity in many entities—the sun, the moon, and the earth, for example—but their divided divinity lacked a Prime Mover or a Great Mind. Lawrence could not accept the notion that human beings were no more than a part of the natural system, no better and no worse than the flora and fauna. Perhaps at the center of his rejection of the Indian "way of consciousness" was its apparent subjugation of the mind to the physical elements. Lawrence had long been on a quest to understand the meaning of existence, and to find that Indian culture not only refused to yield any helpful answers but seemed to be built on a formula that forbade even asking such questions was a deep shock, not completely overcome even in the relatively calm prose of *Mornings in Mexico*.[64]

Dispersed Charisma and the Limits of Enthusiasm

Lawrence's philosophical disappointment with Indianism undercut many of the basic assumptions of the prominent Mexicans whom the bohemians and their compatriots most admired—especially the Marxist muralist Rivera, the philosopher-educator Vasconcelos, and the radical Governor Carrillo Puerto of Yucatan. This varied trio of activists had in common a belief that the rural population—Indian and mestizo alike—could be uplifted through education, land reform, and political awareness to transform Mexico into a unified and effective nation. Their personal influence in Mexican politics and on foreign intellectuals resembled what social scientist Edward Shils has termed "dispersed charisma." Instead of displaying the highly concentrated charismatic power often associated with authoritarian figures, these three individuals projected their particular visions of how the revolution might remake Mexico and used these idealized messages to cultivate a following that was cultural as well as political.[65] Their appeals were especially strong for leftists from the United States.

Rivera's prominence among U.S. leftists was unrivaled by that of any other Mexican. Dos Passos saw his murals as the logical extension of the "enormously rich and uncorrupted popular art" of the people. This uniquely Mexican form of revolutionary art was not artificially ideological or propagandistic; rather, "it was a case of organic necessity. The revolution .... had to be explained to the people. The people couldn't read. So the only thing to do was paint it up on the walls."[66] Rivera and his fellow muralists were, therefore, completing a cycle: they used native techniques and forms to enhance their own creative powers in order to explain the meaning of the revolution to the people who started it and were to benefit from it.

Gruening and Brenner also praised Rivera though with more restraint than Dos Passos. For example, Gruening saw Rivera's work as the most persuasive embodiment of "the spirit of Mexico," but it was art with a didactic purpose. Poster drawings intended to persuade the Indians that their return to the *ejidos* (pre-Conquest communal farms) was not contrary to God's will as explained by the Catholic Church, were, according to Gruening, "a striking example of the fusion in Mexico of art and propaganda."[67] Brenner insisted that Rivera's art could be appreciated only as the intermingling of the aesthetic and the ideological.[68]

It was Brenner, perhaps guided by her Mexican sensitivity to foreigners' perceptions, who rendered the most acute evaluation of Rivera's impact on visitors from north of the border. She discerned a pattern in their reaction to Rivera's colorful, class-conscious version of the brutal exploitation that justified revolution: "Many an American school teacher (or other serious minded tourist) has been shocked and subsequently mellowed, departing to Kansas, Texas, California or New Jersey with a new and disturbing vision, and the phrase on her lips that 'after all it is a matter of the point of view.' That people who think last in terms of painting, and people whose most common language is plastic, may be brought to share a single affection by a man of genius is an achievement significant to all America."[69]

The name of José Vasconcelos did not elicit the same level of recognition in the United States as did that of the flamboyant Diego Rivera, but among the U.S. writers in Mexico from 1921 to 1923, the intense and idealistic education minister inspired a respect.[70] Gruening claimed that he was the only journalist allowed free access to Vasconcelos in his ministerial office. His close observation of Vasconcelos at work in the creation of the nation's first extensive network of rural schools for the peasants and first large system of urban schools for the working class led Gruening to exalt the Mexican leader in continental terms: Vasconcelos's contribution lay "not only in the country's rebuilding, but in molding the future of a race and helping to shape the destiny of half a hemisphere. This may seem extravagant but it is my studied conviction."[71]

Gruening's leaning toward overstatement was matched by the equally excited Tannenbaum, who carried the Vasconcelos story from the comfortable book-lined office to the streets of Mexico City's Colonia de la Bolsa, a haven for "bums, tramps, thieves, pickpockets, burglars, and disreputable women." An untrained and otherwise unprepared "Mr. Orpeza" requested permission of Vasconcelos to establish a school in this hostile environment. Vasconcelos agreed. Orpeza set to work with a combination of free breakfasts, good community relations, and innovative organizational methods. The school flourished with "nine hundred ragamuffins" and a dozen or so dedicated teachers. For Tannenbaum as for most foreign observers, this feat symbolized "the miracle" of the Vasconcelos era: the school—whether in the Mexico City slums or in the mountains of Oaxaca—as a center of community activity with face-to-face relationships among children, parents, and teachers as the driving force behind the remaking of Mexican society.[72]

This rhapsodic praise for Vasconcelos met some cautionary discord from Porter and Beals. Both saw public education as vital to the revolution, but they concluded that Vasconcelos's goals and methods were hardly radical. Porter described the education minister as a "believer in applied Christianity," and Beals cast the entire effort for rural schooling and land reform as fundamentally conservative in that it sought to restore to the native not only land but also benevolent cultural traditions. Porter and Beals did not disparage Vasconcelos, but they did recognize his religious, largely Catholic, values and his cautious approach to the matter of social change in the peasant population.[73]

While Rivera borrowed from native handicrafts in his art and Vasconcelos expressed respect for Hispanic traditions in his educational reforms, Yucatán's youthful Governor Felipe Carrillo Puerto took direct action to mobilize the Indian people. In his brief two years in office he attempted to build a socialist infrastructure, but his work was brutally interrupted by his assassination in December 1923. Tannenbaum had been especially moved by Carrillo's respect for the cultural legacy of the Maya.[74] Gruening saw in Yucatán a left-wing, grassroots "democracy-in-embryo" under the banner of socialism, and reported that the fallen governor had

> called himself a Socialist and over the buildings of the new "leagues of resistence" which in every village served the newly emancipated citizens as a sort of combined ward club, night

school, recreational center, and co-operative society for producer and consumer, the red flag flew. The Indians swore by
it—the Mexican tri-color had been the ensign under which they
had been enslaved. Ninety-five per cent of Yucatan's population
was happy for the first time in its history under what, despite
names and symbols, was as close an approach to public unity as
one finds anywhere on earth.[75]

Carrillo's commitment to leftists ideas underscored the ideological diversity among these three charismatic revolutionaries. Rivera was
an intuitive radical whose devotion to Marxism was more selective than
total. Carrillo was a reader of Marx and Lenin, but his brand of socialism was carefully adjusted to fit the needs of Yucatan. Though they
shared a profession of commitment to the exploited classes, they had
little in common in their grasp of Marxist ideas. Yet the gulf between
Rivera and Carrillo appeared small when compared to their distance
from Vasconcelos on the ideological spectrum; the minister of education
was at heart a Catholic traditionalist whose more conservative nature
surfaced in the late 1920s during his futile presidential bid. The excitement of the early years, however, acted to obscure these differences. In
fact, Vasconcelos sponsored much of Rivera's work and praised Carrillo's education program.[76]

That U.S. writers described this era in a kind of hazy optimism
testified to their immersion in Mexican affairs, which was valuable to
the effort to understand an exotic culture but risky for the effort to
examine a foreign society in a larger context. Gruening, Tannenbaum,
Porter, Beals, and most of the leftists who wrote about Mexico in the
early 1920s placed in their pantheon of revolutionary heroes those who
identified with the Indian, and this onrush of concern for the Indian
distracted attention from the realities of politics that Carrillo's assassination brought into abrupt focus. Vasconcelos's rural schools elicited a
few criticisms, and Rivera's murals spurred conservative protests, but
Carrillo's mobilization of Indian voters and his work in land reform
actually posed a threat to established political and economic powers not
in accord with radical goals. The fragility and impermanence of dispersed charisma became evident later in the decade when Carrillo's
experiments fell into disuse, Vasconcelos's right-wing presidential campaign failed, and Rivera became embroiled in internecine leftist squabbling.

The assassination of Carrillo Puerto occurred in the disruptions
caused by the revolt of Adolfo de la Huerta which, for a few weeks,
seemed to threaten the Obregón government. Soon after that revolt
collapsed, a dismayed Gruening wrote his analysis of these events in a

letter to Beals. Perhaps because of its acerbic tone and dire implications, the following passage never found its way into print:

> I took it for granted from the start that the rebellion never had a chance—in the sense of enthroning de la Huerta. . . . Obviously they [his military allies] would never let him, a mere civilian, get the big prize. But the danger has never been de la Huerta or any one person as much as General Chaos—and that it seems to me the rebellion has definitely achieved. . . . spiritually the damage is terrific. It is easy to wax cheerful on the elimination of scoundrels who went with de la Huerta, but they didn't all go by a long shot, and the pathetic truth is that Mexico is totally lacking in even moderately honest, enlightened, and capable men to hold down the major posts, to say nothing of the many minor ones, who are essential to keep the machinery running.[77]

The de la Huerta uprising and Gruening's pessimism pointed to the side of Mexican national life that many U.S. observers preferred not to see. Despite the charismatic auras of Rivera, Vasconcelos, and Carrillo, the remarkable outpouring of artistic accomplishment, the genuinely hospitable reception for native handicrafts, and the inspirational surge in public education—despite all this, any continuation of the movement for massive social change was dependent upon the apparent sympathy and overt public support of a powerful figure like Obregón in the presidency. Mexican art continued to prosper in its own realm, but the excitement of aesthetic creativity and the stimulation of radical discourse diminished in importance when compared to the bruising and sometimes fatal blows exchanged in the arena of Mexican politics.

The Yankee bohemians and their fellow travelers had witnessed in person and described in print the colorful expressions of the culture of the Mexican revolution, but politics abruptly intervened to break the mood of the early 1920s and to challenge the enthusiastic view of Mexico and its future. U.S. observers, searching for a way to understand the revolution, turned increasingly to ideology as a means of grappling with the complex world of politics.

4

The Limits of the Techniques of Hospitality

Many diplomats and businessmen found the Yankee bohemia of Mexico City objectionable as much for its leftist politics as for its avant-garde life-style.[1] U.S. State Department officials saw a sinister design in the perceived domination of these radicals by the Gruening-Tannenbaum-Haberman "Jewish trinity" with the assistance of Beals. In fact, the tension and rivalry within this quartet made any notion of unified leadership more fantasy than fact; however, the less imaginative assertions of U.S. diplomats that these leftists had some connection with the Mexican government were not entirely groundless. Although documentary evidence that they were on the payroll of the Mexican government is very slim, there is ample evidence that they experienced what sociologist Paul Hollander has termed "techniques of hospitality."[2] The Obregón and Calles administrations arranged easily obtained interviews, planned tours, and in a few cases even small subventions—all creating an atmosphere of cordiality and seeming openness to reinforce the favorable predispositions of the leftist visitors.

Political Pilgrimage and Revolution

The revolution was difficult to understand from any perspective along the ideological spectrum. Conservatives tended to recoil from its chaotic, disruptive aspects and, like U.S. Ambassador James Sheffield, simply imported a ready-made explanation of events. Observers to the left went to the other extreme toward enthusiasm.

Paul Hollander's ideas are useful in the analysis of leftists' responses to revolution. He identifies several cases of aberrant thinking among leftists, or "political pilgrims" from industrialized nations who reacted with exhilaration to what they believed was an authentic social revolution. Alienated from their own society, they turned to some foreign nation committed to a revolutionary movement replete with high-sounding promises. Once within the boundaries of that revolutionary nation, the transient intellectuals saw mostly what they wanted to see: a new age dawning, the promised land, the future of humankind under the aegis of a radical state. Their predispositions found reinforcement in the techniques of hospitality employed by the host government. Tour guides channeled them through carefully chosen landscapes and Potemkin villages. Revolutionary leaders such as Stalin, Castro, and Mao exuded a charismatic appeal that often overwhelmed their visitors. Whether willing or unwilling dupes of such manipulations, these pilgrims failed to see or, at least, failed to describe in their writing the deceptive, arbitrary, and often authoritarian tendencies in these revolutionary states.

The Mexican revolution lacked the awe-inspiring imagery of Marxist-Leninist theory and praxis, but in its own sporadic meandering way it created a radical ambience and carried out some radical social and economic changes. Hollander identified six criteria that justified pilgrimage in the minds of those intellectuals who chose to visit the Soviet Union, Cuba, and China; applying these to Mexico suggests more similarities than differences. First, the revolutionary nation had to be either distant (this leaves out Mexico and Cuba) *or* poorly known—which Mexico was: with the exception of some residents of the Southwest and a handful of academics and journalists, few U.S. citizens knew much about Mexico before or during the revolution. Mexico also fit Hollander's second criterion: that the nation be committed to some "semi-utopian goals" and, to a lesser extent, a "radical social transformation." The country met the third criterion—claiming "some variety of the Marxist ideological legacy"—only briefly, in the 1930s. But for much of the revolutionary period it met the fourth—a hostile international relationship—because of its relations with the United States. Part of this hostility grew out of the military interventions, territorial dismemberment, and economic penetration whereby Mexico satisfied the fifth criterion: it had a "victimized, underdog image." And finally, Porfirio Díaz's push for industrialization fell so far short of the level of modernity in the United States and western Europe that Mexico remained an underdeveloped nation—Hollander's sixth requirement.[3]

The political pilgrims who came to Mexico were important to Obregón, who had struggled for three years to obtain normal diplomatic relations with Washington, and Calles, who labored under the threat of military intervention and the intimidation of brusque denunciations by Secretary of State Frank B. Kellogg. The two presidents shared a preoccupation about the image of Mexico north of the Rio Grande and, aware of the initial sympathies of leftist writers, used the techniques of hospitality with skill and effectiveness to obtain favorable U.S. media treatment. On his arrival in Mexico in January of 1923, Gruening quickly obtained a meeting with Obregón and emerged with the conviction that the Mexican president was "a great man, a statesman."[4] There followed a series of interviews that reinforced this impression. According to Gruening's 1923 article in *Collier's*, Obregón was openly and correctly a socialist who favored the labor movement. His goals included "a new deal—a square deal all around . . . in which the worker shall increasingly receive a greater share of the product of his toil." Gruening saw Obregón's ideology as appropriately radical in that "he has aimed at the *root* [original emphasis] of Mexico's troubles. If the country continues to have similarly radical presidents, these troubles promise to be permanently uprooted."[5]

Tannenbaum and Beals also developed friendly ties with Mexican officials, though not at the presidential level. Tannenbaum knew labor leader Luis Morones fairly well,[6] corresponded frequently with Jesús Silva Herzog in the Department of Statistics,[7] and received office space and staff assistance from the government.[8] Beals relied on Morones's lieutenant, Roberto Haberman, to secure a teaching post in the ministry of education and knew educator and feminist Elena Torres.[9] Both authors wrote optimistic evaluations of the Regional Confederation of Mexican Labor (CROM) under Luis Morones. To Tannenbaum, labor unions offered a political balance against the reactionary military.[10] Beals noted that the more radical, anarcho-syndicalist General Confederation of Workers (CGT) weakened its own cause by internal disputes. In 1923 Beals saw CROM as "the strongest and most representative national organization: the only organization capable of an intelligent, evolutionary solution of working-class problems."[11]

In 1925 and 1926 other commentators joined Beals in depicting CROM's moderation in favorable language. For example, Tannenbaum exhibited unusual emotionalism in his account of the American Federation of Labor meeting with CROM in the border cities of Juárez and El Paso: "[Samuel] Gompers [of the AFL] and Trevino [CROM representative] embraced each other on the International Bridge and called the sky to witness their pledge of eternal comradeship. The scene was fit for poets to describe, the mood one for prophecy."[12]

The dignitaries traveled on to Mexico City for the convention of the Pan-American Federation of Labor, where Gompers embraced Morones before a cheering crowd to symbolize, in Tannenbaum's words, "an international brotherhood which Mr. Gompers was dreaming about and building patiently when death carried him off" soon after the meeting.[13] Gompers's death may have elevated this public display of international working-class unity to a higher plane than institutional reality would support. It was clear, however, that Tannenbaum placed CROM and the AFL in the same category of moderate, reformist unions following the gradualist track to worker uplift.

Gruening had even greater access to President Calles than to his predecessor.[14] He did not match Tannenbaum's ardent essay on Gompers and CROM, but he did abandon references to socialism and radicalism in favor of more moderate commentary. By this time CROM had rejected imported ideologies—presumably Bolshevism and socialism—in favor of practical Mexican solutions to labor's problems, and Gruening endorsed this seemingly pragmatic approach.[15] Although it is difficult to claim that the Mexican state controlled the shift in U.S. leftist commentary from approval of radical socialism in 1923–24 to approval of gradualism in 1925–27, it must be noted that Tannenbaum, Gruening, and Beals experienced heavy doses of the techniques of hospitality at a time when the government was very sensitive to its image in the U.S. print media.[16]

The government's successes were short-lived, however. By 1928 Gruening and Beals had defected from the ranks of friends of the revolutionary state and its labor appendage, CROM. In his magnum opus, *Mexico and Its Heritage*, Gruening admitted to having altered his attitude with "the succession of trips [that] proved useful in noting changes [in Mexico] and the intervals of absence for reflection with the detachment that distance from the scene promotes."[17] Although he recognized the historical context of injustices in the Díaz years that explained CROM's "fighting mood," and was aware that Mexico was sailing uncharted waters because it was the first "backwards nation" with large-scale unionization, Gruening did not excuse CROM's blunders. He insisted that the union had isolated itself "largely because of the 'exclusivism' of its leadership and its attempts to break up rival organizations in order to control their members." This lust for power and wealth caused disputes with peasant spokesmen, who also vied for positions in the matrix of Mexican politics. Perhaps the most damning criticism pointed to the blatant elitism that bestowed great rewards on Morones and left the rank and file with a sense of alienation from their own union.[18]

As early as 1927 Beals noted the growing split between CROM and the less organized peasant movement. CROM, at least at the elite level, prospered under the friendly policies of Calles, while the peasants continued to endure a marginal existence both in the *campo* and the capital. Beals pointed to

> the tendency . . . for Mexican labor to become identified with the process of industrialization, seeking its gains in rapid economic expansion and at the expense of continued low rural standards. Hence the inevitable continuation of the cleavage between labor and peasant movements. Industry and the native industrial worker thus became identified with the western European invasion that began four centuries ago under Cortéz. The peasant movement may ultimately be caught up in the same current; at present it is more closely linked with the great indigenous race surge of the Mexican people.[19]

Confronted with the evidence of the underlying clash between labor and the peasantry and of the corruptive ambition of Morones, Beals and Gruening lost their revolutionary enthusiasm. Had they become more radical, or had Morones's authoritarian methods become more obvious? Probably the latter, since Beals and Gruening agreed— from different perspectives—that Morones was hurting both workers and peasants.

The Divergent Left

The pattern of the leftists' commentary on the accomplishments and then the excesses of CROM paralleled their early praise and later criticism of the revolutionary movement in general. The full expression of their growing doubts, however, was delayed by their protest against the U.S. State Department's harsh denunciation of the Calles regime from 1925 to 1927. Motivated in part by Calles's radical rhetoric and Ambassador Sheffield's phobic perceptions, Kellogg charged in June 1925 that Mexico was "on trial before the world." Calles responded with the techniques of hospitality noted above and conducted his own propaganda campaigns in the *New York Times* and other media.[20]

Calles also took advantage of a seminar for U.S. visitors to Mexico conducted by Hubert Herring, a Protestant minister and social activist. Originating in 1926, the seminar brought in participants from several fields including education, business, journalism, and the ministry. Herring later admitted that the first seminar was "liberally loaded with all sorts of propaganda."[21] The 1927 seminar enjoyed a ninety-minute interview with Calles himself.

The government's combination of carefully contrived hospitality and propaganda contributed to an outpouring of pro-Mexican essays and articles in the pages of the *Nation* and the *New Republic* and also the less polemical *Current History* and *Foreign Affairs*.[22] Though it is difficult to gauge the impact of press criticism on U.S. foreign policy, some historians argue that the sympathetic image of Mexico in the U.S. print media was probably a factor in the softening of the Coolidge-Kellogg policy toward Mexico in 1927-28.[23]

Viewed against this background of favorable press coverage from 1925 to 1927, Gruening's criticism in *Mexico and Its Heritage* (1928) was a significant departure. He had initiated this study with trepidation, he said, in view of the multiplicity of specializations required to gain an understanding of the subject. History, sociology, and ethnology all had much to offer in the study of Mexico, and Gruening laid no claim to expertise in those areas.[24] Yet his 600-page tome carried not only physical bulk but also the weight of extensive if not intensive reading and the prestige of a respected journalist who knew two of Mexico's presidents and several lesser political figures.

In a sense, Gruening gave a positive view of the administrations of the 1920s. He faulted the antigovernment Catholic Church for corruption and excessive wealth. He condemned the overbearing power of foreign investors and the unjust distribution of farmland. But by 1928 Gruening was no longer a political pilgrim. He not only criticized antirevolutionary influences but also perceived unfairness within revolutionary institutions themselves. For example, he sided with U.S. investors to the extent of objecting to the provisions of Article 27 that allowed control of foreign-owned properties, particularly oil holdings, to be retroactive, applying to concessions made before 1917. He also argued that Article 27 could become an unfairly confiscatory device: it might dictate the transfer of property without using fair market value as the basis for compensation. This analysis implied specific limits on the Mexican government's ability to deal with foreign property owners. Apparently, in Gruening's view, the rules of free enterprise should cross international boundaries largely intact.[25]

Yet, though his defense of private property seemingly made him an ally of U.S. business interests, these arguments pertained only to largely hypothetical areas surrounding Article 27. Beyond the possibilities of retroactivity and outright confiscation, Gruening had no theoretical or practical objections to massive land reform under the national government. Much more than unregulated entrepreneurship, he called for the establishment of liberal statism in Mexico, to include the participation of cooperatives and profit-sharing in economic enterprises.[26] The former managing editor of the *Nation* advocated a powerful state in terms that most business executives could not tolerate. He praised the federal Ministry of Industry for its promotion of organized labor as a legitimate actor in the economy and in the courts (though he decried the corrupt practices of Morones). He commended the enlarged roles of the central government in education, the arts, transportation, and banking.

He saw private property as functioning within an environment in part controlled by and in part regulated by a responsible, rational state bureaucracy.[27]

Gruening refined his advocacy of land reform, however, by a critique of current practices in that area, citing political manipulation and gross corruption especially at the state level. His rebuke of federal agrarian officials was mild in comparison with his indictment of the unjustified injection of politics and personal ambition into the system by local officials: "Every type of person and every human impulse is represented in the agrarian movement. It has been betrayed, perverted, constantly used as a cloak for designs unrelated to it, and still more often grievously misrepresented." Gruening argued that the national Ministry of Agriculture with its "high proportion of intelligent and devoted executives" must control the land reform process throughout the entire country, and that this process should be undergirded by federal agrarian laws uniformly applied in all states and localities.[28]

Gruening did not exempt national officials from his high standards of political ethics. He pinpointed Calles's appointment of José Manuel Puig Casauranc to head the Ministry of Education as a major error, compounded by Puig's ejection of respected anthropologist Manuel Gamio from the position of director of the Department of Native Culture.[29] He also implicated Calles in CROM's censorship of the Mexico City press by the application of union pressure against several newspapers.[30] Gruening concluded that the nation's political system was weak and unstable because it was dependent on two men—Calles and Obregón—rather than on laws, institutions, and respect for competence.[31]

Mexico and Its Heritage received plaudits from most reviewers, including historian Herbert Priestley, but one authority on Mexican affairs chose to challenge Gruening on two major issues. Frank Tannenbaum argued first that Article 27 was not really retroactive because it allowed for continued use of foreign-owned resources by the alien owner; then he moved to what he considered the larger issue of land reform. Against Gruening's insistence on a uniform national policy set in Mexico City, Tannenbaum asserted: "The inherent structure of Mexican economic and social organization is such as to require a flexible legal formula for land-holding and land-utilization, one that would make possible a great variety of types of land tenure and rights in land. The great complexity of the primitive cultural groups makes any single legal doctrine for land-holding unworkable."[32]

Gruening saw Mexico as relying heavily on the liberal, activist state, but Tannenbaum argued that peasants and workers had given the impetus to reform, along with state and local authorities. All these

grassroots sources would push Mexico toward a spontaneous, community-based society in which the leaders who arose most directly from
the masses and who worked most directly with them would make the
critical decisions—not an official in Mexico City. In *The Mexican Agrarian
Revolution* Tannenbaum carefully skirted direct criticisms of Mexico's
contemporary political leaders, but the implications of his attitude toward centralized political power were clear: the font of authority should
be at the local level. Land reform instigated locally would create a
nation of vital and prosperous villages.[33] In an analytic and prescriptive
essay in the *New Republic*, Tannenbaum expressed his opinion even
more openly:

> The Mexican Revolution has ... fundamentally changed the
> political structure of the community. It has given freedom of
> movement to nearly one-half of its total population. It has res-
> cued the self-governing village and its relative position in the
> community insuring it a long lease of life; it has reversed the
> position of the Mexican Indian and stimulated a strong racial
> consciousness; it has shifted actual political power from the
> land-owner and foreign investment group into the hands of the
> agricultural and industrial laborer; and finally [it] has tended to
> shape the point of view of the Mexican government toward
> social ends as it was never shaped before.[34]

Tannenbaum's writing in the late 1920s was consistent with his
own admission that he had moderated his anarchistic, World War I–era
belief in direct action against the authorities to a gradualistic version of
grassroots socialism. Yet these writings contained a troublesome contradiction. His continued interest in local "face-to-face" organizations indicated that he did not accept the nation-state as the best vehicle for a
large-scale restructuring of society. Although muted, his anarchistic
tendencies remained evident in his reluctance or perhaps unwillingness, to accept the primacy of the central government—yet this reserva-
tion contradicted his endorsement of Article 27 as the fundamental basis
on which to reshape the Mexican economy and, in particular, the nature
of private property. Without a strong state, such a law would not be
enforceable against the powerful interests inside and outside Mexico
that loudly and effectively opposed it. Tannenbaum's dilemma was that
he supported a strong government to do battle with *hacendados* (large
landowners), corporate executives, and meddlesome U.S. diplomats
and, at the same time, advocated a polity and a society in which the
same government left land reform and union organization to village
and labor leaders far from the center of power in Mexico City.

Tannenbaum's sometime friend and sometime rival Carleton
Beal shared this dilemma but took a slightly different ideological direc-

tion. A left-wing populist from California, Beals, like Tannenbaum, saw the common people of Mexico as central in the political equation. His writings throughout the decade contained an unabashed advocacy of the cause of the masses, both rural and urban, as the rightful beneficiaries of major government programs. If the revolution was in doubt, it was because of the mistakes of the central government. Mexico had a choice of what Beals called "three major highways." The first was the path of Díaz-style dictatorship with its preference for foreign capital and its willingness to exploit the native work force. The second was that followed by Obregón and the early Calles governments, which "allied themselves with the popular aspirations of their own country." But Beals regretfully concluded that Mexico in the last two years of the Calles administration had veered onto the third route, which entailed government action "as a mediator between the popular and national needs on the one hand and Washington and American capital on the other." Even more disturbing was the likelihood that Mexico might turn back to the Porfirian model, which would mean the abandonment of the peasants and workers.[35]

Beals saw the need for an active central government, but he also saw that such a political instrumentality could be turned against the people as easily as it could serve their interests. There was a more subtle problem in the potentially harmful effects of rapid socioeconomic change in rural areas in the name of progress. Such well-intended programs as land reform and rural education might bring unanticipated harmful results, such a large migration of the children of peasant farmers to the cities and/or the rapid expansion of market-driven agriculture in rural areas. In short, Beals saw a possible conflict between the aggressively reformist state and the common people who, at least in theory, were supposed to benefit from the reforms.[36]

The Beals-Tannenbaum mistrust of bureaucratic authority arose from their respective applications of populism and anarchism to the Mexican environment. Their mutual friend Anita Brenner made similar criticism of the nation-state from her own perspective. Brenner, an art historian and critic, emphasized her preference for creative and radical instincts over the potent but sterile mentality of bureaucratic politics. The art, essays, and talk of Díego Rivera, José Clemente Orozco, David Alvaro Siquieros, and their followers, (which even Communist Bertram Wolfe conceded was authentically revolutionary)[37] arose from and was continually influenced by the work of anonymous artists: the Indian mestizo people of the hinterland. Minister of Education Vasconcelos had encouraged both famous and anonymous artists, but this arrangement was only temporary and succumbed to the vagaries of politics. Likewise, the Syndicate of Painters and Sculptors had seemed to promise that revolutionary art would march forward with the unionized factory workers, but it broke up in 1924. Brenner believed that the inevitably political nature of large organizations would offer little help and might do considerable harm to the artist. Her admiration for the free-spirited painter and union activist Siquieros was evident: "A gift of speech and mental agility make him a political figure of consequence. Nevertheless, his position is by conviction not political. His radicalism in labor thinking has been radicalism largely in opposition to the amalgamation of politics and social organization which was the policy of CROM. . . . He races from meeting to meeting on an old bicycle, jacketed in a drab sweater whose pockets are full of holes, but there is no inconvenience because he has nothing to put in them."[37]

By the end of the 1920s, then, the effectiveness of the Mexican government's techniques of hospitality seemed to diminish, and once clear of government pressure and persuasion the former political pilgrims moved in directions of their own choosing. Two fairly distinct positions emerged, both considerably at odds with the friendly media coverage the government had cultivated. Gruening constructed the liberal statist case by positing the U.S. progressive model in which the national government directed economic and social reform and by roundly criticizing official corruption, personal ambition, and other deviations from this model. Independent leftists Tannenbaum, Beals, and Brenner followed separate lines of argumentation to arrive at essentially the same conclusion: the local community and the individual as a collectivist within this community were the basic components in the political process whereby the nation-state, at best, responded to the needs of the masses or, at worst, used bureaucratic devices to subvert the demands of the people and create its own unresponsive centralized power structure. Unlike liberal statist Gruening, these radicals had no more than a reluctant, suspicious tolerance for the nation-state as the progenitor of socioeconomic change. Their attitude toward the state was ambivalent: it could be the savior of the common people, or it might become their scourge. In short, some of the bohemians and political pilgrims of the early 1920s had become skeptics if not pessimistic critics by the last years of the decade.

Reactions on the Left and the Right

While liberal statists and independent leftists pulled away from the official techniques of hospitality to express their own distinctive responses to the revolution, other U.S. observers were grappling with events in Mexico within their own ideological frameworks. The awesome bugaboo of Communism gained an energetic if not always effective advocate in the person of New York–born Bertram Wolfe— and U.S. diplomats saw evidence of Bolshevism in Mexico in his outspoken efforts. Meanwhile, as oil companies and other corporations mounted a public relations campaign against Article 27, a small group of international bankers quietly devised a much more perceptive response to the revolution. This chapter explores the ideas of these various groups, beginning with a dramatic episode from the saga of Bertram Wolfe.

Slightly later than usual on the morning of June 29, 1925, Wolfe dashed out of his apartment on Mexico City's Cinco de Febrero Street to catch the bus to Miguel Lerdo High School, where he was employed as an English teacher by the Mexican government. Wolfe had another job as labor organizer for the small but active Communist Party of Mexico, and his public criticism of the Calles presidency and well-known party membership made him a likely victim of Article 33 of the Mexican constitution, which provided for the immediate expulsion of foreigners suspected of subversive activities. As he ran to the bus stop, he noticed two men in close pursuit. Wolfe had suspected that he might be "33'd," so this chase was not entirely a surprise, but it did contain an element of suspense: pistols, shootouts, and assassinations were not uncommon to the streets of Mexico City in the 1920s. Not blessed with great speed afoot, he decided to face his pursuers. Relieved to find that his fate was deportation and not execution, Wolfe, escorted by two plainclothes policemen, was on a train for the U.S. border that night.

Bertram Wolfe's departure deprived Mexico of a rarity: a genuine card-carrying Communist from the United States, part of the much feared and overrated international Communist conspiracy. His two and a half years in Mexico had been modestly successful from his point of view, but not in the curious eyes of the U.S. diplomats who throughout most of the decade were convinced that somehow the Mexican and Russian revolutions were connected. They feared that Bolshevism would enter the hemisphere perhaps through Mexico City and spread its contagion south and north, placing Central America, the Panama Canal, and all of North America in the grip of the epidemic. This fear and confused thinking led many people in the State Department to jump to the conclusion that Mexico City was a hotbed of Communist intrigue in which Bolsheviks, Mexican radicals, and U.S. fellow travelers came together to plot devious schemes, to agitate the guileless public, and to spread insidious propaganda.

The vast perceptual differences between Wolfe and the U.S. Embassy in Mexico City were typical of the simultaneous but variegated efforts of U.S. observers to grasp the larger significance of events in Mexico. In contrast to the enthusiastic preoccupation with Indian culture in the early 1920s, by the middle of the decade attention was focused on politics and ideology. Most observers believed that a general revolution of some sort was under way, but there was no consensus as to what that meant.

Mexico became a virtual stage onto which various commentators projected their ideological versions of what Mexico (and, by implication, the United States and perhaps the rest of the world) should or should not become. The State Department, the oil men, and the bankers seemed to share the belief that U.S. leftists offered nothing more than a monolithic misperception of Mexico, but they were seriously wrong on this point. Communist Bertram Wolfe's party-serving critique of the revolution was nothing like the liberal statist strictures of Ernest Gruening or the independent leftists' version of revolutionary correctness. The liberal capitalists and the business conservatives underestimated the diversity of the left, which in turn paid scant attention to the gaps between the bankers and their colleagues on the right. It was clear, however, that by the mid-1920s ideas and ideology had come to play a central role in the understanding of events in Mexico among independent leftists, liberal statists, and liberal capitalists as well as Communists of the far left and conservatives (both oil company executives and State Department officials) of the far right.

Communism and the Mexican Government

Bertram Wolfe and his wife Ella were among the arrivals from the United States who knew some of the bohemians but who, for a variety of reasons, remained on the edge of the community. Their main goal was not simply to witness a revolution but to create a rival Communist movement. Born in Brooklyn in 1896, Bertram Wolfe was a product of the City College of New York, and antiwar movement of 1917–18, and the New York Communist Party. Ella, two years younger, shared his adventures and ideology along the left fringe of American politics.[1]

Wolfe recalled his arrival in Mexico as an uplifting experience characterized by brisk, sun-drenched days, cool nights, and pleasantly bustling city streets. But during these "golden days" Wolfe had much more on his mind than this exhilarating setting as he began to repair and expand Mexico's small Communist Party that had nearly collapsed after the departure of Gale, Roy, and Borodin (see Chapter 2). His task was complicated by the intraparty conflicts triggered by the abortive revolt of Adolfo de la Huerta against the Obregón government in 1923. Wolfe advocated support of the government, not out of loyalty but in the hope that Obregón would supply arms to the Communist Party and the unions in the fight against the large number of army units that had defected to de la Huerta. The party secretary, Manuel Ramírez, opposed Wolfe and his friend Rafael Carrillo on this issue. The arms Wolfe had hoped for did not materialize, but because he had supported the winning side, he and his allies in the party were able to oust Ramírez and place Carrillo in the position of secretary.[2]

This experience added one more internal conflict in an organization already torn by dissension. Wolfe's "Report on the Mexican Communist Party," prepared for the Fifth Congress of the Communist International (Comintern), indicated some success in the recruitment of peasants and industrial workers but emphasized the divergence within the party: "The right wing tendencies are a constant danger due to the corrupting atmosphere of a mildly pro-labor government. It is a constant task of the central executive committee to prevent collaboration with other parties on an opportunistic basis and uncritical support of government action. The leftist tendencies are also marked. They arise from the anarco [sic]-syndicalist background of many of the present party members."[3]

Wolfe was also troubled by the high profile of Diego Rivera and other artists in the Mexican Communist Party. In a 1924 article for the *Nation*, Wolfe praised Rivera's artistic talent and sympathy for the proletariat but, at the same time, expressed his doubts about the corrosive influence of the Mexican government's support for the artists. He emphasized that the Mexican state was not unified and that its policies in areas such as land reform and labor organization lacked coherence. In fact, only in the work of Rivera and other artists and a few poets did Wolfe sense any meaningful revolutionary content, and that was limited to words and images. Whether this creative impulse was "the first flush of the dawn or only the red after-glow of a revolutionary sunset, no one can yet decide."[4]

Wolfe enhanced his own status in Mexico by participation in the Fifth Congress of the Comintern held in Moscow in June 1924. Accompanied by Peruvian Victor Raúl Haya de la Torre, Wolfe made a vigorous effort to bring Mexico and Latin America in general to the attention of the congress. Soon after the meeting ended, he wrote to his wife, who had remained in Mexico City: "I can say now, in retrospect, that my trip has not been in vain—far from it. . . . I have placed Mexico and Latin America on the map. They [members of the Comintern] began to know that Mexico is not in South America, the language Mexico speaks, etc. etc. They are beginning to see some importance in an important ally against American imperialism."[5] These claims had at least some validity: in March 1925, G.V. Chicherin of the Central Executive Committee of the Soviet Union called Mexico "a very convenient base in America for Communist expansion."[6]

The Comintern absorbed Wolfe's message but also gave him its own directives. Under instructions to follow the model of the Russian party and to promote the interests of the Soviet Union,[7] Wolfe returned to Mexico to initiate a series of actions that were more indicative of his energy and determination than of strict adherence to the Comintern's instructions. In a speech given in early November in Mexico City, Wolfe described the Russian Revolution of 1917 as "the greatest historical event of our time" and cited improved conditions for Russian textile workers as an example of direct relevance to the Mexican proletariat.[8] In March 1925 he served as the first editor of *El Libertador*, a journal intended to promote the expansion of the Communist Party in Mexico.[9] In the first issue Wolfe attacked "the mildly pro-labor government" of Calles. His unsigned article "Adios, 'Socialismo'!" denounced Calles for stripping Article 27 of its possible retroactive application to foreign-owned oil properties. According to Wolfe, Calles simply surrendered to U.S. oil companies any possibility of exercising control over oil concessions granted before 1917, most of which originated in the Díaz years. Wolfe also attacked Luis Morones and CROM, the labor confederation, as corrupt tools of Calles's counterfeit socialist government.[10]

Another part of Wolfe's campaign was giving courses in the

history of the class struggle to several groups of Mexicans—including the railroad workers' union, one of the most important labor organizations outside the powerful CROM. His central message was simple: the union must support itself and avoid dependence on the state if it was to survive.[11] This challenge could only bring threats of retaliation from the Calles government and CROM. On June 10, 1925, Ella wrote to Carleton Beals that CROM official Roberto Haberman was "rabid for [the] expulsion [of Bert]" under Article 33.[12] Haberman, who by then regretted that he had urged the Wolfes to come to Mexico, believed that unionization independent of CROM was not acceptable under the Calles-Morones regime.

In the deportation of Wolfe the Communists found another reason to accuse Calles of capitalistic inclinations. *El Libertador* labeled the Mexican president a duplicitous collaborator, doing the will of Washington and Wall Street in the expulsion even as he claimed the title of a socialist labor leader.[13]

Wolfe's departure inspired a sympathetic critique of his tactics from independent-minded leftist Haya de la Torre, his companion at the 1924 Comintern congress. Haya, writing from the relative safety of London and with the advantage of hindsight, concluded that Wolfe's methods were "too open" to public and official view and were therefore "very dangerous." Calles had damaged his own image by the expulsion, the Peruvian said, but the greater damage was the loss of Wolfe from the party's ranks in Mexico.[14]

Three years after his expulsion, Wolfe presented to the Sixth Congress of the Comintern his assessment of Communism in Latin America. Despite the party's internal conflicts in Mexico and his own exile, he remained hopeful. Foreshadowing the post–World War II international dichotomy, he declared: "The United States and the Soviet Union represent the two poles of the earth today. Leninism has taught us to seek and find allies against our most powerful enemies. It teaches us now that the whole Comintern must turn its attention to this natural enemy of American imperialism, this natural ally of the proletariat of the world—the revolutionary movements of the Latin American People."[15]

Wolfe had some specific ideas on these "revolutionary movements." He saw the bourgeoisie as weak and vacillating and cautioned against reliance on intellectuals who, like Haya de la Torre, harbored antiimperialist sentiments but easily gave in to the temptation to join non-Communist left-wing movements. In Latin America, Wolfe argued, the peasants and especially the Indians offered the Communist Party a better opportunity because of their exploitation by local landowners and international corporations and their apparent retention of native communal traditions in property ownership and social organization.

Wolfe advocated the formation of a peasant-worker bloc directed by a Communist vanguard. He believed that the peasants and workers should be armed, citing the "incredibly heroic guerrilla warfare" then being waged by the Nicaraguan Sandino against the military intervention of the United States.[16]

Although Wolfe wrote relatively little in the 1920s, his work in the Mexican Communist Party and his brief for Communist expansion in the Americas was known to many U.S. residents in Mexico, including Beals, Weston, Toor, Gruening, and probably Tannenbaum and Brenner. Apparently none of these individuals joined the Communist Party in the 1920s, but they knew of its activism in Mexico.

The Red Scare in the U.S. Embassy

The Wolfes openly plied their trade, and the U.S. Department of State identified them on its list of dangerous radicals in Mexico, while one of its most avidly anti-Communist ambassadors, James Sheffield, was in charge of the embassy. A conservative New York lawyer and an admirer of Theodore Roosevelt's aggressive nationalism, Sheffield had an arrogance toward Mexico and a hypersensitivity for anything that smacked of radicalism.[17] The embassy must have felt some excitement when the expulsion of Wolfe revealed that during Sheffield's first ten months there, U.S. citizen Wolfe had played the undisguised role of Communist organizer in close proximity to the ambassador and his staff. Whether Wolfe's activities exacerbated Sheffield's already intense anti-Communism remains unclear, but there is no doubt that the ambassador became convinced that Mexico was a hotbed of radical activity in which Bolshevism had firmly planted its roots. From mid-1925 until his departure in July 1927, Sheffield conducted a wide-ranging search for Communists and fellow travelers among the U.S. expatriates and visitors in Mexico City.

Sheffield's perceptions of radicalism in Mexico had two prominent features. The first, his fear of the spread of Bolshevism from Russia to the Western Hemisphere, was obvious. The second feature is more difficult to explain because it contained assumptions clearly at variance with the facts. Even though Calles ordered the expulsion of Wolfe and showed signs of hostility toward the Communist Party through the actions of Minister of Industry and Commerce and CROM leader Luis Morones,[18] Sheffield believed that the Mexican government was in league with international Communism. He and many of his advisers felt that Bolshevism was becoming a vital force in Mexico. Counselor H.F. Arthur Schoenfeld and consul general Alexander Weddell, in particular, supplied the ambassador with information that could only reinforce his assumptions.

Sheffield's vision of the Communist menace found important but not total support in Washington. Assistant Secretary of State Robert Olds and consultant Chandler Anderson both agreed with Sheffield, and their influence in the government was quite strong in 1925 and 1926. Secretary of State Frank Kellogg's inclinations seemed to align with Sheffield's for a while, but by 1927 he had pulled away from the rabid anti-Bolshevik alarmists in Mexico and Washington.[20]

Sheffield's suspicions about the Mexican government contributed to his reluctance to speak directly with its officials. Tannenbaum, who had close ties with Morones and other members of the Calles government, took it upon himself to arrange a meeting between the suspicious diplomat and some of the political figures he mistrusted. Sheffield and Schoenfeld met for lunch with Morones, Minister of Agriculture Luis León, and Minister of Education José Manuel Puig Casauranc at the fashionable San Angel Inn on the southern outskirts of Mexico City. Soon after the meeting Tannenbaum wrote Kellogg that the open discussion had benefited all concerned.[21] Sheffield had an entirely different reaction; he sensed that the ideological differences between himself and the trio from the Calles cabinet were as deep as if not deeper than he had previously thought.[22] Tannenbaum's efforts to improve Mexican–U.S. relations apparently had little effect.[23]

An unintended outcome of Tannenbaum's luncheon arrangement was a heightened awareness in the embassy of his activities in Mexico. Even before the San Angel meeting, the State Department had begun to build a file that included his arrest after inciting a street demonstration of the unemployed in New York City in 1914 and military intelligence reports on his IWW activities during World War I. One report noted that he professed a "bias toward the principles of socialism or Communism."[24] In fact, during 1925 and 1926, while the concern about Communist penetration of Mexico was at its peak, Sheffield's staff and Consul General Wedell assembled reports on many U.S. writers, all containing a common assumption: the authors of admiring books and essays on the revolution were Communists or paid propagandists for the Mexican government, or perhaps both. It was Weddell who held that Tannenbaum, Gruening, and Haberman formed a "radical Jewish trinity which has been active in Mexico in recent years."[25] The State Department traced Haberman in and out of the United States and Mexico as a member of the IWW, CROM, and other labor organizations. The same document listed Beals, who was not Jewish, because he allegedly was "in charge of bolshevik propaganda in Mexico" in 1920 and had connections with Haberman.[26] Weddell believed that he had achieved a breakthrough on the question of the relationship between this group and the Mexican government when an informant, Miguel Avila, told him that Beals was in the pay of both the Calles administration and Moscow and that Gruening received a subsidy from Mexico City.[27] Avila was correct in his perception of a close relationship between the Mexican state and these writers, but he proved to be an unreliable source of factual details.[28]

In spite of the ethnic biases and questionable sources of these reports, Sheffield accepted them as valid; it was "a moral certainty," he wrote Kellogg, that Gruening and Beals were on the Mexican government payroll. The names of other North Americans soon appeared on the State Department's list, including "Frances Toor, a woman of Jewish origin [who] . . . is now handling Beals's correspondence for TASS" (the Russian news agency); and Hubert Herring, a Protestant minister who led a group of "American excursionists" to Mexico to view conditions firsthand. The American consul in Guadalajara, Dudley C. Dwyre, reported that Herring's "excursionists," also accompanied by Haberman,

> are in very bad company and it will be impossible for them, even if they desire to know true conditions, to gain an insight when in the custody of the two persons mentioned. The whole affair takes on the appearance of an insidious movement on the part of enemies of the United States, to use a trip to Mexico as a basis upon which to become mouthpieces in the United States, through which to spread propaganda inimical to our interests.
>
> Mr. Herring . . . informed me that he was connected with some protestant [sic] religious organizations in the states, the name of which I cannot remember, but he impressed me as being overbearing and obtrusive.[29]

This accumulation of reports created a highly provocative, occasionally accurate, but fundamentally flawed image of the writers' connections with the Mexican and Soviet governments. Much of the information was presented in strongly charged, self-incriminating, anti-Jewish language, and though it contained partial truths, the conclusions ran far ahead of the evidence. For example, Tannenbaum had been a self-avowed radical in the World War I era but had moderated his ideas considerably in the 1920s.[30] And Beals did write a few short pieces for TASS but did not work for the Russian government or the Communist Party in Mexico.[31] Sheffield, Weddell, and their compatriots were correct, however, in detecting the presence of radical ideas in Mexico in the 1920s. Unfortunately, the State Department's muddled accusations and false assumptions helped to prevent a clear understanding in Washington not only of what the U.S. liberals and radicals wrote about Mexico but also of the larger ideological and political issues at stake there.

The Business Perspective

Sheffield's fears of a Bolshevik epidemic were rooted in his faith in the political and economic system of the United States. In particular, free enterprise capitalism and its concomitant, rugged individualism, had risen in prestige in the late nineteenth and early twentieth centuries at the same time that the economy enjoyed rapid growth. Sheffield and many other prosperous people of his generation believed that free enterprise had proved itself beyond any doubt as the supreme economic formula for nations as well as individuals. Therefore, the ambassador objected strenuously to Mexico's Article 27 because such a law, in his view, could only retard economic growth.

Oil company executives agreed. The tensions in U.S.-Mexican relations in the mid-1920s prompted an extensive public relations effort by Guy Stevens, who was secretary and chief spokesman for the Association of Producers of Petroleum in Mexico, the main public relations organization for American and British corporations operating south of the border.[32] Stevens argued that a general understanding among "civilized nations" guaranteed the protection of the property rights of foreign owners and investors. The Mexican constitution was, in his estimation, clearly in violation of this understanding, and therefore, the threat of its application against U.S. and British oil companies made Mexico a renegade nation that should be cut off from normal channels of capital investment. Furthermore, Stevens claimed that the government's announced justification for its control of private property—the redistribution of wealth to benefit the masses—was not supported by Calles's actual policies: "In all the discussion which has taken place on Mexican matters since the promulgation of the new constitution of 1917, not a single way in which the taking over of these properties by the government . . . would inure to the benefit of the Mexican people has ever been suggested."[33]

I.F. Marcosson, a conservative commentator on international affairs, extended Stevens's argument against the Calles government's claims for social and economic uplift by extensive praise for the long-term impact of private investment in Mexico. Marcosson cited examples of U.S. businessmen in petroleum, banking, railroads, and manufacturing as primary contributors to Mexico's prosperity from the 1870s to the troubled 1910s. The image of Calles in Marcosson's articles for the popular *Saturday Evening Post* was that of an authoritarian leader with Bolshevik and collectivist leanings. In short, Mexico, its people, its resources, and particularly the properties owned by U.S. citizens were in imminent danger, so long as Calles held power.[34]

Marcosson and Stevens represented one part of the U.S. business community, mainly the oil and mining interests, but their widely circulated cries usually drowned out the less strident statements of international bankers Thomas Lamont and Dwight Morrow. Representing the liberal capitalist point of view, the two bankers argued that Mexico's ostensibly revolutionary government was amenable to negotiation and perhaps to persuasion. Through conversations, memoranda, letters, and occasional public statements they quietly but firmly insisted that the Calles administration was made up of reasonable people who, if given the opportunity to compromise in issues relating to property, would indeed compromise.

Neither Lamont nor Morrow believed that business conditions were good in Mexico in the 1920s, but both saw a potential for the growth of private enterprise. Lamont realized that the Mexican government was the central actor in the financial reorganization of the nation. He cited the negotiations that had led to the Bucareli Agreements of 1923 as a model for the peaceful resolution of disputes regarding international debts. (The Harding administration had opened normal diplomatic relations with Mexico in exchange for the Obregón government's informal promise to respect private ownership of property despite the implications of Article 27 for the U.S. oil industry). This model included a central role for the national government in the management of the economy.[35] In a similar fashion, Morrow emphasized that private U.S. lending institutions must understand conditions within the borders of the borrowing nation: "The banker must never be lured, either by the desire for profit or by the desire for reputation, to recommend an investment which he does not believe to be good. But, fundamentally, the reliance of bankers and investors is upon the capacity and, above all, upon the good faith of the foreign government. The foreign government must be able to pay and it must want to pay."[36]

This divergence of views among U.S. businesses active in Mexico sprang from two institutional affiliations. The more rigidly conservative position represented by oilmen Doheny and Buckley in the 1910s and Marcosson and Stevens in the 1920s came out of concern for properties owned directly by corporations, whereas the bankers usually were most heavily involved with loans and investments—commercial paper— which permitted compromise and flexibility as oil wells and copper mines could not. Therefore, the conservative view was essentially pessimistic in its assessment of the radical and, from this perspective, axiomatically irresponsible laws and policies that seemed to undermine the sanctity of private property. By contrast, Lamont and Morrow held that although Mexico's leaders were misguided in many of their policies, they were amenable to negotiation, susceptible to education and persuasion, and sensitive to diplomatic pressure. If these leaders could be brought into the international convergence of business and politics under the Wilsonian world view, Mexico and the United States would find it convenient to adjust their discord while the economies of the two nations became further enmeshed.

What all these factions had in common was an inability to see the whole picture. The Communists' Marxism-Leninism and the conservatives' pro-business ideology reflected the widely separated institutional commitments of the two groups, but both discussed Mexico in terms favorable to their particular institutions and thereby missed much of what was actually happening in the revolution. Even the bankers, with their more pragmatic in their assessments and faith that, eventually, the revolution could be tamed, ignored events and trends in the lower and middle levels of society.

6

The Liberal Mainstream and Radical Undercurrents

John Dewey was a philosopher, not a mountain climber, and the 7,000-foot altitude of the Indian village of Xocoyuacan would have challenged younger men from sea-level cities such as New York. Nevertheless, the sixty-six-year-old philosopher must have felt a sense of pride to find his ideas in use in a teacher-training school in the isolated, ruggedly mountainous state of Tlaxcala. More than four hundred years before Dewey's visit, these tenacious mountain people had successfully resisted the powerful Aztec empire and, after the Spanish Conquest, managed to hold European influence to a minimum. By the 1920s, however, the winds of change had reached the high Sierra Oriental, and Dewey, whose tradition-breaking notions held that school should be a workshop for participatory democracy, witnessed the influence of his philosophy among people who had shunned the outside world for centuries.

Dewey was one of five well-known liberal commentators to follow Ernest Gruening to Mexico in order to gain firsthand impressions of what was happening there. These two and sociologist Edward Alsworth Ross, journalist George Seldes, and philosopher-pundits Walter Lippmann and Herbert Croly were struggling through the general collapse of confidence in progressive ideals after the brutal experience of World War I. That war severely wounded the progressive faith in the capacity of governments to pursue rational, socially responsible policies, but in the 1920s the Mexican revolution seemed to offer the possibility that a New World state could restructure its own society in a way that benefited the vast majority of its citizens.

True, the social and political ferment that gave rise to land reform, labor unionization, and church regulation in the 1920s commanded only a fraction of the press coverage devoted to the spectacular events of the previous decade, such as Madero's revolt against Díaz and the U.S. interventions of 1914 and 1916.[1] Lack of "front page" status, however, did not mean that the mass print media ignored Mexico. Rather, newspapers and magazines placed Mexico on editorial pages, in syndicated columns, and in essays of analysis and opinion often written by leading intellectuals such as Dewey, Croly, and Lippmann. Publishing houses, particularly Century and Viking, produced a modest number of books on Mexico in these years.

Most of these authors were near the center of the ideological spectrum, but their intellectual predispositions split them into two different camps: the liberal statists (Gruening, Dewey, and Croly) placed their confidence in the Mexican state as the defender and benefactor of its people; the liberal capitalists (Ross, Seldes, and Lippmann) saw the state and the revolution as factors to be reckoned with and eventually absorbed by the liberal capitalist world order. These two trios of liberals quickly became prominent commentators on Mexico, despite their limited exposure to the complex nuances of politics and social change there. The writing of veteran Mexicanists such as Tannenbaum and Beals slipped out of the mainstream of media commentary, and their perspective—much more critical of the government in Mexico City than was that of the liberals—also receded into the background.

Taming the Revolution

One way in which the liberal capitalists differed from their statist brethren was in their methods of observation. For example, Seldes and Lippmann limited themselves to a rather narrow political environment, whereas Dewey and Croly ventured into areas familiar only to a handful of Mexicanists (including Gruening). Seldes and Lippmann and Ross attempted to make quick studies of the Mexican situation by skimming across the political surface, but as Gruening (or Beals or Tannenbaum) could have warned them, such exercises in selective observation and facile generalization seldom permitted a grasp of the larger picture—particularly the socioeconomic dynamics and cultural nuances that were so important in a nation where for centuries the politics of decision making had been largely divorced from the lives of the common people. The Mexican state of the 1920s was apparently attempting to end this estrangement by responding to the voices of the previously neglected masses, though with varying degrees of success. Any analysis that omitted this new and volatile context was highly risky and subject to errors of a large magnitude.

University of Wisconsin professor Edward Alsworth Ross seemed to relish his self-designated role of roving sociologist. He had gained his reputation as a major liberal thinker with his 1901 book, *Social Control*, in which he argued that human intelligence could combine with governmental action to solve social problems. But his subsequent experiences in Latin America challenged that optimism. A peripatetic observer who stretched the perimeters of academic specialization, Ross published a commentary on South America in 1915 in which he found fault with the continent's Hispanic social and political tradition. Corruption, elitism, and excessive centralization greatly diminished the effectiveness of most governments. The direct application of human intelligence through a smoothly functioning state seemed unlikely in this climate.[2]

His South American venture acquainted Ross with Indo-Hispanic traditions not dissimilar to those of Mexico. He was actually in Mexico for only eleven weeks in 1922, but this brief exposure did not inhibit his inclination to generalize. A conspicuously conservative bent to his liberalism grew out of his assumptions on the relevance of intelligence tests in the evaluation of the capacities of Indians and mestizos. Yet though he accepted without question the verdict that the Mexican had an inferior mental ability, compared with the west European, this cultural bias did not lead Ross to conclude that Mexico should surrender itself completely to the United States for tutelage and protection. Instead, he argued that Mexico had a chance to improve itself, mainly through public schooling. Even if the predominantly mestizo peoples were intellectually inferior to Caucasians, they were capable of working with machinery and tilling the soil, provided they could break through the native tendency toward passivity and indolence—characteristics that were socially and not biologically determined. While Ross disagreed with José Vasconcelos's emphasis on "ornamental" subjects such as the classical writers of Europe, the Wisconsin sociologist believed that the new government had an opportunity to remake Mexico—not in a few years, perhaps, but within a generation or two.[3]

Ross saw gradualistic reform and private enterprise taking hold. As examples, he cited land reform that promised to bring into existence "a great body of yeomen like our American farmers"[4] and a labor movement whose rank and file were committed to moderation: "The labor movement beyond the Rio Grande is, on the whole, normal and healthful. Without it, workers will reap little from the revolution. Their leaders are probably no more rabid than were the American labor leaders thirty-five years ago. Dangerous tendencies, instead of growing, will slowly disappear, as Mexican labor registers economic and social progress and comes to feel itself strong and secure."[5] The sociologist also saw private property as a source of stability. Ross quoted an unnamed "wise man who held a high post under Carranza" as an advocate of revising the Constitution of 1917 in order to encourage private initiative "by making property rights more secure."[6]

Large portions of Ross's book were out of date by 1925, when new tensions appeared in Mexican-U.S. relations. George Seldes, veteran journalist and self-described descendant of the muckrakers, visited Mexico in his 1927 tour of world trouble spots, which included Italy, Russia, and the Middle East. He began his report with notations of misperceptions and misinformation in the U.S. press about these foreign lands, followed by attempts to penetrate the fog of journalistic bias and government manipulation to give his readers some grasp of his version of reality. Seldes paraphrased the eminent Lippmann on the notion that "false ideas are frequently more effective than true ones" in reaching the public mind, a provocative challenge for an avowed enemy of censorship and propaganda.[8] In his coverage of Mexico, Seldes saw the main problem as the ethnic and cultural biases of U.S. editors and reporters who focused on revolts, instability, and bloodshed at the expense of less dramatic but more meaningful events. There was a dark side to Mexico, however, where Seldes found parallels with what he had seen in Italy and Russia: the rise of dictatorial government.[9]

Yet Seldes's efforts to penetrate to the "facts" of the Calles administration did not carry far beyond Mexico City and the major rail lines. In his stated purpose of exposing distortions in the U.S. press, he was successful, but he did not delve into the social and economic problems of the peasant and the worker nor explore the effectiveness of the Calles government in dealing with these problems. In seventy-six pages of text on Mexico, Seldes devoted only one paragraph to land reform.[10] In brief, he judged Mexico by the standards of the U.S. Constitution's First Amendment and the free flow of information that it protected. If he gained valuable insights on the issues surrounding state-directed social change, these were not evident in his analysis.

Lippmann joined Seldes in trying to unravel the political reality behind the barrage of press information during these critical years. Calles's announced intention of enforcing Article 27 and the Coolidge-Kellogg announced opposition to that intention led Lippmann to conclude that U.S. military intervention was a genuine threat. Like most U.S. liberals and radicals in Mexico, Lippmann was appalled by the Coolidge administration's repeated charges that Bolshevism had taken hold under Calles in Mexico and from there threatened the rest of Latin America. In an editorial outburst in the pages of the *New York World*,

Lippmann charged that "the thing the ignoramuses call bolshevism in these countries is in essence nationalism, and the whole world is in ferment with it."

Lippmann focused his considerable acumen on the property question. His judgments as revealed in his January 14, 1927, *New York World* and in *Foreign Affairs* placed him unequivocally in the camp of Dwight Morrow (then ambassador to Mexico) and other liberal capitalists:

> In the last analysis the security of American investments abroad must rest, as Mr. Dwight Morrow pointed out in the last issue of *Foreign Affairs*, on the faith of the borrowing nations. They must believe that American capital profits them, and is consistent with their own national interest. If they do not believe this, pressure which forces them to act contrary to their convictions can give only temporary advantages to American business men. The victory on one point can be won only at the cost of arousing a general ill will against American capital and the American Government. Such a general ill will is more threatening to the security not only of capital but of the nation than any one Latin [American] policy, however inconvenient, however ill-considered. And nothing would be so certain to arouse still further this ill will as the realization in Latin America that the United States had adopted a policy, conceived in the spirit of Metternich, which would attempt to guarantee vested rights against social progress as the Latin American people conceive it.[11]

But Lippmann did not explore or explain "social progress as the Latin American people conceive it." As Ronald Steel has observed, Lippmann's stance had "nothing particularly 'leftist' about" it. More precisely, Lippmann was working closely with his friend Dwight Morrow, representative of the House of Morgan and, more recently, a man with presidential ambitions. Lippmann's analysis grew out of the banker-diplomat perspective that held sway on the Council of Foreign Relations and in other institutions in the urban Northeast. The matters of land reform, labor organization, and public education carried little weight in this approach. For Lippmann and Morrow the main issue was foreign ownership of property, which in their view was largely a problem to be handled by the denizens of bank boardrooms and diplomatic conferences.[12]

Lippmann, Seldes, and Ross measured the Mexican revolution against the U.S. models of economic advance and journalistic openness. Though no one in this trio found cause to celebrate world-shaking innovations in the Obregón-Calles years, they did express a fair amount of confidence in the Mexican leaders' capacity to find their way into the liberal capitalist system.

Liberal Statist Ambivalence

Dewey and Croly delved into the Mexican milieu to discover levels of political and social interaction that their liberal capitalist colleagues did not see. The property question and the Coolidge-Kellogg policy of intimidation seemed to shrink in importance when considered beside changes under way in rural Mexico. Croly, deeply disillusioned with the proximate future of humankind as a result of the horrors of the First World War, was somehow able to find a cause for hope in Mexico. Relying on Carleton Beals and Hubert Herring as guides, he probed the politics of the revolution and saw Calles as a dictator who redeemed his authoritarianism by furthering social experiments intended to benefit the common people.[13] He recognized the inconsistency between reform in the name of uplift and enlightenment and the employment of excessive executive power, but to Croly that was a problem for the Mexicans to solve on their own, without the interference or intervention of the United States.[14] The national government of Mexico might not satisfy the definition of democracy as understood in the United States, but it did respond to the wants of the people:

> The Mexican nation is, for the first time, practicing self-government. Its form of self-government does not as yet involve the free and honest expression of the popular will in elections, but it is, in its own way, expressly responsible to the Mexican people. It has promised to provide for them a measurable quantity of social welfare and to stand or fall by the result. It differs from all previous governments in Mexico in that it is trying to stimulate the ambition, diversify the opportunities and enlarge the outlook of the Mexican Indian. Its practical program is thoroughly enlightened and has already achieved a small measure of success and popular approval. There is taking place in Mexico something in the nature of a national renaissance. Its spokesmen hope to build up a Mexican culture and society which is based, not upon the exploitation of the peon, but upon his deliverance and education.[15]

Such an attempt at massive social reform necessitated government regulation of economic investment and business operations; therefore, said Croly, the controversy surrounding Article 27 was largely an external reaction to changes that were taking place within Mexico. To delay or block the Calles government's implementation of its policies would be disastrous not only for Mexico but also for the liberal cause in the United States. Croly saw this issue as a test case for all progressives: "who are defending the right of Mexico to pursue a national policy, which for the time being, is justified in being suspicious and even defiant of the United States. . . . If they [the progressives] cannot safeguard her from the peril to her independence created by the alliance between aggressive capitalism, narrow legalism, and racial snobbery in this country, they will themselves in the long run have to submit to treatment as rough and as unfair as that to which the State Department and the oil interests are now subjecting the Mexican government."[16]

Dewey agreed with much of Croly's analysis of Mexico's internal dynamics. The Columbia University professor took a particular interest in the educational aspects of the revolution, just as Mexican government officials exhibited an intense interest in the application of his theories in their school programs. Vice-Minister of Education Moisés Sáenz, a graduate of Columbia University, provided Dewey with a guided tour of rural schools in the state of Tlaxcala.[17] After his 1926 trip to Mexico, Dewey wrote a series of three articles for the *New Republic* that conveyed his perception of "vitality, energy, sacrificial devotion," and hard work as the chief characteristics of the public education movement as well as of the revolution in general.[18]

Yet Dewey had less confidence in the Mexican government than did Croly. Probing the Mexican ambience through armchair rumination and personal observation, he began to have doubts about the possible consequences of the kind of experimentation that he and Croly had praised. A founding father of modern liberal optimism, Dewey tested his faith in the progressive school and its cultural concomitants and found that the changes initiated by the Mexican central government in the name of and for the benefit of the common people did not necessarily bring positive results. Instead, he saw confusion and contradiction: "The coexistence of customs that antedate the coming of the Spaniards, that express early colonial institutions, and that mark the most radical of contemporary movements, intellectual and economic, accounts for the totally contradictory statements about every phase of Mexican life with which the visitor is flooded; it makes impossible any generalization except that regarding the combination of the most stiff-necked conservatism and the most unrestrained and radical experimentation."[19]

Ernest Gruening also had doubts, and he was much more specific in his assessment than were his liberal statist colleagues. He did not follow Croly's tendency toward slightly qualified praise of the government's reformist efforts, nor was he as ambivalent about the consequences of social change as Dewey. Gruening's *Mexico and Its Heritage* identified at least three weaknesses in Mexican polity: the uneven and often unfair application of land reform laws;[20] the manipulated elections in the state governments, which "reveal irrefutably the utter failure to date of any growth of democratic practices";[22] and the violent, undisciplined, and rapacious conduct of army officers who threatened political stability on the national level and the well-being of local citizens at the local level.[23] With such large systemic problems, Mexico, in Gruening's estimate, faced severe challenges in the stimulation of socioeconomic change. The Calles administration had made a beginning in land reform and had awarded organized labor legal and political support, but the operations of the nation-state in Mexico remained subject to the whims of politics and the impingements of violent opposition. Any president, whether possessing the military prowess of Obregón or the Machiavellian savvy of Calles or a combination of both, had very little margin for error.[24]

Placed on a continuum, this trio of liberal statists ranged from the cautiously optimistic Croly to the profoundly uneasy Dewey to the reluctantly pessimistic Gruening. Yet these differences were not nearly so great as their discord with the liberal capitalist views of Ross, Seldes, and Lippmann. Among possible influences accounting for this sharp contrast, probably the key determinants were their perspectives within the framework of international history. These mobile intellectuals were involved in an international environment that linked the modern metropolises of New York and Washington with rapidly modernizing Mexico City; from the Valley of Mexico, slender but growing lines of communication tied regional cities and rural communities to the nation's capital. Liberal capitalists rarely ventured beyond the familiar cosmopolitan setting of Mexico City, but liberal statists Dewey and Gruening plunged into the hinterland, trying to grasp the nature of the socioeconomic change under way there. What they found was not a world of noble peasants eagerly embarking on the road to modern agriculture but a congeries of complex and often ambiguous interactions between the progenitor of change—the national government—and the rural communities.

This message moved from the observers' personal perceptions of rural Mexico through the communications center in Mexico City to the publishing center in New York and out across the United States in the mass media. But the internal workings of a social revolution in a neighboring nation had lost the excitement of a daring and brutal Pancho Villa and did not have the menace of the great international Bolshevik conspiracy. The international communications system that linked the inhabitants of Tlaxcala and Tepoztlán with the citizens of Main Street conveyed a series of provocative and even poignant messages, but the Main Street audience, averse to foreign affairs and impatient with ambiguities, generally ignored them.

The liberal capitalists chose to minimize the peasant component of this international context, but they did so at some risk to the validity of their analyses. Observers of the liberal capitalist stripe, perceiving the crises in Mexico as problems involving relations between Mexico City and the New York-Washington axis, found solutions in open channels of communication and trade, exploration of diplomatic solutions, and reliance on gradualism. By contrast, observers who followed the approach of the liberal statists saw these crises as products of social and political struggles in which peasants and workers were active participants. Their projected solutions included heavier emphasis on the internal forces that swirled around and within the revolution. The shift in perspective from Washington or New York to Mexico City and then from Mexico City to Tepoztlán or Tlaxcala introduced U.S. liberal statists to a world in which the sociological generalizations, diplomatic formulas, and political agendas of previous decades seemed irrelevant and outmoded.

Shifts in perspective also gave the foreign observer a deeper appreciation of Mexico and a sympathetic understanding of the difficulties involved in the establishment of what was, at least in name and sometimes in fact, a revolutionary program. Nevertheless, whatever their on-the-scene insights, neither Croly nor Dewey nor even Gruening completely lost faith in the activist state as the inevitable and perhaps appropriate if often malfunctioning engine for the generation of a new socioeconomic structure. To a large extent the persistence of their idealism was a function of their experience in the United States as much as their experience in Mexico. They saw Mexico's difficulties as obviously more intractable than those of U.S. society, but they did not fully sever the intellectual underpinnings of liberal statist theory. Despite fundamental cultural and structural differences between the two nations, the liberal statists believed that Mexico could, with great effort, overcome these differences to join the select community of progressive nations.

The "Godless State" and the Catholic Church

It was not the uncertainties of socioeconomic change but the grossly exaggerated perception of international Communism in Mexico that attracted widespread public attention in the United States. Some of the most acute fears of radical excess arose from the Calles administration's anticlerical policies. Rumors of Bolshevism and the posturing of a strong man in the presidency, combined with the unequivocal and widely publicized hostility of Calles to the Catholic Church, led many excitable people north of the border to the conclusion that atheistic, totalitarian Communism had arrived in Mexico. In reality, totalitarian Communism was not present, but a virulent anticlericalism was.

The roots of the desire to weaken and regulate the Catholic Church did not spring from any external political or ideological influences but rather were embedded in four centuries of Mexican history during which the church had come to possess extraordinary material and political power as well as spiritual and cultural dominance. Calles, a son of the arid, partially "Americanized" state of Sonora, had no sympathy for the Catholic faith and no tolerance for the political and educational remainders of clerical prerogatives that continued even after Benito Juárez had stripped the church of much of its wealth in the 1850s and 1860s. Calles wanted to complete what Juárez had started.[25]

The anticlerical hyperbole of Calles created such a controversy that Lippmann and Morrow took on special responsibilities to help resolve the crisis and reduce pressures on the Coolidge administration for military intervention. Their involvement marked another episode in international history in which U.S. commentators attempted to bridge the wide gaps separating Main Street and Pennsylvania Avenue from the Zócalo in Mexico City, and from the political center to the bastions of peasant religiosity in rural Mexico. Lippmann secretly joined a group appointed by Ambassador Morrow to serve as unofficial mediators between Mexican Catholics and their coreligionists in the United States. Lippmann spent nearly all of March 1928 in Mexico City deeply involved in negotiations between the Calles administration, various Catholic elements in both countries, and the papal office in Rome. The result was a settlement satisfactory to all parties directly involved, and Morrow emerged with much favorable publicity; he became, as Lippmann had hoped, a major force in the Republican Party. According to Ronald Steel, "Although Lippmann's part in the settlement was considerable, he gave Morrow the entire credit."[26] Lippmann's 1930 article in *Foreign Affairs* gave no indication of its author's involvement, but it did offer testimony to his belief that responsible negotiations involving national leaders could minimize antagonisms between the two nations.[27]

As unofficial diplomat Lippmann performed an impressive service for Morrow, but as commentator on current events he missed an important part of the story. The negotiations in Mexico City, Rome, and Washington satisfied presidents, prelates, and diplomats, but the war in the name of the Catholic faith as understood and defended by the peasants of west central Mexico did not cease with the signing of the documents. The story was more complicated than Morrow and Lippmann thought. Herbert Croly senses the gulf between the peasants and the political power brokers and turned to Carleton Beals for help. Beals left the relatively secure environs of Mexico City to travel to the state of Jalisco, where for two years the peasants had been engaged in a bloody war against the Mexican army. Beals was no friend of the Catholic Church and had often denounced it in his earlier writing,[28] but what he found in Jalisco caused him to question his previous conclusions. After much thought, he wrote an article for the *New Republic* in which he criticized the military for extreme abuse of the peasant population. In this civil strife, called the Cristero War, murder and rape and plunder seemed to be the guidelines for some army units. Beals realized, however, that a blanket condemnation of the Calles government's policies in Jalisco would encourage Mexican and U.S. Catholic opponents of the regime, some of whom had joined the most extreme conservative enemies of the revolution in seeking U.S. military intervention. Therefore, he singled out brutal army field commanders and held back serious criticism of the Mexico City officials.[29]

While the significance of the Cristero War to Mexican church-state relations escaped Lippmann and Morrow and perplexed Beals and Croly, it engendered disagreement between Gruening and Tannenbaum. Gruening saw a church-led guerrilla campaign against a national government that was simply trying to enforce the laws of the land. His account of rebel excesses relied on the announcements of government agencies. He admitted that U.S. citizens would not accept the religious restrictions of the Mexican government, but "neither would [they] tolerate a clergy of the character of the Mexican. The entire story and the entire picture are different. The repression which is now visited on the church, however unjust it may seem, and be, is the fruit of the Mexican church's own past and present performance."[30]

Tannenbaum argued that Gruening exaggerated the importance of the church in contemporary Mexico and painted an unjustifiably negative image of corruption, infidelity, and material excess among the clergy.[31] Tannenbaum did not explicitly defend the role of the Catholic Church in Mexican history, but in his 1933 book, *Peace by Revolution*, he came close to Beals in his depiction of the church-state conflict. The main actors in this historic struggle were upper- and middle-class urbanites who defended the expansive authority of the modern state against the peasant practitioners of Mexican Catholicism. Like Beals, Tannenbaum identified with the peasants and their communities where, he believed, Catholicism of a special Indo-Mexican variety not only survived but flourished: "What Mexico has had through all the centuries is a local religion—the religion of the village, with an occasional greater saint in the neighborhood for special veneration. . . . What has happened is that the superstructure of the church has been well nigh destroyed. But it really never existed in the minds of the people of the villages and in the mountains among the Indians. Whether the Church is re-established or whether the priest is allowed to come again every six months, the local religion of the village will go on as it has in the past."[32]

The commentary of Beals and Tannenbaum on the church-state conflict placed them in their customary positions on the ideological spectrum—not only to the left of liberal capitalists Lippmann and Morrow but also to the left of and in sharp disagreement with liberal statist

Gruening. Again the matter of perspective helps to explain these differences. Beals and Tannenbaum attributed prime importance to the *campesinos* and their communities, where the churches provided a cohesive, comforting influence. Gruening, by contrast, moved toward Lippmann on these issues, seeing the clash as an outgrowth of the centuries-old competition between the state and the church for legitimacy and authority within a given nation. This view led to the conclusion that the government must triumph in a world dominated by nation-states. And since liberal capitalists Morrow and Lippmann and liberal statist Gruening all believed that Mexico under Calles had cast its fate within the bounds of some form of progressivism, they thought the Mexico City government worthy of a place in international affairs, free from impediments raised by the Catholic Church, whether in Rome or in Jalisco.

The Tannenbaum-Beals perspective revealed another factor in the matrix of church-state relations: a peasant population devoted to its own version of Catholicism. This grassroots faith had little to do with the political and diplomatic maneuvers in Mexico City, Washington, and Rome. As historian Jean Meyer confirmed a generation later, the guerrilla war against the government came very close to success, despite its lack of substantive support from urban Catholics. Military assistance furnished by the U.S. government helped Calles to triumph in the field of battle, but the faith of the peasants remained unchanged or, perhaps, even strengthened in defeat.[33]

The Primacy of the Peasantry in the Resilience of Radical Doubt

When the discussion shifted from the specific issues of church-state conflict to broader concerns about the overall effectiveness of government programs in rural Mexico, the independent leftists again disagreed with both liberal camps. The divergence between independent leftists and liberal capitalists was larger and easier to discern. To the liberal capitalists, Mexico was a pubescent, predominantly Hispanic version of the United States, tentatively moving ahead on the path of sensible reform. The independent leftists saw a nation of preindustrial peasants in the grip of a maldistribution of wealth, their grinding poverty moderated by a benign communalism that they were attempting to reconcile with the onrush of modern necessities and temptations. Consequently, the liberal capitalist formula for the resolution of Mexico's problems through open trade and communication, gradual reform, and appropriate international agreements carried little credibility with the independent leftists.

The distance between the Tannenbaum-Beals-Brenner perspective and that of the liberal statists was smaller but still of signal importance. Croly, Dewey, and Gruening believed that in ways they could not specify, the well-intentioned politicians and civil servants in Mexico City could fashion a series of programs that would smooth the path for the rural people to enter the modern world. Occasionally, Dewey and Gruening caught glimpses of the interaction between the metropolis and the countryside that unsettled their assumptions, but in general they clung to their progressive model, with some variations. The independent leftists, on the other hand, usually constructed their prescriptions on what they saw as the inner dynamics of rural segments of Mexican society. Their community-based model (or set of assumptions) came largely from firsthand observations in the backlands and barrios.

As a result, the independent leftists were often opposed to programs the liberal statists championed, such as aggressive anticlericalism and centralized land reform. In the strongholds of the peasantry, the fluid interaction of land and water, harvest and fiesta, birth and death simply did not connect with these intrusive political-bureaucratic inventions, however benign. Tannenbaum, Beals, and Brenner explored the gap between the expansive, modern industrial civilization of Mexico City and the remote, peasant-populated world of the intermontane valleys and concluded that plans concocted in the city would not work in rural areas.

A similar void appeared between the modern values typical of many U.S. visitors and the perspective of an independent Mexican leftist when Anita Brenner recorded her reaction to a dinner conversation. Her own complex qualities—a blending of Mexican, Jewish, and bohemian values with a growing sense of populistic radicalism— emerged in her evaluation of the tendency of the leading talkers, Gruening and the ostensibly radical Dos Passos, to impose their patterns of thought on Mexico:

> Their minds work differently, I guess. I am very Mexican about some things, and this mania for classification seems strange to me. They were talking about how strange Mexico is but I was almost at the other end of the telescope. I place things by their human plane, not by date or place or sociological significance, and this makes me inaccurate in research work, I think, because I don't give numerical or source accuracy much importance, unconsciously. I can, of course, but none of this stuff "me convence [convinces me]." They seem bourgois [sic] about their own convictions, that is bourgois in their class. Flippancy is tabu with them, as with the trade, and all in all they take life and themselves much too seriously, or rather solidly. Dos Passos seems pleasant enough personally, however, and Gruening is the broadest I believe. Nevertheless the atmosphere lacks perspective.[34]

Quantification and categorization seemed out of place in traditional Mexico, where life followed a holistic pattern and the individual's role was seldom in doubt. Brenner sensed that Gruening and Dos Passos viewed Mexico from a distance, through a telescope focused on details in the landscape, and never grasped the value of examining a broad visa. Brenner did not share their narrow, highly focused way of looking at humanity.

Beals managed to escape the "mania for classification" that was often embedded in the values of the visitors. Both Dewey and Gruening traveled into the backlands, but neither could match the freewheeling, impulsive adventures of Beals; in his admittedly subjective leftist journalism he exceeded both in providing a sympathetic defense of the way of life of the peasantry. Beals was not a defender of the status quo in rural Mexico, but he cautioned that the sudden injection of an internally contradictory mix of revolutionary activism, market economics, modern transportation, and mass-produced consumer goods would overwhelm the peasants and their cultures. Citing the village of Tepoztlán, Beals warned that the rural people faced the challenge of: "an alien culture that ruffles their inner harmony and sullenly struggles for its place. And the freshly seared scars of revolution! These brusque, uprooting factors are well concealed, but bit by bit the stoic, stark independence of the inhabitants is becoming darkly overcast.. In the brimming cup of their normal unaffected lives whirls the backwash of the tempest of the changing world. They feel subtly, uncomprehendingly, the tug of these conflicting influences; yet they little realize how much they are puppets of grotesque, gigantic forces."[35] Obregón and Calles may have had good intentions, but their backgrounds in partially "Americanized" northern Mexico provided them with limited understanding of the central and southern regions.

Tannenbaum agreed with Beals that the political elite in Mexico City (and, by implication, the liberal statists) had at best a limited and sometimes misguided understanding of the nation's rural conditions. The previous elite generation, under the imposed order of the Díaz regime, had attempted to thrust modern commercial agriculture into many parts of Mexico and, in the process, impoverished or destroyed many villages by the seizure of their communal lands. The revolution of 1910 and the emergence of cultural leaders such as Diego Rivera and Manuel Gamio had brought the Indians and their traditions to the attention of a new and seemingly revolutionary elite, but Tannenbaum remained uncertain whether this mixture of politicians, generals, and intellectuals—located in the treacherous, labyrinthine government and political bureaucracies—would grasp the needs of the peasant communities. The peasant revolutionaries had demanded an end to economic exploitation but provided no consensus as to what was to replace the old system. The utopian oratory, imported ideologies, and political demagogy that seemed to dominate the debates about land reform gave Tannenbaum reason to doubt that any policies arising from such an unhealthy concoction could actually bring beneficial change to the rural people.[36]

In sum, neither the liberal capitalist model (drawn from the modern, urban context of the interconnected realms of diplomacy, politics, and international economics) nor the liberal statist model (refined by a large but heavily "Americanized" awareness of the ambiguous impact of socioeconomic change on the rural and urban masses) found much acceptance among the independent leftists. Tannenbaum, Beals, and Brenner often placed a community-based outlook at the center of their discussions. The premodern, culturally specific roots of village life provided these observers with varied sources for their writing, but their departures from the expectations of liberal-minded readers in the United States cost them an important audience and both intellectual and political influence. The dominant image that flowed through the international communications system contained the message that Mexico had begun the process of modernization, and the independent leftists created only a turbulent undercurrent of political criticism and ideological divergence beneath the smooth surface of favorable mainstream liberal commentary. Throughout the 1920s, the writing of Gruening, Dewey, Croly, and even Ross, Seldes, and Lippmann conveyed the impression that Mexico had embarked on the path to progress under the guidance of a benevolent if undemocratic government. Although most independent leftists had agreed with this thesis in the first years of the decade, the conclusions they reached in the late 1920s undermined their confidence in the Calles administration. John Dewey leaned in their direction through his philosophical uncertainty about the jagged edge of change, and Ernest Gruening was even closer to the independent left with his specific critique of the Mexican government. He expressed a decided lack of confidence in the Mexican political system, first in a private letter to Beals in 1923 and, most openly, in *Mexico and Its Heritage* in 1928. The independent leftists went still further in their criticism of the Mexican polity, but given their smaller readership, their observations had little public impact compared with the pronouncements of diplomatic successes from the State Department, the Coolidge White House, Ambassador Morrow, and his supporter Walter Lippmann.

As the Tannenbaum-Beals analysis of the Cristero War indicated, they and other radicals no longer idealized the Indian and Indian art as symbols of the rise of the downtrodden. Rather, they began to understand the complexity and diversity of rural Mexico, to appreciate the sincere attachment of the people to their religion and their generations-old folk cultures, and to recognize the importance to any national reform impulse of their resistance to outside influence and aversion to sudden change.

These radical writers were probing the outlines of a major problem that, despite its submergence in the 1920s and 1930s, would resurface in international history and the study of social revolutions in Third World nations after World War II. The consequences of large-scale modernization in peasant communities has continued to provoke debate along the same lines that divided liberal and radical commentators in the 1920s. The superficial confidence of liberal capitalists and the heavily qualified confidence of liberal statists in the positive results of externally stimulated socioeconomic change found continuations in the studies of development by W.W. Rostow, S.N. Eisenstadt, Robert Heilbroner, and Seymor Martin Lipset and in the foreign policies of the Eisenhower, Kennedy, and Johnson administrations.[37] The populist-anarchist critique of massive, intrusive centralized reform programs found echoes in the work of Albert O. Hirschman, Ivan Illich, E.F. Schumacher, and Kirpatrick Sale.[38]

The Absent Comparison

Neither the superficiality of the two liberal views nor the tentative groping of the independent leftists was accompanied by any attempt at comparative analysis of the Mexican with other revolutions. The Russian Revolution was a near-obsession with some U.S. leftists, who saw in the Soviet experiment a replacement for the discredited progressive visions of the prewar years. Yet most U.S. leftists simply ignored Mexico. The notion that these two movements might be comparable or, at least that their differences should be explored apparently did not occur to the prominent students of revolution. Lyford Edwards's pioneering study was typical in including the Russian example but not mentioning Mexico.[39]

Dewey and Ross traveled to both countries and published books and articles about them but did not include any comparative analysis. Only in passing did Dewey note that both nations were undergoing an energetic expansion of interest in art and culture; he did not carry that thought any further.[40] Ross observed that "sometimes organized labor [in Mexico] aspires to intervene in management in a way that smacks of Bolshevism," but even this limited comparison was unusual. The roving sociologist saw as much evidence of mimicry of U.S. models in representative government and institutional organizations as agitation to follow the Soviet example.[41] By implication rather than explication, the two liberals expressed differing degrees of acceptance of the two state-directed revolutions, but they ignored the larger task of comparative analysis.[42]

It was Bertram Wolfe who gave the most thought to a comparison of the two revolutions, but his purpose was far from disinterested. He hoped to convince the leaders of the Comintern that the Mexican revolution and similar movements elsewhere in Latin America offered a well-trained cadre of Communist organizers the opportunity to gain the upper hand. The Mexican revolution had brought into power not genuinely radical leadership but clever opportunists such as Calles, who were capable of mouthing socialist rhetoric with no intention of building socialist institutions. Wolfe insisted that the Lenin of Mexico would have to go beyond the urban workers and petit-bourgeois intellectuals to conduct a wide-reaching campaign among the peasantry, especially the Indian population. By his revisionist Marxist-Leninist standards, Wolfe found the Mexican state a jury-rigged combination of bourgeois interlopers and misguided *narodniks* who, even in their best moments, were far inferior to the government of the proletariat in the Soviet Union.[43]

Two Errant Pilgrims and an Anthropologist

A trio of books appearing in 1930 and 1931 suggested that Mexico was still a mainstream issue in the United States. The Great Depression affected the ideas and ideology of many commentators, including at least two of the authors of these books. Stuart Chase, a well-known critic of private enterprise, turned from the scrutiny of industrial process to search for a haven in Mexico's frequently studied village of Tepoztlán. Social critic Waldo Frank had been seeking an alternative to the potent union of pragmatism with the material culture of the industrial revolution. The collapse of the U.S. economic system gave his quest in Mexico (and Latin American in general) a new relevance.

Chase and Frank were more interested in escaping the travails of modern technological society than in promoting an understanding of Mexico. But anthropologist Robert Redfield studied rural Mexico from the perspective of his academic discipline, and his findings on the people of Tepoztlán had much more to say about Mexico and its revolution. In his own way, Redfield found common ground with Tannenbaum and other independent leftists.

Stuart Chase and the 1930s

Chase came to Mexico in search of utopia or something close to it. A youthful, athletic forty-two in the summer of 1930, the journalist-economist from Connecticut chose to live in the village of Tepoztlán for two months to experience Indian life firsthand. He brought in his intellectual baggage Robert and Helen Lynd's *Middletown*, a sociological study of the onset of industrialization in Muncie, Indiana; Robert Redfield's *Tepoztlán*, a recently published anthropological study of peasant life in that Mexican community; and the conclusion shared by many liberal and radical thinkers in 1930 that capitalism was on the verge of extinction. A liberal statist in the 1920s, Chase was seriously tempted to join the ranks of the rural escapists with the collapse of the economic system that he had hoped to tame through government regulation. Unlike many leftists, Chase did not identify the Soviet Union as the alternative but concentrated his hopes on the Valley of Tepoztlán some sixty miles south of Mexico City.[1] He was closer to the ruralism of the southern regionalists (who issued their manifesto against capitalism as the midwife to industrialization in their book *I'll Take My Stand*) than to the writers who flocked to the far left and often the Communist Party.[2]

What Chase's intellectual baggage did not include was also important. An expert on the modern U.S. economy, he knew little about Mexico or its history and had a limited background in the anthropology, sociology, and the economics of areas outside industrialized urban centers. He seemed to be familiar with the liberal and radical praise heaped upon the Obregón government and the early Calles regime by writers such as Beals, Tannenbaum, and Gruening, but he showed little awareness of their criticisms of the national government after 1926. He had pointed out the harshness of the Soviet state after his 1927 trip to Russia but gave only brief mention to the Callista push toward authoritarian methods. Although he deplored Mexican militarism and corruption, Chase confidently concluded in 1931 that "no powerful reactionary group has seized the central power."[3] The result of his Mexican sojourn was a provocative and controversial book that presented village Mexico in a flattering light and minimized the realities of politics, poverty, and provincialism.

In his focus on the world of the villager, Chase deliberately avoided spending much time in Mexico City, the historical seat of power for five centuries and the center of political machinations in the early 1930s. This flaw in his methodology was the opposite of the liberal capitalists' omission of rural Mexico from their surveys in the 1920s. Where Seldes and Lippmann devoted much attention to the Calles administration, Chase made little mention of the high-stakes game of maneuver and manipulation involving the First Chief and his predecessor, Obregón. The all-important image of stability the two had managed to create suddenly disappeared when an assassin's bullets removed the one-armed ex-president from the scene in 1928. Mexico seemed bound for trouble as Calles, whose drive for power was obvious and often crude, stood as the only bulwark against the extremes of political disintegration and military dictatorship. Labor unions, peasant leagues, and ambitious politicos lashed out at one another to create an environment in which the First Chief could justify the exercise of extraordinary power as necessary to avert catastrophe. Instead of blatant caudillismo, however, Calles opted for the creation of an official political party cloaked in revolutionary rhetoric, the National Revolutionary Party (PNR), which soon acquired a life of its own beyond the intentions of its founder.[4]

Stuart Chase arrived too late to join the U.S. expatriate-traveler community that had flourished in the mid-1920s. This group had broken up by the end of the decade, for a variety of reasons. Edward Weston was the first to depart, leaving in 1926 because of personal unhappiness and artistic restlessness. His former mistress and the source of his jealousy, Tina Modotti, ceased to be a leading light in the group when the Mexico City police accused her of complicity in the 1928 murder of Julio Antonio Mella, a refugee Cuban Communist.[5] Carleton Beals traveled between Mexico City and New York to attend to his rising career as a freelance journalist.[6] Anita Brenner married a New York doctor, David Glusker, and began to visit Mexico's various regions in order to prepare an English-language tourist guide.[7] And Diego Rivera achieved renown as Mexico's greatest muralist at the same time that he became involved in bitter left-wing controversies surrounding the Communist Party. The dispersal of these individuals ended the luncheons and fiestas that had flourished in the 1920s and deprived Chase of an opportunity for informal conversations with people who had been trying to understand Mexico and its revolution for most of the previous decade.

Howard Phillips, the editor of *Mexican Life* (an English-language magazine founded in Mexico City in 1924), became a prominent figure among U.S. visitors in the 1930s. Phillips knew many writers and artists from the previous decade and kept track of their comings and goings in the "Personal Notes" section of his magazine. He also built *Mexican Life* into a forum for serious discussion of contemporary Mexico. He published articles by Beals, Brenner, and many visitors from the north—including Stuart Chase, whose contribution, "Mexico Knows How to Play," later became a chapter in his book.[8] To this varied fare Phillips added his own thoughtful editorials.

The Mexico City that Chase avoided and where Phillips resided was the focal point for the expansion of several leftist groups in the early 1930s. These groups seemed to feed on the repercussions of the worldwide economic collapse and the growing malaise in the nation's political system. The extent of the depression's impact on Mexico remains the subject of debate among historians, but apparently there was a decline in employment and wages in the export and industrial sectors during the first few years of the decade.[9] Economic downturn was only part of the explanation for the agitation in Mexican politics, however. The Calles-PNR machine began to lose credibility with the public and, at the same time, conducted a repressive campaign against the Communist Party. In this environment of economic and governmental troubles, several new movements emerged on the left quite apart from the severely wounded Communists.

The charisma and talent of philosophers and artists no longer provided the government with an image of revolutionary spontaneity. José Vasconcelos, the philosopher-educator-administrator, had turned against the government by 1929 and attempted to win election to the presidency. His unsuccessful conservative, pro-Catholic campaign and his subsequent self-imposed exile marked the removal from Mexico of one of the most dynamic figures of the previous decade. At the other ideological pole, Diego Rivera remained an important cultural figure in both Mexico and the United States, but his place in the rough-and-tumble of his nation's politics was ambiguous because of his ties to an increasingly rightist government, his identification with the Communist Party, and his involvements with large, well-funded mural projects in the United States.

With Vasconcelos and Rivera entering a kind of political limbo, new personalities entered the scene to raise old issues in more radical terms than either Obregón or Calles had been willing to tolerate. Vicente Lombardo Toledano elbowed his way into the forefront of the labor movement, using a Marxist vocabulary and impressive oratory to win a large following in the working class just as Luis Morones was on the decline.[10] In the state of Veracruz, agrarian radicalism gained a foothold with the work of Governor Adalberto Tejada and peasant organizer Ursulo Galván. Tejada increased the tempo and extent of land reform and announced plans for cooperative farms.[11]

Chase seemed unaware of the incipient radicalism in labor organization and land reform as he turned his attention to what he believed was the essence of the country—the rural village, as exemplified by Tepoztlán. During his five months in Mexico he apparently did not seek out any government official, nor did any come to him. The absence of any mention of assistance from national or state sources in his book and the absence of his name in the records of the presidency and the Foreign Relations Ministry strongly suggest that Chase—unlike Beals, Gruening, and Tannenbaum—did not experience any of the techniques of hospitality.

Chase's central purpose was to compare life in Tepoztlán with the urban-industrial character of the Lynds' "Middletown." He found that the worker in Muncie was imprisoned by factory walls and work schedules, whereas the village craftsman worked in harmony with the seasons and even his own mood. Chase praised the products of the villagers' labor. Despite their decline since the Conquest, the traditional handicrafts, he said, "are still amazing enough. Their freshness and vitality cause the traveler on his return [to the United States] to wonder why American shop windows look so lifeless."[12] At play as well as at work the life of the peasant was superior to that of the people of Muncie. The fiesta was an intuitive, all-inclusive form of community celebration, far more functional and beneficial than the motor-driven amusements of Coney Island and its version in Muncie. Although Chase issued caveats regarding the absence of health care and the presence of disease and poverty in rural Mexico, his assessment clearly placed the "machineless men" ahead of their mechanized counterparts.[13]

Still, the visitor from Connecticut readily admitted that a few components of modern life would do no serious harm to Tepoztlán. While insisting that the basics of village life should remain unaltered, he listed public sanitation, electrical power, and scientific agriculture as acceptable innovations; motorized transportation and motion pictures, by contrast, were risky because they carried the threat of inundation by factory-made products and alien values. The first set of changes would make small compromises with the modern world in order to improve village life without challenging the organic existence of the peasant.[14]

The depression seemed to offer overwhelming evidence in support of Chase's defense of the village:

> What is going to happen to us [Americans] in our declining years, say when middle age arrives—with industry refusing to hire men over forty? What is going to happen to us in a business slump, if we cannot go a month on our cash reserves? . . . The house and the car, the overstuffed davenport, and the new refrigerator are all very nice but they are not paid for yet, and how long are they going to last?
>
> Necessities for us are a blurred mass . . . [and] we have no conception of what our basic biological and psychological needs are.

Tepoztlán had no such problems: "It works, plays, worships, attires itself, composes its dwellings in the normal rhythm of homo sapiens upon this planet, without abnormal effort, without waste. It knows what life is for because every move it makes contributes to a legitimate form of living." Chases's final verdict was inevitable: "The future hangs like a great black raven over Middletown. In Tepoztlán the sky is clear. The corncrib takes the place of mortgage and installment contract. There is no care, no electric refrigerator, but there is economic security."[15]

This conclusion led Chase to warn against the gradual extension of such Yankee values as materialism, individualism, and the primacy of technological change: "I found it difficult to become overheated as to American imperialism—old style—in Mexico. A billion dollars [of U.S. investment in Mexico] is dangerous anywhere, but it is not so threatening as it once was. A greater danger to my mind lies in the invasion of gadgets, ideas, and habit patterns."[16] The carriers of this plague were U.S. tourists and residents of Mexico with their pantheon of automobiles, advertising, radios, motion pictures, and quick lunch restaurants. The most profoundly infected part of the nation was Mexico City which—as a hybrid of Madrid, Paris, London, and, increasingly, Hollywood—combined these influences in an awkward and superficial way to deny its own native heritage for the sake of artificial modernity.[17]

The New World of Waldo Frank

The appearance of Chase's *Mexico* coincided with the publication of another comparative study of the United States and its neighbors to the south, Waldo Frank's *America Hispana*. Frank included not only Mexico but most of Latin America in his highly subjective quest to understand the nature of change wrought by industrialization. A social critic as well as a novelist, he enjoyed wide acceptance in Spain and Latin America, where his criticisms of the United States matched the deep concerns about the aggressive homeland of Theodore Roosevelt and Woodrow Wilson. *America Hispana* confused his U.S. readers, however; those who expected a travel account or literary commentary found instead a complex philosophical exposition on the struggle between the individualistic, materialistic culture of the United States and the communal, aesthetic values of the Latin American nations.

Frank arrived at his conclusions after more than a decade of travel and rumination that took him to Taos, New Mexico in 1918, then to Spain, and in 1929 and 1930 to Mexico and South America. He first explored the clash between the two cultures in his 1919 book, *Our America*, and expanded on this theme ten years later in *The Rediscovery of America*. In both volumes he argued that the fusion of Calvinistic Protestantism and capitalism in the United States had resulted in an "atomistic society" where individuals were set against each other in furious competition and even further dehumanized by the growth of technology and the resulting machine culture.[18]

Frank's ideology defies simple categorization. Nominally a Communist and certainly a fellow traveler, he produced a unique admixture of Marxism and pro-Hispanic idealism. His focus was not on class conflict or the formation of a revolutionary vanguard but rather on the ponderous impact of the Protestant-capitalist-pragmatist culture, which denied the individual a sense of fulfillment in its pervasive rejection of the spiritual side of life.[19]

The danger of an expansive United States was, therefore, in Frank's view, more cultural than economic or political. Modern industry's need for enlarged markets and new sources of raw materials enticed bankers, merchants, and engineers into the southern part of the hemisphere, but it was the structure of their cultural beliefs—"the premises and promptings of the dissociate personal will"—that brought forth the isolated, materialistic loner who threatened the communal and aesthetic character of a harmonious society.[20] The proper response to this invasion would involve politics and economics, but the essential issue was cultural, and the historical headwater for Mexico and most of South America was Spain. Frank believed that the political-economic factors flowed from "the tradition of cultural unity through Spain and through the heritage (if not the creed) of the Catholic Church."[21]

Frank's hope for the Western Hemisphere lay in Latin America, with its potential for a healthier balance between the material and the spiritual. The unfolding of the Mexican revolution from 1910 to 1930 provided him with a case study of the struggle between the two cultures. In Frank's truncated political analysis, Mexico's presidents Obregón and Calles had attempted to fight against U.S. economic influences by the enforcement of legal restrictions on foreign business enterprises, but in the struggle, the chief executives had succumbed to the temptations of policies based on materialistic values and had neglected the spiritual-aesthetic component of human nature.[22]

In the 1929 presidential campaign, José Vasconcelos captured Frank's admiration with his projection of a capacity to restore the spiritual balance to Mexican national life. According to Frank, Vasconcelos's "aim was to free the will of bread-and-power [materialism] from the North American obsession by linking it, for the first time, with the religious impulse [spiritual strength] of the people." But Vasconcelos failed to see that cultural transformation must precede political change, and his effort to engender cultural change through a political campaign became entangled with the controversies concerning Mexico's Catholic right. His defeat marked a major failure of the revolution, but it also freed the philosopher to carry his cultural campaign to the broader stage of Latin American civilization.[23]

Frank prescribed a two-level approach to save Mexico and the rest of Latin America from the capitalist flood. At the first level he gave tepid recognition to politics in his assertion that regional federation must begin as soon as possible; Mexico was to be included in "The Confederation of the Central Sea" along with Central America and the

Spanish Caribbean. The more important level of activity, however, was "human regeneration," which would ultimately create a unified "organic world" in which the individual personality and the national culture would exist in harmony. As this individual-national vitalization spread through the hemisphere in a movement simultaneously personal, national, and international, the threat of capitalist culture would diminish, and Spanish America would offer the world an example of healthy balance between the instinctive urges for "bread and power" and the spiritual need for wholeness.[25]

The writings of Chase and Frank on Mexico posed special problems for their critics. At times it seemed that these two commentators were talking about different countries, and to some extent they were. Chase saw the Indian community as the center of Mexico's culture; Frank looked to the opposite side of that nation's turbulent history, the Hispanic institutions imposed during and after the Conquest. Frank turned to Mexican hispanicists Vasconcelos and Antonio Caso, who shared a vision of Mexico's future; Chase, to Mexican Indianists Moisés Sáenz and Manuel Gamio. Although their books both appeared in 1931, only one reviewer compared them, and his preference for Frank's abstract approach did not include a thorough exposition of their differences.[26]

What both authors had in common was a confidence in Mexico that had begun to fade from the writings of most observers from the United States. Gruening, Tannenbaum, Beals, and Toor continued to write about Mexico in the early 1930s but with a growing pessimism about the dictatorial methods of Calles, an authoritarian drift that coincided with a slowdown in land reform and rural education. Chase and Frank had the misfortune to locate their alternatives to capitalism in Mexico at the very time that Mexico itself was confronting serious crises in both economics and politics.[27]

One of Chase's harshest critics deplored *Mexico: A Study of Two Americas* as an example of the literary results of the futile search for a pristine Arcadia. Howard Phillips held back none of his cynicism in evaluating the motives of Chase and other U.S. writers who claimed expertise after a quick visit to Mexico: "They came hither escaping the ravages of a mechanized society that has gone on the rocks. . . . Since there is no solace for the sensitive soul in our contemporary scheme of machine-ridden Christendom . . . there is but one way of eluding ultimate despair. The poet turns his back to today and seeks assuagement in antiquity."[28] Phillips claimed that Chase and his colleagues created an image of rural Mexico that glorified privation and ignored the cruel realities of an existence so heavily dependent on nature. The editor of *Mexican Life* lamented that although Redfield's *Tepoztlán* conveyed a much more accurate view of village life, Chase's book outsold Redfield's by a ratio of one hundred to one—a clear indication that misguided "norte-americanos prefer fiction to facts."[29] Gruening agreed, though in less strident terms. In a letter to Anita Brenner he complained about those who rushed to Mexico and " 'discovered' all kinds of things which, as you say, were discovered some time ago by others."[30]

Critical reaction to Chases's *Mexico* was more direct than the response to Frank's *American Hispana*. Frank escaped unscathed or, perhaps more accurately, largely ignored. Gruening, one of his few reviewers with a background in Mexican affairs, admitted that "following him through the intricacies of his thought and the complexities of expression was often difficult and, at times, impossible for this reviewer."[31] By contrast, Chase's attempt to popularize rural Mexico coupled with his straightforward prose made his ideas more accessible to reviewers. Gruening's judgment was positive in many respects, but he did agree with Phillips and other commentators that Chase often ignored the darker side of life in many areas of the Mexican countryside—the famine, illiteracy, and religious fanaticism—in favor of generalizations based on a narrow selection of facts.[32]

Robert Redfield

Chase acknowledged his debt to Redfield's *Tepoztlán* but did not incorporate all of the anthropologists's major findings in his own text. Even if Chase's goal of popularization justified such omissions, there were additional important differences between these two versions of life in Tepoztlán. Redfield was not concerned with direct and immediate U.S. cultural influence; instead, he concentrated on the impact of urban influences emanating from Mexico City. The problem was not the arrival of Buick-wielding Yankee tourists in Tepoztlán but the migrations caused by the revolution, including the movement of Tepoztecos to Mexico City, their experiences there, and their return to their home village with new ideas and attitudes.

Redfield's review of *Mexico* emphasized Chase's failure to comprehend this difficult situation:

> In Tepoztlán some people are halfway out of the folk world and halfway in the modern city world; therefore, they feel sensitive, and ashamed, and sometimes miserable. After all the Mexican villages are on the edge of our world; they are in ferment and remaking through the enzymes poured onto them from the city civilization. Mr. Chase would have them keep the good and refuse the bad; keep their handicrafts and disregard of money, clocks and hurry; acquire modern hygiene, hydroelectric power and scientific agriculture and yet reject hustle, Sunday motor-

ing, and nervous breakdowns. But can these things be separated? We must study more closely the process of becoming
civilized or citified, and see if and just how these things are
linked.[33]

Redfield's study, unlike the escapism of Chase and the abstractions of Frank, served as a reminder that this community in particular
and Mexico in general were still reverberating to the uncertain sounds
of revolution. Redfield reported that to the common people of Morelos
the fallen revolutionary Emiliano Zapata was a mythic figure. Revered
because he stood up for the cause of the downtrodden, "Zapata as a
symbol embodies the group consciousness of the Indians of Morelos
which developed during the revolution."[34]

The strength of the Zapata myth, however, could not counteract
the disruptive impact of the revolution, which over the years acted to
accentuate the divisions within Tepoztecan society. The common folk
clung to the memory of Zapata and seemed to change little, but the
correctos (the educated and more affluent residents) ventured onto a
new path that led them to become reformers and traditionalists at the
same time, with an uncomfortable recognition of the power of modernity and the security of custom: "Los correctos . . . develop an intelligen-
sia who live in two worlds, in two cultures, the city and the folk, and are
correspondingly restless and unhappy. The periods of revolution
sharpen the self-consciousness of the intelligentsia; drawn together as
temporary expatriates, they idealize their home community and at the
same time deprecate its shortcomings. This dissatisfaction and unrest
finds an expression in programs of reform [in Tepoztlán]."[35]

Had Chase given more attention to Redfield's description of the
case of "R.G.," an Indian male of Tepoztlán who attempted to bridge the
chasm between village life and the modernity of Mexico City, he might
have acquired a greater awareness of the burdens inevitably thrust
upon rural folk by the urban world. After several years in Mexico City,
R.G. returned to Tepoztlán to transplant carefully selected modern
ways. He worked for "civic reform, . . . new roads, new street lights, and
a school only to meet apathy and failure." Redfield's conclusion cast
R.G. in a role of symbolic importance for the revolution: "R.G. can best
be understood partly in terms of his particular temperament, but partly
in the light of that development of racial and national consciousness
that has so marked the last two decades in Mexico. As he sees Tepoztlán
partly through the eyes of a man of wider city-world, so are the folk of
Mexico coming to see themselves. His dreams and despairs, his crudi-
ties and sensitiveness, are those of this country."[36]

Redfield's Tepoztlán was not the enclave of security and stability
that Chase believed the village to be. Instead, it was a community

caught up in the early stages of the arrival of modern culture, which undercut the displaced generations-old traditions and divided the residents into two groups: the *tontos*, who continued to live by the old skills and values and whose mentality was genuinely "timeless" (they did not use clocks); and the *correctors*, who strove for a competitive shrewdness in the politics and business that linked the village plaza to the outside world. Tepoztlán was, in Redfield's words, an "intermediate community."[37]

Waldo Frank's abstract endorsement of Hispanic values as a defense against the modern world was no more congruent with the views of Redfield than was Chase's estimate of rural Mexico. Like many visitors over the previous twenty years, Frank and Chase remained faithful to their own ideological and cultural predispositions and, in so doing, missed the complex essence of contemporary Mexico—from the burdens of past injustices to the vagaries of revolutionary politics. Redfield, a pioneer in the study of revolution and social change among rural, nonindustrial peoples, was much closer to the people of Mexico.

8

Pilgrims without a Shrine

Chase and Frank projected onto Mexico their solutions to the economic and cultural crises of modern times just as the revolution was collapsing upon itself. Among veteran U.S. Mexicanists the pessimism of the late 1920s deepened in the early 1930s. Former head of state Calles and three short-term presidents—Emilio Portes Gil, 1928-30; Pascual Ortiz Rubio, 1930-32; and Abelardo Rodríguez, 1932-34—dominated this period known as the Maximato. Social and economic reform declined, while behind-the-scenes machinations sapped the nation's political energies. Political pilgrims who had been drawn by a vision of revolution found this fragile optimism shattered under the weight of authoritarian ambition.

The Literary Abandonment of Revolution

Katherine Anne Porter's writing in the early 1920s had contained an element of hopeful sentimentalism for the Indian peoples, but some of the short stories that brought her acclaim as a writer of serious fiction revealed her growing pessimism about the revolution. Her first published doubts appeared in 1923 in "The Martyr." The main character, a fictionalized version of Diego Rivera, degenerates into a pathetic gluttony in which he loses "both his artistic purpose and revolutionary aim."[1] If the radical could not sustain his revolutionary fervor, the larger movement was in doubt.

Darlene Unrue has identified Porter's first questioning of the revolutionary ethos in "Flowering Judas," a short story outlined in early form in 1921 but not published until 1930. The main male character, Braggiani, captures the attention and admiration of Laura, an idealistic visitor who has come to Mexico to participate in the revolution. Unrue quotes at length from the 1921 sketch of her character. This penetrating description of the naiveté of a recently arrived revolutionary sympathizer easily coincides with Hollander's characterization of the prototypical political pilgrim:

> Being born Catholic and Irish, her romantic sense of adventure has guided her very surely to the lower strata of revolution. Backed by a course of economics at the Rand School, she keeps her head cool in the midst [of] opera bouffe plots, the submerged international intrigue of her melodramatic associates.
>
> She had meant to organize the working women of Mexico into labour unions. It would all have worked beautifully if there had been any one else in the whole country as clear and as straight minded as Mary [later Laura]. But there wasn't and she has got a little new pucker of trouble between her wide set grey eyes, within four weeks of her arrival. She doesn't in the least comprehend that revolution is also a career to the half dozen or so initiates who are managing it, and finding herself subtly blocked and hindered at every turn, she set it down to her own lack of understanding of the special problems of labor in Mexico. . . . She has been bludgeoned into a certain watchful acquiescence by that phrase. So that now she has the look of one who expects shortly to find a simple and honest solution to a very complicated problem. She is never to find it.[2]

Depiction of this unsophisticated zeal precedes an equally impressive portrayal of idealism abandoned. Laura's view of Braggioni refocuses to reveal not the protagonist of revolution but the self-serving hypocrite mouthing radical slogans with no intention of working for them. At the end of "Flowering Judas" Laura joins the ranks of the betrayers of the revolution who act out a meaningless charade. Porter was probably the first of the expatriates to lose her leftist ideals and begin to detect flaws in the attitude of the typical political pilgrim. In her view, the revolution met its defeat, in part, because of the character flaws of those who claimed to lead it.[3]

Probably Porter's most devastating critique of the political-bureaucratic perversion of revolutionary zeal was her 1932 short story "Hacienda." Based on the abortive efforts of Russian filmmaker Sergei Eisenstein to create an epic about the Mexican revolution, "Hacienda" abounds in political commentary as well as psychological insights. Porter's disdain for the image-conscious bureaucrats and radical poseurs surface in the following paragraph:

The government officials still took no chance. They wanted to improve this opportunity to film a glorious history of Mexico, her wrongs and sufferings and her final triumph through the latest revolution; and the Russians found themselves surrounded and insulated from their material by the entire staff of professional propagandists, which had been put at their disposal for the duration of their visit. Dozens of helpful observers, art experts, photographers, literary talents, and travel guides swarmed about to lead them aright, and to show them the most beautiful, significant, and characteristic things in the national life and soul: if by chance anything not beautiful got in the way of the camera, there was a very instructed and sharp-eyed committee of censors whose duty it was to see that the scandal went no further than the cutting room.[4]

Though Porter's main audience was made up of readers and critics of serious fiction, her statements on the revolution and people close to it placed her, at least momentarily, in the camp of the independent leftists. Her sympathies for the native peoples had been central in her first grasp of the Mexican environment, but as politics and corruption grew larger in her view of the situation, her mood became increasingly one of disappointed expectations.

Labor and the Lost Revolution

Porter's Laura came to Mexico to organize the working women of the lower class. The disappointment of this fictional character matched similar attitudes among U.S. observers in the early 1930s. The promises of the pro-labor Article 123 of the constitution seemed as vacuous as they had in 1917. The Labor Code of 1931 marked a major shift in the balance of power from employer to the unions and the government, but the state's intrusion met with much criticism, especially from Communists and other leftists who saw incipient fascism in this trend. Such polemics aside, it seemed that the labor movement, like other attempts to benefit disadvantaged groups, had fallen into a period of uncertainty and perhaps retrogression. From the workers' perspective the demise of the corrupt CROM left a vacuum at the very time that labor needed strong leadership.

During this critical period an academic specialist in labor affairs, Marjorie Ruth Clark, came to Mexico to make a scholarly investigation of the unionization movement. Her 1934 study, *Organized Labor in Mexico*, added a healthy dose of restrained if not dispassionate analysis to the often polemical literature on this aspect of the revolution. As in her earlier history of the French labor movement, she presented the strengths and weaknesses of worker organizations in Mexico but with a presumption in favor of a vigorous labor organization independent of the state. In this sense, she held to a nonsectarian, independent radicalism that made autonomous trade unionism the protagonist of her study.[5]

Clark was unhesitatingly critical of abuses and corruption in CROM, but she saw the extension of the power of the unions as inevitable and appropriate for contemporary Mexico. She cited the portions of the 1931 labor code that favored the workers, but she observed that the current government was unlikely to further the cause of the unions in any meaningful way. She perceptively called attention to Vicente Lombardo Toledano as the likely successor to the deposed Morones. In her final evaluation, Clark implicitly rejected the rural escapism of Chase and the Hispanic traditionalism of Frank. Her findings indicated that effectively run labor unions would benefit the urban working class, a rapidly growing group that neither Chase nor Frank had considered in their assessments.[6]

Clark's carefully argued case for independent unionism, expressed in the language of scholarly discourse, offered a sharp contrast to the polemical and inflammatory commentary of Joseph Freeman, a U.S. Communist. With interests in literature, art, and labor, Freeman brought to Mexico an explosive combination of ideological and political commitments. His arrival in Mexico City in the summer of 1929 coincided with the government's anti-Communist campaign that nearly destroyed the party. His handwritten notebook reveals an intense opposition to this repressive policy and to Mexico's then proposed labor code. He claimed that the government involvement in the new code would result in passive labor unions in the grasp of a fascist state.[7] The same notebook contains bitter attacks on Ursulo Galván and Diego Rivera, two party activists of the 1920s who, Freeman said, had deserted it in its hour of great need. Galván's "stupid and vulgar accusations" against the party and Rivera's fraternization with petit-bourgeois leftists justified their expulsion by Mexico's hard-pressed Communist Party.[8]

Freeman believed that he was witnessing the demise of the Mexican Communist Party. The organization that Bertram and Ella Wolfe had labored so diligently to build was the victim of both Callista repression and its own internal dissension. The government, weakened by the Obregón assassination and the deepening depression, cracked down on the small Communist Party in 1929 and 1930. Officials arrested several party leaders and suppressed its newspaper *El Machete*. At this critical time, Diego Rivera's prominent public persona cast him in the role of popular symbol of the party, even though he was far removed from its day-to-day operations. Rivera enraged Freeman by distancing himself even more with his acceptance of a government appointment to head the San Carlos Academy of Fine Arts in Mexico City. The party responded by expelling its most famous member. Enervated by its losses, the Mexican Communist Party went underground in the early 1930s and for a few years virtually disappeared from the political arena. Unfortunately for Freeman, he arrived just at the beginning of this decline.[9]

Freeman's acidic commentary was not limited to the Mexican government and backsliding Communists. In "The Well-Paid Art of Lying," his diatribe against liberal commentators on the revolution, he attacked Stuart Chase and Anita Brenner as examples of "the Mexican-as noble-savage school." These bourgeois writers, limited by their own connections (both conscious and unconscious) with imperialism and fascism, chose to distort conditions in Mexico. In an opinionated but revealing contrast of liberal attitudes toward Mexico and Russia, Freeman charged that these untrustworthy fellow travelers had a tendency to

> lie about the Soviet Union as other writers lie about Mexico, only the other way around. It is very simple: Mexico—where imperialism and fascism oppress the people, where peasants are robbed of their lands, where masses of workers are unemployed, where misery, illiteracy, and political murder prevail; where the population is kept in feudal oppression and darkness—this Mexico is a haven to which you look wistfully—(and safely)—from a skyscraper window in New York; but the Soviet Union—where the workers run the country, where a planned socialist economy steadily improves the physical and spiritual lot of the masses of the population, where illiteracy and superstition and race hatred are disappearing, where the entire resources of the county are directed toward building a socialist civilization in which poverty, ignorance, and violence will be only prehistoric memories—that is a hell which you must curse in the pages of the *Saturday Evening Post*.[10]

Freeman's earlier sojourn in the Soviet Union and his subsequent paeans for its socialist experimentation marked him as a typical political pilgrim, but he held no illusions about the rough and simple life of the Mexican peasant. For Freeman, Chase's admiration of the condition of the native was an endorsement of exploitation, poverty, and ignorance for the sake of continued profit for the capitalist in league with the feudal landlord. Had he directed his anger against the Hispanic vision of Waldo Frank (who was active in the U.S. Communist Party in the 1930s),[11] he would probably have condemned the Catholic Church, the landlord, and the caudillo in comparison with the noble Soviet idea.

In early 1932 Freeman's antipathy toward Rivera erupted in a heated confrontation with aftershocks that continued for several years.

Freeman charged Rivera's movement away from the party was symptomatic of the muralist's desertion of the cause of the working class in general. Freeman saw this desertion as an outgrowth of Rivera's "political evolution" from his revolutionary period, in which the artist achieved considerable acclaim for his radical synthesis of Mexican history, to this current stage of "painting for the bourgeoisie." Using Rivera's move to the right as example in a larger condemnation of the Mexican government's lurch toward conservatism, Freeman alleged specifically that Rivera had changed his design for one mural: "The original design for the mural in the National Palace showing Mexico as a gigantic woman holding a worker and a peasant in her arms was altered; for the worker and peasant, no doubt a painful sight to the government officials who pass the mural every day, were substituted harmless natural objects such as grapes and mangoes."[12] Unfortunately for Freeman, this accusation was apparently based on dubious evidence. Many liberals and radicals claimed that it was false, thus putting Freeman on the defensive. His antagonists included Edmund Wilson and Frances Toor, and their rebuttals served to obscure Freeman's basic thesis—that the government had betrayed the revolution.[13]

In this broader critique of the rightward shift in Mexico's politics, Freeman was in agreement not only with Clark but with Porter, Beals, and Phillips that the revolution was running amok. The academic student of labor and the Communist labor critic focused on the rapidly growing urban life of Mexico with its factories, warehouses, suburbs, public schools, and government offices. Neither the conveniently myopic, Calles-dominated government of the period nor the authorial meanderings of Chase and Frank addressed the needs of urban workers in these crucial years.

Revolutionary Change at the Grassroots

Frank Tannenbaum produced the most extensive, albeit indirect, refutation of Chase and Frank. In Tannenbaum's view, both the existing conditions of poverty and ignorance in rural Mexico and the nation's tenaciously conservative Hispanic heritage justified the intensification of the revolution. Disillusioned with the nation-state, he fell back on the local rural community as the foundation for revolutionary change. Tannenbaum subjected the political elite and its power base in Mexico City to special criticism in a private letter to Narciso Bassols, the Marxist minister of education who was attempting to upgrade the nation's schools in rural areas: "I wish you the best of luck in your efforts to bring to the consciousness of the Mexican educated classes an appreciation of the needs of the nation, which is, as you see truly, in the Indian and mestizo, and not in the spoiled darlings of Mexico City."[14]

In his interpretive 1933 book, *Peace by Revolution*, Tannenbaum portrayed the temptations of political power and urban life that tended to co-opt young Indian leaders: "The repeated rebellions during the last twenty years have been from one point of view, the sending up of new leaders to take the place of the old ones for a time, until they too have been overcome by the good dinners, the automobiles, the flattery of friends, the adoration of leeches and parasites, the ambition of family, the ease, comfort and good will of the city."[15] Tannenbaum also explored the psychological dimensions of the peasant leader's conversion: "He wakes up one morning and discovers that he thinks differently. He has not changed his mind; his mind has been changed for him. He begins to be more careful, more conservative, less ardent in his old beliefs, less accessible to his former companions in the country. The more he becomes like others in the city, the more favor he wins, the more he becomes like the people who favor him. He has become swallowed up by the city."[16]

Although Tannenbaum was sharply critical of the ethos of national politics, he avoided specific indictments. He even praised Luis Morones—the most obvious example of corruption—as the founding father of unionization in Mexico.[17] Calles and his successors, short-term presidents Emilio Portes Gil and Pascual Ortiz Rubio also escaped direct criticism. Tannenbaum's apparent reluctance to toss a blanket condemnation over the Calles-Morones group is difficult to explain.[18] Perhaps his intention to continue research in Mexico led him to refrain from publishing commentary that would create enemies within the government or the newly formed national political party.

Yet Tannenbaum did not lose all hope for a remaking of Mexico. The Constitution of 1917 provided the legal basis for a new, more egalitarian society. Article 27 gave the national government controls over private property that could establish a foundation for land reform and the regulation of foreign corporations. Article 123 promised an advanced code and a substantial shift of power to unionized workers and away from private businesses. Though many U.S. businessmen and diplomats saw these provisions as genuine threats, Tannenbaum saw them as the initial steps toward a new social and political order and a more viable economy for the nation.[19]

Nevertheless, Tannenbaum's mistrust of the national state and his rejection of Chase's rural escapism and Frank's Hispanic revivalism thrust him upon the horns of the independent left's difficult dilemma. Mexico's rural society required profound socioeconomic change and looked to the national government for the resources to carry out such change. But that government was highly corruptible and potentially dictatorial, and even the native sons of the villages who entered the urbanized, politicized capital seemed incapable of surmounting the temptations of material gain and personal power. The national government's commitment to reform was subject to abrupt shifts seemingly determined by the prevailing mood in Mexico City and perhaps Washington and New York.

Tannenbaum attempted to resolve this dilemma by hypothesizing a mutually hostile but symbiotic relationship between the village and the capital. If the political elite did not move the nation-state to carry out reforms, then the villages would resort to arms in the Zapatista fashion and thereby compel Mexico City to act. The "peace" in the title of his book, therefore, could arise only out of a rural "revolution" that would grant the peasants the lands they wanted. The "peace" of a stable and just society would come only after a massive redistribution of property. If the government rejected this course, violent convulsions would result.

There were alternative answers to the independent left's dilemma. Perhaps the most acceptable type of change—at least in theory—would be the self-generating variety that started at the grassroots. Sprouting from the basic units of the society and polity, these movements contained the potential for authentic structural change carried out by those directly concerned. U.S. visitors who saw at least a narrow sampling of Mexico's rural communities in the 1920s and early 1930s found it difficult to generalize in a meaningful way, but they did not ignore the existing signs of spontaneous activity.

In his explorations of the huge gap between the promise of revolutionary change and the multiple dimensions of rural Mexico's travail, Tannenbaum revealed an understandable ambivalence. His early research, published in *The Mexican Agrarian Revolution* in 1929, resulted in a pessimistic view of life in the villages. His description of isolation, illiteracy, unsanitary living conditions, and debilitating poverty contained little evidence of hope for self-generated social change.[21] According to Tannenbaum, only Morelos, Yucatán, and the sparsely populated Campeche had initiated significant land reform, and these were only precariously flickering lights in an otherwise dim landscape.[22] Four years later, however, Tannenbaum found an institution that stirred his optimism: the rural school. Even though it was funded in Mexico City and run by teachers with urban backgrounds, "the school," he insisted in *Peace by Revolution*, "is not from the outside, but from the inside, so to speak. It has fitted into the village democracy and become a source of stimulus and strength to that democracy."[23]

Ernest Gruening was more dubious than Tannenbaum about spontaneous initiatives in education and land reform. Largely inexperienced in village politics and society, Gruening concentrated on the states, and his conclusions offered little hope for the redress of economic grievances at that level. His study of politics and government in fourteen of Mexico's states convinced him that public education, like other ostensibly reformist programs, was inadequate because of corruption and ineptitude.[24] He found one promising example of land reform in the state of Hidalgo, but it was the product of federal initiatives in property redistribution, banking, and education—not the work of local officials.[25]

Robert Redfield's anthropological study of Tepoztlán offered a persuasive but unexpected case of self-generating social change at the local level. In spite of Chase's claims and Frank's implications to the contrary, the Tepoztecos had begun to migrate to Mexico City to explore the world of urbanity and commerce. These changes, however, came from commercial profit-seeking as well as revolutionary activism. Redfield claimed that in the village itself, civic reformers and merchants were the main agents of change and that they operated from atop the social structure. The majority of the town's inhabitants, generally poor and illiterate, remained on the fringe of these innovations. If meaningful (and often painful) social change was under way, it emanated from the *correctos*, or dominant group within the community, and involved economic competition as well as education and land reform.[26]

Carleton Beals surveyed a broad cross-section of regional Mexico, and his conclusions, though more impressionistic than those of his colleagues, contained a similar ambivalence. After a swipe at the insensitivity and ignorance of the Maximato's ruling clique, charging that "few Mexican leaders have any vital conception of the ethnological and sociological pattern of the country,"[27] he proceeded to describe a half-dozen rural communities. He included the frequently visited Tepoztlán and Milpa Alta, just south of Mexico City, and Amecameca on the slope of the volcano Popocatepetl. More distant from Mexico City were the mountainous Tlaxcala to the northeast; Oaxaca's Valerio Trujano to the southeast, and the Tarascan village of Paracho in Michoacán. His discussions of the villages identified no clearly defined pattern beyond the frequently mentioned clash between tradition and modernity; each case seemed to be unique. Mexico's leaders may have been ignorant, but they were ignorant of a complex subject.[28]

Beyond the beginnings of foreboding change in Tepoztlán, Beals identified two of the six areas as centers of spontaneous activity. Civil violence had nearly destroyed Paracho early in the revolution and scattered its inhabitants—some as far as the United States. Later they returned to take up the task of reconstruction as the local political boss used land reform to build public support. In Valerio Trujano the villagers had confronted a nearby *hacendado* and won some small but important victories. Here Beals stretched his evidence and ventured as close to optimism as anywhere in *Mexican Maze*:

> Valerio Trujano is far from the highways of modernity. But its problems are eternally modern: thirst for freedom, for knowledge, for decency. Their spirit of communal freedom is watered by the sweat of the brow, flowering with joy and pain in the heart. But though the problems of the humble village are modern and practical, the people have the grace, the aesthetic appreciation, the hospitality and the refined courtesy of the ancient high-born, which is always and forever startling to the outsider observing their soil-woven, toil-worn lives. . .
>
> Here is the flowered pattern of thought and culture as mysterious as that of any of the unknown continents, doubly mysterious to one like myself bred in a nation doomed to the present prosperity. Their problems may seem petty, but they link up with the common struggle of mankind to conquer his environment and to conquer his own soul. And in this backstream eddy of a corner of Oaxaca is all the fertile silt of the broader stream of dark-skinned people everywhere in Mexico and in many places in the world, flowing inevitably to a destiny unknown, a destiny some day to be linked closely, perhaps fearfully, to our own.[29]

The Dwindling of Revolutionary Hope

Obviously, the evidence cited by all these observers was far from exhaustive. They tended to ignore the northern tier of states—the strongholds of Obregón, Calles, and Portes Gil—where dynamism in business and politics had become accepted practice. Further, they simply did not see a great deal of Mexico because mountains, deserts, and jungles made travel difficult, even for Beals and Tannenbaum. Nevertheless, a synthesis of their writing gives a valuable if not comprehensive assessment of the work of village and state politicians in response to the demands of their constituents. In a handful of communities such as Paracho and Valerio Trujano and in a few states such as Morelos and Yucatán, local leaders had decided to assert the interests of their followers, often through land reform and public schooling. Gruening probably would have argued that they could not possibly succeed, but Beals, Redfield, and Tannenbaum—more knowledgeable about the rural village— seemed to detect a small but encouraging strand in the fabric of village life: a pragmatic recognition of the inevitability of change and a wishful anticipation of a better day.

Even at their most optimistic, however, Beals and Tannenbaum understood that a self-inspired, locally controlled transformation of Mexican society was unlikely. Given the complexity of the problems and the dearth of persuasive solutions, both liberal statists and independent leftists were unsure how Mexico should proceed in the early 1930s. By this time, two issues—the efficacy of the nation-state, and the relationship between the nation-state and the lower strata of society— were paramount in the writing of both groups. The excesses of the Maximato came close to discrediting the government as a reliable mechanism for the stimulation of socioeconomic change. Porter, Beals, and Tannenbaum all testified to this paralysis. The hopes of Croly and other liberal statists of the 1920s seemed out of date half a decade later. Death took Croly in 1931, and Ross, Gruening, Lippmann, and Seldes turned their attention elsewhere. Among the independent leftists, only Tannebaum devised a theoretical resolution of the crises, but his peace-by-revolution formulation contained as much faith as substantive evidence. He apparently borrowed from John Dewey's philosophical confidence in the will of the common people and applied it to Mexico's resilient class structure. Yet the villagers had few grassroots organizations and no national spokesman. Only the labor unions had the structural potential to put pressure on the government, and as Marjorie Ruth Clark noted in the early 1930s, the old organization (CROM) was virtually defunct and the new unions still in an embryonic stage. As a result, the means by which the threat of revolution from below was to be communicated to those above remained unclear. And an overt revolution seemed difficult in the wake of the Cristero defeat by the Mexican military.

There was sense of futility in the writing of most independent leftists. Porter described the tendency of idealists to turn to self-aggrandizing corruption while encircling themselves with the aura of the revolution. Beals found that the government was no longer a progressive, reformist state but had slipped into the still dominant Hispanic proclivity for autocracy. In a passage that Waldo Frank would have deplored and Frank Tannenbaum would have applauded, Beals claimed: "The revolutionary Mexican government. . . . is still square within the Roman-Spanish super-state tradition; and the Indian leaders who have risen to power during the past hundred years, establishing themselves by one program of liberation or another, have inevitably, once they gained office, been swept out of the popular current into the closed confines of the super-state, and there developed an arbitrary semi-feudal psychology unrestrained by direct and active public opinion."[30]

Beals, one of the most outspoken critics of the central government's mishandling of socioeconomic reform, was apparently the only disillusioned political pilgrim to experience personally the heavy hand of the frustrated nation-state: his published condemnations of the Maximato resulted in his arrest and brief detention by Mexican military police in February 1930. The episode indicated the government's continuing concern with its image in the United States press and also a collapse of its efforts to practice the techniques of hospitality. After his release, however, Beals continued to lash out at the nation's ruling clique.[31]

As they lost faith in the nation state, most U.S. leftists were equally uncertain about the effects of widespread social change in Mexico. Although they saw the need for such innovations as public schools, labor unions, land reform, irrigation and fertilization, they also hoped that the stable, communal aspects of traditional life might survive. Spontaneous change was possible but rare and therefore not a universal solution. The government had great potential for both harm and good. It could struggle up the mountainside as guardian of benevolent traditionalism and selective modernization, or it could pull the people into a swamp of parasitic corruption and suffocating power, or—somewhere between the lofty heights and the murky depths—it could take the initiative as the aggressive catalyst of innovation on a massive and disruptive scale. U.S. observers did not reach a consensus on these alternatives. Liberal capitalist Lippmann and liberal statist Gruening held generally favorable views of the Calles government's church policies and the elitist-controlled outcome of the church-state dispute; they believed that the problem was solved. But Beals and Tannenbaum took the peasant point of view and saw an oppressive central government at work.

For most U.S. intellectuals who wrote about Mexico in these years, the revolutionary state had failed to provide a model for effective action in a time of crisis. Political pilgrims such as Beals, Tannenbaum, Porter, and eventually even Gruening found no shrine at which to worship. Their search for a new social and economic order seemed to have been in vain.

Mexico under Cárdenas

By the mid-1930s most U.S. observers regarded Plutarco Elías Calles as a sinister figure utilizing dictatorial legerdemain to retain control of the Mexican government. Interim presidents from 1928 to 1934 (Pascual Ortiz Rubio, Emilio Portes Gil, and Abelardo Rodríguez) had to reckon with and try to maneuver around this power behind the scenes. They had little success. In the writing of many liberals and radicals from the United States, Calles had undergone a remarkable transformation from leftist leader of an enlightened government in 1925 to the embodiment of the much-detested phenomenon of caudillismo in 1935.

At this point, when many had relegated Mexico to the list of fascist or near fascist states, an unexpected challenger emerged: thirty-nine-year-old Lázaro Cárdenas who, against heavy odds, turned Mexico sharply to the left.

The U.S. writers in Mexico in the mid-1930s were considerably different from those who had assembled in Mexico City a decade earlier. The old camaraderie was gone, and most of the bohemians and their acquaintances had dispersed. Carleton Beals married again and settled in Connecticut. Anita Brenner was married, had young children, and lived in New York City. Edward Weston was in California, and Tina Modotti remained a controversial and distant figure, surrounded by doubts concerning her role in the murder of Julio Mella. Ernest Gruening had moved to Franklin D. Roosevelt's Department of the Interior en route to the governorship of the territory of Alaska. Of the old group Frank Tannenbaum, Lesley Simpson, Eyler Simpson, Frances Toor, and

Howard Phillips either lived in or frequently visited Mexico, but the conviviality and freewheeling discussions of the 1920s seemed to have had no counterpart in the 1930s. Even the remaining and returning veterans were drawn in separate directions.

In the international communications system that connected Mexico with the United States, the work of journalists and other observers became more routine. Improvements in transportation made travel less an adventure and more an everyday matter. Newcomers and veterans alike moved around Mexico with little difficulty, whether they received help from the government or planned their own itineraries. Perhaps the increasingly routine nature of travel throughout the republic helps to explain the absence of a community similar to the bohemian group of the 1920s. Students of Mexico simply passed through the hotel-apartment section of Mexico City between the Zócalo and Reforma on their way to a political meeting, a regional city, or a rural village. Accompanied by and often resentful of the ever growing flocks of tourists, they seemed to go in different directions in search of new vistas and unspoiled villages off the well-worn paths of the previous decade.

Easier travel meant that the migration of liberals and leftists to Mexico had considerably less resemblance to the conditions of political pilgrimage as outlined by Paul Hollander. Also, the ascendancy of the New Deal and the spread of cooperative values in the United States reduced the sense of alienation that had been typical of many pilgrims of the 1920s who had sought a better way of life in a foreign land. The other end of the process of political pilgrimage, however, was vigorously restored: deployment of the techniques of hospitality was very much in evidence under Cárdenas, who seemed to have a special talent for capturing and retaining the sympathies of travelers to the left of ideological center—particularly Waldo Frank and Frank Tannenbaum.[1]

The Expropriation

Lázaro Cárdenas climaxed two decades of tense relations between the Mexican government and foreign oil companies with his dramatic and, to many conservatives and liberal capitalists, drastic expropriation decree of March 18, 1938. This decision to seize the oil properties was the consequence of a dispute between the Mexican petroleum workers' union and the foreign companies. Standard Oil led the corporate defiance of the Mexican government by refusing to abide by the decisions of an arbitration board and the Mexican Supreme Court. With the credibility and legitimacy of his government in question, Cárdenas acted decisively.

Four days later, a ballerina turned writer witnessed the massive emotional outburst of 200,000 people in front of the National Palace. She was not a detached foreign observer but a Mexican by marriage and by personal choice. After five years in Mexico, Verna Carleton Millan had developed an acute awareness of the nuances of Mexican politics and society. Similar public demonstrations in Hitler's Germany or Mussolini's Italy contained ominous elements of militaristic nationalism, but Millan was confident that Cárdenas—in her view the St. George of Mexico—and his nearly unanimous public were justified in celebrating their infliction of severe wounds on that special group of dragons: the U.S., British, and Dutch oil companies that had for four decades dominated one of the nation's most valuable resources. A veritable explosion of national pride overwhelmed everyone present on the Zócalo that day, including Millan. Far from objective, her description of what she saw and felt indicated the political and social forces at work:

> There was a moment of absolute madness when Cárdenas' voice swept the multitude. I doubt if anyone heard a word he said. The cheers were deafening; people screamed from sheer nervous tension; bands clashed forth the strains of Mexico's anthem and the International, taken up by thousands of voices. Showers of green, white, and red confetti, the national colors, drifted from nowhere and the bright gleam of the Mexican sunshine blurred them into an iridescent haze.... The parade began at nine. It was after three when we wearily returned home.
>
> Whatever the future might bring, this much can be said: On that day, the Mexican people attained a unity which had never been possible before. An entire nation, accustomed for centuries to the perpetual humiliation of the underdog, reared its head proudly for the first time. Cárdenas gave his people a national consciousness, a sense of historic responsibility and above all else a feeling of pride. It meant something to be Mexican that day. No more humble pie, no more kowtowing to arrogant foreign officials; the Mexican people began to breathe freely as though a weight had been taken from them.[2]

The oil companies and their supporters had a different point of view. The presence of radical labor organizations and elements of the Mexican Communist Party among the demonstrators and Cárdenas's preference for collective farms and support of militant labor unions convinced many corporate officials that the oil expropriation was one giant step on the road to state socialism. Many conservative commentators had already been deeply disturbed by the apparent leftward trend of the Roosevelt administration, and their selective perception of events in Mexico reinforced their willingness to believe the most extreme claims of success from the lips of Mexican leaders such as Marxist Lombardo Toledano. In short, they saw Mexico rushing headlong toward Communism.

The colorful ideological expressions of muralists José Clemente Orozco, Diego Rivera, and David Alfaro Siqueiros on the walls of public buildings in the United States added to Mexico's leftist image,[3] as did the adoption of socialist education as official policy and the acceptance of a communal basis for agrarian reform. Both leftists and rightists were caught up in the excitement, a potent mixture of emotion and ideology that led many otherwise astute observers to accentuate the enthusiasm that seemed at times to engulf them. Like Millan, many leftist writers joined the celebration as participants as much as observers. Conservatives felt the confluence of emotion and ideology with a sense of revulsion rather than elation. The words and images that flowed across the border to the United States captured the elan of the moment but, in most cases, offered little depth of analysis.

Cárdenas and his advisers were concerned that they would not receive a fair hearing in the U.S. media after the expropriation. The support of leftists such as Tannenbaum and Frank was helpful, but mainstream newspapers and journals of opinion reached a larger and more influential readership, and—as Francisco Múgica and Ramón Beteta quickly observed—conservative and even moderate print organs were producing a torrent of anti-Mexican coverage. Both urged Cárdenas to mount a publicity campaign in English to counter this negative image.[4]

The Mexican government did devise its own English-language responses to U.S. conservative attacks,[5] and Cárdenas also found volunteers among liberal statists. William Cameron Townsend was a California-born missionary and Bible translator who worked for five years in Mexico; his patience and persistence among the Indians had won the president's admiration. Cárdenas "requested" an invitation to dinner from Townsend and his wife (who lived in a "shanty" in the village of Tetelcingo) six weeks before the expropriation. On that occasion, the chief of state explored the deepening oil-labor controversy with his host. The two men corresponded regularly thereafter; in a January 30, 1939, letter Townsend detailed the U.S. lecture tour in which he intended to present the Mexican government's case. He also wrote a sharply worded defense of the Cárdenas administration in a pamphlet for U.S. readers. Another volunteer was Hubert Herring, also a Protestant minister by training. Though not as close to Cárdenas personally, Herring became one of the Mexican president's most persistent champions in the U.S. press. A frequent contributor to *Current History* and *Harper's*, he was an insistent liberal statist, praising the use of government activism to uplift the masses.[6]

With Townsend, Herring, and others writing favorable articles and books based on their own convictions, Cárdenas, Beteta, and Múgica found that their cultivation of U.S. writers continued to bear fruit. The president's quiet, apparently effortless charisma seemed even more effective in the crisis atmosphere after the expropriation. Waldo Frank of the far left had common cause with Herring and Townsend of the center in their support of the mestizo from Michoacán. There was agreement among extreme and moderate leftists on the historical, legal, and economic bases for the expropriation. Millan, an intuitive socialist and a Mexican nationalist, presented the most powerful indictment of the economic abuses and ethnic prejudices that had been associated with the exploitation of petroleum in her 1939 book, *Mexico Reborn*:

> This was the epoch of get-rich-quick overnight when beach-combers became millionaires and small-town speculators hit a lucky well that ran ten thousand barrels a day, when oil was converted into gold and the gold strewn in reckless profusion over the land because there was plenty more where that came from, or so they thought. Nothing like these days has been seen since the Klondike gold rush, and even that was small fry compared to Tampico. The red-faced Gringos who showered diamonds on their mistresses plucked from the cream of Tampico's brothels, their arrogant wives, product of Southern farms and Minnesota ranches who suddenly discovered aristocratic blood in their veins, their children, educated in Europe and the United States, all made one mistake, however. They thought Mexico's oil was theirs by some God-given right, to hold and exploit and use at will without ever taking into consideration the country that had made this possible. Indeed, if they thought of Mexico at all, it was with sullen contempt.[7]

The Debate in the Roosevelt Administration

Although there was no open expression of "sullen contempt" in the Roosevelt administration, there was a serious debate. Secretary of State Cordell Hull, the stolid former senator from Tennessee, was a determined Wilsonian internationalist and an archenemy of high tariffs and barriers to free trade. He was outraged by the expropriation and, for at least six months thereafter, took a firm stand for immediate compensation for the oil companies. In private conversations with Mexican ambassador Castillo Nájera and Secretary of the Treasury Henry Morgenthau Jr., Hull denounced Mexico as a nation lurching recklessly in the direction of Communism. In public, Hull attempted to discredit the Cárdenas administration's plans for economic structural change by linking them to what he saw as the illegal seizure of the oil properties.[8] His sharply worded unpublished and public statements had considerable support among Foreign Service officers who, according to historian Clayton Koppes, "were largely Republican and opposed to the New Deal and the Good Neighbor Policy to say nothing of nationalization."[9]

Hull's pointed rebuke of the expropriation appeared in a front-page story in the *New York Times*. He placed Mexico in the category of outlaw nations because of its apparent abandonment of the widely accepted practice of immediate compensation. Mexico's position was based on "astonishing theory," whereas Hull claimed as his precedents "the basic precepts of international law and of the law of every American republic as well as . . . every principle of right and justice upon which the institutions of the American republics are founded."[10]

In the left wing of the State Department and very much in disagreement with Hull was Josephus Daniels, the populist newspaper editor from North Carolina. Appointed to the Mexico City embassy in 1933 by his old friend Franklin Roosevelt, Daniels was not a professional diplomat, and many of Hull's advisers saw him as easily misled by Cárdenas. While Hull had fretted and fumed about the expropriation of U.S. citizens' agricultural holdings in 1936 and 1937, Daniels had accepted those actions and expressed confidence that Mexico would eventually compensate the former owners at a reasonable level.[11]

Daniels justified his position in terms typical of leftist populism in the 1930s. The ambassador sided with the Mexican oil workers in their quest for higher wages and better working conditions, and he saw a parallel between the labor movements on both sides of the Rio Grande. He admitted that Cárdenas might have miscalculated in the abruptness of the expropriation, but there was no doubt that the Mexican president enjoyed the support of his nation. Any hint of surrender to the demands of the oil companies would not only arouse the anger of a unified Mexican populace but would threaten to discredit the noninterventionist principles of the Good Neighbor Policy throughout the hemisphere.[12]

Daniels took some risks in disagreeing with his boss, Secretary Hull, but the wily former newspaper editor was not nearly as naive as many of his State Department critics believed. Biographer E. David Cronon discovered that Daniels kept a newspaper clipping of Roosevelt's April 11, 1938, news conference in which the president stated his view of the Mexican situation. Without mentioning the oil companies by name, Roosevelt left no doubt that he held a very dim view of large business operators such as W.R. Hearst, who "bought a state legislature, bribed officials and acquired title . . . to hundreds of thousands of acres of land for practically nothing except the cost of the bribe, or they paid three cents an acre for it, things like that, and then claimed all kinds of damages in a sum far in excess of the amount of money that he had actually put in. We do not have much sympathy with trying to collect that excessive sum for him."[13]

The Daniels view ultimately prevailed. He was not the key decision maker on this issue, but his arguments captured the mood of the Roosevelt administration and anticipated the policy that the State Department did ultimately employ. In 1942 the United States and Mexico reached a settlement in which the oil companies received modest compensation, and Washington furnished the new administration of Manuel Avila Camacho (the moderate successor to Cárdenas) with financial support.[14] Daniels's approach was a decided break with the narrowly conceived Sheffield-Kellogg defense of private property through intimidation and bombast and with the Morrow-Hull advocacy of liberal capitalism through diplomacy and manipulation, which acted to slow the pace of government-directed reform. Daniels argued that the United States must stay out of the internal affairs of Mexico; he saw no reason to stand in the way of that nation's assertion of control over petroleum, land, and other resources for the benefit of the masses.

Conservative and Liberal Capitalist Responses

Daniels and Hull represented only two positions along a broad ideological spectrum of U.S. responses to the mid-1930s manifestations of the Mexican revolution. If Cordell Hull had sought support for a much harsher policy—perhaps to the point of military intervention—he could have found it in mainstream publications that attempted to revive the 1920s fears of Bolshevism. Veteran journalist Owen White in the pages of *Collier's*, disillusioned New Dealer Ray Moley in *Newsweek*, and Henry J. Allen in the *Reader's Digest* and the *New York Herald Tribune* were among the conservatives who expressed the belief that a dictatorial Communist government was a real possibility in Mexico if not a *fait accompli*. Writing in 1936, White saw Mexico's golden ages in the time of Porfirio Díaz and in the fourteen years of Obregón-Calles rule. The chaos of the mid-1910s was about to return in the mid-1930s but with important differences: the Six Year Plan, Marxist rhetoric, labor-peasant agitation, and government expropriations convinced White that Communism was close at hand. He cited a pamphlet distributed by the Ministry of Foreign Relations as evidence of radicalism. The pamphlet was full of phrases such as "class war," "insurgency of the proletarian class," and the particularly sinister call for the "creation of a new state to realize progressive socialization of [the] means of production."[15]

After the oil expropriation, White seemed to conservatives to have been a prophet of remarkable vision. Ray Moley saw "the doom of private property" under Cárdenas, who had moved "away from the strong, intelligent guidance of Plutarco Calles" to follow a course that led to expropriation, "the crowning act of stupidity."[16] Henry J. Allen visited Mexico in the summer of 1938 and found much evidence of growing Communist control. The head of the powerful labor union, the

Confederation of Mexican Workers (CTM), was the unabashed and eloquent Marxist Vicente Lombardo Toledano, whose harangues seemed to confirm Allen's worst fears: an "irrepressible craze that is sweeping Mexico hell-bent for industrial and commercial chaos."[17]

These conservatives found eager allies among the oil companies, which from 1937 to 1942 were locked in a struggle with the Mexican government. Standard Oil and others financed an extensive public relations campaign to gain support for their defense of the rights of private property against the Cárdenas government. For example, they paid for the publication of a special issue of the *Atlantic Monthly* and a compilation of newspaper editorials by former *Literary Digest* editorial staffer Burt McConnell.[18] Neither one of these publications, however, contained a comprehensive conservative critique of the revolution. Roscoe Gaither's book *Expropriation in Mexico* moved beyond the alarmism and propagandistic tone of this subsidized work, but his specialized legal arguments, though appropriate for the courts, were restricted in overall breadth and depth and left many issues—land reform, collectivization of agriculture, government control of the print media and education, and radical ideology—essentially untouched.[19]

Conservatives who wrote out of a sense of immediacy and urgency found it difficult to gain historical and ideological perspectives on the revolution. Numerous radicals and liberals went to Mexico and traveled through both city and country at an easy pace, visiting places they wanted to see or were advised they should see, whereas very few conservatives stayed there for any extended time during these years. With an apparent aversion to the liberal-radical writings of the recent past, the conservatives generally fell back on the deeply held and seldom questioned belief that somehow events in Mexico were a part of the overall Communist design for world domination.[20]

Among the most comprehensive and systematic critiques of the Cárdenas administration by U.S. writers came from the pens of Frank Kluckhohn, a *New York Times* correspondent stationed in Mexico, and Virginia Prewett, a Tennessee-born journalist who, like Kluckhohn, had covered the Spanish Civil War earlier in the decade. Although neither was a doctrinaire conservative, they both combined robust journalistic skepticism and a capacity to resist the low-keyed charisma of Cárdenas with a preference for liberal capitalist policies.

Kluckhohn was by far the more controversial of the two; his clashes with the Mexican government ended in his expulsion in December 1938. The exact reasons await further study in Mexican government archives; the Mexican Consulate General in San Antonio, Texas, announced that Kluckhohn had excited "the ill will of foreign people against us [Mexicans]," but there were no detailed charges. Whatever the circumstances, Kluckhohn held the distinction of being the only foreign correspondent so treated by the administration of Cárdenas, who was sensitive to U.S. press opinion.[21]

In spite of his troubles with the government, Kluckhohn produced a coherent analysis of the Cárdenas regime and the revolution in general. A large, good-humored veteran of frontline journalism in Spain, he struggled with the canons of reportorial objectivity and the priorities of his personal ideology (which emerged more clearly in his book than in his newspaper dispatches). His was a brand of liberal capitalism amended by a progressive acceptance of the regulation of private enterprise through government agencies. The New Deal's recently appointed governor of Alaska, Ernest Gruening, seemed to slide from his liberal statist position when he called Kluckhohn's *Mexican Challenge* "the most realistic book about Mexico in half a decade" and praised the author's ability to balance "his sympathy for the Mexican people" with "the first evaluation in some years unclouded by sentimentality, wishful thinking, or partisanship."[22]

Prewett joined Kluckhohn in resisting the temptation to measure the Cárdenas administration on the spectrum of contemporary European politics. The two journalists evaluated Mexico in its own terms. Their verdicts on the massive land reform project in Laguna (a region spreading into the states of Coahuila and Durango), labor control of the oil fields and refineries, and government controls on the national press were all negative, however. The cottonfields in the north were inefficient under the communal (*ejido*) pattern. The oil workers, who had the technical skill to do their jobs, found their corporate bosses replaced by equally venal labor bosses. The nationalization of land and oil not only threw valuable resources under inefficient managers but also turned away private investment, both foreign and Mexican, from an economy that needed capital. The government, saddled by huge foreign debts, could not meet its basic fiscal needs.[23]

The hectic atmosphere in Mexico in 1937 and 1938 was, for both writers, symptomatic of a nation moving rapidly toward disaster. Abrupt and far-reaching actions had augmented the power of the nation-state, but wounded the capacity of the private sector and accomplished virtually nothing to improve the welfare of the workers and peasants. According to Kluckhohn: "The rapid land nationalization . . . and the widespread confiscation of private property . . . have created a tangled economic and social morass in the midst of which general hardship has increased rapidly. Behind the smoke screen of unrelenting propaganda, the labor leaders, the government farm agents, and the generals have increased their domination of the common people."[24]

In Kluckhohn's prescription for alternative policies, he singled out the cordial relationship between Ambassador Dwight Morrow and the president–power broker Plutarco Elías Calles as the path that Mexico should have followed. Morrow, the banker-diplomat, was well schooled in the practice of regulating large corporations in the United States and seemed to have provided Calles, his prize student, with valuable lessons for Mexico. Although Morrow's policy "has been in force for almost fifteen years, Mexico's officials have unfortunately failed to recognize it. Instead of seeking Washington's co-operation in order to get a larger income from foreign corporations and to bulwark reasonable regulations, a sense of having been wronged, fear, internal politics, and greed have led to the rapid seizure and elimination of foreign property."[25]

Writing in 1941, two years after Kluckhohn, Prewett noted a potential return to the Morrow-Calles pattern, an ideological pendulum at work in the Cárdenas presidency that resembled the policy shifts of the Calles years. Both men started on the far left, with land reform and the expropriation of foreign-owned property. During his last two years in office Cárdenas, like Calles during the Maximato, became more cautious and conservative, and in 1940 he agreed to the nomination and election to the presidency of the moderate friend of free enterprise, Manual Avila Camacho. There was investment capital in Mexico, but investors had not used it because of their lack of confidence in Cárdenas. Prewett saw this attitude changing as the rise of Avila Camacho began to restore the confidence of the private sector.[26]

Both Prewett and Kluckhohn combined a trenchant critique of the manipulations and dishonesty of peasant and labor leadership with a rejection of the program of nationalization which, in effect, created a large bureaucracy in which these ambitious refugees from the lower classes could pull their way up the political-administrative ladder. Kluckhohn believed that the continued ascension of organized labor within important state agencies posed a threat to the survival of "private industrial capital."[27] Prewett, though less pessimistic on this point, agreed that the oil and land expropriations were omens of what an arbitrary government might attempt in later years under similar circumstances. Such acts could only isolate Mexico from its traditional and natural trading partner, the United States, and in the long run frustrate Mexican as well as foreign entrepreneurs.[28]

Kluckhohn and Prewett wrote the most persuasive critiques of the Cárdenas administration from the right side of the political spectrum. White, Moley, Allen, and Gaither, sniping at Cárdenas from their highly particular conservative points of view, did not provide the same breadth or depth of analysis. Both Kluckhohn and Prewett advocated free enterprise, but they did so within a Mexican context that included not only the well-being of Wall Street but also the requirements of sustained economic expansion of local and national industries.[29]

The Far Left: Momentary Discord

The Kluckhohn-Prewett brief for Mexico's adoption of the liberal capitalist model did not draw heavy fire from the left, perhaps because U.S. leftist writers were so caught up in the excitement of converging ideological and political trends in the late 1930s that the journalists' critique seemed almost irrelevant. In general, liberal statists, independent leftists, fellow travelers, and even some Communists found the intuitive, idealistic socialism of Cárdenas and many of his followers not only acceptable but admirable. Factional disputes were minimal, despite the presence in Mexico of the doomed Leon Trotsky and the intrigues that surrounded him.

There were at least two exceptions to this general euphoria, however. One was the experienced Mexicanist Bertram Wolfe. In 1936, on his first visit to the land of Diego Rivera since his expulsion in 1925, Wolfe expressed the enthusiasm of a political pilgrim in a letter to his wife: "What a day—my first in Mexico. I'm just full to bursting. Every sight, every sound, every smell brings back a flood of emotions. Now I know what we've been missing since 1925. And the city has made itself a hundred times more beautiful than you and I knew it to be."[30]

But Wolfe's enthusiasm was short-lived. He soon located Rivera, and the two of them began collaboration on a book of black and white photographs of the artist's murals, accompanied by the writer's brief text on Mexican history and politics. Wolfe's twenty-one page discussion of Cárdenas was the most virulent attack by a U.S. leftist in the decade. He accused the president of being a petty dictator who clung to power only because he had the support of the Mexican army and Washington. Wolfe insisted that Cárdenas's policies benefitted Wall Street and its Mexico City lackeys because he was unwilling to wield presidential authority in the area of economic planning.[31] Wolfe even accused Cárdenas of having used inside information from the U.S. Treasury to make a fortune for himself in the silver market.[32] This charge of personal corruption aroused the ire of the Mexican president, who wrote a categorical denial in a private letter to William Cameron Townsend: "Wolfe wrote in his book *Portrait of Mexico* that I took part in 'un juego de bolsa' that made me a millionaire. It is a lie. Money does not interest me. My goal is only [to maintain] the power to carry out my duty."[33]

Maurice Halperin was another Communist who had unkind words for the Cárdenas administration. A member of the University of Oklahoma faculty, Halperin wrote a series of articles for *Current History,* the *New Republic,* and the *New York Times* between 1934 and 1938 in which he described Cárdenas as leading the way through "the middle ground, the path that leads to liberal capitalism"—an insult of sorts from a Marxist.[34]

If the Wolfe-Halperin criticisms damaged the Cárdenas image in the United States, Waldo Frank's 1939 return to Mexico and his subsequent pieces in the *Nation* and *Foreign Affairs* did much to repair it. Frank had established a fairly close relationship with the Mexican president, as revealed in their correspondence and in the fact that the two toured Mexico together from Chihuahua to Oaxaca in May and June 1939. Frank's influence on Cárdenas is difficult to assess, but there is little doubt that the Mexican president took their relationship seriously. On March 18, 1938, the day of the oil expropriation, Cárdenas had sent Frank a brief letter that contained no mention of that event (it may have been written before the decision was made) but revealed that Mexico's chief executive took time to communicate his concerns about the plight of Spanish Republicans and his interest in Frank's plans for a new book.[35] Frank's claim that Cárdenas found guidance in *The Rediscovery of America* for his decision to expropriate the oil company properties finds some support in a letter from the president to his friend written about three months after the act.[36] Their respect was mutual; in the pages of the *Nation* and *Foreign Affairs* Frank rendered a resounding endorsement of the Cárdenas presidency.[37]

The *New Masses* added its support to the Mexican cause. Unaffected by Wolfe's charges of corruption and Halperin's view of Cárdenas as insidious capitalist, this New York–based organ of the U.S. Communist Party blasted the greed of the oil companies and the "vicious" attacks and "scare stories" in the U.S. press. Cárdenas was, in the estimate of the *New Masses,* squarely in the center of the "people's front program." His actions brought immediate benefit to those Mexicans who toiled in the workplace and were of symbolic importance for all the struggling masses.[38]

The commentary of the *New Masses* and Waldo Frank was typical of U.S. leftists' writing on the last years of the Cárdenas regime. After March 18, 1938, neither Wolfe nor Halperin publicly criticized the president. Other factors may have contributed to their unwillingness to do so, but the ouster of the oil companies made it extremely difficult to sustain the argument, at least in public that Cárdenas was "soft on capitalism."

The Mainstream Press

The immediate economic turmoil resulting from the expropriations largely escaped the enthusiastic supporters of the Cárdenas program.

With their eyes turned toward the ideals of social justice, these leftists seemed to believe that the dislocations, shortages, inflation, and general confusion associated with the land and oil expropriations were short-run phenomena that would eventually disappear.[39]

The leftist writers who presented an image of Mexico as a social-ist state in the making—a state populated with Marxists, an occasional Communist, and a potpourri of left-wingers—sought to stimulate ac-ceptance, not revulsion and fear, in their reader. They received welcome but probably unexpected support in the pages of mass circulation pub-lications. In the late 1930s, leftist ideas found legitimacy if not popular-ity in the United States. The continuing severity of the business collapse, the eclectic experimentation of the Roosevelt administration, and the ascent of leftist cultural values in the United States gave discussions of Mexican communal agriculture, socialist education, and government management of large sectors of the economy a familiar and even recep-tive context. In a general sense, Roosevelt and Cárdenas seemed bound in the same direction, although they had started from different locations on the scale of socioeconomic development. In 1938 Cárdenas appar-ently thrust his country's underdeveloped economy several steps ahead of the New Deal in the regulation and, in some cases, socialization of critical elements of production. Mexico obviously lagged far behind the United States in per capita industrial and agricultural output, but in the 1930s, announced intentions and symbolic actions carried much weight in politics and in public opinion.[40]

John Gunther, the roving journalist who specialized in quick studies of large and complex regions of the world for a popular reader-ship, visited Mexico in 1941—after Avila Camacho was in office—to find the radical impetus of the Cárdenas administration still very much in evidence. Gunther accepted the idea that Cárdenas has "attempted to fulfill the social promises of the revolution." The result was not a com-plete revamping of Mexico's distribution of wealth and power, but in Gunther's words the former president had "made a prodigious effort." The journalist singled out Mexico in his 18,938-mile tour of the lands south of the Rio Grande as "the only country in Latin America with an advanced social-economic program, with definite collectivist aims, principles, and accomplishments."[41] He specified Article 27 of the Con-stitution of 1917 as the basis for Mexico's collectivist orientation and in low-keyed tones described the land reform program and the oil expro-priation as typical policies arising from such a leftist approach.[42]

Betty Kirk agreed with much of Gunther's commentary, but in *Covering the Mexican Front* she provided a deeper political analysis and used the crucial word that Gunther seemed to avoid: "socialism." Kirk was an experienced journalist who came to Mexico in 1936 and, unlike

Gunther, remained there for most of the next half-decade. She arrived with no obvious political commitments and an apparent but circumspect liberal statist ideology. She wrote regularly for the *Christian Science Monitor* and occasionally for the *New York Times* and *Life* magazines. After five years on the scene, she had no aversion to socialism in Mexico.[43] Carleton Beals's review of her book characterized her as a typical U.S. liberal seeking the middle way, which, as she found in Mexico, had shifted to the left.[44]

Kirk stated her view forthrightly: "Cárdenas dedicated his government to a socialistic program built on a healthy labor base when he said that its objective was to raise the living standard for the poorer classes and to level out the existing inequalities of wealth."[45] She saw an extension of the commitment to socialism beyond 1940 into the Avila Camacho presidency and paraphrased the new president's minister of foreign relations, Ezequiel Padilla, on post–World War II Mexico and general international economic conditions: "The devastation throughout the world will be so enormous that no private initiative could attempt to cope with it; it will become the problem of the state to rebuild civilization, but on the principle of the greater good for the greatest number. . . . In the course of time, private initiative will again function, but in co-operation with the state. He [Padilla] calls this 'a form of socialism' "[46]

Although socialist education created a furor in Mexico and a loud debate in the United States, many leftists defended the radical policy. Journalist J.H. Plenn argued that it was a success within certain parameters, largely limits imposed by the influence of education itself. For Plenn, the new program's emphasis on rationalism and science was a healthy trend that moved away from the traditional stress on aesthetics and abstract philosophy. Educators George Sánchez and George Booth made even larger claims for the socialist school, placing it in the vanguard of a social and cultural order that would elevate urban workers and village peasants to new standards of literacy and communality.[47]

The image of Cárdenas as a benevolent socialist appeared in two of Henry Luce's publications: *Life* and *Time*. In September 1937 *Life* presented a three-page photographic essay with a brief text by Betty Kirk. The story's title captured its essence: "Socialist President Cárdenas Visits Mexico's Lower Classes."[48] In August 1938, eleven months after the *Life* coverage and five months after the expropriation, *Time* featured Cárdenas on its cover and published a lengthy and favorable discussion of his presidency. The piece concentrated on Cárdenas's personal qualities, particularly in its account of his visit to a hacienda that had been the scene of recent peasant unrest. The incident brought out the president's stern moralism and determination to carry out a sweeping redistribution of property:

> After stopping the night ... with a young Mexican owner of
> some 50,000 acres, President Cárdenas invited his host to accompany him in riding over the estates. Presently they clattered up
> to some still-smoking hovels and a group of dispossessed peons
> standing abjectly in the road. The peons explained to the President that they were squatters who had refused to be dispossessed until finally the landlord's men had burned them out of
> their shacks. Said Lázaro Cárdenas in a cold rage to his host:
> "Don't you know that it is the duty of the rich and fortunate to
> help the poor? Are you not ashamed to burn the houses of a few
> poor peons because they want a little piece of land? Don't you
> know it is the duty of the government to help poor peons to
> become citizens?"
> "Si," answered the landlord, without enthusiasm. "Yes."
> President Cárdenas crooked his finger at the local head of
> the Agrarian Commission, ordered him to have the burned
> houses of the peons rebuilt at once, to supply them with farming
> tools, guns and ammunition.
> "I want rifles and plows to be here together, and that not
> ten days later than this date!" commanded the President, then
> turned to the bewildered peons. "The arms I have ordered for
> you are to make sure that your homes will not be burned again.
> But you have the responsibility to keep the peace in this neighborhood not only for yourselves but for all. You must protect
> everyone, including the owner of the plantation here. And I
> urge you not to permit the establishment of drinking places. If
> you do not stay sober you will not keep the peace." [49]

This Cárdenista blend of idealistic populism and benevolent paternalism emanated from the person of the president, the massive land reform and oil expropriation and from the national government he headed. His role as leader of this activist state won the confidence of *Time, Life,* and many Americans who seemed to accept this form of socialism as appropriate for Mexico at this stage of its history. Perhaps the most unusual aspect of his acceptance among U.S. observers was its breadth—extending from liberal statists such as Townsend, Herring, and Kirk to populists such as Beals and Daniels to Communists and fellow travelers such as Waldo Frank. For them, Mexico of the late 1930s was a laboratory of socioeconomic innovation in which the experiments seemed to have a good chance of success.

In their public discussion of Mexico, however, political predispositions and propagandistic efforts frequently outweighed careful thought. Words were more often ideological weapons than tools for cogent analysis. The flow of printed praise from the left and the phobic anti-Communism of the right combined to produce the impression that large-scale radical experimentation was under way. Millan's exuberant description of the expropriation celebration and White's alarmist account of Communist inroads in Mexico were typical respectively of leftist and rightist hyperbole. *Time's* less extreme but perhaps more persuasive description of the simple, personal president-peasant relationship touched the sentimentalist inclinations of many leftists, just as Cordell Hull's condemnation of Mexico as an outlaw nation stimulated the fears of conservatives and liberal capitalists. But with the exceptions of those by Kluckhohn, Prewett, and, to some extent, Kirk, all these discussions generally lacked depth. There was no widely accepted definition of the nature of the radicalism apparently in vogue. Observers seemed to dwell on large images and symbols (such as the expropriation), impressive personalities (mainly Cárdenas himself), and bits and pieces of evidence (government-issued, Marxist-slanted pedagogy and pamphlets)—the kind of information that quickly implied a pattern, but a pattern that may have had little substance. The visual and verbal rhetoric of the revolution had spawned its own dimension, and in the excitement of the late 1930s and early 1940s, many foreign observers seemed content to stay there.

10

The Revolution beneath the Revolutionary Image

The fears of right-wing critics and the excitement of left-wing sympathizers created the impression that Cárdenas had led Mexico a considerable distance down the path to socialism. A closer reading of these polemics makes clear, however, that neither camp rendered their respective verdicts on the basis of a comprehensive, widely accepted definition of socialism. The rightists (with the exceptions of Kluckhohn and Prewett) wrote mainly in terms of exaggerated fears that skewed their perceptions. Many leftists held exaggerated hopes that skewed their perceptions in the other direction. As the preceding chapter indicates, their capacity for enthusiasm seemed to outweigh their commitment to analysis—a condition typical of political pilgrims.

The lack of a consistent definition of socialism within the Cárdenas administration and the often rambling commentary of U.S. sympathizers led some students of Mexican history to conclude that the revolutionary image of these years was more rhetoric and intention that policy and accomplishment. This critique was especially compelling for those who held up the Marxist-Leninist model. Yet both the excited, ideologically inspired observations of contemporaries and the more analytical retrospectives of later writers tended to overlook the presence of a sociopolitical base of support for Cárdenas among workers and peasants and a set of policies directed toward these supporters that did constitute a socialist revolutionary movement, at least for a few years.

History does not stop just because the protagonists have no broadly accepted, ideologically pure definition of key terms. More recent studies of the Mexican revolution, particularly those of Alan Knight, Heather Fowler Salamini, Paul Friedrich, and, to some extent, Nora Hamilton identify a pattern of sociopolitical change in which statism and populism interacted to produce forces that flowed between the nation-state and the partially mobilized peasants and workers.[1] Their model of statist populism provides a conceptual framework within which to study the serious analyses of the Mexican revolution in the late 1930s. Admittedly, leftists writers did not focus their appraisals through an ideologically precise lens, but they had in common their concentration on this interaction between the government and the masses.

Many U.S. observers became convinced that the Cárdenas brand of intuitive, populistic state activism was an appropriate variant of socialism. Contained within (and partially obscured by) the many discussions of Mexico's manifestations of radicalism was an explanation of the form of socialism that Cárdenas attempted to put in place piece by piece from 1935 through 1938. To socialists and many nonsocialist leftists in the United States, the government was not limited to the regulatory functions of the model envisioned by liberal capitalists Morrow, Kluckhohn, and Prewett, or even to the more expansive role advocated by liberal statists Gruening and Herring. Neither was it, at least in Cárdenas's plans, the potentially abusive Spanish superstate that Tannenbaum and Beals feared nor the tightly planned economy of the Soviet Union. Some leftists believed that Cárdenas humanized the government and harmonized its workings with the needs of the common people at the same time that peasant and worker activists placed demands on the political system. This interaction was not a sentimental, charisma-based symbiosis between a leader and a people but a working relationship in which popular demands pushed the government to make structural reforms—sometimes in ways unanticipated by officials. The chief executive seemed to do something for or to everyone: he both stimulated and harnessed the workers and peasants; he won the allegiance of and then reined in the restive military; he threatened and later conciliated Mexican industrialists; and he challenged and eventually compromised with the Catholic Church. For a relatively brief three years of the three decades of revolutionary activity, the common people and the government worked together toward socialism—at least in the eyes of some U.S. leftists.

The State and the People

The most provocative and probably the most influential book about Mexico published in English during the Cárdenas presidency was *The Ejido: Mexico's Way Out*, by Eyler Simpson. Although the book appeared in 1937, the author completed his research and writing in 1934, apparently several months before Cárdenas rose to national prominence. Holder of a doctorate in sociology from the University of Chicago, Simpson applied the conceptualizations of his discipline and the ideology of socialism to Mexico. At first glance, Simpson's staid personality did not seem to match the confrontational message of *The Ejido*. Even in his mid-thirties his boyish face carried the quiet, pleasant expression of a midwestern boy-next-door rather than the look of the almost humorless scholar he was. Carleton Beals, his friend and frequent traveling companion, poked lighthearted fun at Simpson's futile efforts to impose schedules and clocks on the backlands of Oaxaca. Guggenheim Foundation official Henry Allen Moe also made friendly jokes about the hardworking, highly structured life-style of his organization's Mexico City representative.[2] But Simpson's devotion to the modern world's conceptions of time and organization reflected deeply held beliefs that surfaced not only in his personal life but also in his prescriptive study of Mexico. Beneath the calm, youthful exterior was a forceful advocate of modernization through socialism.

Simpson was highly sensitive to the role of politics in land reform. Mexico's land reform program as of 1934 was a hodgepodge of broken promises, bureaucratic inefficiency, and budgetary inadequacies sprinkled with a few examples of success. One of the main culprits in the record of neglect and abuse was politics or, a bit more specifically, "backstairs intrigue," favoritism, and reactionary manipulation at the local, state, and national levels. The root of the problem may have been the absence of peasant mobilization in the villages: "The majority of the ejidos which are unorganized or disorganized at the present time are in this unhappy state for the very good reason that they have never been organized. In many cases the laws have simply not been enforced at all and the ejidos have been abandoned to their own (inadequate) resources to work out their own salvation as best they may."[3]

Simpson saw another side to peasant politics, however—signs of arousal among the land-poor and landless that included speeches and organization as well as pistols and fisticuffs. The violence was regrettable, but given Mexico's generations of elite-dominated politics, it may have been unavoidable. In the political bases scattered throughout the nation Simpson discovered what he believed was a growing movement that came into conflict with the resilient machine of ex-president turned political boss Calles. The Callista agrarians, known as *veteranos*, favored distribution of land to individual owners, who could then enter the open market as agricultural entrepreneurs. This approach to land reform, in vogue for over a decade, faced a challenge from the recently aroused peasants known as *agraristas*. Their demands included a collective system close but not limited to the traditional village *ejido*: land held in common by the families of the village.[4]

The *agrarista* movement had an unmistakable impact in 1933 and 1934. Led by Graciano Sánchez, an energetic political insurgent, the *agraristas* challenged the Callista-authored Six-Year Plan and succeeded in changing some of its provisions. Of special importance to Simpson was the inclusion of the *acasillados* (landless peons who lived and worked on the large estates) as potential participants in the ejidal land reform system.[5] A second triumph was the passage of the national Agrarian Code of 1934, which marked "the culmination of the reform in agrarian legislation of the veterano-agrarista polemics of 1933." The new code gave the national government a much larger role, cleared a way through bureaucratic red tape, and thereby made it possible at least on paper—for a village to obtain a "provisional ejidal grant" within 150 days and a definitive grant soon thereafter.[6] Simpson cited statistics to show that the number of definitive grants of ejidal property to villages jumped dramatically: nearly seven times as many in the first half of 1934 as during the entire year of 1933.[7]

Simpson's weighty tome took on the quality of a revolutionary pamphlet as the academic threw off the cloak of objectivity. With the announcement "It is time for the analyst to become the advocate," Simpson's prose moved from third person to a first-person endorsement of agrarian socialism: "There is a way out for Mexico. There is a sword which, wielded with strength and skill, will cut the knot of many a Mexican problem. . . . I repeat, there is a way out for Mexico—and that way is the ejido!"[8] The urgent demands that he directed at Mexico's political leaders were, in his estimate, a statement on behalf of the *agraristas*: "It is imperative that the Revolution accept the principle of the socialization of the land with all that it implies, . . . but also, if the agrarian reform is to succeed, it behooves its leaders to achieve a new conception of the future role of the ejido in the social and economic organization of the nation. And the first step in this direction is an agreement that the ejido is not a transition or a stepping stone to anything, it is an end in itself and an institution in its own right."[9]

Simpson envisioned a land reform program in which the government responded to the demands of the peasant population. The villagers, *acasillados*, and rural wage laborers would pressure the state to make use of Article 27 and the new Agrarian Code; the resulting land reform, organized through the national government, would include not simply the soil but also credit, water, transportation, and technology to provide a state-centered socialized agricultural economy.

Cárdenas as Catalyst

The name of Lázaro Cárdenas did not appear in Simpson's index nor, apparently, in his text, but a broad outline of the Cárdenas rural program seemed implicit and in come cases explicit in the book. The *ejido* became the centerpiece of Cárdenas's efforts in land reform.[10] The political nexus that linked the assertive *agraristas* and the activist state also continued, on an even larger scale than Simpson had described. Cárdenas used a powerful array of weapons, including personal charisma and political astuteness, to take advantage of a golden opportunity: a left-leaning government in Washington represented by a sympathetic populist ambassador in Mexico City. The result of this unusual alignment of factors was more than an assertive president with an attentive following; it was a functioning political system in which a mobilized peasantry joined newly revived labor unions to apply pressure on a government that was willing and able to respond to those pressures.

A few writers grasped the internal dynamics of this revolutionary movement. Beals and Herring explored the ideological and sociological parameters of the Cárdenas administration and uncovered some of its linkages with peasants and workers. Beals, for example, identified a pattern in Cardenista politics that was, from his independent leftist perspective, a pattern at odds with the expectations of most observers. The recently restructured and renamed PRM (formerly the PNR, now the Party of the Mexican Revolution), according to Beals,

> has become a party in its own right in a more pluralistic system. To those who see government as a neat dogmatic pattern instead of a general trend, for those who put ideological clarity above all else, the result is as appalling as President Roosevelt's efforts are for the extreme radicals and the "economic royalists." . . . Perhaps compromise and concessions to widely different groups blur the picture and postpone the final reckoning, but in the meantime Cárdenas has been able to give Mexico a great impulse toward land reform, education, progress and reconstruction as have few presidents in its history.[11]

Anita Brenner's concerns had evolved from a bohemian preoccupation with art to an independent leftist stance in the 1920s, and in the 1930s she saw new ideological possibilities. For a while she was close to the Communist Party in the United States, but she rejected it and its sister organization in Spain when she perceived the devious (and, in Spain, cruel) methods of its leadership.[12] After several weeks of research in Mexico for *Fortune*, she wrote an explanation of the ideological and political context of the oil expropriation for that magazine and the *New York Times*. To her dismay, neither one would accept her work; she believed that their editors saw her conclusions as distorted to favor the

Cárdenas government. In a November 1938 manuscript originally intended for the *New York Times*, she evaluated the movement toward socialism in Mexico at that time,[13] and this passage finally appeared in her 1943 book, *The Wind That Swept Mexico*:

> There are three doctrines: complete socialization, middle ground through co-operatives, and capitalist organization. The cycle of official doctrine goes from the first to the third, depending on which set of pressures—those from Washington or those from the unappeased eighty percent [of Mexicans]—is most immediately ominous. Politicians shift to meet each pressure, and when the pressure becomes a danger, administrations shift—or appear to. There is a recurring pattern, often marked at the shifting point with explosive violence. Administrations with strong left-wing direction give way to "pacifiers" and those in turn usher in business booms, appease foreign capital, and are then, as a rule, ousted by threatened revolt. Each time the lefts come in they are more sharply radical.[14]

Nathaniel and Sylvia Weyl agreed with Brenner that there was more "ideological clarity" in Cárdenas's regime than Beals described, and the young husband-and-wife team wrote an incisive study of his administration. A member of the Communist Party in his college days at Columbia University in the early 1930s, Nathaniel had worked in the New Deal's Agricultural Adjustment Administration before moving to journalism and away from Communism. Sylvia served as translator in their interviews with Mexican officials. The Weyls saw Cárdenas leading Mexico toward a unique form of socialism in which the "state is an ally of the workers and peasants in the peaceful transformation of hybrid feudalism and capitalism into socialism."[15]

They secured an interview with Minister of Public Works and Communication Francisco Múgica, who corroborated Cárdenas's commitment to an intuitive form of socialism. Múgica had known the president for fifteen years and characterized him as "a self-taught man" in political ideology, one who learned from books and personal observations of the "harshness of land control and the helplessness of manual workers in a country like Mexico where industry was unstable and oppressive, salaries did not even cover the bare necessities of life, and land was cultivated under primitive methods with a workday twelve hours long." Múgica believed that Cárdenas had accepted socialism in the mid-1920s: "I can assure [you], because we worked together from 1926 to the beginning of 1928, that his ideas were then clearly defined as to socialism being the proper doctrine to be used in solving Mexico's problems."[16]

From this interview and their own observations the Weyls concluded:

> Cárdenas has added nothing to the content of the socialist goal,
> but he has displayed profound originality in evolving a new
> pattern for the hard journey from one social system to the other. . . .
> In the economic sphere, he has developed new forms of worker
> control and explored fruitful paths toward collective agricul-
> tural organization. . . . In the political sphere, Cárdenas has
> evolved a new role for the state. . . . Cárdenas's approach differs
> from European social democratic theory in that the State be-
> comes the conscious organizer of trade unions, the guide of the
> people in the class struggle, and the custodian of an educational
> procedure that trains the new generation for the specific tasks of
> the long period of social revolutionary change. In its emphasis
> on the intrinsic values of democracy, cultural multiformity, and
> the right of the individual to dissent, the Cárdenas viewpoint
> differs markedly from that of contemporary Russia.[17]

The Weyls admired these innovations, but they also saw weaknesses in
Cardenista politics. The long, difficult road to a revolutionary restructuring of Mexican society required political strengths that Cárdenas
lacked: "The president faced the urgent task of consolidating left-wing
power. He needed a disciplined battle organization, not a laboratory for
democratic experimentation."[18]

The Weyls cited the ejidal land reform supported by the national
government's agricultural banking facilities as evidence that a unique
agrarian collectivism was working in Mexico. They were aware of bureaucratic inertia, official corruption, and *hacendado* sabotage, but despite these and other stumbling blocks, they endorsed the essence of
Eyler Simpson's view that Mexico should move rapidly toward a socialized system of production in agriculture. Again, they were emphatic in
their assertion that Mexico was far removed from the Soviet model:
"Oblivious to the significant structural differences between Cárdenas
and the Soviet paths of agricultural reorganization some will brand
(incorrectly) the new giant agrarian co-operatives as Bolshevik importa-
tions. . . . Mexico has evolved new techniques and strategies in her
battle against feudalism. The form and function of the land banks and
their role as directing organs are specifically Mexican creations."[19]

In the PRM—an open system in a state of flux, certainly not
centralized, and lacking in discipline—the Weyls saw both strengths
and weaknesses:

> "The Party of the Mexican Revolution is not an organization of
> the elite, such as the Communist of the Soviet Union, the Italian
> Fascist Party, and the German N.S.D.AP. It is essentially a coali-
> tion of existing organizations. . . . The PRM, moreover, lacks a
> coherent body of doctrine that could serve as the articles of faith

of its membership. The bulk of its members are within the Party because of a decision taken by the leadership of their organizations. Hence they feel little responsibility toward it and cannot always be persuaded to carry out its mandates. Its only cohesive force is the prestige of Cárdenas the willingness of the Mexican people to fight for the preservation of the harvest of the Revolution.[20]

The Weyls saw additional problems in the PRM's failure to appeal to the middle class. Educated middle-class women supported Cárdenas because of his stand in favor of female suffrage, but the bulk of middle-class voters (all male) disagreed with the administration's leftist policies. Professionals, lawyers, middle-level managers, small industrialists, and merchants resented the government's tilt toward workers and peasants.[21]

In their forecast for the future of the revolution in Mexico, the Weyls' hopes for long-term change collided with their perception of the left's lack of an internally cohesive political organization, its uncertain base of support among the lower classes, and the right's capacity to revive. Although they were wrong in their anticipation of a rightist coup attempt, their estimate of conservative strength was close to the mark:

> Cárdenas's faith in liberalism and democracy has been ill-rewarded. The people have been left to the mercies of a venal press, while the enemies of social reform have been permitted to use their wealth and hired eloquence to mislead working people into fighting their battles.
>
> The Mexican reaction has not confined itself to parliamentary methods of struggle, and Cárdenas has stubbornly driven himself into a political impasse by granting it the liberties appropriate to a civilized opposition. The political organization of the working classes within a democratic framework has not proven sufficient to obviate the dangers of civil war. Failure to destroy the capacity of the old order for continued resistance may prove to be the chief weakness of the Cárdenas regime.[22]

Power From the Machine

An essential element in the socialists' understanding of the mutually reinforcing relationship between the Mexican government and the common people was the former's promotion of industrial modernization in ways that would benefit the latter. Turning from politics to economics, many leftists considered modern industrial technology a vital component in the remaking of the nation. In the early 1920s some visitors had romanticized the virtues of peasant existence, and, in 1931 Stuart Chase had regarded Mexican rural life as an enclave safe from the storms of the business cycle. By the late 1930s, however, many radical commentators were opposing this brief against the viability of industrial society.

Eyler Simpson's frontal assault on Chase's conclusions established the pattern. In the forceful concluding chapter of *The Ejido*, Simpson cited architect and art critic Lewis Mumford, particularly to support the idea of small-scale, village-based industries that would utilize small electrical motors wired into a power grid, alongside an extensive transportation network, all planned and supported by the national government. Central to Simpson's approach was a view of the village and the region as economic units. Modern technology was to usher in modern society in a fashion acceptable to the common folk. "The application of industrial technology to ejidal agriculture," he said, would be "a normal and natural part of the ejido program viewed as an undertaking for agrarian and agricultural reform. But note how in carrying out our plan we have already introduced many of the basic elements of industrialism—machinery, inanimate power, division of labor, interdependent markets, credit, and specialization of productive functions. Is it not natural that we should take the next step and bind into our system industry itself?"[23] Many leftists followed Simpson's lead but later devised arguments based on their own observations. In general, their acceptance of the modern industrial machine in Mexico's garden was related to a broader tendency among liberals and radicals to see some form of modern technology as inevitable and, if properly handled, potentially beneficial for the masses.

The Weyls too assumed that industrialization would play an expanding role in the economy, and, on a scale much larger than Eyler Simpson had in mind. Although they expressed doubts about the efficiency of worker-run factory cooperatives, they did not question the importance of industrialization for the long-term march toward socialization of the nation's economy. Major challenges remained, such as the internal political problems of labor unions and the lack of management experience in government agencies. But none of these problems, the Weyls stated bluntly, could justify a slowdown in the adoption of the machine: "Only through industrialization and the utilization of modern technology can the masses drag themselves out of the dark caves of poverty and ignorance into the light of a civilization of abundance."[24]

Though less explicit than Simpson, Anita Brenner accepted his approach and, with sensitivity nourished by nearly three decades of living in or close to Mexico, pointed out the contrast between the 1920s emphasis on the revolution as a manifestation of the nation's Indian heritage and the 1930s emphasis on the need to bring the country into the modern world. It was a change that reflected her own ideological migration from bohemian views to the independent left in the 1920s and to something approaching socialism in the late 1930s:

> Ten years ago political and cultural Mexico was in love with its ancient image. The Indian's face, the native way of life, the archaeological and popular arts were the springboard of both

art and demagogy. Today these things are left to the tourists and the students. Today both cultural and political Mexico is in love with industrial technique. The peasant, who formerly played, as he talked, with a flower perhaps, now contemplates with thrilled absorption a tire gauge. The craftsman, who spent hours delicately lacquering a chair or a bowl, now tinkers lovingly with the insides of a jalopy. The government, which spent its extra pesos on imposing buildings and eloquent frescos, now pumps them into more roads, more dams, and more machinery.[25]

Far left commentator Bertram Wolfe also accepted the importance of industrialization, and even Wolfe's artistic collaborator Diego Rivera included modern machinery in his murals to symbolize the liberation of workers and peasants from the drudgery of less efficient means of production.[26]

Waldo Frank's endorsement of the expropriation seemed to be, on the surface, inconsistent with his earlier warnings that individualistic, pragmatic materialism—usually associated with the machine—posed a threat to the organic, spiritual wholeness of Hispanic culture. As historian Michael Ogorzaly has observed, however, Frank had a talent for elevating the thrust of his central thesis so far above the facts he cited in support that the connection between conclusion and evidence was not always clear. In Ogorzaly's words, "the factual information is correct: but its interpretation is always subordinated to the demands of the argument."[27]

In Frank's system of thought the main question of contemporary Mexico hinged on the revolution's capacity to transform the still powerful Indo-Hispanic culture into "a modern civilization that will enhance, not lose, its essential values." How this transformation could be accomplished, Frank admitted, was "a question without an answer."[28] Yet on the streets of Torreón, the regional city of the Laguna, Frank witnessed what was for him a synthesis of Hispanic-Indian values with the technology of iron, oil, and plastic as "labor-saving tools" wielded by the benevolent state under the guidance of Cárdenas:

> I stood one evening in the chief square within the cars and crowds and the cries, sensing the Indo-Hispanic flavor of this people whose seeming main concern was to buy an American refrigerator or to see an American movie. I felt an intuition of what Mexico may be if this complex, potent human plasm finds constant water and good roads for itself, and steel by the new process that employs Mexican oil and Mexican iron; if the frontier houses of modern Torreón (hideous as those of London) disappear with the hovels of yesterday before the fresh plastic structures already foreshadowed in every town from Monterrey

to Chiapas; if a people in no hurry but no longer neurotically
delayed by their own conflicts learn to wield their labor-saving
tools with that tenderness and sensitivity which created Mexico's cult of flowers and which, thwarted by want of proper
tools, twisted this cult into the dark love of death.[29]

Frank, like most of this fellow leftists, believed that with Cárdenas at the helm there was little reason to object to this combination of a
powerful state wedded to a nationalized petroleum industry which, in
turn, had no choice but to employ modern technology. Eyler Simpson's
1937 case for village-based industrialization in rural areas seemed to
have been lost in the drama of 1938; by 1939 the Weyls, Waldo Frank,
and most radicals accepted with few reservations the role of the nation-
state as propagator and manager of large-scale, centralized industrialization.

Mexico's Socialism in an International Context

For anxious conservatives in the United States, the analytical commentary of the Weyls and Brenner reinforced the pro-Cárdenas exuberance
of the radical Millan and the liberal-to-moderate voices of Kirk and
the editors of *Time* and *Life*. The Cárdenas story, from a conservative
point of view, was an account of a rapidly spreading socialist virus
(European, non-European, or a combination of both). Fatal infections
had already struck the president, the minister of public works and
communications, the head of the CTM, and the upper echelons of the
labor movement, the ministry of education, and thousands of school
teachers. Even some of the English-language travel writers seemed
afflicted, with their boosting of Mexico as a fascinating place to visit.
Readers who shared the concerns of Moley, White, and Allen believed
that Mexico was approaching the status of a lost cause, that it was a
nation under the spell of radical ideologues who were guiding their
people away from the model of laissez-faire capitalism and abandon-
ing the tenets of liberal statism.

This rightist perception of rampant, expansive socialism in
Mexico was an exaggeration, but there was a political and ideological
foundation for believing that the Cardenista brand of statist populism
encompassed socialistic policies: collectivist land reform, labor activism
in government programs, socialist ideas in public education, and, most
dramatically, the government's expropriation of privately owned oil
properties. Commentators such as Eyler Simpson, the Weyls, Brenner,
Herring, Beals, and Frank—going beyond the ebullient endorsements
of Millan, Kirk, and Townsend and the quick generalizations of Gunther, *Time*, *Life*, and the *New Masses*—found a social basis for Mexico's
radical politics. They emphasized that the linkages between Cárde-

nas, his government, and the peasant-worker masses had formed a species of revolutionary socialism (temporary in duration and limited in scope) that would take Mexico along the path to statist socialism.

In a part of the political culture of the United States this image of the Cárdenas regime fit quite comfortably. Roosevelt's New Deal accompanied its programs for material relief and socioeconomic change with a strong commitment to what historian Robert McElvaine has called "cooperative individualism," a set of values somewhere between rugged individualism and stifling collectivism.[30] Here the *ejido* program of the Laguna, the traditions of the communal village, and the populistic ideals of Cárdenas seemed to harmonize with the New Deal. Socialists, some liberal statist and independent leftists, and even a few Communists and fellow travelers found sufficient cause to praise the political moods on both sides of the border.

The oil expropriation brought Mexico to the forefront of public discussion in the United States in the late 1930s, much as Pancho Villa's raid and Calles's threat of expropriation had done in earlier years. While the oil issue did not include all of the seemingly radical experiments going on in Mexico, it did serve as a symbol of the U.S. public's perception of the Cárdenas administration. The results of a 1939 public opinion poll on the expropriation found the U.S. population evenly divided: about 39 percent opposed the use of force to protect American-owned property faced with seizure, and the same percentage favored military intervention.[31] With public opinion divided, and popular magazines such as *Time* and *Life* and leading journals of opinion such as the *Nation* and the *New Republic* sympathetic to Cárdenas, the Roosevelt administration seemed to have considerable room to maneuver in its dealings with Mexico.

The State Department was not ignorant of the leftist opinions expressed in various popular and academic media in the United States, but its leadership was deeply divided on the Mexican issues. Hull and most professional foreign service officers took a liberal capitalist stance on the expropriation question, but their cause failed in confrontation with the Daniels approach, which seemed to approximate Roosevelt's own point of view. In short, while many U.S. media conveyed images of a Mexico striding toward socialism, the State Department conducted its own internal debate and, in the end, agreed to negotiate with this apparently radical government on issues that cut deeply into traditional American beliefs regarding the sanctity of personal and corporate ownership of material resources.

The unusual alignment of forces brought to bear on Mexico in the last 1930s differed from the pressures that dominated the late 1920s.

In both situations there were three main sources of power: the government in Mexico City, caught in the middle between the other two sources; the external pressures applied from Washington (and Rome in the late 1920s, London in the late 1930s); and the internal pressures coming from aroused peasants, workers, and other domestic groups. In the late 1920s the external powers combined with the Calles-controlled nation-state to quash the Cristero rebellion and thereby strengthen Mexico City's ties with the outside world. By contrast, in the late 1930s the U.S. government, although engaged in an internal debate about the expropriation, seemed supportive of Cárdenas and was committed to negotiations on the oil question. Meanwhile, the Cárdenas administration had turned its energies not only to land reform and the labor movement but also to the arousal of the Mexican masses: peasants and workers were demanding broad social and economic changes. Unlike the divided peasantry of the Cristero era, the activist popular sector under Cárdenas included a wide cross-section of the nation's population. Thus all three sources of power—the amorphous but aroused lower strata, the nation-state under Cárdenas, and the New Deal in Washington—pointed in the same direction: to substantial social and economic change guided by the government. This alignment, like an unusual arrangement of planets in a solar system, created a unique display of forces, but one that lasted for only a short time.

The Washington-Rome-Mexico City alignment of the late 1920s elicited the expected commentary across the ideological spectrum, but in the next decade a new international alignment produced an entirely new set of reactions. In response to the Cristero crisis, liberal capitalists Morrow and Lippmann saw the church-state conflict as a matter of negotiations involving Washington, Rome, and Mexico City, thereby omitting the general populace from their calculus. Liberal statist Gruening held that the Mexican government could devise policies that would ultimately resolve the problem. Independent leftists Tannenbaum and Beals criticized the political-diplomatic outcome as harmful for the people and perhaps fatal for the revolution.

In the 1930s the left held the high ground on both sides of the Rio Grande. Independent leftist Brenner came to agree with Eyler Simpson and the Weyls that the Cardenista brand of socialism was appropriate for Mexico. The "unappeased eighty per cent" had, for a while, found a leader who used the machinery of the state to try to benefit the masses. But Brenner also saw a "recurring pattern" at work in which pressures from the United States could redirect Mexico toward free enterprise and away from state planning. Brenner and the Weyls sensed the fluidity and fickleness of a revolution subject to the often countervailing forces of international powers, a generally self-serving nation-state, and the partially mobilized masses. The uniqueness of the 1930s implicit in the analyses of Simpson, the Weyls, and Brenner was that all three factors pointed in the same leftist direction in these years.

Also influencing the U.S. acceptance of Mexico's defiant actions was the deterioration of the situation in Europe. By 1938 Germany's clearly aggressive intentions had made Western Hemisphere solidarity increasingly important. Historian Bryce Wood has argued that the Good Neighbor Policy and its dedication to nonintervention had achieved a life of its own just as Hitler's threats to peace in Europe seemed to extend their potential impact across the Atlantic.[32] Whether the Roosevelt administration was motivated by fear of Axis inroads in the Americas or a sincere wish to build on the improved intrahemispheric relations of the previous five years, or both, the results were clear: a willingness to treat the Mexican state as a legitimate actor in world affairs and to respect its internal economic and political conditions in a time of serious international crises.

There is no claim here that the Roosevelt administration embraced all the radical programs and projections of the Cárdenas government—neither the vague socialism described by the enthusiasts nor the more carefully delineated populist statism of Eyler Simpson and the Weyls. My central thesis is much more limited. The lesson that the Cárdenas regime, the leftist commentators, and Roosevelt's Mexican policy provided for later generations was that the existence of an ongoing social revolution (however flawed because of ineffective programs, partial because of the survival of a large private sector, and destined for derailment by internal as well as external factors) need not mean that the diplomatic resolution of serious international conflict was impossible. The U.S. government reacted with patience and calm for the most part, evincing a reluctant tolerance of the Mexican formula for social revolution. The conservative turn in Mexico during and after the election campaign of 1940 was not in evidence until nearly two years after Washington had committed itself to the application of the Good Neighbor Policy in response to the expropriations in Mexico.

11

Friendly Dissenters

Amerian liberals and radicals accorded Mexico such high esteem in the late 1930s that the handful of sympathetic critics who expressed doubts about the revolution did so in near-obscurity. Yet this variegated group—from independent leftists to liberal capitalists—revealed their immunity to the techniques of hospitality and the aura of revolutionary elation in penetrating commentary that was a small but vital segment of the American response to the Mexican revolution. As previously noted, liberal capitalists Kluckhohn and Prewett were highly skeptical of both the radicalism and the authority that seemed to be concentrated in the Cárdenas presidency. Other observers were receptive to or at least tolerant of the Cardenista radicalism on a theoretical level but saw problems in the enactment of such broad policies. In a period when the U.S. left became divided on Stalin's dictatorial policies in the Soviet Union[1], a few commentators warned of excesses of power in the nation that had produced Porifrio Díaz. Their warning found little support, however, in part because the presence of Cárdenas in the cottonfields of the Laguna and the oil fields of Tampico inspired confidence in the government as the benefactor of the people.

Ironically and perhaps unintentionally, however, Cárdenas's inspirational persona and organizational skills superseded local initiative and imposed the imprint of the nation-state on crucial activities throughout the nation. For example, the Communists of the Laguna were among the most active advocates of land reform in the region, and early in the process, they were among the most effective of the local leaders. But soon Cárdenas overshadowed them all. He personally supervised the agricultural expropriation in the fall of 1936, and government officials directed most key events thereafter. Soon the Laguna *ejidos* were integrated into the national agrarian bureaucracy. Local initiative had become a small part of a larger centralized system. Presidential charisma and institutional centralization replaced grassroots collectivism, a point that most leftists reported without critical commentary.[2]

This omission was not unusual among U.S. liberal and radical visitors to Mexico at the time. The achievements in land reform and labor unionization and the public ebullience that followed in the wake of Cárdenas's personal appearances overwhelmed questions about the advisability of extending the bureaucracies of the national government, the PNR (PRM after 1938), and the CTM into the states and localities. The anarcho-syndicalist theorizing in the Cárdenas campaign speeches and the government's responses to spontaneous activism at the lower rungs of society seemed to indicate that the revolution was at work. The incandescence of presidential charisma was so bright and the kinetic thrust of large institutions so amorphous that only a few visitors grasped the nature of the change at the local level as the traditional culture and politics of the *campesino* interacted with the power politics of Mexico City.

Dissent on the Independent Left

Among those who did harbor serious doubts about the direction of the revolution were journalist Carleton Beals and novelist Max Miller. Although an admirer of Cárdenas, Beals had misgivings about the intrusion of modern ways of life into Indian areas, whether they resulted from the political ambitions of a local cacique or the arrival of a bureaucrat from Mexico City. The mannerisms of a local community leader furnished Beals with a revealing example of the dark side of this interaction: "Where an Indian leader has been traduced by the trappings of power and by western European psychology, he goes to the extreme of flamboyant ostentation, showiness, luxury, wastefulness, sexual excess, and sadistic cruelties—such was the story of many an Indian dictator of Latin America, of many a Mexican revolutionary leader, of most of its generals."[3]

Max Miller, a native of Oregon, was thirty-three years old when his 1932 novel, *I Cover the Waterfront*, claimed the praise of many literary critics. A traveler who relished rugged terrain, he had already seen the icy wastes of Alaska and northwestern Canada.[4] The tropical valleys and mountains of southern Mexico promised new experiences. A free spirit who seemed akin to the independent left in its ethos if not its ideology, Miller made no pretense of objectivity. Disliking tourist-worn trails, he chose distant Chiapas and the isolated mountain regions of Morelos to escape not only the gringo gawkers but also the Mexico City politicos. His hero was Emiliano Zapata, and his guide, ex-Zapatista Teodomiro Ortiz, introduced him to the deceased rebel's sister and wife. Miller found the condition of the peasant class largely unimproved in the fifteen years since Zapata's death, and the explanation he fashioned out of his own observations and his cynical view of government officials was close to the populism of Beals and, to some extent, the anarchism of Tannenbaum.[5] Miller saw no redeeming virtues in the typical labor leader who went to Chiapas in the name of reform: "He is on the side of the law now, of course, the government being a labor government. Yet had the government been a dictatorship, as in the slavery regime of Díaz, most of these smart labor racketeers would probably have been slavers. It makes no difference to them so long as the side they are on is the safe side."[6]

Miller's aversion to the modern world of tourism and labor politics led him to look for an "unspoiled village" where Indians still lived in traditional ways. He did not want to join Stuart Chase in finding a way of life superior to that of Muncie, Indiana; instead he hoped to prove to himself and his readers that such a village existed. A sympathetic Mexican government official took him to Tetelcingo, an isolated village in the rugged recesses of Morelos. Its inhabitants had successfully resisted the Spanish Conquest and other outside influences and had also aided Zapata of their own volition. But even in Tetelcingo, Miller was disappointed. He found that an American student of native languages had lived there for nearly a year and had left only a few weeks earlier. The villagers greatly admired this linguist, whom Miller called William Thompson (actually William Cameron Townsend, discussed in Chapter 9). Miller did not fault Townsend's work but was discouraged by the outsider's lasting impact, which provided a foothold for an alien culture. He also complained of the consequences of the Mexican government's largess—a truck for the village. Now the *campesinos* had to increase their commercial activities in nearby towns to earn enough money to keep the truck running. Miller lamented: "The zest has been killed in me. For no matter now deeply I might have gone [into the mountains] and how many burros I might have had to ride to get there, I felt quite positive that some American would have been there ahead of me—and perhaps another truck."[7]

Beals and Miller sensed that Mexico's balance between centralization and local autonomy had shifted, and on the basis of their wanderings they fashioned informal critiques of the expanding power of the nation-state and the arrival of commercial values. Although pungent and provocative, these observations were impressionistic and lacked sustained analysis.

A more penetrating analysis of policies eventually adopted by the Cárdenas administration appeared in the published writing and private correspondence of Frank Tannenbaum. In *Peace by Revolution* and more emphatically in *Whither Latin America?* he argued against large-scale industrialization in Mexico (and Latin America in general). He cited the widespread poverty that greatly limited the consumer market for manufactured goods, the lack of capital, and the scarcity of critical resources such as coal and iron. He admitted that some elements of industry were necessary in urban centers and for mining and petroleum production, but he relegated these activities to a minor position within the predominantly rural, agricultural, village-oriented economy of the nation.[8]

By 1934 Tannenbaum was a widely recognized authority on contemporary and historical Mexico and had secured a position in the prestigious Department of History of Columbia University.[9] Given his prominence in the field and the force of his argument, Tannenbaum's case against industrialization elicited a rebuttal from Princeton's Eyler Simpson. The sociologist conceded that the form and scale of industrialization in Mexico would not necessarily follow the patterns of the United States or western Europe, but he claimed that the application of modern mass-production technology in Mexico was both necessary and potentially beneficial. He saw Tannenbaum's position as thoughtful but misguided. For example, the assertion that the dearth of consumer demand created an insurmountable roadblock was, in Simpson's words, "one of those tail-chasing arguments" that could be refuted by observing the increase in consumer demand for manufactured goods in peasant communities where such items were available. Simpson foresaw the growth of this domestic market as a response to the expansion of highways, currency, and education.[10]

Tannenbaum did not respond directly to Simpson—perhaps because of the latter's unexpected death at age thirty-eight, only a short time after his book appeared. Tannenbaum did, however, express his judgments in 1937 in a personal letter to Cárdenas that testified to the nature of the relationship between the two men:

> I want to talk to you about a problem that is giving me a great deal of concern in relation to the economics of Mexico. . . . I have a strong feeling that some of my Mexican friends forget that the mass of people live and must continue to live from agriculture, but that the income of the government comes from [taxes on] industry. Looked at as a whole, Mexican industry is not very important except that it provides income for the Mexican gov-

ernment. Without industry the Mexican government would not have any money to spend for the benefit of the mass of the people who are agriculturalists. It therefore seems to me that in the long run the Mexican government ought to look to increasing its income from industry because, unless it does, it will not be able to carry out the promise of the Revolution for the agricultural peasant. The Mexican industrial population and Mexican industry is [sic] so small that it is a mistake to overemphasize its significance to the disadvantage of the agricultural population.

I am saying all of this to you and with all this frankness because I think that the whole industrial policy of the Mexican government ought to be reconsidered with the point of view in mind that its importance to the nation is primarily the income it gives to the Mexican government for expenditure among the Mexican agricultural people.[11]

Tannenbaum applauded Cardenista agrarianism, but after March 18, 1938, he expressed little if any praise for the government's industrial policies. He was surprised by the oil expropriation, terming it "drastic and ill-considered" in a letter to the State Department's Lawrence Duggan, a bright young professional diplomat and a protégé of Undersecretary of State Sumner Welles. Duggan had a special interest in social and economic development issues in Latin America. Tannenbaum used his influence with Duggan and Welles to plead for a peaceful settlement of the dispute. Tannenbaum's deepest commitment, however, remained with land reform. In a letter of December 16, 1936, to Cárdenas, he had called the expropriation of the Laguna and the subsequent *ejidal* organization of those lands "the most important single step that has been taken so far towards making the Mexican Revolution successful."[12] And in a lengthy letter to Duggan he argued against immediate compensation for U.S. citizens whose agricultural properties were turned over to the peasants because such a requirement would severely hamper the land reform process.[13] Compensation for foreign owners of petroleum and agricultural properties involved similar situations, but Tannenbaum's comments to Duggan on the oil issue were brief and lacking in historical and economic analysis.

Like the oil expropriation, the spurt of Marxist writings and speeches in Mexico in the 1930s made little positive impression on Tannenbaum. The flood of plans for socialist education and the Marxist (or neo-Marxist) books and articles by recent Mexican converts to this radical creed left him disappointed.[14] In a November 1937 letter to Narciso Bassols, a well-read Marxist who had remained aloof from much of the discussion about socialist education, he deplored the quality of contemporary publications by Mexicans about Mexican affairs: "I am writing this to you with such frankness because I hungered for such a long time for some honest writing in Mexico about Mexican problems and you will agree with me that there has not been any or so little that it is hardly worth mentioning."[15] Bassols, a former minister of education then serving as a diplomat, replied in the affirmative to Tannenbaum's bleak assessment.[16]

The energetic, peripatetic Lombardo Toledano earned the admiration of Millan, Plenn, and the Weyls[17] but not of Tannenbaum, whose skepticism was evident in a letter to Carter Goodrich of the International Labor Organization: "Lombardo Toledano himself is an unstable Latin American type of intellectual—brilliant, energetic, ambitious—full of vague notions about the proximity of social revolution, anti-American but sincere and personally honest. Without governmental support the leadership of the Mexican trade union movement would slip from his hands overnight."[18]

By the end of the decade Tannenbaum was a friend and confident of Cárdenas, but this personal relationship did not sway the veteran Mexicanist's opinion of policies that conflicted with his own analysis. By omission, Tannenbaum indicated that he rejected Marxism and its various permutations,[19] and by direct communication to Cárdenas he rejected the contemporary vogue of industrialization. He had observed firsthand the cohesiveness of the village community; at the other end of the power structure he had seen the mischief, ineptitude, and corruption in the national government. Cárdenas—the dedicated, honest man of the people—was the exception, he thought, not the rule.[20] But the excitement of expropriation, the drive for land reform, and the reassuring presence of Cárdenas in the presidency would soon be gone—leaving a powerful administrative structure rooted in Mexico City, a national commitment to industrialization and urbanization, and the confused and unpersuasive fragments of an ideology that could not match the inertial inevitability of the state and the machine.

Graham Greene: Fugitive Priest

A critic of the Mexican government from a very different perspective was Graham Greene, the British novelist, who arrived in Mexico in late February 1938 with the express purpose of writing a defense of the embattled Catholic Church. Having converted to Catholicism in 1926 at the age of twenty-two, in heavily Protestant England, Greene had a strong sense of identification with the beleaguered faithful of Mexico. In both *Another Mexico* (1939), a travel account, and *The Power and the Glory* (1940), a novel, he took the church's point of view. The central character in the novel was modeled on the martyred Father Pro, a priest who fell before a firing squad in 1926. Greene knew the analyses of anti-Catholic policies in *Red Mexico* (1928) by Francis McCullough, a Catholic layman and professional journalist, and *Mexican Martyrdom* (1936) by Wilfred Parsons, a Jesuit priest. His Catholic contacts and the antigovernment slant of his writing led many critics to see another conservative attack on the leftist Cárdenas administration.[21] This conclusion, however, missed some key points. After a close reading of these two Mexico-based volumes and a review of Greene's lifetime commitment to the left, biographer Norman Sherry and literary critic Maria Couto found a populistic, even anarchistic, perspective not far removed from that of the Tannenbaum-Beals-Miller school.

Probably more than Parsons and McCullough, D.H. Lawrence sparked Greene's interest in Mexico's religious situation in the pages of *The Plumed Serpent*.[22] Yet Greene was much more at ease with the world of the Indian than was Lawrence. Greene's purpose—to witness and describe the struggles of faithful Catholics under an anticlerical regime—was considerably less ambitious (but more risky) than Lawrence's futile quest for an alternative to the values of European civilization. For Greene, the Indian transformation of Catholicism into a force that was compatible with their traditions resulted in a syncretic religion that actually recaptured some of the more vital elements of historical Catholicism. On seeing the rough, giant, wooden crosses erected by the Chamula Indians on a hillside in isolated Chiapas, he wrote in admiration: "This was the Indian religion—a dark tormented magic cult. . . . in the mountainous strange world of Father Las Casas, Christianity went its own frightening way. Magic, yes, but we are too apt to minimize the magic element in Christianity—the man raised from the dead, the devils cast out, the water turned into wine. The great crosses leaned there in their black and windy solitude, safe from the pistoleros and the politicians."[23]

Safety from "the pistoleros and the politicians" was important because, for Greene, the combination of armed violence and bureaucratic power was the greatest threat to the spiritual life of the common people of Mexico. The doggedly determined lieutenant who pursues and ultimately captures the unnamed protagonist priest of *The Power and the Glory* is a model of devotion to the cause of anticlericalism. In Greene's characterization, however, he is little more than an automaton—emotionally "flat and dead"—even after his capture of the priest.[24]

The fugitive priest and the Catholic faithful are arrayed against the state, which cleverly juggles the meaning of words as easily as it dispatches its soulless hunters. In concepts that anticipated some of the later writings of his contemporaries George Orwell and Rebecca West, Greene found that "treason" had a new meaning in Mexico—loyalty to the faith: "And that, I suppose, is treason too. For the State puts its own interpretation on the word treason - and never punishes anyone for his religion. It is the technique the totalitarian State has always employed: in the time of Elizabeth in England, just as in Mexico, Russia, and Germany today."[25]

Beneath the surface of this grim tale, however, lay a deep confidence in the survival of the faith. On the last page of the novel, the distraught Mexican boy who has befriended the ill-fated priest finds a new source of hope. A stranger appears at his door: " 'If you would let me come in,' the man said with an odd frightened smile, and suddenly lowering his voice he said to the boy: 'I am a priest.' " The boy lets him in. The faith of the people will survive.[26]

The Historians' Ambivalence

A trio of historians joined Greene and Tannenbaum in the expression of doubts about the direction of change in Mexico. Despite their shared concerns, these three—Herbert Priestley and Lesley Simpson of the University of California at Berkeley, and Henry Bamford Parkes of New York University—held different ideological perspectives. Priestley, who became interested in Mexico before Carranza gained the presidency, was a liberal capitalist; his younger Berkeley colleague, who first went to Mexico in the 1920s, was an independent leftist; Parkes was new to Mexican affairs in the 1930s and as a liberal statist occupied a place between Priestley and Simpson on the ideological spectrum.

Lesley Simpson used his skills as a trained linguist and an intuitive historian to find a Mexico that his ideological inclinations did not want to accept. In a frank letter to his longtime friend Carleton Beals, Simpson unburdened himself in words that were apparently too sharp to find their way into print: "It's a mistake to come down here and smell the stench of Mexican politics again. It gives one the horrid feeling that there is no hope for a country with the tradition of irresponsible exploitation by public officials. Gruening and Eyler Simpson had an easy time, comparatively, because they believed in some sort of happy destiny, but here I come along struggling under the weight of history, which tells me that Mexico is sodden with corruption, and that, in all probability, the Revolution will succumb eventually (if it hasn't already) to the [inevitable]."[27]

Somehow transcending these trepidations, Simpson went on to write *Many Mexicos*, a singular survey of Mexican history that combined literary grace with astute historical judgement. His knowledge of the labor systems of colonial Mexico provided him with a sensitivity to the extensions of the past into the present. The announced revolutionary aims of the Cárdenas government, he wrote, ran headlong against the vital remnants of "an authoritarian society, in which the ruler ruled and the people obeyed, at least in theory, and everything was fixed in a rigid order which was meant to last until the Judgement Day."[28] Even at the center of the widely praised land reform program, Simpson detected an outcropping of the past. The ejidal projects depended on the ejidal banks, whose control of the purse strings gave them considerable power over the villagers. According to Simpson: "The bank is caught in the same dilemma as the ancient encomendero; it has to make a living with Indian labor, but it must not use coercion. The bank becomes, in fact, the administrator of a huge estate and it must make good."[29]

Simpsons's ideology was complex and his assessment of Mexican affairs correspondingly subtle. On the surface he seemed to be a liberal statist with the socialistic inclinations of Betty Kirk, not far from the socialism of Eyler Simpson. His historically rooted pessimism, however, drove him to the populist wing of the independent left. Although he saw the Constitution of 1917 as a welcome radical departure from the laissez-faire ideals of the Díaz elite and praised the pragmatic, strong-willed Obregón and the announced goals of Cárdenas, Simpson concluded that the ideology and politics of the revolution fell apart when pressed into the real world of economic and social affairs. The performance of the railroads and the oil industry under labor leadership in the late 1930s had dashed cold water on fervid liberal statist and socialist idealism. Simpson was explicit: "In the workers' administration of the oil industry and the railroads, the Utopians received another shock. They discovered that the unions were just as anxious to make money at the public expense as the corporations had been and they were less easily controlled. The number of employees on the payroll increased, despite lowering demands. Overhead charges tended to eat up what little profit could be made in a restricted market. The workers' administration of the railroads was so bad that it approached disastrous."[30]

For Simpson and Beals and Tannenbaum—who had been visiting and writing about Mexico since the 1920s—it was a surprise when a newcomer, thirty-four-year-old Henry Bamford Parkes, published what became a widely used college text. Few of the veteran Mexicanists knew the English-born, Oxford-trained Parkes, whose previous study of British colonial North America gave no indication that he was developing an interest in Mexico.[31] If the dedication of *A History of Mexico* can be taken as an explanation, it was Herbert Weinstock of Houghton Mifflin who "persuaded" Parkes to write the book, presumably to meet a perceived demand for a college text.[32]

Whatever its origins, Parkes brought to the endeavor a wide range of interests and a facility for written expression. His caveats and restrained judgments in *Mexico* created some uncertainty as to his ideology, but his pointed attack on the guiding light of the far left in *Marxism: An Autopsy* made clear his liberal statist credentials. Though largely ignored by students of U.S. intellectual history, the latter book caused enough of a stir to draw a favorable review in *Time* magazine. The book condemned Marxism mainly because of its perversion by its chief practitioner in the 1930s, Joseph Stalin. The Marxist-Leninist-inspired dictatorship did not benefit the workers for whom, in theory, the Russian revolution came into being. Parkes advocated a regulated market economy with a powerful, impartial government as referee to see that material goods would be distributed fairly.[33]

A tinge of the maverick in his liberal statism, however, led Parkes to express uncertainty about the efficacy of the nation-state. Benito Juárez emerged as champion of a moderate liberalism that steered between the radical Jacobins and the reactionary clerics of the nineteenth century.[34] The 1917 Constitution set advanced goals for government-directed socioeconomic change.[35] Lázaro Cárdenas took large steps to implement these aims with a government that "was the most honest . . . since Juárez."[36] Yet the presence of Cárdenas was not enough to reassure the dubious Parkes. Like Lesley Simpson, he saw the ejidal bank as carrying an awesome responsibility, and as of 1938 the limits of the bank's credit placed the Laguna experiment in jeopardy. Also, the oil expropriation weakened the nation's productive capacity and reduced the government's tax revenues. Therefore, Parkes saw Mexico on the verge of crises, since "the stability of the Cárdenas regime probably depended on a rapid success of the new cooperative ventures and the new experiments in government ownership."[37]

Parkes added one more concern that did not seem to trouble Simpson: the specter of a Mexican form of Bolshevism. The 1930s generation of leaders took the Constitution of 1917 seriously but also felt the attraction of the Soviet model. Parkes chose his words carefully in his claim that: "the Mexican reforming movement, which had spoken French through the nineteenth century, was now beginning to speak Russian. To what extent these young men would remain loyal to their ideals only time would show. They seemed more capable of sincerity than any of their predecessors since the generation of the reform."[38] Yet in *Marxism*, he identified the deceptions and dangers inherent in the Russian example. "Loyal to their ideals" was not a phrase that fit easily into a discussion of the contributions of Stalinists to recent Soviet history.

The arrival of Marxism was one more indication that Mexico was being pulled inexorably into the modern world. Parkes believed that all of Mexico, even remote Indian villages, would be a part of this complex of international interactions, even though the revolution seemed to have no counterpart in the U.S.-European world; not even the Marxist-Leninist formula as devised for Russian circumstances fit the Mexican example. He used language that suggested what analysts after World War II would call "the third world" in his attempt to place the Mexican revolution in a comparative context:

> Foreign observers frequently tried to fit the Mexican system into one or other of the dominant ideologies of the post-(World War I) world. If foreign industrialists often regarded the Mexican dictatorship as a dictatorship of the proletariat, foreign radicals—even during the regime of Cárdenas—were apt to discover resemblances to Fascism. In reality, however, the Mexican system was sui generis; and in spite of the Fascist tendencies of the Callistas and the admiration cherished for the Soviet Union by the intellectuals of the CTM, it owed more to native traditions than to foreign ideologies. The central creation of the Revolution, the ejido, was a return to the institutions of pre-Cortesian Mexico. The closest parallels to modern Mexico were to be found not in Germany or Russia but in those countries, such as Turkey and China, which had been the scene of an analogous national reawakening.[39]

The appearance of the Parkes textbook posed a special problem for Herbert Priestley, who had been both mentor and colleague to Lesley Simpson at Berkeley. The sixty-three-year-old historian had been working on a study tentatively titled "Mexico since Porfirio," which, if grafted onto a revised version of his *Mexican Nation*, would have been a rival to Parkes's text.[40] Therefore, Priestley's review of *A History of Mexico* carried an element of generational conflict. One might also have expected it to indicate ideological differences, but that sort of disputation was noticeably lacking. Although Priestley disagreed with some of Parkes's generalizations on pre-twentieth-century trends, the Berkeley historian expressed his sympathy with his New York University colleague's view of the revolution. Priestley praised Parkes's "acceptance of the vitality of the current Revolution; it is by far the most significant fact in the history of the continent today. The acceptance of the revolutionary ideal is certainly not bias; it is point of view. If it were attempted to show the Revolution as better or more successful than it is; or to show it less so, that would have been bias."[41]

Priestley's death in 1944 after several years of debilitating illness deprived him of the opportunity to complete his own study of recent Mexican history, but several of his manuscripts survive and suggest the direction of his thought. One 1936 essay conveyed both trepidation and optimism about Cárdenas: "The strength of the [land reform] movement of which he has made himself the glittering-eyed Apostle, lies in the approval of the masses of the workers in town and country, and in the persistence with which he follows the ideal of organization of all the laborers, urban and rural, into a Central Organization."[42] This open-minded liberal capitalist's respect for the resilience of history clashed with his sensitivity to the impact of innovation and led him to express some of the ambivalence shared by Parkes and Simpson about the current government in Mexico. The vision of a "glittering-eyed Apostle" in command of a rural-urban worker combination conveyed a certain note of alarm, but this same mobilization of the masses meant that Mexico had turned from militarism and the barracks coup toward civilian politics: "It will not likely be so easy in the future for generals to betray their cause by taking their unquestioning troops over to the highest bidder. A rise in the literacy of the masses, and a more general understanding of the objects of the Revolution, have made the old style of winning revolutions anachronistic"[43]

Even through Priestley saw too much ardor in the young president's efforts to produce socioeconomic change, the historian argued that the Cárdenas government deserved a chance to see its experiments carried through to their conclusion. Priestley believed that the "extreme wing of the Revolutionary Party" wrote the Six-Year Plan and that Cárdenas took it "as a mandate," but the flexible liberal capitalist insisted that the United States should compromise with Mexico on these issues in view of Germany's willingness to deal with Mexico City. There was no condemnation of Cárdenas's ideological assumptions, which Priestley at one point termed "state socialism." His selection of quotations from Cárdenas carried the impression that he wanted the Mexican government's justification for the expropriation to have a fair and extended hearing in the United States.[44]

In sum, this trio of historians held that the announced goals of Lázaro Cárdenas were commendable but that the burdens they imposed upon him were too great. For Lesley Simpson, the burdens originated with the legacy of governmental corruption and public cynicism. Parkes looked to the future and saw huge hurdles: the temptation of the Marxist-Leninist siren, and the abrupt and debilitating absorption into the process of worldwide modernization. Priestley was probably the least pessimistic of the three, but he too was very aware of Mexico's inescapable political traditions and the universal uncertainties of sudden change.

Warren Susman and Richard Pells, historians of the depression decade in the United States, argue that the chief function of the intellectual of the 1930s was the recognition or creation of myths, devoid of ideology but full or references to the proper functioning of the government, the economy, and culture.[45] Many U.S. leftists who studied Mexico, however, found in Lázaro Cárdenas a political leader who used both myth and ideology. He was a charismatic populist who created a partially socialized economy in the name of the workers and peasants. Writers who witnessed his visits to rural villages often saw the mythic Cárdenas, a living embodiment of the unity of the government and the people.

The small but significant group of observers who disagreed were unable to join the celebration. From several different ideological positions, they pinpointed flaws in the revolutionary program. Although they wrote in a sympathetic spirit and accepted the revolution itself as a legitimate if risky phenomenon, they simply did not believe that Cárdenas could pull the entire nation—twenty million people of varying ethnic and cultural backgrounds, uneven levels of technological and economic development, and incongruent political and religious practices—into the industrialized modern world by the force of his own idealism, honesty, and hard work. Further, those whose seismic sensors detected the upward thrust of an ominously powerful central government concurred on the dangers of the nation-state in the hands of ambitious politicos and well-intentioned champions of industrialism. Their warnings, however, went largely unnoticed.

12

The Changing Image

In the 1930s Mexico's image in the U.S. popular media took on a more positive tone. Conventional assumptions about ethnic inferiority and political retardation gave way under the cumulative effect of the writings of sympathetic U.S. observers in the 1920s., the emergence of new leadership in Mexico in 1934, and the upwelling of a broad-based, intercultural sense of identification with the underdogs of society during the depression years.

Yet the old image died hard. In the early part of the decade, fiction, travel accounts, tourist guides, and films still borrowed heavily from the easily recognizable stereotypes. In 1934 the popular author of adolescent fiction Franklin W. Dixon sent his main characters, Frank and Joe Hardy, to the rugged deserts and mountains of Chihuahua in pursuit of a missing witness in an oil company scandal. The English-speaking son of a *hacendado* family made an instant companion for Joe and Frank. The villain, Vincenzo, was a swarthy, scheming, dark-browed Latino. The inevitable bandits were also swarthy but stout (resembling Wallace Berry's character in the film *Viva Villa!* which opened in the same year that Dixon's book, *The Mark on the Door*, appeared). The austere, athletic Indian guide who bore the name and reputation of Yaqui saved the lives of the Hardy brothers but was not present in the final chapter when the "good guys" got their rewards. In the end, the light-skinned Yankees and their upper-class companion triumphed over the swarthy evildoers.[1]

Stereotypes began to yield to more complex, politically sensitive

images as the discussion of Mexico shifted to include more clearly
delineated ideological content. The media in which these issues were
explored widened to include not only journalistic, academic, and creative print organs but also tourist guides and motion pictures, usually
directed to mass audience. Media commentators soon discovered that
the Mexico of Cárdenas made "good copy," in harmony with the New
Deal ethos, with John Steinbeck's humble but noble Joads in *The Grapes
of Wrath*, and with the respectful portraits of ordinary folk in *Let Us Now
Praise Famous Men* by James Agee and Walker Evans.[2]

The presence of Lázaro Cárdenas was an important key to understanding the improving perceptions of Mexico in the American mind in
these years. As Frank Tannenbaum wrote in 1937, "Mexico has never
known anything like him—so completely disinterested, so devoted to
the public good."[3] The three preceding presidents had been, in the eyes
of many U.S. observers, puppets of Calles, the revolution's corruptor.
Cárdenas ended all that and turned his nation emphatically to the left
again—much further to the left than the reluctant Obregón and Calles in
his early years had ventured.

The Popular Image: Film

Motion pictures in the 1930s provided the American public with a steady
diet of escapist adventures and brought Hollywood producers steady
profits, except during the decline from 1931 to 1933. One well-estab-
lished formula involved tales from tropical lands where the scenery and
the culture offered a marked contrast with the contemporary United
States.[4] Hollywood had often set such stories in Mexico and had fallen
into the habit of portraying Mexican males as bandits in the style of the
widely known but erroneously perceived Pancho Villa—mindless, bes-
tial practitioners of random violence. The Mexican government and
individual Mexicans protested this image, and by the middle of the 1930s
the California film industry had begun to make changes.[5]

The resilient bandido figure dominated two films however:
Warner Brothers' *The Bad Man* (1930) and MGM's *Viva Villa!* (1934). In
the first, although veteran actor Walter Huston carried off the Villa-like
title role of Pancho López in the usual bandido style—with "musta-
chios, enormous eyebrows and glistening white teeth, a large sombrero
and chaps"—he imbued his performance with enough humane concerns and clever philosophizing to win praise from the *New York Times*
critic.[6] When Metro-Goldwyn-Mayer cast Wallace Beery as Villa in the
1934 film, the gruff actor exhibited a wide range of moods from wrath-
ful to sentimental; his version of the wrath of Villa, however, was very
close to the bandit stereotype and generally dominated the film.[7]

Warner Brothers produced two film vehicles for Paul Muni that presented different images of the Mexican male. In *Bordertown* (1935) Muni played the part of a high-minded young Mexican-American lawyer who fails to win a place in the U.S. legal profession and, in a throwback to the older image, turns to gambling.[8] The more ambitious *Juárez* (1939) finally broke through the Hollywood stereotypes. Muni used extensive makeup and absorbed the advice of two superannuated Juaristas to project an interpretation of the statesman as a reserved, soft-spoken Zapotec Indian who relies more on determination, patience, principle, and idealism than fiery rhetoric and sporadic violence to achieve his goals.[9]

Some film critics and historians deprecate Muni's version of Benito Juárez because, in their view, Brian Aherne dominated the film as the kindly, equally idealistic, but fatally naive Maximilian, whose outgoing personality outshone that of the "stoic" Indian.[10] But this judgment ignores the importance of Muni's escape from Hollywood's Mexican stereotype and the screenplay's heavy emphasis on ideas as an integral part of the film. Benito Pablo Juárez was a man of the people who, when faced with mutiny, literally turned to a street filled with compatriots and, in his own subdued fashion, rallied them to his cause in a triumph of democracy over backroom political connivance. President Cárdenas viewed *Juárez* with enthusiasm and arranged for its public showing in Mexico City's Palace of Fine Arts. The Mexican audience, highly sensitive to and usually critical of U.S. films about their country, greeted the production warmly and even broke into applause when Muni's Juárez condemned foreign domination in the name of national autonomy.[11]

The epitome of the U.S. film industry's attempt to understand Mexico and the Mexicans in their own terms came in the independently made *Forgotten Village*. Shot on location in Mexico in 1940, this film told a simple but compelling tale of the struggle against epidemic disease and native superstition in a village geographically close to but culturally far from Mexico City. Essentially a scripted story line acted out by villagers and filmed in documentary style, *The Forgotten Village* had an authenticity previously lacking in movie depictions of Mexico.

John Steinbeck, at the peak of his acclaim as author of *The Grapes of Wrath*, provided a screenplay that was both powerful and simple. Young Paco becomes ill. His family takes him to the local *curandera* (witch doctor), who treats him for "evil airs," but he dies. Other children soon become ill with the same sickness, and the local schoolteacher (the only person in the village who has ever traveled in the outside world) and one of his pupils, Juan Diego go for a doctor. The doctor diagnoses the disease and calls for antibiotic injections for the sick and chemicals to disinfect the water in the community well. These changes are too

much for the villagers, who run the doctor off and Juan Diego with him.
Before his expulsion, Juan Diego manages to give his sister a shot and to
disinfect the well. Then, with the help of the doctor, he goes to school to
learn the ways of the modern world.

Steinbeck spent several difficult months in Mexico working on
the film. The rural location created rugged conditions that would have
defeated most film crews, and MGM executive politics intervened: the
studio abandoned the project to independent producers. But more important was Steinbeck's intellectual struggle with the impending arrival
of the modern world in rural Mexico.[12] As the film made clear, the
transition would not be easy; the schoolteacher and the doctor had
influence on only one person in the village—Juan Diego. Steinbeck's
narration sounded a clear note of optimism, however:

> Changes in people are never quick. But the boys from the vil-
> lages are being given a change by a nation that believes in them.
> From the government schools, the boys and girls from the vil-
> lages will carry knowledge back to their own people. . . .
>
> And the change will come, is coming; the long climb out
> of the darkness. Already the people are learning, changing their
> lives, learning, working, living in new ways.
>
> The changes will come as surely as there are thousands of
> Juan Diegos in the villages of Mexico.[13]

Since the 1910s many liberal and radical writers had implored
the public as well as the government to take the revolution seriously
and to look at the Mexican people without prejudgment. The film
industry had been as laggard as any segment of U.S. culture to follow
this advice, but by the end of the 1930s the one-dimensional bandido
had given way to the calm, tenacious idealist projected by Muni in his
portrayal of Juárez and the sensitive, sincere Juan Diego. This new
filmic perspective coincided with two leftist points of view: Juárez was
the liberal statist who could rally the people to his cause; Juan Diego
symbolized a spontaneous reaching of the common people for a modern and presumably better way of life—much as Tannenbaum and Beals
emphasized local initiative as the basis for change. Juárez was committed to national autonomy, and his firm hand on the machinery of state
guided the nation through a time of troubles. His victory was a triumph
of popular, constitutional authority over a reactionary plot. As the symbol of legitimate government, he was in accord with and worked to
benefit the common people, but foreign intervention and war prevented
the enactment of the reforms he favored. By implication, the villagers
had to wait for change. In *The Forgotten Village* the teacher and the
doctor brought the benefits of modernity—science and medicine—in a
patient, humane manner, only to meet rejection by all the villagers but

one. These two films highlighted the differences between the two leftist positions. In *Juárez*, the state and its leader were the key factors in change; in *The Forgotten Village*, the state could assist, but the impetus for the new ways had to come from within the peasant world.

The Popular Image: Travel Literature

Travel writers also began to take Mexico seriously. In these years, as Paul Fussell has observed, flocks of visitors on guided tours that took them from hotel to hinterland and quickly back again began to replace the intrepid traveler who risked the unexpected in foreign lands.[14] In Mexico the handful of expatriates and adventurers who had sought unique, extended first-person experiences were replaced by hundreds and then thousands of short-term tourists who took pleasure in walking and gawking among pyramids, mountains, and no-longer-isolated villages. In Mexico for a few days, they became likely consumers of tourist guides and travel books and, for better or for worse, embodied a profound change in the nature of international communications.

Only a few travel writers went beyond the customary evaluations of hotels, restaurants, rail service, and pyramids to touch on controversial topics. The adventurous Harry Franck had an intriguing idea for a travel book: he used W.H. Prescott's account of the Spanish Conquest to follow the footsteps of Hernando Cortez from Veracruz to Mexico City. The result was *Trailing Cortéz through Mexico*, a book spiced by Franck's own willingness to climb high mountain trails and explore Indian villages far beyond the reach of the average monolingual tourist in street shoes. Nor did Franck ignore the revolutionary currents that had swept through Mexico since his first visit in 1911. He incorporated his own observations and quotations from Mexicans and foreigners on issues such as land reform, the church-state crisis, and national politics. In one choice quotation a Mexican conservative conveyed his point of view and at the same time incriminated himself: "Said a Mexican professional man of high standing, both in his profession and socially, a very religious conservative, 'Under Díaz we were under the pleasant tyranny of those who bathed and changed their underwear; now we are under the far harder tyranny of those who do not bathe and probably don't use underwear.' "[15]

Like Steinbeck, Beals, Tannenbaum, and most U.S. writers who came to Mexico in the 1930s, Franck had a ready sympathy for the common people. Besides reassuring the tourist that Mexico possessed excellent opportunities for travel, he stated that waitresses, maids, streetcar conductors, and even many peons had abandoned their passive, humble ways to seek a better material existence; they were joining their fellow workers in the United States in asserting their rights.

Franck wrote for a growing readership; in 1934 and 1935 Mexico experienced a substantial increase in visitors from the United States—most of whom, however, eschewed the Cortez route for the new Laredo–Mexico City highway. The Mexican government had actively promoted tourism at least since 1929, and the completion of this highway, plus improvements in rail, ship, and plane service, brought more visitors from the north. The obvious benefit for the government was increased tax revenue from the tourism-related businesses such as hotels, restaurants, and transportation.[16]

The outpouring of guidebooks stimulated by the increase in travel to Mexico ranged from Franck's venturesome approach to much more routine listings of places to go and things to see. Experienced travelers such as Frances Toor, T. Philip Terry, and Anita Brenner joined newcomers Jean Austin, A.L. Moats, and others to provide a shelfload of volumes portraying a fascinating land of colonial churches, ancient pyramids, and Indian villages spread among mountains, valleys deserts, and jungles—in short, the kind of locale that U.S. visitors had seen on the motion picture screen and could now see in person.[17]

Eduardo Villaseñor, Mexico's consul general in New York, monitored his nation's public image in the United States and found that the tourist guides presented a positive view at a critical time.[18] In the mid-1930s U.S. Catholics were issuing denunciations of the Mexican government's restrictions on religion, openly charging that the anticlericals had a Communist orientation. Jean Austin, however, confirmed Villaseñor's confidence in tourist literature by answering the charges of Bolshevism with the observation that Mexico was "brown" not "red"— a nation of Indian-mestizo people for whom radical politics was less important than their native heritage.[19]

Erna Fergusson, like Franck, had little patience with pushy, insensitive tourists who dashed from one spot to another in order to claim a fleeting but obviously uninformed presence at various sites of, to them, dimly understood importance. Fergusson's interest was in fiestas, the centuries-old indigenous celebrations of local communities throughout Mexico. Her descriptions of their origins, color, and vitality were similar to the writings of Frances Toor, but Fergusson sounded an unexpected note of alarm: she argued that the Mexican government's anticlerical campaign posed a threat not only to the survival of the fiesta but also to the religious basis of native culture. The prohibition of religious symbols in public places removed the heart of many fiestas. While the government claimed to be the protector of the Indian, it was seeking to make native festivals into secular celebrations, not religious

Left, Pancho Villa is caught in a brief moment of apparent repose belied by the energy and intensity of his eyes. This 1914 photo shows him at the peak of his power, at a time when he inspired disagreement between observers John Kenneth Turner and John Reed. Prints and Photographs, Library of Congress.

Emiliano Zapata (above, left) and young Lázaro Cárdenas (above, right) both fought for land reform between 1910 and 1919, Zapata in Morelos, Cárdenas in his home state of Michoacán. Zapata died in the struggle; Cardenas went on to become president of Mexico in 1934. Photos from Anita Brenner, *The Wind That Swept Mexico*, courtesy of the Anita Brenner Estate.

These two West Coast radicals went to Mexico to witness and describe the revolution. John Kenneth Turner (above, left) criticized the Díaz regime and defended the revolution as a social movement for nearly a decade before Carleton Beals (above, right) arrived in 1918. Beals continued to write about Mexico and its revolution for three decades. Turner photo courtesy of the Bancroft Library, University of California, Berkeley. Beals photo courtesy of Special Collections, Mugar Memorial Library, Boston University.

Katherine Anne Porter's walk along this sunny path in Mixcoac in March 1931 is in sharp contrast to the dark disillusionment with the revolution that she shared with other U.S. writers who visited Mexico in the 1920s. Courtesy of Special Collections, University of Maryland at College Park Libraries.

Diego Rivera (below) attracted an
international following as one of
Mexico's leading muralists. The
youthful Anita Brenner (right)
discussed Rivera's work and the
mural movement in general in her
pioneering study of Mexican art,
Idols Behind Altars. She remained in
Mexico for most of her life, working
as a journalist and publisher. Rivera
photograph from author's collection.
Edward Weston photograph of
Brenner (mid-1920s) courtesy of
Brenner Estate.

Above, President Alvaro Obregón (at right) strikes a dignified pose after gaining official recognition from the government of China in 1921. At the time he was deeply disturbed by the refusal of the Harding administration to recognize his regime. Prints and Photographs, Library of Congress.

Carleton Beals snapped this blurred photo of a December 1923 demonstration for Adolfo de la Huerta in the Zócalo in front of the National Palace, part of a revolt that threatened the Obregón government. Although by this time Obregón had secured U.S. recognition and was able to control the revolt, Ernest Gruening, Beals, and other U.S. observers were distressed by this revival of political instability. Author's collection.

The close working relationship between U.S. Ambassador Dwight Morrow (at right) and President Plutarco Elías Calles helped explain the improvement in U.S.-Mexican relations in the late 1920s. Here they attend opening ceremonies for a public school. Prints and Photographs, Library of Congress.

This massive demonstration in the Zócalo celebrated the 1938 oil expropriation as an act of assertive nationalism against foreign-owned corporations. From Anita Brenner, *The Wind That Swept Mexico*, courtesy of the Brenner Estate.

Several Hollywood films depicted aspects of the Mexican revolution. Above, in John Steinbeck's *The Forgotten Village* (1941), the schoolteacher carries part of a casket for a child who died from drinking contaminated water. Below, in the 1939 film *Juárez*, Paul Muni dons a stovepipe hat to portray Benito Juárez as the Mexican leader rouses his followers to the cause of democracy against a military *golpe* and, in other scenes, against French imperial intervention. Both from Museum of Modern Art Film Stills Archive.

Marlon Brando's performance in the 1951 film *Viva Zapata!* assumed romantic and heroic proportions. In the scene below, his expression conveys Zapata's dawning recognition that he has become the agent of a centralized, self-serving, authoritarian state—exactly what he had rebelled against in the first place. Both from Museum of Modern Art Film Stills Archive.

By the 1950s flocks of fashionably dressed tourists trod the ancient steps of Teotihuacán in a commercialized procession that would have surprised and probably disturbed many of the radicals and liberals of the 1920s and 1930s. From Anita Brenner's *Mexico This Month* of March 1959. Her May 1959 issue charted the progress of Mexico's highway network with the photo below showing a winding paved road through the mountains of Chiapas. Thirty-five years later, a rebel group in this state claimed the name of Zapata to emphasize their opposition to the regime in Mexico City. Both courtesy of the Brenner Estate.

rituals: "The village Indian probably misses the fine distinction when his government refuses permission for indigenous dances when performed in the old way on the saint's day and encourages those same dances when done for a visiting president or at a school program. It sometimes happens that, even when dances are actually not forbidden, rulings are made [by the national government] which cause deep resentment."[20]

The Popular Image: Folk Tales and Fiction

Fergusson's concern for native culture placed her on the left side of an imprecise spectrum that featured intense but unfocused polemic between two practitioners of popular historical fiction. The conservative H.H. Dunn's *Crimson Jester* was a sweeping and, in places, vicious attack on the legend of Emiliano Zapata. Dunn's opponent, Edgcumb Pinchon, first attempted to move Pancho Villa out of the category of despicable bandit and into the hallowed company of Robin Hood. Pinchon's 1933 *Viva Villa* did not convince the critics, but eight years later his response to Dunn's brutalization of the Zapata legend found a warmer reception. According to Zapata biographer John Womak, Pinchon devoted a year to research in Mexico and wrote "a good popular biography" that managed, despite its "invented characters and scenes," to capture "the essentials of personality, theme, and purpose very well."[21] Perhaps Pinchon tended to overestimate Zapata's influence after 1919, but the dramatic death of the peasant leader of Morelos underscored the danger inherent in any challenge to the nation's political establishment from the lower rungs of provincial society.[22]

Two authors widely read in the United States in the 1930s dealt with Mexican fiction and folklore. The outgoing Texan J. Frank Dobie and the reclusive, mysterious B. Traven each managed to convey, in his own distinctive style, a provocative estimate of Mexican reality. Where the gregarious and loquacious Dobie seemed to amble through northern Mexico in search of friendly conversations, local color, and native stories, the secretive and enigmatic Traven combined his observations on the lives of common folk with a doctrinaire, didactic, essentially anarchistic view of life. Yet both writers invested the mountains and deserts with a kind of nobility that overshadowed and, at times, controlled the human conflicts they hosted. More important, both saw in the common people a vitality and veracity worthy of extensive discussion and thinly veiled admiration.

Dobie accorded *vaqueros* (Mexican cowboys), hunters, and *curanderas* a kind of respect lacking among the disciples of modern medicine and industrial society. With the change to daylight saving time under the Calles regime, he asked people whether they preferred it to standard time. His respondents rejected both in favor of astronomical time, based on the perceived movement of the sun across the sky, and a reverence for the natural rhythms of life. The new system was a tool of the "coyotes and hawks of the government" who had little understanding of day-to-day existence in the rugged sierras.[23]

In the huge desert of the north, the Bolsón de Mapimi, which stretches from the border southward through western Coahuila and eastern Chihuahua to Durango, Dobie heard and recorded stories of the nature of justice and the justice of nature:

> The last stir of human life on the Bolsón de Mapimi was during the Mexican Revolution that began in 1910. In the early winter of 1913 old Don Luis Terrazas, his scores of descendants, and half a hundred other rich Chihuahua families fled up the Chihuahua Trail for the safety that lay north of the Rio Grande. They fled from Pancho Villa. Terrazas owned, some say, seven million acres of land in the state, some say fourteen million. He owned a large portion of the largest state in the republic of Mexico, and a large part of this land lies within the Mapimi desert. Don Luis was the State. On the hegira he took with him 5,000,000 pesos in specie—so they say—and left 600,000 secreted in or under the pillars of his bank. . . . There were over 3,000 of the refugees. . . . no animal crossing the Bolsón de Mapimi carried anything more precious than a gourd of water. The trail was marked with carcasses. In the mountains of the Big Bend on the Texas side men yet look for the treasure that [Pascual] Orozco and other refugees are supposed to have secreted there.
>
> Four years later Pancho Villa, retreating from Carrancistas, set out from the ancient mining town of Mapimi with 1,200 men; when four days later he reached Los Jacales to the west, he had only 900 men and many less than that number of horses. During the four days neither man nor beast had come to water, for the sparse aguajes to right and left were guarded by the enemy. The men singed prickly pear for their horses; they ate prickly pear themselves. But the prickly pear is sparse where the Bolsón is worst. Had the men and the horses alike not belonged to the desert, few indeed could have thus traversed it.[24]

B. Traven cultivated an air of mystery about himself in part to cover his past as a refugee from the turmoil of post–World War I Germany. Although he wrote mainly for a German audience in the 1920s, English translations of his novels won favorable reviews and a small but avid readership in the United States in the 1930s. Traven experienced a burst of confidence about Mexico's political leadership in his first few years in the country, but by the 1930s, when he began to address his audience in the United States, he had returned to his earlier anarchist outlook. He saw himself not so much a novelist as an ideologist who placed his characters in situations intended to exemplify a larger point. He found in Mexico numerous examples of indigenous communities caught up in struggles with the bureaucratic central government and the profit-seeking corporations, both of which in his view, regarded the common people as mere objects for their own manipulations and self-agrandizements.[25]

Traven's trio of vagabond gold seekers in *The Treasure of the Sierra Madre* (1935) know the tribulations and dangers of dealing with local, state, and national officials, Fred C. Dobbs and his partners Curtin and Howard agree that they should not register their claim because

> on filing the claim with the authorities the exact location of the field had to be given. The three men were of little consequence; even the American ambassador could give little protection should it happen that they got into trouble. It happened in this country that chiefs of police, mayors of towns, congressmen, and even generals were implicated in cases of kidnaping for ransom and in open banditry. The government, both state and federal, could at any time confiscate not only the whole field but every ounce of gold the men had mined with so much labor and pain. While the three miners were at work they would be well guarded. Only when on their way back with their hard-earned loads would they be waylaid or highjacked by a party of fake bandits acting under orders from someone who was paid by the people to protect the country from bandits. Things like that have happened even in the country to the north; why not here? It is the influence of the atmosphere of the continent.[26]

In *Government* (a less popular novel than *Sierra Madre* but a more powerful statement of the author's main ideological position), Traven vividly described a scene of grassroots democracy in action among the residents of an Indian village. Historian Heidi Zogbaum argues that this tale had its origins in north German culture and was probably intended for a German readership during the rise of Adolf Hitler, but its application to Mexico of the early 1930s also pointed directly to the political power of the tenacious Calles. It left no doubt as to Traven's attitude toward governmental authority and the need to discipline it through popular participation. The force and clarity of the description of the transfer of power from the old chief to his successor justify extended quotation:

> Now a chair was brought up. It was a low chair woven of wickerlike twigs. The seat had a hole in the middle.
>   The new chieftain pulled down his white cotton trousers and sat on the chair, while all the men who had crowded around to watch the ceremony laughed and made ribald jokes.
>   Holding the ebony staff with its silver knob in his right

hand, the chief sat solemnly in the chair, his face turned to all the men of his nation standing before him. He sat there with majestic dignity as though he were performing the first solemn act of his office. The laughing and joking of the crowd was stilled, to show that the first weighty utterance of their new chief was awaited with due respect.

But now three men came up, sent by the barrio which was to elect the casique [chief] for the following year. These men carried an earthenware pot with holes bored into its sides. The pot was filled with glowing charcoal, glowing brightly because of the holes.

One of the men explained in rhymed verses the purpose that the pot of fire would serve, and when he had concluded, he put the pot of glowing charcoal under the seat of the new chief.

He said in his speech that the fire under the chief's posterior was to remind him that he was not sitting on the seat to rest himself but to work for his people; he was to look alive even though he sat on the chair of office. . . . If he tried to cling to his office they would put a fire under him that would be large enough to consume both him and his chair.

As soon as the pot of glowing charcoal had been placed beneath the chair, rhymed sayings were recited, first by a man of the barrio of the retiring chief, next by a man of the barrio who would elect the chief for the following year, and by a man of the barrio of the newly appointed chief.

The new chief had to remain seated until these recitals were at an end. It depended on his popularity with the people whether the men who recited these sayings chanted them in slow and measured tones or as fast as they possibly could without openly giving the show away. If the last man to recite thought the two who spoke before him had recited too quickly, he would make up for it by reciting his verses twice as slowly. . . .

When the charcoal died down the chief got up slowly. . . . Great blisters had been raised on his skin and in places it was so well roasted that it could be smelled from a distance. . . . The new chief would not forget for weeks what he had had under his seat. It helped him considerably during his period in office to carry out his duties as his nation had expected of him when it elected him.

Workers would be advised to adopt this well-proven Indian method of election, particularly with the officials of their trade unions and political organizations—and not only in Russia, where it is most necessary. In all other countries, too, where Marx and Lenin are set up as saints the militant working class could achieve success much more surely if they lit a good fire yearly under their leaders' behinds. No leader is indispensable. And the more often leaders are put on red hot seats, the more lively the political movement would be. Above all things, the people must never be sentimental.[27]

Traven was stating in even stronger terms essentially the same message that Dobie, Fergusson, and Franck attempted to deliver on the incompetence or venality of government officials. They demonstrated the vast distance between the politico-cultural center of Mexico (and its appendages in the urban-based, profit-oriented tourist business) and the authentic life of the Indian and mestizo rural population. The politico in the capital and, even more emphatically, the Yankee tourist could visit a centuries-old Indian community and fail to understand the boundless differences that separated the world of clocks, schedules, and interest rates from the world of the *petate*, the *curandera*, and indigenous restraints on political authority. Yet for liberal statists, an active national government and sweeping social change were necessary for Mexico. Paul Muni's Juárez, the champion of the antiimperialist nation-state, represented the liberal statist case; John Steinbeck's Juan Diego, the ostracized, small-scale importer of modern medicine, represented a version of the independent left's uncertain prescription for change in Mexico from the anarchist/populist perspective.

From Selective Amnesia to a New Liberal Orthodoxy

In reviewing the changes in U.S. intellectuals' views of Mexico from 1910 to the early 1940s, it is helpful to think of the observers as using binoculars to focus on events and trends across the border. Their eyes were fixed on Mexico, but their feet and also their ideologies and other cultural baggage remained planted in the United States. The history of Mexico in this period was so complex that they usually found some figure or occurrence to sustain their prejudgments.

The most blatant carriers of prejudice were the ethnically biased writers who went to Mexico during the first years after the fall of Díaz. Richard Harding Davis and Jack London saw a "half-breed" nation descending into chaos with little hope of salvation except through the tutelage of Anglo-Saxon Uncle Sam. The revolution was merely a severe spasm within a body politic well known for such involuntary, violent thrashing.

In the next decade Ernest Gruening, Herbert Croly, and other liberal statists adjusted their lenses to peer further into Mexico and found tendencies that placed the revolution in a more favorable light. They saw the Constitution of 1917 as a legitimate expression of the will of the nation, a guide to sorting out the meaning of recent disorders. Seemingly connected with the constitution was the presidency of Alvaro Obregón and the work of leaders such as José Vasconcelos, which exemplified the means whereby the goals of the constitution could reach the people.

Mexico in the 1920s became a kind of ideological battlefield for

U.S. observers. On the far right Ambassador James Sheffield continued to see Davis's stereotypical Mexican: a hopeless, hapless inferior being now drawn into the international Communist conspiracy. By contrast, liberal capitalists—typified by Dwight Morrow and Walter Lippmann—located rational, bureaucratic, and business-minded leaders in Mexico City who resembled their counterparts in the United States; consequently, they believed that revolutionary Mexico could be dealt with by normal diplomatic and business methods. Those further to the left—liberal statists, independent leftists, and some bohemians—applauded Plutanco Elías Calles's start as a fire-eating nationalist but deplored his transformation into a dictator who used the power of the government and the new political party to push for stability at the expense of reform. Therefore, Stuart Chases's depression-evoked paean to poor but stable Tepoztlán met resounding rebuttal from the left. To veteran Mexicanists, the images of Mexico in the mainstream writings of both Lippmann and Chase (though quite different) contrasted with their own view of a nation victimized by a predatory dictatorship.

The 1930s brought an unprecedented convergence of views on Mexico. Although never achieving unanimity in every ideological group, the favorable perception of the Lázaro Cárdenas administration ran from liberal statists to socialists and some Communists, to a few hesitant independent leftists, into mass culture through films, popular fiction, and travel books, and even into the Roosevelt administration. The common assumption was that a social revolution was under way in Mexico, though only a few observers explored in depth the implications of the experiments in collective land reform, an aggressive labor movement, the nationalization of the rail and oil industries, and the use of radical ideas. Independent leftists such as Frank Tannenbaum quietly decried the expansion of the central government but shared a sympathetic view of the intentions of the Cárdenas administration. The coalescence of this vision and the general acceptance of its implications for U.S.-Mexican relations produced a breakthrough in the understanding of social revolution in the United States. Even when the revolution devoured property owned by U.S. citizens, this perspective retained firm, ideologically diverse support. Although Roosevelt and his advisers made decisions on the basis of their own judgments (which included the danger that Mexico might shift toward the Axis powers), this broadly based leftist point of view at least reinforced Washington's willingness to negotiate with the Cárdenas administration.

In 1942, then, one might have concluded that after three decades of discord and distrust punctuated by brief periods of tenuous harmony, the two nations had at last learned to live together, largely because the United States had finally accepted the political legitimacy and economic necessity of revolutionary change. Such a conclusion, however, would have been premature. Over the next two decades the government in Washington and many liberal statists forgot—or chose not to remember—the lessons of the revolutionary period in Mexico. This selective amnesia grew out of major changes in the ways that U.S. intellectuals and policymakers viewed their own nation and its relations with the postwar world.

From Good Neighbor to Cold Warrior

The Second World War was an unexpected and, for many U.S. observers, a little-noticed impetus for further reconciliation between the two countries. A common enemy, lethal German submarines along Caribbean shipping lanes, elicited naval and military cooperation between the two neighbors at the same time that Mexican petroleum, other mineral resources, and food products were in great demand. The residue of tensions surrounding the oil dispute slid into the background as collaboration took priority on both sides of the border. The United States prosecuted the war in the name of democracy and in opposition to fascism—an ideological position acceptable in both nations.[1]

The warm postwar afterglow in U.S.-Mexican relations lingered for many years. Frank Tannenbaum's social anarchist perspective led him to a vigorous skepticism on most arrangements reached by political leaders, but even he expressed the hope that the success of the expropriation negotiations would mark the opening of a new era:

> In a strange and unexpected way the original statement that Mexico was free to work out its own policies, even if it injured the interests of United States nationals, and that the territorial integrity and political independence of Mexico were inviolate has, like bread cast upon the waters, returned a thousandfold. It has increased the moral and political role of the American people and given our government a place of trust and leadership in the world which it could not have achieved by a mere show of force. American foreign policy has been hammered out on the Mexican anvil.[2]

Emerging in a new generation of Mexicanists, thirty-eight-year-old Howard Cline echoed Tannenbaum's optimism but added a broader interpretation of events since 1910. According to Cline, the U.S. response to the expropriation and other revolutionary acts revealed that such a movement, if treated with respect, would be "successfully amalgamated with the main traditions of Western-style democracy."[3] Although Cline was much more at ease with evidences of modern institutions in the U.S.–western European mold than was Tannenbaum, both historians agreed that the United States had taken the high ground in political and moral leadership in world affairs. As later events were to show, however, they greatly overestimated the importance of this experience not only in Washington's policies on a worldwide scale but also within the Western Hemisphere.

In 1950, the year in which Tannenbaum's optimistic prediction appeared in print, diplomatic and military specialists in the administration of Harry Truman were moving to a more aggressive, less neighborly set of foreign policies. Assistant Secretary of State Edward G. Miller used general terms to warn that while nonintervention was a noble doctrine, it was not a binding commitment for the United States; he suggested that some unspecified form of "collective intervention" might become necessary for the well-being of the hemisphere. Where Miller left much unsaid, the newly formed National Security Council sent to President Truman a report known as NSC 56/2, which recommended military aid to and collaboration with Latin American governments against possible Communist adventurism. Miller's public statements and the secret NSC document indicated that the Truman administration's concern about Communism—greatly exacerbated by the outbreak of the Korean War in June 1950—was beginning to have an impact on its Latin American policies. In the following year it began to send military aid to selected Latin American governments.[4]

The U.S. response to the Bolivian revolution of the early 1950s gave little indication of the willingness cited by Tannenbaum and Cline to tolerate movements similar to the Mexican example. The vaguely leftist Bolivian National Revolutionary Movement (MNR), which included radical miners and peasants, came to power by revolt in April 1952. The new government nationalized the nation's tin mines and began to consider extensive land reform. The Eisenhower administration, caught in the grip of McCarthyism and committed to the support of national militaries as a weapon against Communism, poured massive amounts of foreign aid into the coffers of the moderate sector of the MNR and purchased large amounts of Bolivian tin to strengthen the revenue base of the new government. These moves diverted leftist tendencies, and once a defanged MNR was in power, the United States sent material support to the Bolivian military as a buttress against any slippage toward the left. The example of negotiations with and accommodation to Mexico's meandering but usually independent policies in nationalization and land reform had no counterpart in the wheeling and dealing in Bolivia. True, the United States did accept the tin mine nationalization (U.S. investors held only a small interest in these properties), but the influx of economic aid, business contracts, diplomatic pressure, and military support gave the United States by 1954 an even greater presence in Bolivia than before the revolution. Where Carranza,

Obregón, and Calles had wrestled with the power of U.S. diplomatic and economic influence and Cárdenas had forcefully challenged it, Bolivian President Victor Paz Estenssoro quickly submitted to it. He was so careful to maintain good relations that when conservative Senators John Bricker and Homer Capehart visited Bolivia in 1963, they found no reason to sound the anti-Communist alarm. In short, the United States threw a heavy blanket of aid, trade, and political pressure on the fires of the Bolivian revolution and within two years snuffed it out.[5]

Although the Eisenhower administration combined the enticements of material support with the restraints of firm diplomacy in Bolivia, it had no comparable reservations in dealing with the leftist governments of Guatemala under Juan José Arevalo (1945-51) and Jacobo Arbenz (1951-54). Historian Bryce Wood charged Eisenhower and Secretary of State John Foster Dulles with "dismantling the Good Neighbor Policy" and its commitment to nonintervention in their dealings with that Central American nation.[6] Eisenhower, Dulles, and their advisers saw an incipient Communist takeover of a reformist state and ignored the Mexican model.

Eisenhower was aware of the parallel between Guatemala and Mexico, but his clouded memory of the latter made the 1952–54 situation of the former seem even more perilous for the United States. In his memoirs he recalled his time as "a young lieutenant" on the Texas-Mexico border prior to U.S. entry into World War I. Pancho Villa's "irregular incursions into our territory" were the main problem, he said, but after the war the border troubles had ended for the most part. He dismissed the two decades of tension that centered on Article 27 and other challenges to U.S. interests with one sentence: "After World War I conditions [in U.S.-Mexican relations] gradually improved, although even in President Franklin Roosevelt's time many in the country called for war when Mexico decided to nationalize its oil industry, in which some of our citizens had invested heavily."[7] Eisenhower alluded to Mexico again, 187 pages later, but only to indict Guatemala in a contrast based on erroneous assumptions about the influence of Communists in both countries: "Expropriation itself does not, of course, prove Communism; expropriation of oil and agricultural properties years before in Mexico had not been fostered by Communists."[8]

Eisenhower did not probe deeply in comparing the two revolutionary situations, but he did see some complexity in the Latin American left. One brief flash of insight indicates that he was more uncertain than many of his top-level advisers were willing to admit about Guatemala (and other Latin American nations): "where resentments against the United States were sometimes nurtured by groups other than Communist cells, it was difficult to differentiate positively between Communist influence and uncontrolled and politically rebellious groups." Apparently unaware, however, of the leftist (or socialist) image of Cárdenas; the Communist involvement in Mexican education, labor unions, and agrarian reform; Lombardo Toledano's vehement Marxism; or the *ejido's* challenge to individual private property; Eisenhower charged that the Guatemalan leadership was dominated by Communists: "The Communists busied themselves with agitating and with infiltrating labor unions, peasant organizations and the press and radio. In 1950 a military officer, Jacobo Arbenz Guzmán, came to power and his actions soon created the suspicion that he was a puppet manipulated by Communists."[9]

Guatemalan Communists had a closer relationship with Arbenz than Mexican Communists had enjoyed with Cárdenas, but the Guatemalan party had at best a marginal impact on national policies. Piero Gleijeses's study of revolutionary Guatemala details the relationship between Arbenz and the Guatemalan Labor Party (PGT), which, in the early 1950s, was a small but growing Communist organization. The PGT did not control the government, however, and Arbenz, its main benefactor, was not a member. The party's strengths lay in its ties with Arbenz and its inroads into the government's agrarian reform agencies—which were distributing land to private holders, not to rural collectives.

Nevertheless, these ambiguities were enough to arouse right-wing fears in the McCarthy era. The United Fruit Company's public relations expert Edward Bernays devised an effective media campaign that emphasized the leftist tendencies in Guatemala. While John Foster Dulles plied the hypersensitive press with speeches that portrayed Arbenz as an agent of international Communism, his brother Allen, director of the Central Intelligence Agency, undertook an ostensibly covert campaign (although it was known to some journalists and politicians in the United State and the Caribbean) to overthrow the Guatemalan president. The CIA worked with anti-Arbenz rebel Carlos Castillo Armas, using false radio broadcasts to give the impression that a large invasion force had crossed the Honduran border. The resulting public fears were intensified by aerial bombing of Guatemala City. Without the support of the army and with rapidly dwindling public confidence, Arbenz chose to resign.[10]

The CIA, the State Department, the United Fruit Company, and the White House projected an image of Guatemala as a nation about to slip into the grip of Communism, but no direct link between Guatemala City and Moscow ever surfaced. Barely five weeks before the coup John Foster Dulles admitted to a Brazilian diplomat that he had no proof of

Communist subversion but was operating on the "deep conviction that such a tie must exist." A year after the overthrow, U.S. intelligence investigators had found no evidence in the Guatemalan government records of such a connection.[11]

The overthrow of Arbenz meant that, to paraphrase Tannenbaum's 1950 statement, the United States had abandoned its "place of trust and leadership in the world." Howard Cline's prognosis for the amalgamation of revolution into "the main tradition of Western-style democracy" likewise never had the opportunity for a fair test. By 1954 the Cold War revulsion to revolution had taken hold in Washington. The Mexican revolution—if not simply forgotten—fell into the category of an irrelevant episode of the recent past, and reminders of it fell outside the main flow of discussion.

Selective Amnesia

At the 1954 meeting of the Organization of American States in Caracas, Mexican Foreign Minister Luis Padilla Nervo compared his nation's recent revolutionary past with events in Guatemala in the presence of Secretary of State Dulles: "I remember the time when Mexico stood alone and we were going through an economic and social reform, a revolution, and if at that moment you had called a meeting of the American states to judge us, probably we would have been found guilty of some subjection to foreign influences."[12]

Nervo's memory served him well, particularly for the Cárdenas years. No Guatemalan leftist matched Minister of Labor Lombardo Toledano, who had traveled in Russia and loudly avowed Marxism on his return. Many more Mexican labor leaders and schoolteachers had been members of or openly sympathetic to the Communist Party than were their Guatemalan counterparts fifteen years later. Cárdenas was an unflinching supporter of Soviet-backed Republican Spain and made no apologies for cohabitating with Communists on that issue. Finally Cárdenas threw the full weight of his presidency behind peasants and oil workers in the expropriation of foreign-owned agricultural and oil properties. Arbenz took only the least-used parts of United Fruit Company lands through a carefully structured system of compensation for the previous owner, whereas the abrupt action of Cárdenas required nearly five years of difficult negotiation before arrangements for compensation could be completed.[13]

Obviously, however, Nervo's history lesson had little effect on his listeners from the United States. The logic of clandestine paramilitary operations against left-wing governments had captured the minds of foreign policy planners in Washington. By 1954, respect for what Tannenbaum had called the "moral leadership in defense of the right of the little nation to a dignified place in the community of nations" seemed to be a curious anachronism.

A few commentators outside the Eisenhower government attempted to explain land reform and other elements of the Arévalo-Arbenz programs by implicit and explicit comparisons with the Mexican revolution but found U.S. editors and publishers unreceptive. Veteran liberal statist and Mexicanist Samuel Guy Inman published a favorable description of the Arévalo years in 1951, but both he and Carleton Beals found that by 1954 any probing essays on the revolution in Guatemala or the CIA-directed coup met with a cold reception even in leftist journals of opinion.[14].

Some members of the post–World War II generation of social scientists looked at Guatemala within the context of the worldwide process of rural modernization. Nathan Whetten, Kalmon Silvert, Richard N. Adams, and John Gillin wrote analyses of the social dynamics and political nuances of change in peasant communities, which laid the foundation for a comparison with the Mexican experience, but their studies reached only a small academic readership, and the wave of anti-Communism that swept the United States in these years heavily colored Whetten's attempts to synthesize recent research on Guatemala and compare it with studies of Mexican land reform. Like most academics, Whetten accepted the validity of the message, amplified by Bernays and the Eisenhower-Dulles State Department, that Communism had penetrated Guatemala. It is important to note, however, that Whetten concluded his analysis of Arbenz's land reform with the contention that except for the alleged presence of the Communists, the Guatemalan program was "roughly similar" to the Mexican system. In other words, subtract the tracings of anti-Communist hyperbole from the works of Whetten, Silvert, Adams, and Gillin, and there emerges an imprecise but useful analogy between the two movements. Whetten stated frankly that "although there were some important differences, the two programs were roughly similar." The major contrast involved the Communist issue in Guatemala, where

> large land owners and many other members of the middle and upper classes feared that the land reform program was actually a major step toward communization of the entire country, which might bring the people and their institutions under the control of the Soviet Union. Their fears were intensified by visits of Guatemalans to countries behind the Iron Curtain. Many of these visitors returned singing publicly the praises of international communism and denouncing western imperialism. They quickly obtained for themselves key positions high up in the advisory councils of the Arbenz regime. Such persons were permitted to exercise decisive influence on the agrarian pro-

gram as well as other government programs. This contributed greatly to the intensification of fear and unrest at home as well as to the growing apprehension abroad, especially in the United States and adjoining Central American countries, lest international communism be establishing a permanent beachhead for its operations in the Americas. All of these fears tended to create a climate favorable to resistance which finally culminated in the invasion by the liberation army and the overthrow of the Arbenz government.[15]

The CIA ouster of Arbenz in 1954 encouraged a similar effort against Fidel Castro in 1961 which turned out to be a disaster for the United States. Given a high priority during the waning months of the Eisenhower presidency and the entire thirty-five months of the Kennedy administration, the Cuban revolution seemed to foreign policy and defense experts a direct function of international Communism, with few if any roots in Cuba or the Latin Caribbean. There is no doubt that by late 1960 Castro was firmly and openly tied to Moscow, but during the gestation period of his movement, he had resided in Mexico and studied its record of revolution with special emphasis on land reform under Lázaro Cárdenas.[16] The influence of the Mexican revolution on Castro, though more suggestive than objective, was nevertheless a factor deserving more attention than analysts have yet given it.

The uses of comparative analysis came through clearly and, perhaps for some, with surprising results in Frank Tannenbaum's brief synthesis of his four decades of research and thought, *Ten Keys to Latin America*.[17] Always wary of a caudillo's proclivity to grasp for power, Tannenbaum in 1960 wrote one of the first leftist indictments of Castro. The sixty-seven-year-old academic laid his historical groundwork by recalling the Hispanic (not Communist) tendency toward personalized authority, which could be dislodged only by political upheaval. Then he cited Cárdenas, who "once remarked that the people of Mexico must learn that they can be governed without violence. Cárdenas, however, had qualities of leadership which made violence unnecessary and governed Mexico that way." Twenty-six pages later, Tannenbaum presented a different image of Castro: "The announcement that he is organizing a political party—it makes no difference whether it is called communist or any thing else—is in his case insignificant because his followers expect him to govern, to make every decision, to lead them and to impose his will on everyone who opposes him. If he is making a social revolution, it is because he wants to make it. If he does not make one, it is because he does not want to make one."[18] Castro had no plans to emulate the Cárdenas example. Cárdenas had exercised authority with a sensitivity to the needs and wishes of the people as he saw them; he carried out a six-year left-wing populist administration and then retired from the presidency. When Castro set out to build a party and a state, he had little intention, in Tannenbaum's view, of sharing power or walking away from it.[19]

At the heart of Tannenbaum's indictment was the accusation that Castro incorrectly applied Mexico's model of land reform to Cuba. The two countries were fundamentally different at the time of land redistribution: Mexico was predominantly rural with isolated villages rooted in traditional culture, whereas Cuba was, in Tannenbaum's estimate, over 60 percent urban and tied directly to the international (mainly U.S.) sugar and tobacco markets. Cuba was too deeply involved in the modern world economy for the Mexican example to work: "If most of the population is urban and if the entire population lives on a money economy, the Mexican model for revolution is a bad one."[20]

Tannenbaum's comparative analysis placed Castro's revolution in a harsh and unflattering light that exposed its defects. He saw "social revolution" not as a single, immutable phenomenon but as complex and highly varied sets of trajectories that would take different forms according to their economic, social, and political circumstances. He recognized the existence of Communist theory and methods in Cuba but relegated them to a subsidiary position in his discussion—which most Americans would have found confusing if not suspicious.

The Mexican revolution served as an imprecise but important prototype not only for Cuba, but for other populist movements in Latin America, from Peru to Guatemala to Bolivia in the 1940s and 1950s, with indirect influences in Argentina and Venezuela. Analysts Donald Hodges and Ross Gandy insist that the Mexican model, not the Cuban, has continued as "the mainstream of the Latin American revolutions."[21] But the U.S. State Department, most political leaders, and the media in general saw mainly Communism at work. By the time of the rise of Castro the relevance of the Mexican revolution had been lost to all but a handful of Mexicanists, most of whom were academics. Instead, U.S. observers took Castro at his word after 1960 and saw only Marxist-Leninist doctrine at work. The late 1950s fascination with the novelty of a bearded rebel became by the early 1960s a narrow-minded obsession with the major demon of Cold War mentality.[22]

The question is not whether there was a precise analogy between the Mexican revolution and the Bolivian, Guatemalan, and Cuban revolutions of the 1950s but, rather, why the State Department, the CIA, and other responsible U.S. agencies failed to explore the possibility of such an analogy. If the recent past supplies usefully similar situations for decision makers to consider, then their minimal mental exercise should be to recall the relevant events.[23] Apparently, Mexican history from 1910 to 1942 had dropped from the memory of official Washington by the 1950s, which could see analogous situations only in Russia of 1917 and China of 1949.

The New Liberal Orthodoxy

The demise of the leftist image of revolutionary Mexico might seem to be another of the many casualties of the Cold War. The story, however, is more complicated. The right-wing hysteria of the era certainly did nothing to reinforce open-mindedness about revolution, but the rapid fade-out of the leftist image of U.S.-Mexican cooperation resulted largely from monumental shifts in liberal statist and liberal capitalist ideology. In fact, this seismic change was sufficiently large to merit a change in terminology at this point. The reformulation of liberalism in the United States in the 1940s was particularly significant with respect to analyses of the nations and peoples of Latin America, Asia, the Middle East, and Africa. The writing of Robert Packenham, Michael Hunt, Richard Pells, Walter LaFeber, Emily Rosenberg, and others necessitates the introduction of the term "third world liberalism" to describe the set of assumptions and doctrines utilized by postwar liberals to shape policies toward what they came to call third world nations—a grouping that included Mexico.[24]

Third world liberalism arose in a period of wrenching contradictions for the United States. At the very time that the nation emerged as the world's great power, the public immersed itself in a bath of patriotism and parochialism, an unembarrassed wallowing in the traditional values that seemed to explain military victory and apparent economic and cultural superiority. One consequence of these antagonistic inward and outward pressures was the imposition of the U.S. model of political, economic, and sociocultural development on the outside world—in particular, on third world nations. Third world liberalism differed from the Wilson-Morrow-Hull liberal capitalism in its new fascination with social science models that specified the paths progress should take. It differed from liberal statism in that the new formulas for development contained a much deeper revulsion toward revolution in general and Communism in particular, often revealing these attitudes in the models themselves.

Third world liberalism seemed to sweep aside the older liberal ideologies by incorporating their main ideas in a kind of consensus among foreign policy experts and commentators. It was a more potent force than liberal statism had been in the prewar years because it also claimed much of the old liberal capitalist position. Third world liberalism posited a mixture of the 1920s and 1930s Gruening-Croly-Herring notions of large-scale government activism with liberal capitalism's preference for private-sector expansion. By combining the statist and capitalist wings of liberalism, this new formulation dominated the center of the spectrum. Further, its antirevolutionism and anti-Communism were resonant with the far right. In vogue in the higher echelons of government, the executive offices of multinational corporations, and the campuses of large universities, third world liberalism had an apparently unassailable position.

One reason that the memory of the Mexican revolution virtually disappeared was the postwar liberals' single-minded focus on the Lenin-Stalin revolutionary model. By 1960s, sociologist Daniel Bell had detected the appearance of what he termed a "new left" in the United States, a movement that lacked maturity in judgment. When examining upheavals in places such as Cuba or Africa, said Bell, these new leftists had "an alarming readiness to create a 'tabula rasa,' to accept the word 'Revolution' as an absolution for outrages, to justify the suppression of civil rights and opposition—in short, to erase the last forty years with an emotional alacrity that is astounding."[25] The still overwhelming presence of Stalin's excesses of the 1930s overshadowed other factors in Bell's view of revolution in the nations of Latin America and Africa. A comparative analysis of the Cuban and Mexican examples might have yielded results more like Tannenbaum's.

In 1950 Louis Halle, an official in the State Department, had reached conclusions close to Bell's later criticisms of the "new left." Halle warned that "public opinion in the United States today tends to be more impatient than it used to be with Latin American failures in democracy." For more than a century the United States had provided the correct example for mature, stable democracy, but the Latin American states simply had not emulated the preceptor. Halle denied the presence of paternalistic elements in his ideas, but his conclusions smacked of ethnocentrism:

> The very fact that these nations are, in so many respects, younger than we, and much weaker, should persuade us to maintain an attitude of noblese oblige. We North Americans, by our nature, feel better when we are conducting ourselves in a broad and generous way than when our behavior in the world is mean, quarrelsome, and niggardly. That is our natural instinct. but we have a mortal fear of being "suckers" that impels us constantly to throttle our instinct. In the case of the other American republics we can afford by virtue of our preponderant strength to fulfill our capacity for greatness.[26]

Neither Halle nor Bell gave much attention to recent history south of the Rio Grande. Halle saw nation building as key in the formulation of U.S. foreign policy in the Cold War. Nation-building theory drew heavily on the predictions of social scientists that representative democracy and economic modernization were within the grasp of any nation that followed the example of the United States. Typical of U.S. postwar cultural and political leadership was the tendency of intellectuals and policymakers to assume away the past or, at least, large portions of it that pertained to U.S.-Latin American relations. Halle's eagerness to see progress in the direction of U.S. style political and economic systems overrode tolerance for experimentation and radicalism. The patience of Josephus Daniels in the face of the abrupt 1938 oil expropriations and the favorable commentary of Hubert Herring and Waldo Frank on collective farming and a Marxist-led labor movement found no parallel among the Cold Warriors of the late 1940s and 1950s.

Robert Packenham, a Stanford political scientist, has provided valuable insights on the origins and basic assumptions of U.S. policy toward third world nations. He located the origins of this policy in the 1947 Marshall Plan, which, he insisted, "remains the most successful program in the history of American foreign aid."[27] The United States funneled over $10 billion into the reconstruction of war-torn western Europe, with impressive results. This use of economic aid as a buttress against the spread of Communism left an indelible impression on Washington policymakers.

For a decade and a half after the start of the Marshall Plan, foreign policy experts analyzed the results, gathered information on third world areas, and devised theories on what became known as the nation-building process. Packenham isolated the four main assumptions that came out of this experience; these, considered in the context of the leftist evaluations of the Mexican revolution over the three decades before 1940, provide some explanation as to why that particular body of information and analysis was irrelevant to postwar designers of U.S. foreign policy.

Packenham identified the first liberal assumption in the simple statement "Change is easy." In other words, the movement from a rural, agrarian, nonliterate, hierarchical society to an urban, industrial, literate, democratic society can flow smoothly with few disruptions.[28] The early writings of Gruening in the 1920s and those of Eyler Simpson, Waldo Frank, Herring, and Kirk in the 1930s were similarly optimistic in tone, but most leftist writers—from the later Gruening (in his 1928 *Mexico and Its Heritage*) to Porter, Traven, and Beals in their fiction and essays in both decades, to Miller, Tannenbaum, Redfield, Millan, and Lesley Simpson in the 1930s—raised cautionary notes and even dire forecasts about the rigors of socioeconomic change for the peasant population, the uncertain consequences of large-scale industrialization, and the fragility of representative government. A thoughtful perusal of their work would have encouraged the advocate of modernization to question if not to refute this first assumption.

Packenham explained the second assumption as the belief that "all good things go together": that is, as economic development proceeds, political and cultural maturity will follow close behind. In the enthusiasm of the Obregón presidency and the excitement of the Cárdenas years, a few observers did seem to believe that Mexico would progress quickly along all fronts, but most of those who took time to study their respective ambiences found considerable evidence of uneven or lopsided development. For example, as economic recovery took hold in the mid-1920s, Gruening did not hesitate to criticize the authoritarian arbitrariness of the Calles government. Tannenbaum, Beals, and Porter exposed the excessive power of the central government in the Maximato and the potential for the state to do harm to the nascent peasant and labor movements. Tannenbaum saw a possible resolution of the problem in the peasants' propensity to rise up against an unjust state, but this solution would hardly have satisfied the adherents of third world liberalism, who sought balance and stability, not imbalance and unrest.

The epicenter of the clash between postwar liberalism and the leftist image of the Mexican revolution involved the related issues of revolution and radicalism. Packenham summarized the third assumption succinctly: "Radicalism and revolution are bad." For Packenham's liberals, revolution meant the kind of violent upheaval that ravaged Mexico from 1910 to 1920. He defined radicalism as the tendency to "reject exclusively political definitions of freedom, equality, and democracy" for a "social and economic" emphasis on these issues. In other words, the radical sees political solutions as inadequate and opts for much larger projects to change the structure of society and the economy.[29] Although most leftist observers from Gruening to Tannenbaum to Millan deplored civil strife,[30] they were nearly unanimous in their acceptance of massive undertakings such as land reform and labor organization, as well as important programs in art and public education. The most significant episodes of Mexico's turbulent three decades after 1910 clearly did not fit into the mold of third world liberalism.

The fourth liberal assumption, in Packenham's words, was that "distributing power is more important than accumulating power."[31] Liberal trepidation about the concentration of authority contradicted a broad spectrum of praise by Tannenbaum, Beals, Porter, and Gruening for Obregón's consolidation of power in the early 1920s, and by Freeman, Weyl, Millan, Brenner, Kirk, Herring, Townsend, and Frank for the activist state under Cárdenas in the late 1930s. Significant exceptions to this earlier leftist espousal of centralized government were the growing skepticism or outright rejection of Traven and Miller, and the later observations of Beals and Tannenbaum. On the whole, however, the post–World War II liberal assumptions represented a clearly divergent path from that laid out by the pro-Obregón, pro-Cárdenas leftists of the previous decades.

The synthesis of modern world history by Theodore Von Laue reinforces Packenham's propositions on a wider scale. According to Von Laue, the United States emerged from the war with a huge range of responsibilities, a global economic and military reach, and a remarkably narrow ideological frame of reference. Unlike the tolerant, somewhat eclectic attitudes that characterized the Good Neighbor Policy and its application in Mexico, the postwar ideals of U.S. foreign policy experts seemed to be rooted in "a single perception of modernity": it had to follow the onward and upward curve of inevitable material progress as enacted by the United States.[32] Both Von Laue and Packenham touch on the same critical flaws in the U.S. outlook toward the third world: the inability to recognize the uniqueness of the American experience without spouting self-defeating arrogance, and an unwillingness to work through peaceful means with nations that depart from this pattern.

Advocates of third world liberalism did have their intellectual challenges. Several critics of U.S. foreign policy agreed with Walter Lippmann's objections in his 1947 attack on the nascent containment policy intended to block the spread of communism by various means including nation-building in crucial regions. Seymour Martin Lipset, H. Stuart Hughes, and others saw limits to U.S. power on a global scale and warned that the White House and the State Department would have to learn to live with anti-Americans of many ideological shadings.[33] Yet they did not persuade the pre-Vietnam policymakers; their arguments, though more widely known, ultimately suffered the same fate as the conclusions of the earlier Mexicanists.

Third World Liberalism's Perception of Mexico

In the 1940s it became clear that three decades of revolutionary activism had not brought a leftist millennium to Mexico. After Cárdenas stepped down in 1940, President Manuel Avila Camacho steered Mexico on a centrist course. Cooperation with the United States in hemispheric defense during World War II was a priority in his government. With the end of the fighting, Avila Camacho and his successor, the even more conservative Miguel Alemán, encouraged closer economic ties with the booming U.S. economy. Neither president saw fit to raise questions relating to land reform, new limitations on foreign-owned property, and the need for a fully mobilized proletariat and peasantry.[34] The conservative mood in Mexico matched the ideological shift in the United States as the New Deal fell out of fashion, to be replaced by an aggressive anti-Communism, a somewhat restrained capitalism, and a quest for social stability.[35]

As both nations moved to the right, a new generation of U.S. Mexicanists arrived on the scene. Largely the products of graduate training in political science and economics, as well as history and anthropolgy, their work was indicative of the growing acceptance of Latin America in general as a field of study in major universities. They used the prevailing assumptions of the times within the highly competitive and generally conformist world of scholarship. The writing of two leading figures can provide some insight into the ideas typical of their generation.

In 1959, University of Illinois political scientist Robert Scott published the preeminent analysis of the Mexican political system, *The Mexican Government in Transition*. The notion of "transition" was central; according to Scott, upheaval, disorder, and socioeconomic experimentation had given way to a period of transition in which the nation's major political as well as social and economic institutions were exhibiting characteristics associated with modernity. Scott posited that the governmental structure was top-heavy because of the extraordinary powers vested in the presidency as it evolved under Alemán and Adolfo Ruiz Cortines (1952-58), but he saw signs of change. The participation of the masses within the framework of national politics promised to make presidential government more responsive to the needs of the general public: "evidence of the effectiveness of increasing popular pressures upon the official party [after 1946 known as the PRI or Party of the Institutional Revolution] suggests that within the foreseeable future mass participation in the political process is both possible and probable. This should be the next stage in the evolution of the revolutionary party."[36]

Third world liberalism's aversion to revolution was neatly sidestepped by the assertion that the revolution of 1910 to 1940 had become an evolution: an inexorable shift to modern institutions and values. To Scott, this political modernization was symptomatic of larger changes, a proposition that went along with the assumption that "all good things go together": "Democracy as a political system cannot long coexist with social or economic inequity and, conversely, a fluid society and viable economy are apt to produce conditions favorable to democratic government, for all human activities and values must be reasonably consistent with each other if stability is to exist in a given society."[37]

After applying these concepts to Mexico of the 1940s and 1950s, Scott concluded that "the evolutionary process already is well advanced" and that the "positive factors favoring responsible government are in the ascendancy in Mexico today."[38] One hope for the bridling of presidential authority was the arrival of "a cadre of career officials" who would respond to law and regulations more than to personal and pecuniary interests and thereby "provide a predictable and constructive pattern" for the individual citizen in his or her relations with the government's bureaucracy.[39]

Scott's acceptance of these and related concepts led him not only to evaluate contemporary Mexico in such terms but to engage in what historians call "presentism," or the imposition of present-day concerns on the past.[40] For many social scientists, the middle class became the core of democratic tendencies and a transferable feature of U.S. society that was taking root in many third world countries. Scott saw this not only as happening in the 1950s but also as having happened in the 1930s, when Lázaro Cárdenas "in many ways was the prototype of the new Mexican middle class." As such, Cárdenas had chosen the moderate course, seeking to resolve conflicts for the sake of social stability and political harmony—a generalization that fit his last two years in office but certainly not the land reform and oil expropriation crises that dominated his presidency.[41]

Historian Howard Cline shared Scott's optimism about Mexico's evolution toward a better future, basing his view on the familiar assumptions about democracy and prosperity. Although Cline admitted that problem areas existed—especially the abandonment of land reform—his 1953 book, *The United States and Mexico*, exuded a confidence in the capacity of modern technology to overcome weaknesses and inequities that the revolution did not solve. The continuation of rural poverty could not be denied, but Cline believed that it was amenable to "technical agrarianism," which included irrigation, electrification, highways, tractors, and fertilizers.[42]

Cline believed that Mexico could surmount the twin challenges of rural backwardness and the migration of poor farmers to already overcrowded cities:

> If figures show anything at all, they indicate that peons are being upgraded both in rural areas and as they drift into cities. The ambitious campesino can thus go to town, and the higher production of his former fellows will feed him. As rural income rises, he will soon begin to pay more for their products. Presumably the cityward trek will continue until conditions—economic and social—between urban areas and countrysides reach an equilibrium. Under the twin drives of industrialism and technical agrarianism, some of the wide gaps between city and country are slowly being bridged, not by "ruralizing" the nation but by "urbanizing" it.[43]

A brief glimpse of historical wariness did surface in Cline's limited foray into the underside of Mexican social change: "No one expects the final balance to be achieved overnight. It is a slow, painful, expensive process in terms of money and human lives."[44] But this momentary lapse was overwhelmed by his faith in the industrialization process. Under Avila Camacho and Alemán, Mexico had steered a course between free enterprise and socialism in a state-directed economy that emphasized flexibility and practicality over ideology. Cline's prime example was the government's Nacional Financiera, which guided private investments into economic sectors in need of special help.[45] By 1953 the advisability of expanding modern industry was no longer a question open to debate for Cline: "The only useful basic premise from which to discuss the modern Mexican economy is that such industrialization has arrived as a permanent, dynamic, and central feature of national life. It has by far passed the stage of inquiring 'should we?' In its train, industrialization has brought numerous problems. Others yet will appear. But the venture has passed the point of no return. In general it can be said that the auguries for successful industrialization are favorable."[46]

And then, like Scott, Cline averred that "all good things go together": "Potentially Mexico has a wide assortment of resources, natural and human: it has capital and markets; it has a successful and stable democratic government; and it is on good terms with its neighbors in the hemisphere and throughout the world."[47] Finally, the Harvard-trained historian detected a determined yearning for achievement, an attitude that any hard-working Yankee could understand: "More important than all of these, perhaps, is the driving will to overcome any obstacles that may appear until unqualified success is assured."[48]

This combination of Mexico's turn to the right, the expansion of the nation's industrial sector, and the acceptance of third world liberalism among students of Mexican affairs helped to bury the earlier leftist image of the acceptable revolution beneath a flurry of studies claiming that the revolution's greatest triumph was its having given birth to the modernizing nation-state and economy. The perception of presidential and bureaucratic responsiveness to public need, the growth of a middle class, and the application of up-to-date credit systems and modern technologies meant that Mexico was on the way toward the highest ideal of third world liberalism: emulation of the U.S. model of modernization.

14

The Persistence of Doubt

In the 1940s and 1950s the independent left again found itself swimming against the currents of mainstream government, business, and academic opinion. The two decades after the oil expropriation seemed to be a golden age for Mexico. Its stable government and expansive economy attracted much favorable commentary from U.S. observers. For example, historian Hubert Herring and biographer William Cameron Townsend, two outspoken defenders of the Cárdenas administration, extolled the "institutional revolution" of the 1940s and 1950s. Herring, who had settled in as a professor of history at California's Claremont College, published a successful college text on Latin American history in 1955. His section on Mexico praised the industrialization that had accompanied World War II and seemed to take Avila Camacho at his word that "honesty and efficiency" were requirements of his administration. Democracy was still a distant goal, but Herring observed that "the progress of the last fifty years gave promise of better things to come."[1] Townsend concluded his 1952 biography of Cárdenas with a similar upbeat observation: the 1938 expropriation, he said, "guarantees Mexico the benefits of its own oil and economic freedom. Beside it stand countless public works feverishly continued by Alemán, lands for the masses, uplift for the Indians, the civil service law, and a Lincoln-like attitude of 'Charity toward all and malice toward none.' "[2]

This effervescent optimism flattened out in the writing of Henry Bamford Parkes. Like Herring and Townsend, Parkes believed that

Mexico had a place among the most rapidly advancing of the developing nations, but by 1960 he foresaw irregular progress. He anticipated "continued economic and technological development" but thought that "it might not proceed so smoothly, with so little class conflict, as in the forties and fifties."[3]

Veterans of the Independent Left

Not quite everyone agreed that development had proceeded all that harmoniously. Looking at the 1940s, Lesley Simpson found little evidence of smooth political and economic change from the perspective he chose to employ—that of the lower-income groups in Mexican society. Expressing views typical of the anarchist-populist independent left of the 1920s and 1930s, he saw an "endemic shortage of food stuffs" verging on famine in some areas. He recounted a tale of rampant caciquismo and exploitation of banana workers in Tapachula, Chiapas, similar to the writings of B. Traven two decades earlier. The improvement of the literacy rate was admirable, but the public suffered from low pay and government indifference to their plight. And, Simpson charged, the apparent World War II prosperity was a myth. Industrial output increased, but the accompanying inflation imposed a terrible burden on urban workers and the unemployed. A 1945 peso would buy only one-fifth the beans that a 1934 peso had purchased. The appearance of factories, highways, and skyscrapers indicated prosperity for the minority—the new group of businessmen and their middle-class employees—but not for the majority. For Simpson, measuring the Avila Camacho and Alemán administrations by the same standard he had used to assess previous governments, what was needed was a primary commitment to alleviate the stubborn poverty that characterized "the desperate plight of the rural workers."[4]

Writing in the 1960s, Carleton Beals agreed. Though not opposed to the industrialization projects that originated in the Cárdenas era, Beals was appalled by the rightward drift in the 1950s, during which worker and peasant activists seemed to disappear from the political landscape. He damned the administration of Adolfo López Mateos (1958-64) in typically inflammatory language, predicting that "unless civic rights are restored and respected and the steady destruction of the great land reforms halted, another revolution will be the unfortunate answer."[5]

Frank Tannenbaum, the unyielding social anarchist, had reached similar conclusions. His foremost concern had consistently been the rural village, and he watched with dismay as the government's commitment to industrialization grew from its initial spurt under Calles to a sizable expansion under Cárdenas to a veritable passion under Avila

Camacho and Alemán. In his 1950 book, *The Struggle for Peace and Bread*, Tannenbaum reinforced his original thesis with arguments derived from his perception of the barriers to industrialization in Mexico. Its people did not have sufficient income to provide the capital savings necessary to underwrite the building of the physical plant required by an industrial economy. Protective tariffs for selected industries such as textiles merely elevated prices for consumers, who in effect subsidized the industry out of their meager incomes. Forced savings and tariff barriers, then, were more harmful than helpful—and the other alternative, reliance on foreign investment, seemed inconsistent with the nationalism and nationalizations of the past.[6]

Tannenbaum was dismayed by the determination to achieve large-scale industrialization that had taken hold in Mexico City and other urban areas. Upper- and middle-class urbanites could not resist the temptation to "make big plans, procure large foreign funds, organize great industries, discover some magic in 'industrialization,' and have a national economy served by a national market at any cost, even if in their hearts they suspect that it is chiefly a dream, which, because of inadequate resources, cannot be realized. But the ideal of bigness is upon them, and they will copy and make plans for the impossible, even if the majority of the Mexico they love must be sacrificed to their notion of 'progress.' "[7]

The ideal of bigness also manifested itself in the central government, where it met similar criticisms from the Columbia University historian. While his friend Lázaro Cárdenas was extending the power of the nation-state into many areas, including control of the national railways, land reform, and the oil industry, Tannenbaum had quietly approved or remained silent.[8] When Cárdenas left the presidency, however, Tannenbaum sensed that the rare qualities of integrity and selflessness had departed with him. Thereafter, the nation not only lacked democratic institutions; it also lacked responsible political leadership at the national level. The rapid expansion of government agencies created heavy burdens for the people rather than solutions for their problems. These two processes together—bureaucratization of the government and industrialization of the economy—constituted a formula for potential crisis: neither "the efficiency of government [nor] the integrity of the politically dominant bureaucracy [has] kept pace with the increased powers of the government over the national economy."[9]

Tannenbaum believed that bigness in government and industry diverged from and was destructive of the original intentions of the revolution. The Indian and mestizo masses had risen up to demand a place in the life of the nation and a plot of land for themselves. Without a Lenin or a Mao to guide them, they had persisted in their demands until they found Cárdenas who began, at least, to move in the direction they wanted through his land redistribution, labor, and education policies.[10] But even the dedicated, sympathetic Cárdenas had veered off course.

Tannenbaum pointed out ways to regain the original path of the revolution. Since the little agricultural communities, "those microscopic bits of society," constituted the core of the Mexican nation and the essence of the motive force of the revolution, the role of the central government was to provide the techniques, the training, and the financial resources for local, small-scale modernization that would make the villagers more efficient producers and more effective citizens.[11] Tannenbaum cited Switzerland and Denmark as models for Mexican development—not the United States. As he had for a quarter-century, he saw the origins and ends of the revolution in these villages, where the state had an obligation to provide "what modern science and skill can make available for the needs of the little community without making it increasingly dependent on a national market."[12]

Reinforcements for the Independent Left

Like these veteran leftists, some members of the post–World War II generation of Mexicanists could not accept third world liberalism. Anthropologists Ralph Beals and Oscar Lewis, sociologist Nathan Whetten, and economists Sanford Mosk and Raymond Vernon, writing in the terminologies and concepts of their respective disciplines, warned against potential imbalances between a powerful national government in close alliance with a modern industrial economy and the weak, widely dispersed rural communities on the fringe of or entirely outside this concentration of authority and wealth.

Nathan Whetten, who fell under the spell of the rabid anti-Communism of the early 1950s in his work on Guatemala, had had no such difficulty in dealing with the Mexico of a decade earlier. He attempted a sweeping survey of the countryside, based largely on his research. His appointment as a specialist in rural sociology for the U.S. Embassy from 1942 to 1945 afforded him the opportunity to travel extensively, touching every state in the republic. Drawing on this firsthand research and his family background (he was born in turn-of-the-century northern Mexico of parents who were pioneer farmers), Whetten produced a text of nearly 600 pages that rivaled Eyler Simpson's work not only in bulk but also in sympathy for the revolution. But by the time he completed his manuscript in April 1947, some serious doubt had been cast on his apparently optimistic preliminary judgments.

Whetten's verdict on land reform was positive but considerably more subdued than the earlier Herring-Kirk evaluations in the Cárdenas years. Land redistribution was a partial success, but ejidal and small-owner properties remained inefficient, and the farmers uninformed of modern techniques—especially in the prevention of soil erosion. Education remained important, but only the national government had the resources to finance rural schooling, and at the national level politics often handicapped this critical function. Rural education and agricultural policy in general suffered from Mexico's deeply ingrained elitism and a propensity for corruption. In sum, Whetten saw many cultural and political barriers to the rural policies begun so energetically in the 1930s.[14]

The Cárdenas dynamism had begun to dissipate by the 1940s. Two anthropologists, the well-known Robert Redfield and Ralph Beals—younger brother of Carleton and a rising member of the University of California, Los Angeles faculty—completed field research in widely separated areas but reached similarly cautionary conclusions. In an intensive study of Cherán, a Tarascan community in the state of Michoacán, Ralph Beals found that economic activity seemed to be moving ahead at a steady pace, partly as a result of Cherán's unusually facile adjustment to European civilization in the colonial period. Redfield detected favorable signs also in Chan Kom, an isolated Yucatecan Maya bush village that transformed itself into a relatively prosperous, formally organized town in the 1940s mainly by the determination and hard work of its residents. Yet both men saw signs of trouble. According to Beals, Cherán faced too many "major problems" in the "under-productivity of the soil and agricultural technology, inadequate mechanization, [and] the probable existence of an overly large population to permit any marked rise in economic status." Likewise, Redfield foresaw a decline in soil productivity and an increase in population pressure in Chan Kom.[15]

It seemed that these two relatively prosperous communities had achieved as much as local resources and the local residents could manage. To push beyond their extant standard of living would require an extension of economic and political activism far beyond the communities' own capacities. As Redfield said of Chan Kom in 1950: "To go outside the municipio (local government) for attachment of ambitions and recognition of responsibilities, the people would have to think of themselves as leaders in the world managed by the dzul [a person not of a Maya village, usually a 'white' person of town or city]. They would have to become political leaders of the state of Yucatán. And this would require an extension of their sense of solidarity and breadth of social and political purpose which they are far from having."[16] Only by becoming involved in more intensive and ultimately more productive agriculture, larger and more complex market systems, the bewildering entanglements of state and national politics, and the uncertainties associated with fluctuations in commodity prices, political factions, and cultural values could such communities continue to expand. Redfield's concluding paragraph made his doubts clear: "The people of Chan Kom are, then, a people who have no choice but to go forward with technology, with a declining religious faith and moral conviction, into a dangerous world. They are a people who must and will come to identify their interests with those of people far away, outside the traditional circle of their loyalties and political responsibilities. As such they should have the sympathy of the readers of these pages."[17]

While Redfield was completing his work on Chan Kom, he faced a challenge on another front. In 1943 a Columbia University–trained anthropologist, twenty-nine-year-old Oscar Lewis, began an in-depth community study of Tepoztlán, a follow-up to Redfield's earlier work there. Lewis disputed Redfields' findings and employed more than a little overstatement in the process. Twice he accused Redfield of falling into the Rousseauean trap of portraying "primitive peoples as noble savages."[18]

It is true that Redfield had been reluctant to describe many of the harsh aspects of life in Tepoztlán, but he had not presented peasant existence as idyllic or even comfortable (as his review of Chase's *Mexico* made abundantly clear).[19] He and Lewis did have substantial disagreement on the nature of change in rural Mexico, but the discord was less profound than the younger anthropologist alleged. Both insisted that the Tepoztecans were caught up processes of change that the villagers did not understand and that brought more harm than benefit. Even though Lewis derided Redfield's folk-urban continuum as too simplistic to provide an explanation of the nature of change among the rural people, his concluding paragraph revealed that they shared a concern about the seemingly random incursions of "civilization":

> We have seen that in the increased contact with the outside world in recent years, Tepoztecans have taken many new traits of modern life. They now have Coca-Cola, aspirin, radios, sewing machines, phonographs, poolrooms, flashlights, clocks. . . . They also have a greater desire to attend school, to eat better, to dress better, and to spend more. But in many ways their world view is still much closer to sixteenth century Spain and to pre-Hispanic Mexico than to the modern scientific world. They are still guided by superstition and primitive beliefs; sorcery, magic, evil winds, and spirits still dominate their thinking. It is clear for the most part, they have taken on the more superficial aspects and values of modern life. Can western civilization offer them no better?[20]

Lewis's *Life in a Mexican Village* met favorable reviews and gave him an academic steppingstone to a successful career as a widely read author and public figure specializing in the subject of urban poverty. A precocious son of Jewish parents who operated a guest house in a rural area near Liberty, New York, Lewis also frequented New York City in his youth. After graduating from the City College of New York, Lewis came under the influence of Ruth Benedict at Columbia University, where he completed his doctorate in 1940. His writing career followed the pattern of his youth in its transition from a rural to an urban focus. Lewis followed one of the Tepoztecan families to Mexico City, where he began his study of urban poverty, a condition that abounded there in the 1950s. From a perspective that echoed the independent left of the interwar years and also foreshadowed the antiestablishment left of the 1960s, Lewis saw the grim world of poverty firsthand, staying in the impoverished homes of Mexico City's poor to observe their day-to-day struggles. His *Five Families* (1959) and *The Children of Sánchez* (1961) laid bare the myth of Mexico's push for progress through industrialization.[21] The latter book's despondent and even ominous assessment of the condition of Mexico's urban poor contained more than an echo of Tannenbaum's concerns over three decades:

> Even the best-intentioned governments of the underdeveloped countries face difficult obstacles because of what poverty has done to the poor. Certainly most of the characters in this volume are badly damaged human beings. Yet with all their inglorious defects and weaknesses, it is the poor who emerge as the heroes of contemporary Mexico, for they are paying the cost of the industrial progress of the nation. Indeed, the political stability of Mexico is grim testimony to the great capacity for misery and suffering of the ordinary Mexican. But even the Mexican capacity for suffering has its limits, and unless ways are found to achieve a more equitable distribution of the growing national wealth and a greater equality of sacrifice during the difficult period of industrialization, we may expect social upheavals, sooner or later.[22]

Lewis was in agreement with Redfield in this case, along with Ralph Beals and Whetten. All four rendered gloomy appraisals of the place of common people in Mexico in the 1940s and 1950s. Along with many other anthropologists and sociologists of the middle twentieth century, these Mexicanists began to recognize urbanization and technological change as central factors in their analyses of culture. By 1956 Redfield saw that his "folk-urban continuum" had expanded to include more people and a more rapid rate of change, energized by the powerful attractions of the city:

In every part of the world, generally speaking, peasantry have been a conservative factor in social change, a brake on revolution, a check on that disintegration of local society which often comes with rapid technological change. And yet in our days many peasants are changing very rapidly. . . . Peasants now want to be something other than peasants. They are pulled by the city into industrial work. . . .

These are times in which even the isolated and backward experience discontent. Quite plain people want to be different from what they have always been; peasantry develop aspirations.[23]

Mavericks of Third World Liberalism

Anthropologists and sociologists were not alone in questioning the impact of the changes embedded in the industrialization process. Two young economists, though less concerned about the effects of modern technology on the peasants' ways of life, turned to other subtle issues often overlooked by adherents of third world liberalism. Sanford Mosk, a professor of economics at UCLA, saw a potential for continued economic growth in Mexico, but his scenario included serious problems. He examined the attitudes and entrepreneurial activities of a generation of young businessmen he called the "New Group," who had begun their rise during the 1930s. They retained an identification with the nationalistic, antiforeign policies of Cárdenas, but they also (in something of a contradiction) adopted the United States as a model for economic development. In their attitudes toward collectivization of agriculture and government support of labor, they quietly but firmly parted company with Cárdenas. Their main goal was private-sector industrial expansion, and to this task they brought, in Mosk's words, "energy, determination, and the skill necessary to make that zeal count."[24] This drive toward modernity presented a stark contrast to conditions in rural Mexico. Despite the efforts of the Cárdenas administration, Mexican farmers lagged far behind the New Group in both material productivity and the capacity to exploit change. Mosk warned of a fundamental imbalance between the city and the countryside if poor peasants were unable to buy the output of the New Group's factories: "The rate of industrial development must be linked to the rate of agricultural development. Otherwise Mexico is destined to find herself with an industrial capacity in excess of what her market can absorb; and with an unbalanced economy that will one day require drastic measures to set it on an even keel."[25]

For more than a decade after Mosk's assessment the Mexican economy continued to expand, but in 1963 another scholar pointed out similar underlying weaknesses. A specialist in the burgeoning field of international business, Raymond Vernon identified what he believed was a dilemma confronting Mexico's leaders. Although not at all hostile to the promotion of industrial growth, Vernon outlined elements similar to those identified in earlier pessimistic critiques. The boom that had begun during World War II had run its course and depleted its fiscal resources by the end of the 1950s. Like Mosk, Vernon saw that extensive poverty meant a small domestic market for manufactured goods; he added that the lack of capital meant a shortage of resources and investment in industry. A continuation of economic expansion, therefore, would probably involve some significant decisions that could bring unhappy results. Reflecting on Mexican history, Vernon judged that the most likely consequence was a "reversion to the 'strong president' " as the arbiter in the decision-making process. Centralized political decision making on economic problems reinforced by the government's fiscal power may have worked for two decades, said Vernon, but he was not certain it could continue to do so.[26]

Hubert Herring came to share this uncertainty. His 1955 textbook had praised the industrialization program, but the 1968 edition revealed an abrupt change. After noting that the PRI "is neither 'revolutionary' nor a 'party' but a formula that works for the moment," Herring used a touch of sarcasm in observing that the party had worked out "a pleasant consensus in which almost everyone is content—almost everyone, that is, except perhaps the 60 per cent or more of Mexicans who have gained little from the new affluence."[27] Quoting Lewis's *Children of Sánchez*, he described frustration feeding upon pathos: "Here is the stuff of which rebellion is made. But the Mexican poor have few spokesmen and there is little sign of revolt."[28]

Two young historians with post–World War II doctorates exemplified a subtle, seldom-noticed shift from third world liberalism toward informed skepticism. Charles Cumberland of the University of Texas and Stanley Ross of Columbia University produced overlapping biographies of Francisco Madero in which the initiator of the revolution appeared as a symbol of democracy and state-directed socioeconomic reform. In Cumberland's words, Madero was the progenitor of a state that was to assume the "responsibility for the welfare of the masses."[29] Both Cumberland and Ross emphasized Madero's sincere commitment to democratic forms and his role in the arousal of the common folk, as well as his fatal inability to control devious generals and politicians. Neither historian argued that change had come easily to Mexico, but both saw an evolutionary aspect to the nation's recent history in which Madero's vision of a progressive, reformist state had gained at least some legitimacy from democratic principles.[30]

Yet like Herring, the two scholars recognized the uncertainties accompanying the boom years. Cumberland's 1968 textbook, though heavy on the positive aspects of the recent surge, also noted that "Mexican economic gains have been funneled into a small segment of the population, with the vast majority benefiting only slightly from the impressive gains after 1950."[31] Ross's seminal article "Mexico: The Preferred Revolution" contained a similar message. Observing that U.S. leaders had begun to praise the Mexican revolution as "a preferred solution for the hemispheric problems of change and development"— especially in contrast with the Cuban and Soviet examples—Ross reminded these latter-day enthusiasts that a generation earlier Mexico's widespread disruption, violence, and experiments with radical policies had shocked and dismayed many U.S. observers. He cited Mexican historian Juan Ortega y Medina on the possibility that Mexico might become a Cold War ideological battlefield where the United States and the Soviet Union each deployed its own propaganda devices in order to gain strategic advantage, even at the expense of historical accuracy. "We . . . have the obligation of knowing the opposed points of view in order to avoid, on the one hand, being converted into noxious instruments of imperialist reaction or, on the other hand, into noxious instruments nourishing pseudo-revolutionary demagoguery: in sum, we must prevent the ideas that are at stake from falling into ingenuous, wicked, stupid, or ignorant hands."[32]

It is doubtful that the voices of Ortega y Medina, Ross, Cumberland, Herring, Tannenbaum, Redfield, Lewis, Mosk, Vernon, and the Beals brothers were heard by those academics and policymakers who flocked around the third world liberalist model. Much like the independent left's questioning of the Cárdenas policies of the 1930s, the post-1946 critique of the PRI and its leadership in Mexico became an easily ignored minority report. The independent leftist views of Tannenbaum, Carleton Beals, and Lewis and the maverick liberal statist outlook of Herring, Mosk, and Vernon barely penetrated the bureaucracies of government and met quick rebuttal in the academy.

Viva Zapata!

The historians and social scientists who sustained the independent left's criticism of intrusive governmental and industrial modernization did, however, receive support from the Hollywood film industry at a time when such support seemed highly unlikely. John Steinbeck's long-term interest in the common folk of Mexico and the directorial talent of Elia Kazan merged with producer Darryl Zanuck's decision to make "a big western" of the Hollywood type about the life of the legendary Emiliano Zapata.[33] Steinbeck wrote a script based on Edgcumb Pinchon's 1941 biography and then worked with Kazan in the production of the film.

Zanuck's expectation that the final product would resemble a traditional western perhaps explains how a film with a subtle but nevertheless apparent independent leftist message emerged in 1952 amid the right-wing hysteria of the McCarthy era. *Viva Zapata!* has a large portion of visual excitement, including fisticuffs, machete slashes, and gunfights, but Steinbeck and Kazan made their ideological intentions quite clear. Zapata, played by Marlon Brando, gives a convincing, low-voiced challenge to the aged Porfirio Díaz in the opening scene. His quiet insolence in demanding the return of farmland to the villagers triggers the dictator's suspicions and notifies observant viewers that this film is going beyond the traditional Hollywood struggle between outlaws and lawmen.

But the filmic Zapata is not a revolutionary who feels drawn to the Communist model. Most of the film is set in the 1910-17 period, of course—before the Bolsheviks took power in Russia—but a Marxist-Leninist version of Zapatismo would have been possible, if risky, in the early 1950s. Steinbeck and Kazan, however, emphasized the ominous fictional figure of Aguirre, who personifies the professional revolutionary. The script does not identify Aguirre as a Communist, but he is clearly operating from what Kazan termed "a communist mentality"— a cold, mechanistic understanding of the politics of revolution.[34] Zapata reluctantly works with Aguirre for a while but eventually rejects him in a dramatic denunciation: "Now I know you. No wife, no woman, no home, no field. You do not gamble, drink, no friends, no love. . . . You only destroy. . . . I guess that's your love. . . . And I'll tell you what you will do now! You will go to Obregón or Carranza [the most powerful leaders at that time]. You will never change!"[35]

The ideological message in the film was clearly not Marxist-Leninist but rather the independent left's melange of social anarchism and populism. Steinbeck and Kazan seemed to paraphrase some of the words of Lázaro Cárdenas (without approving his implementation of state activism and modern industrialism) in Zapata's brief talk to his peasant followers at a crucial moment in the film: "This land is yours. But you'll have to protect it. It won't be yours long if you don't protect it. And, if necessary, with your lives. And your children with their lives. Don't discount your enemies. They'll be back. . . . About leaders. You've looked for leaders. For strong men without faults. There aren't any. There are only men like yourselves. They change. They desert. They die. There's no leader but yourselves." And a few moments later the soon-to-be-assassinated Zapata warns: "I will die, but before I do I must teach you that a strong people is the only lasting strength."[36]

Viva Zapata! stimulated criticism from the Marxist-Leninist left *and* the McCarthyite right—a predicament familiar to independent left-ists for several decades—yet did not broaden public interest in the anarchist and populist perspectives. The independent left remained a marginal component of the larger, embattled left in the United States.

15

A Relevant
Legacy

Had government, business, and academic observers in the United States managed to overcome the effects of selective amnesia and consider the implications of the Mexican revolution in the context of the Cold War, they would probably have found that the commentary on this revolution, though voluminous, offered no quickly phrased, universally accepted answers to the issues raised by such movements. This book makes no claim to resolving the debate about the nature of the Mexican revolution; it aspires only to analyze the discussion of this revolution in the United States in the half-century after 1910. Though the Bolshevik revolution in Russia inspired sharp and transcendent polemics, philosophical debates, and assertions of Marxist-Leninist and liberal capitalist certainties—engaging the attention not only of government officials, journalists, and academics but also of the general public—events in Mexico provoked few monumental exchanges and considerably less public attention. Yet commentary on the Mexican revolution seemed to contain at times a deeper awareness of the inner workings and the underside of revolution: its weaknesses and flaws, its potential for massive disappointments, and its capacity for the unintended and the unpredictable. These observations usually came from three schools of thought—the socialist, the independent left, and the liberal capitalist—but their insights were often overshadowed by the opinions of the liberal statists (before 1945) and the practitioners of third world liberalism (thereafter) and by the heated and often overwrought pronouncements of Communists, conservatives, and racists.

Of the seven basic schools of thought identified in this study, it was liberal statism that dominated the field. A complete explanation of its hegemony is difficult, but its most obvious strength had little to do with Mexico: liberal statism had been powerful if not dominant in the United States since the progressive era. After a decline in the 1920s it returned in the next two decades to take hold in politics, journalism, academics, and broad areas of popular culture.

Given this background, most observers sought and generally found evidence that the national government in Mexico was following a pattern similar to the progressivism that guided the United States through a depression and two world wars. In particular, Franklin D. Roosevelt's New Deal appeared to be a model. Though radical in selected areas—such as the Tennessee Valley Authority and parts of the Works Progress Administration—the New Deal left most of the free enterprise system intact. For liberal statist observers of Mexico, what remained after the excitement of the Cárdenas administration had worn off was a large, potentially powerful, centralized government that seemed, at least in the 1940s and 1950s, to have good intentions in its relations with the Mexican people. As liberal statism evolved into third world liberalism in the post–World War II era, the prevailing view of the Mexican revolution underwent a similar metamorphosis (see Chapter 13): its historical image shed its rough edges to appear mainly as a transition from social disorder to responsible and respectable modernization. In the McCarthy period of the early 1950s the Mexican revolution virtually disappeared from public discourse in the United States, conveniently forgotten somewhere along a path on which "evolution" overtook and devoured "revolution."[1]

Another reason that liberal statism–third world liberalism gained the upper hand was the weakness of the opposition—especially of the self-serving, narrowly conceived commentary of Communist, conservative, and racist observers. The writing of Communists, particularly Bertram Wolfe and Maurice Halperin, held the interest of the Communist Party at first and placed events in Mexico in a light that favored the party. Conservatives Edward Doheny and Guy Stevens used the same approach with similar results, except that their interests were of course influenced by their ties to large oil corporations rather than the Communist Party. Overtly racist commentators fell into extensive exaggeration as their conclusions simply followed the assumptions they carried in their cultural baggage. The ethnic jingoism of Richard Harding Davis added little of substance to the discussion of Mexico, and because this approach had few adherents among serious students after the mid-1920s, it was of limited importance thereafter.

The level of influence of the three remaining ideological catego-

ries fell somewhere between the hegemonic position of liberal statism–
third world liberalism and the marginality of Communism, conservatism, and racism. These three schools of commentary, each in its own
distinctive way, made important contributions to the U.S. understanding of the Mexican revolution. Yet the decline of socialism after
1940, the aversion to statism and implicit pessimism in the messages of
the independent left, and the submergence of pre-1945 liberal capitalism in the flood of third world liberalism meant that none could com-
pete with the expansive optimism that dominated the flow of
information and ideas in the international media during the Cold War.
Despite their relative obscurity, however, they testify to a vital diversity
and skepticism in the discussions of the Mexican revolution.

Socialism and the Independent Left

Socialist ideology, though its span of prominence was short, played a
crucial role in the discussion of the Mexican revolution. The open advocacy of socialism as practiced by Eyler Simpson and the Weyls in the
1930s was an aberration rooted in the intellectual climate peculiar to that
decade, but these writers had a particular awareness of what was happening in Mexico. Simpson explored and was moved by the grassroots
ferment of the early years of the decade and prescribed a government-
directed nationwide system of *ejidos* as Mexico's way out of its problems.
The Weyls saw the Cárdenas presidency up close and believed that they
were witnessing an innovative implementation of socialism that, despite
its flaws, constituted a major contribution to radical praxis.

   This surge of populism and state socialism in the 1930s had its
antecedents, however vague and insecure, in previous years. The Weyls
found more evidence of socialism in the Constitution of 1917 than did
the impatient Eyler Simpson, but all three agreed that Article 27 established the legal potential for government control of crucial resources:
farmland and petroleum. The irregular activism of the Obregón administration and the vacillations of the opportunistic Calles tended to emphasize in fits and spurts the expansion of public education, the public
art of the radical muralists, and the assertive rhetoric (but seldom the
enaction) of land reform. In all these areas there was a lurking socialism,
seldom explicit except in the work of the muralists but present in
sufficient amounts to worry the far right and to inspire the hopes of
some protosocialists on the left.

   Obviously, these tendencies did not reach their potential in the
1920s, but they resurfaced in the next decade with a new vigor inspired
by the apparent collapse of capitalism, the rise of newly aggressive
peasant and labor movements, and the leadership of Lázaro Cárdenas.
By the early years of the Cold War, however, the confident acceptance of

the assertive but short-term populist state socialism of the 1930s seemed out of place. Such left-wing, ideologically charged positions were unpopular and even seen as dangerous in both the academic and the public media. Further weakening of the socialist cause came with the bureaucratized routinization of many of the Mexican government's ostensible redistributive functions in the years after Cárdenas. The Weyls had detected the possibility that the fragile Cárdenas coalition would fall victim to a combination of bureaucratic politics and administrative inertia, and this kind of institutionalization did indeed become an acceptable variant of third world liberalism after 1945.

The independent leftists and their academic allies advocated a different type of revolution. They searched for and sometimes discovered examples of spontaneous peasant and worker movements that contained the seeds of community and individual betterment, with or without the aid of central authority. Katherine Anne Porter and Anita Brenner sensed expressions of ethnic pride in the Indian art forms in the 1920s. Carleton Beals located promising activism in the villages of Paracho and Valerio Trujano, and Frank Tannenbaum found inspiration in Mexico City's "miracle school" and many rural schools scattered throughout the countryside. Max Miller overcame his cynicism to relish the folk memory of the legendary Zapata in the hills of Morelos, and John Steinbeck's fictional Juan Diego transcended local traditions and the modern world.

These experiences with local agents of substantial change offered only temporary hope, however. In a way they paralleled the intense but brief life of the Cárdenas coalition's push toward socialism. Many independent and academic leftists eventually saw and described the sources of their disillusionment. Tannenbaum, Beals, Miller, Traven, and other like-minded observers had ventured onto ground sometimes occupied by those who postulated, according to French social critic Pascal Bruckner, "the romantic view of the primitive" (which in a sense approximates Paul Hollander's analysis of the political pilgrim's penchant for seeing the peasant-proletarian as a modern version of the noble savage).[2] The temptation to do so was quite strong during the Indianism of the early 1920s and again a decade later, when the enormity of the international industrial collapse made the economic simplicity of the Indian-mestizo communities seem an appealing alternative.

Stuart Chase reiterated the larger outline of this argument in his quickly written book *Mexico: A Study of Two Americas*. Bruckner's criticism seems to apply to the Indianists and Chase: "In sum, we are the masters and slaves of technology to which we have lost our souls, are indebted to other cultures for the power of survival. On these tiny, backwards societies the Golden Age is projected, and it is imagined that what once was believed to exist only in the past, is in existence there now."[3]

Chase's hasty work probably benefited experienced Mexicanists, who sought to separate their analyses from his popular book. Although Tannenbaum, Beals, and others on the independent left placed more weight on the validity of the values of the peasantry than on the invasion of tractors, trucks, fertilizers, and hybrid seed imported by Mexico City entrepreneurs and bureaucrats, they came to acknowledge the inevitability of change, moving beyond Chase's version of Tepoztecan economy. Still, they retained the hope that the local people's sense of cultural identity would endure.

The academic discipline of anthropology, which led its practitioners to take a look at human activity "from the bottom up," brought conclusions similar to those reached by the independent left. Whatever their varied field methodologies and other disagreements, Redfield, Ralph Beals, and Lewis all identified high costs associated with peasant involvement in rapid social change. The common points in their analyses centered on the personal and social turmoil introduced by change and the growing size of institutions. They saw change as inevitable but disruptive, full of both promise and pain for the native communities where threats of disease and bad harvests made life certainly less than idyllic. Ralph Beals's 1946 study of Cherán, Michoacán, found signs of economic stasis and even decline within an essentially cohesive rural community. In the same decade Oscar Lewis analyzed the impact of rural to urban migration and included new levels of biographical detail, without losing his grasp of the fact that jobs and homes in the city did not mean prosperity and happiness for those who left the village.

Anthropologists and journalists who expressed admiration and sympathy for rural peoples facing the onrush of modernization often managed nevertheless to avoid the romanticism that Bruckner has pinpointed as a major cause of misunderstanding between interested intellectuals and the peoples of developing nations. Why were they able to escape the "tears of the white man" syndrome as identified by Bruckner? One explanation is the ideological predisposition or academic training of the observer: Tannenbaum's social anarchism; Carleton Beals's left-wing populism; and Redfield's, Ralph Beals's, and Lewis's anthropological sensitivity to the impact of change on communities and individuals. But Bruckner's critique suggests another important factor: the practice of "authentic travel," in which the foreigner gives up ready-made, selective perceptual and attitudinal predispositions in order to explore the uncertain world outside partially modernized cities and towns. Bruckner implored the "authentic traveler," instead of seeing the peasant as a reincarnation of Rousseau's noble savage, to risk seeing reality, or what passes for reality, in the native's community:

> Travel means coming to welcome the other on his own territory. It means declaring that a man is more my neighbor than people like me or my family. It means giving up the required identification of race, camp, party, ideology, and language in favor of the free choice of a country I want. It means giving priority to uncertain relationships rather than hereditary ones, borrowed identities rather than kinship and citizenship, choosing an intimacy of the heart rather than one of flesh and blood. Travel is, therefore, the homage that friendship renders to distance. However fragile it may be, it is proof that no spiritual or physical distance can overcome the similarities that impel people to meet and gather together. I have only to choose between two postulates that are both contradictory and necessary—I cannot be involved in the fate of this far-off other, but I cannot live with him, either. I am obsessed by people whose existence obliges me to leave my country, but I am unable to blend into their way of life. And so, I am caught in the emotional situation described by the adage, "I can't live with them and I can't live without them."[4]

A half-century before Bruckner wrote of the contradictions of authentic travel, D.H. Lawrence understood its risks and experienced its sometimes frightening consequences. Lawrence demeaned those Europeans and North Americans who conjured up a sentimental vision of Native Americans, but the English novelist and social critic was deeply disturbed by his own experiences in indigenous Mexico, especially the vast gulf that separated Indian values from those of his culture. Katherine Anne Porter and Carleton Beals objected strenuously to Lawrence's view of the Indian; however, they and many other observers avoided the excesses of sentimentality criticized by Lawrence in the 1920s and by Bruckner in the 1980s.

Many of the critics of massive, nationwide socioeconomic innovation were attempting to confront these problems several decades before terms such as "third world" and "modernization" became part of the vocabulary of the social and political sciences. Tannenbaum, the Beals brothers, Lawrence, Porter, Redfield, Miller, and Lewis observed the native villages and the condition of the rural people on a day-to-day basis. Lesley Simpson and Lewis walked the *colonias* of Mexico City to study the situation of the migrants from the country. As Bruckner postulated in somewhat overstated terms, the authentic traveler can gain knowledge of the native people without a transcendent sense of identity with them: "The very failure of travel is its success. No discomfort can diminish my hunger for going abroad, or bring down the fever that rages in me. The more the other reveals himself to me, the more I push toward him without reaching him. Soon the witless desire to be the other gives way to a desire for the other insofar as he is not me. Of course, this is still an illusion, but it is the best one to be under."[5]

We are left with the image of the authentic traveler and the authentic peasant peering at each other, their vision impaired by their particular cultural preconceptions, but both nevertheless aware that they are caught up in a turbulent pattern of change and shifting perceptions that taxes their intellectual capacity and yields no single universal solution to the travails of disruptive change.

The Problems of Political Power

The struggle to understand the process of change carried foreign observers along dusty paths into small villages, but the problem of the use and abuse of authority vested in the national government carried them into the busy streets of Mexico City and along the corridors of power in the National Palace. Liberal statists Gruening, Croly, and Herring, and even socialist Eyler Simpson, seemed content to measure the results of the revolution largely in terms of how the government used its power; they tended to assume that expanding state authority was a benefit for the general public. Were the independent leftists who disagreed with this assumption merely stubborn skeptics, out of step with one of the main thrusts of modern history? Or had they found in the Mexican revolution a theme of broad importance for future generations? Since the records of many nation-states in the twentieth century are far from admirable—from the horrific extremes of Hitler's Germany and Stalin's Russia to the equally grotesque examples of the Somozas' Nicaragua, Pinochet's Chile, the "dirty war" of the Argentine generals, and the last years of Castro's Cuba—it seems clear that the arrival of modern governmental bureaucracy, even if it brings significant material resources, is far from being an unmixed blessing.

From their first episode of doubt in the mid-1920s to their sharp castigation of the Calles satrapy in the early 1930s, independent leftists lashed out against political corruption and administrative excess. Their case against the expansive power of the central state was most profound, however, in the broad (and admittedly imprecise) area where political and cultural factors interact. Tannenbaum, who tended to avoid hostile commentary on individual politicians, joined the fray at this level beside Carleton Beals, Brenner, Lesley Simpson, and literary figures such as Porter, Traven, Miller, and Dobie. Although these individuals had their own particular approaches and often disagreed, a fairly clear theme emerged in their writing: the concentration of power vested in or assumed by the national government was a tool for those who craved power and wealth more than a vehicle for the liberation and fair treatment of the masses.

Lesley Simpson was probably the most articulate exponent of the notion that the unfortunate heritage of colonial Hispanic politico-cultural history bore down heavily on modern Mexico. A student of Spanish colonial institutions, Simpson used his research trips to Mexico from the 1920s to the 1950s to gain a wide-ranging awareness of the forces at work in the nation's politics. A strong opponent of the "black legend" school of historians who painted Spanish and Spanish American history in only the most unfavorable light, Simpson nonetheless had profound doubts about Mexico's past. His bold and pessimistic analysis in a private letter to Carleton Beals encapsulates a central theme in much of the independent left's writing on Mexico: "the horrid feeling that there is no hope for a country with the tradition of irresponsible exploitation by public officials."[6] He noted with a tinge of resentment that Gruening and Eyler Simpson could envision a more promising outcome for the revolution "because they believed in some sort of happy destiny"[7]—a presumption common to liberal statists and socialists but not to independent leftists.

Touching on a longitudinal interpretation of all Latin American political history, Simpson carried his readers back several centuries to place the Mexican revolution within the context of a broad and deeply rooted cultural pattern. Many of his contemporaries, particularly Tannenbaum and Carleton Beals, agreed that the tendency toward the centralized state and the voracious aggrandizement of power by those who held high office within it constituted a problem during the revolutionary regime as much as it had during the Díaz administration and the period of colonial government. This continuum of concentrated power in the hands of an elite remained a focal point for scholars of a later generation, among them Charles Hale, Peter Smith, William B. Taylor, Kalmon Silvert, Roderic Camp, and Glen Dealy.[8]

The Hispanic propensity for centralized government was only one of two major influences that pushed Mexico in that direction. The second was, perhaps ironically, the revolutionary state itself, the political entity that claimed the intention of eradicating or at least diminishing the pernicious side of the Hispanic traditions. Clearly, the centralized state was one of these traditions. Two other revolutionary targets, however—the pervasive Catholic Church and the regnant landholding class—could be dealt with only by an aggressive government— a fact that made this apparent contradiction seem less contradictory. Most independent leftists, however, argued that the effectiveness of the revolution had to be considered in terms of the responses of the state not only to its enemies but also to its intended beneficiaries—peasants and workers. The accumulation of power at the political center was, from this perspective, a threat to those on margins of national life, and the national government more menace than servant.

Although Tannenbaum's view of the grassroots sources of the Mexican revolution was in many ways opposed to Theda Skocpol's emphasis on the statist essence of modern revolution in general, they did have at least one point in common. Tannenbaum portrayed the transformation of the sincere, naive peasant revolutionary into the self-seeking, cynical politician, and his hypothetical peasant rebel was the eventual victim of what Skocpol described as the "centralized, mass incorporating, bureaucratic state." That interpretation was reinforced by Nora Hamilton's views of the processes of assimilation and co-optation during the Calles, Cárdenas, and post-Cárdenas years. According to Hamilton, Cárdenas presided over a period of popular political activism and government-directed redistribution of property. But after 1940 his fluid "progressive alliance" gave way to bureaucratic statist and party structures that turned away from peasants and workers and toward the rising entrepreneurial class with a firm commitment to government–private sector collaboration.[9]

Tannenbaum also recognized but could not resolve the contradiction between the centralized bureaucracy's creation of political distortions and social imbalances on the one hand and, on the other, the need for a strong national administration to deal not only with the church and the *hacendados* but also with the international threats posed by foreign governments and corporations. The determination of presidents from Carranza to Cárdenas to enforce Article 27's limitations on foreign ownership of property met effective opposition from U.S. diplomats, bankers, and industrialists for two decades before Cárdenas nationalized the oil company properties in 1938 and thereby dealt a severe blow to foreign control in that area of the economy. Yet Tannenbaum did not believe that the industrial development so energetically pursued by the Cárdenas administration and its successors would work harmoniously for the small economies of village Mexico. The same resourceful state that expelled the U.S. and British oil companies also rushed its program for modernization into the countryside, where the outcome of the quest for a nation unified by the benefits of modern technology and material culture remained uncertain.

Unlike what many political pilgrims believed they saw in the Soviet Union, independent leftists did not see the Mexican revolution as a single transcendent movement. Instead, these Mexicanists regarded events and people as finite fragments of a larger entity. The revolutionary state, whether under the shifting and shifty leadership of Calles or the straightforward guidance of Cárdenas, was to be watched carefully with the expectation that those at the top were capable of self-serving connivance or muddled decision making or both, all in the name of righteous reformism.

Liberal capitalists had their own critique of excessive bureaucratization. The Frank Kluckhohn–Virginia Prewett brief against the Cárdenas government called for a return to what they believed were the laudable policies of Dwight Morrow's confidant, Plutarco Elías Calles. The Morrow-Calles formula posited a stable polity supporting an expanding economy that would entice and hold foreign as well as domestic investment. The political openness that allowed electoral competition, opposition parties, and public criticism was neither prohibited nor essential in this formula. Although Kluckhohn and Prewett did not endorse dictatorship, they saw the political stability associated with it as essential for economic growth.

Wilsonian Cordell Hull joined Kluckhohn and Prewett to argue that Mexico should reverse the tendency toward state-worker-peasant management of large sectors of the economy. The workers' inefficient and sometimes corrupt administration of the railroads and the oil industry gave the liberal capitalists ample ammunition for attacking the revolution. They used the mixed performance of the *ejidos* (particularly the apparent decline in agricultural production) as additional support for their position. They prescribed for the state the role of referee: it should provide laws and other guidelines for the private sector without overstepping the primacy of private property, as Cárdenas had done in 1938. Following the Morrow-Calles formula, the government was to serve as a coordinator of foreign investments and domestic enterprise to ensure the maximum availability of capital for economic, largely industrial, growth. The partnership of the regulatory nation-state and business would result in the efficient allocation of resources, eventually benefiting peasants and workers through an expansion of the entire economy, which would generate greater demand for agricultural products and an increased demand for industrial workers.

Acceptance of Mexico's dependence on foreign capital and markets implied acceptance of corporate decisions reached in the boardrooms of New York and London. Though not an ideal circumstance, the dominance of foreign powers in Mexico was a necessity because these same powers had the financial resources, technology, and consumers that a developing Mexican economy needed. It was a tentative marriage of convenience, though neither separation nor divorce seemed practicable.

The liberal capitalists wrote only an outline of these positions, but their selective observations and piecemeal analyses formed one of the first relatively dispassionate responses to a twentieth-century revolution from an ideological position on the right of the spectrum. One can detect the evolution of similar judgments in the writing of diplomat-historian Dana Munro, historian Samuel Flagg Bemis, political scientist Graham Stuart, and, in more recent years, diplomat-politician Jeane Kirkpatrick, historian Mark Falcoff, and sociologist Paul Hollander.[10]

Both liberal capitalists and independent leftists, then, opposed the erection of the machinery of centralized governmental authority, but they did so for different reasons. The liberal capitalists defended the private sector and its individual entrepreneurs; the independent leftists took up the cause of the peasant community and the labor union. The two schools were far from agreement. If the Maximato was the epitome of the liberal capitalist formula, it permitted the independent left to launch charges of authoritarianism. Furthermore, Morrow, Hull, Kluckhohn, and Prewett—mainly concerned with the continued transformation of enclaves already involved in the commercial-industrial world—gave only passing attention to the impact of socioeconomic change on the peasantry, the working class, and those caught up in the difficult transition from tradition to modernity—the people on whom Tannenbaum, the Beals brothers, Redfield, Lewis, Traven, and Miller focused their attention.

International History and Ideological Perspective

The end of the Cold War, the dissolution of the Soviet Union, and the consequent revisions of Marxist-Leninist ideas and institutions in recent history open the way for a reassessment of revolution, both as a theoretical formulation and in the more concrete terms of historical events. The decline and near-demise of the Mexican revolution as alleged in recent historical writing now seems a bit overstated. This revolution had shortcomings—corruption, authoritarianism, elitist leaders with only a temporary commitment to the common people—but most revolutions have suffered from these or similar failings. In a comparative historical sense the Mexican revolution reemerges as one of several movements (French, Russian, Chinese, Cuban, and maybe Turkish, Bolivian, North Vietnamese, and Nicaraguan) that fell far short of their utopian goals but did bring about significant, often unanticipated and unintended social and economic change.

United States government officials, journalists, academics, and the public in general focused on the Soviet example for seven decades after 1917 and seemed to measure any revolution or revolutionary situation by the Marxist-Leninist standard. Contemporary observers of the Mexican revolution had quite different tales to tell. For example, liberal capitalists warned against nationalist policies that would drive out foreign investments and discourage native business ventures but did not couch their analyses in the phobic hysteria of the anti-Communist far right. Morrow, Lamont, Kluckhohn, and Prewett assumed that these matters were negotiable. In short, there was no ideological Armageddon under way, in their view, but rather a time of sudden and drastic change in which free enterprise could take hold as easily as state activism. Liberal statists, socialists, some Communists, and some independent leftists agreed with much of what Cárdenas attempted at the apogee of radicalism in his administration, and, under highly unusual circumstances, the Roosevelt government decided to negotiate with Mexico.

Other independent leftists, considering central government activism a dubious solution at best, introduced a heavy dose of the peasant-worker perspective into this complex mixture of international politics and economics. In a world caught up in implosive tendencies not only in communications and trade but also in mass politics and massive migrations, their ideological perspective has much to offer those who want to grapple with the continuation of these tendencies into the present.

Although Emily Rosenberg had in mind the genesis of capitalism in peripheral nations, her comments could just as easily apply to the work of U.S. independent leftist and liberal capitalist observers of the Mexican revolution: "As the central actors . . . become less the traders, bankers, and politicians in London or New York and more the inhabitants in particular villages in Peru [or Mexico] or plantations in the West Indies, the focus of the larger theoretical framework [about the nature of revolution] . . . changes. Viewing systems of power from the periphery helps to transcend grand abstract models of development or of underdevelopment and to recall the necessity of contextuality, both in terms of time and place."[11]

The place of the periphery in international history helps to explain why independent leftists had an advantage over the other ideological schools in penetrating the depths of the Mexican revolution: the anarchists and populists chose to look away from the central government and large international commercial and media institutions to see what was happening outside Mexico City; their work evinced a sensitivity to spontaneous, autonomous activity. Of course, the independent leftists sought out unrelated kinds of activity—strong-willed village leadership often had few political connections with mass peasant and labor movements—but the types of social and cultural change they reported were just as significant in their own ways as the arrival of government programs from Mexico City and the incursions of multinational corporations from New York.

Liberal capitalists from Morrow to Kluckhohn located their version of reality in Mexico City and other enclaves of the international economic system. They saw international business and national politics as the decisive forces in Mexico, not the small-scale agriculture and markets of the countryside. The role of the national government was to smooth the way to modernization by creating a favorable environment for foreign and domestic investors. Calles made use of this formula in the late 1920s, but Cárdenas abandoned it with his expropriations and his encouragement of peasant and labor activism.

It remained for the third world liberalism of the 1940s and 1950s to build a sweeping and persuasive amalgam of liberal statism with liberal capitalism. Under its broad formula there was ample room for both the activist promotional state and the aggressive expansionist corporation to operate in a kind of tentative symbiosis. This government–private sector collaboration pushed in several directions at once, but perhaps the most obvious outcome was increased bigness virtually across the board: government agencies, private corporations, urban centers (especially Mexico City), and agricultural enterprises.

Third world liberalism became a powerful ideology. It seemed to offer something for most of the key players in recent Mexican history: government and corporate elites, peasant and labor leaders, intellectuals, foreign investors, and the advocates of international economic integration. Yet nagging questions remain concerning local and national identity, just and equitable treatment of workers and peasants, environmental problems, and the political and social consequences of popular reactions against the massive intrusions of multinational businesses. Mexico and the United States moved to a more intimate economic relationship through the shift of factories and investments to the south in the 1970s and 1980s. In the debate surrounding the North American Free Trade Agreement, opponents and proponents on both sides of the Rio Grande emphasized the extent to which economic integration had taken place even before the treaty was ratified in November of 1993. The January 1994 peasant uprising spearheaded by the Zapatista National Liberation Army underscored the independent left's warnings about the excesses of sudden and unbalanced modernization. The forces pulling the two economies together seem immense and inevitable, yet the independent leftist position devised over half a century of observation and commentary, remains relevant not only for Mexico and the United States but also for many nations caught in the vortex of international economic integration. The rapid rate of socioeconomic change and the uncertainties and inequities that usually accompany uneven thrusts of modernization provide a large potential for narrowly based improvements in material well-being, accompanied by exploitation (both perceived and real), frustration, disorientation, and even alienation in many communities both large and small. Under these circumstances the subject of revolution or, at least, revolutionary movements remains important. Despite the collapse of Marxist-Leninist, Stalinist, Maoist, and Castroite mystiques, the discontent that spawned social instability and political volatility continues to be a prominent factor in world affairs.

The varied experiences of U.S. observers of the Mexican revolution offer some relevant lessons on these issues. Most commentators from the center and the left lauded—at times to excess—the Cárdenas blend of liberal statism, socialism, and respect for popular elections—a mixture that has little in common with the authoritarian traditions of Lenin, Stalin, Mao, and Castro. Many independent leftists were uneasy about the Cárdenas approach; they did not present a comprehensive consensus on the nature of revolution and the path to modernization, but they did provide useful and provocative insights into the turbulence of a world where the juggernaut of expansive capitalism, often supported by eager and pliant politicians, collides head on with the struggles of common people for material subsistence and cultural substance.

The Mexican revolution is no more the prototype for other revolutions than was that of Russia, China, or Cuba. It was, however, a genuine revolution that deserved (and deserves) a place in serious comparative analyses that can yield helpful insights into events in other areas and other circumstances. The role of national governments and the nature of socioeconomic change will continue to spark debates among liberals and conservatives as well as radicals. The work of American observers on the Mexican revolution, obscured by a half-century of Cold War polemics, is relevant to if not resonant with a world of ever more closely connected nations, dominated by huge economic and media systems imposed uneasily upon hopeful but insecure and often resentful peoples.

Notes

Abbreviations

AGN   Archivo General de la Nación
AHR   *American Historical Review*
CBC   Carleton Beals Collection. Mugar Library, Boston University. Boston, Massachusetts
CERM   Centro de Estudios de la Revolución Mexicana Lázaro Cárdenas. Jiquilpan, Michoacán, Mexico
D.S.   U.S. Department of State
FBI   Federal Bureau of Investigation
HAHR   *Hispanic American Historical Review*
JAH   *Journal of American History.*
JLAS   *Journal of Latin American Studies*
MID   U.S. War Department, Military Intelligence Division
SEP   *Saturday Evening Post*

Introduction

1. Gordon S. Wood, *The Radicalism of the American Revolution* (New York, 1992).

2. Barry Carr, *Marxism and Communism in Twentieth Century Mexico* (Lincoln, Neb., 1992), 1-141.

3. Michael Hunt, *Ideology and U.S. Foreign Policy* (New Haven, Conn., 1987), 12.

Chapter 1. Revolution in Context

1. Frederick Katz, *The Secret War in Mexico* (Chicago, 1981), 253-326; Clarence Clendenen, *The United States and Pancho Villa* (Ithaca, N.Y., 1961); and Linda B. Hall and Don M. Coerver, *Revolution on the Border* (Albuquerque, N.M., 1988), 57-77.

2. Hall and Coerver, *Border*, 93-106; and Katz, *Secret War*, 158-66, 298-26, 496-503.

3. For discussions of the term "intellectual," see Edward Shils, "Intellectuals," in *International Encyclopedia of the Social Sciences* (New York, 1968), 7:399-415; Roberto Michels, "Intellectuals," in *International Encyclopedia of the Social Sciences* (New York, 1937), 118-24; Steven Biel, *Independent Intellectuals in the United States, 1910-1945* (New York, 1992); Russell Jacoby, *The Last Intellectuals* (New York, 1987); and Thomas Bender, *Intellect and Public Life* (Baltimore, Md., 1993).

4. Useful studies of the broad and interconnected aspects of cultural and intellectual history include Warren Susman, *Culture as History* (New York, 1973); Richard Pells, *Radical Visions and American Dreams* (New York, 1973); Casey Nelson Blake, *Beloved Community: The Cultural Criticism of Randolph Bourne, Van Wyck Brooks, Waldo Frank and Lewis Mumford* (Chapel Hill, N.C., 1990); Hunt, *Ideology*; T. Jackson Lears, *No Place of Grace* (New York, 1981), and "The Concept of Cultural Hegemony: Problems and Possibilities," *AHR* 90 (June 1985): 567-93; Clifford Geertz, *The Interpretation of Cultures* (New York, 1973); Ronald G. Walters, "Signs of the Times: Clifford Geertz and Historians," *Social Research* 47 (Autumn 1980): 537-56; Robert Kelley, "Ideology and Political Culture from Jefferson to Nixon," *AHR* 82 (June 1977): 531-62; and Lawrence A. Levine, *Highbrow and Lowbrow: The Emergence of Cultural Hierarchy in America* (Cambridge, Mass., 1989). On the history of racist attitudes, see Reginald Horseman, *Race and Manifest Destiny* (Cambridge, Mass., 1981); and Arnaldo de León, *They Called Them Greasers* (Austin, Tex., 1983).

5. Michael Doyle develops this broad theme in his book *Empires* (Ithaca, N.Y.: 1986), but does not include U.S.-Mexican relations.

6. Emily Rosenberg, "Walking the Borders," in *Explaining the History of American Foreign Relations*, ed. Michael Hogan and Thomas G. Paterson (Cambridge, England, 1991), 24-25. The Hogan and Paterson volume contains a valuable selection of articles on the new international history.

7. For two stimulating approaches to the impact of Mexican Culture in the United States see Helen Delpar, *The Enormous Vogue of Things Mexican: Cultural Relations between the United States and Mexico* (Tuscaloosa, Ala. 1992) and Lester Langley, *MexAmerica: Two Countries, One Future* (New York, 1988).

Additional thoughtful discussions of international history are: Christopher Stone, *Border Crossings. Studies in International History* (New York, 1988); Akire Iriye, "The Internationalization of History," *AHR* 94 (Feb. 1989): 1-10; Ian Tyrell, "American Exceptionalism in an Age of International History," *AHR* 96 (Oct. 1991): 1031-55; Michael McGerr, "The Price of the 'New Transnational History' " and "Ian Tyrell Responds," *AHR* 96 (Oct. 1991): 1056-72; John Lewis Gaddis, "New Conceptual Approaches to the Study of American Foreign Relations," *Diplomatic History* 14 (Summer 1990): 405-25; and William Walker, "Drug Control and the Issue of Culture in American Foreign Relations," *Diplomatic History* 12 (Fall 1988): 365-82. A unique and provocative study is Frederick Pike, *The United States and Latin America: Myths and Stereotypes of Civilization and Nature* (Austin. Tex., 1992).

On the reporting of international events, see Robert W. Desmond, *The Information Process: World News Reporting to the Twentieth Century* (Iowa City, Iowa, 1978); Anthony Smith, *The Geopolitics of Information* (New York, 1980); Jeremy Tunstall, *The Media Are American* (New York, 1977); Daniel Czitrom, *Media and the American Mind* (Chapel Hill, N.C., 1982), esp. 145-82; Edward W. Said, *Covering Islam* (New York, 1981); Philip Knightly, *The First Casualty* (New

York, 1975); Thomas A. Bailey, *The Man in the Street*, (New York, 1948); and Ken Ward, *Mass Communications and the Modern World* (Chicago, 1989).

8. Crane Brinton, *Anatomy of Revolution*, rev. ed. (New York, 1952); Barrington Moore, *Injustice: The Social Origins of Obedience and Revolt* (White Plains, N.Y., 1978); James A. Billington, *Fire in the Minds of Men: Origins of Revolutionary Faith* (New York, 1980); and Michael Kimmel, *Revolution: A Sociological Interpretation* (Philadelphia, 1990). For Alan Knight's analyses, see his *The Mexican Revolution*, 2 vols. (Cambridge, England, 1986), and "The Rise and Fall of Cardenismo, c. 1930-c. 1946," in *Mexico since Independence*, ed. Leslie Bethel (Cambridge, 1991), 240-320.

9. Theda Skocpol, *States and Social Revolutions* (Cambridge, Mass., 1979); Jack Goldstone, ed., *Revolutions: Theoretical, Comparative, and Historical Studies* (New York, 1986); Samuel Huntington, *Political Order in Changing Societies* (New Haven, Conn., 1968); John Dunn, *Modern Revolutions* (London, 1972); and Martin Carnoy, *The State and Political Theory* (Princeton, NJ, 1984). On the Carranza government, see Douglas Richmond, *Venustiano Carranza's Nationalist Struggle* (Lincoln, Neb., 1983); and Charles Cumberland, *The Mexican Revolution: The Constitutionalist Years* (Austin, Tex., 1972).

10. See, e.g., Ramón Eduardo Ruíz, *.The Great Rebellion: Mexico 1905-1924* (New York, 1980); Lorenzo Meyer, *El conflicto social y los gobiernos del maximato* (Mexico City, 1978); and James D. Cockroft, *Mexico: Class Formation, Capital Formation, and the State* (New York, 1983).

11. Nora Hamilton, *The Limits of State Autonomy: Post-Revolutionary Mexico* (Princeton, N.J., 1982), examines this pattern in Mexico. Alan Knight has challenged Skocpol's view of statist revolutions and Nora Hamilton's application of these concepts to Mexico in "The Mexican Revolution: 'Bourgeois'? 'Nationalist'? or Just a 'Great Rebellion'?" *Bulletin of Latin American Research* 4, no. 2 (1985): 1-37. John Hart poses his alternative to Skocpol and Hamilton in *Revolutionary Mexico: The Coming and Process of the Mexican Revolution* (Berkeley, Calif., 1987). Another study that differs with Skocpol's emphasis on the importance of the state in revolutions is Fariden Farhi, "State Disintegration and Urban Based Revolutionary Crisis," *Comparative Political Studies* 21 (July 1988): 231-56.

12. Hunt, *Ideology*, esp. 92-198. A helpful study is Leon Baradat, *Political Ideologies: Their Origins and Impact* (Englewood Cliffs, N.J., 1988). Working from a different conceptual framework but also useful is Mona Harrington, *The Dream and Deliverance in American Politics* (New York, 1986).

13. Clifford Geertz, *The Interpretation of Cultures* (New York, 1973), 219-20.

14. Brooks Adams, *The Theory of Social Revolution*, (New York, 1913), and "The Collapse of Capitalistic Government," *Atlantic Monthly* 111 (April 1913): 433-43. See also Arthur F. Beringause, *Brooks Adams* (New York, 1955).

15. O. Henry, *Cabbages and Kings*, (New York, 1904), 8-9.

16. Paxton Hibben, "Why Is a Revolution?" *North American Review* 198 (July 1913): 60-74.

17. Lyford Edwards, *The Natural History of Revolution* (Chicago, 1927), 16.

18. Crane Brinton, *Anatomy of Revolution* (Englewood Cliffs, N.J., 1938), 7.

19. Frank Tannenbaum, *Peace by Revolution* (New York, 1933).

20. Jackson Lears, "The Concept of Cultural Hegemony," 567-93; Hunt, *Ideology*: David McClellan, *Ideology* (Minneapolis, Minn., 1986); John K. Roth and Robert C. Whittmore, eds., *Ideology and the American Experience* (Washington, D.C., 1986); Carnoy, *State and Political Theory*; Baradat, *Political Ideologies*; and Donald C. Hodges and Ross Gandy, *Mexico 1910-1976: Reform or Revolution?* (London, 1979).

21. For insightful discussions of anarchism, see Alan Ritter, *Anarchism: A*

Theoretical Analysis (Cambridge, England, 1980); George Woodstock, *Anarchism: A History of Libertarian Ideas and Movements* (Cleveland, Ohio, 1967); and John Hart, *Anarchism and the Mexican Working Class, 1860-1931*, 2d ed. (Austin, Tex., 1987). On populism, see Craig Calhoun, *The Question of Social Struggle* (Chicago, 1982); Lawrence Goodwyn, *Democratic Promise: The Populist Movement in America* (New York, 1976); Norman Pollack, *The Populist Response to Industrial America* (Cambridge, Mass., 1962); and Michael Conniff, ed., *Latin American Populism in Comparative Perspective* (Albuquerque, N.M., 1982). For a critique of modern liberalism from a perspective not far removed from that of the anarchists and populists in this study, see Arthur A. Ekirch Jr., *The Decline of American Liberalism* (New York, 1967).

22. Some general studies of Communism in the United States include Paul Buhle, *Marxism in the USA* (London, 1987); Theodore Draper, *American Communism and Soviet Russia* (New York, 1986); and Harvey Klehr, *The Heyday of American Communism* (New York, 1984).

The apolitical or partially politicized bohemian writers and artists held a cultural rather than an ideological point of view. Sometimes overly sentimental toward the Indian or sharply critical of the workings of the Mexican government, the bohemians provided frequently astute but subjective observations. To place them in any one category would be misleading; their sympathies lay with the masses, and their art, essays, and fiction might fit into any of a number of slots to the left of center. On bohemianism in the United States, see John P. Diggins, *The American Left in the Twentieth Century* (New York, 1973), 73-106; Emily Hahn, *Romantic Rebels* (Boston 1967); and Leslie Fishbein, *Rebels in Bohemia* (Chapel Hill, N.C., 1982).

23. Eyler Simpson, *The Ejido: Mexico's Way Out* (Chapel Hill, N.C., 1937. For general studies on the state as the prime factor in economic development, see Carnoy, *Political Theory*; Skocpol, *Social Revolutions*; and a specialized study on Mexico in the 1920s and 1930s, Hamilton's *State Autonomy*.

24. James Kloppenberg, *Uncertain Victory* (Oxford 1986); Ellis Hawley, *The Great War and the Search for a Modern Order* (New York, 1979); Robert Wiebe, *The Search for Order* (New York, 1967); and Charles Forcey, *The Crossroads of Liberalism* (Oxford, 1962).

25. Discussions of various progressive attitudes toward foreign policy in general and imperialism in particular are found in William Leuchtenberg, "Progressivism and Imperialism: The Progressive Movement and American Foreign Policy, 1989-1916," *Mississippi Valley Historical Review* 39 (Dec. 1952): 483-504; Gerald Markowitz, "Progressivism and Imperialism: a Return to First Principles," *Historian* 37 (Feb. 1975): 257-75; Robert Dallek, *The American Style in Foreign Policy* (New York, 1983) 62-122. See also two books crucial for this study: Mark Gilderhus, *Diplomacy and Revolution: U.S.-Mexican Relations under Wilson and Carranza* (Tucson, Ariz., 1977); and *Pan American Visions: Woodrow Wilson and the Western Hemisphere* (Tucson, Ariz., 1986).

26. Hunt, *Ideology*, 92-139; Lloyd C. Gardner, *Safe for Democracy* (New York, 1984); Josefina Zoraida Vázquez and Lorenzo Meyer, *The United States and Mexico* (Chicago, 1985); N. Gordon Levin Jr., *Woodrow Wilson and World Politics: America's Response to War and Revolution* (New York, 1968); William Appleman Williams, *America Confronts a Revolutionary World* (New York, 1975); and John Milton Cooper Jr., *The Warrior and the Priest* (Cambridge, Mass., 1987).

27. Robert Schulzinger, *The Wise Men of Foreign Affairs* (New York, 1984), 11.

28. Robert Freeman Smith, *The United States and Revolutionary Nationalism in Mexico* (Chicago, 1972), 229-59.

29. Wiebe, *Search*, 133-63; and Robert Schulzinger, *The Making of the Diplomatic Mind* (Middletown, Conn., 1975).

30. I use the word "conservative" in a fairly specific sense; many academic and popular writers define it more generally to include "liberal capitalists." For some provocative studies, see Clinton Rossiter, *Conservativism in America* (New York, 1962); Milton and Rose Friedman, *Free To Choose* (New York, 1979); Daniel Boorstin, *The Americans: The Democratic Experience* (New York, 1973); and Robert Higgs, *Crisis and Leviathan* (New York, 1987).

31. Horseman, *Race and Manifest Destiny*; Hunt, *Ideology*; and de Leon, *They Called Them Greasers*.

32. For perceptive discussions of the role of the border region, W. Dirk Raat, *Los Revoltosos: Mexico's Rebels in the United States, 1903-1923* (College Station, Tex., 1981); william Beezley, *Insurgent Governor: Abraham González and the Mexican Revolution* (Lincoln, Neb., 1973); Hall and Coerver, *Border*; and Hector Aguilar Camín, *La frontera nómada* (Mexico, 1977).

Chapter 2. A Search for Meaning

1. Hunt, *Ideology*, 46-150.

2. John J. Johnson, *Latin America in Caricature* (Austin, Tex., 1980), 136-39, 144-49, 226-29.

3. Allen L. Woll, *The Latin Image in American Film* (Los Angeles, 1980), 6-16.

4. Kevin Brownlow, *The Parade's Gone By* (Berkeley, Calif., 1966); New York Times, May 10, 1914; Woll, *Latin Image*, 10-12; and W.A. Swanberg, *Citizen Hearst* (New York, 1961), 352-54.

5. Raat, *Los Revoltosos*, 280.

6. Herbert Ingram Priestley, "Into Mexico and Out" (unpublished MS, Priestley Papers), 3.

7. Quoted in John Perry, *Jack London: An American Myth* (Chicago, 1981), 281; see also *Nation* 99 (July 2, 1914): 7.

8. Jack London, "The Trouble Makers in Mexico," *Collier's* 53 (June 13, 1914): 14.

9. Ibid., 13-14.

10. Ibid., 25.

11. Richard Harding Davis, *Three Gringos in Venezuela and Central America* (New York, 1896); Scott Osborne and Robert L. Phillips, *Richard Harding Davis* (Boston, 1978), 60-63, 80-82; and Arthur Lubow, *The Reporter Who Would Be King* (New York, 1992).

12. Quoted in "How Davis Got a Story," *Literary Digest* 48 (May 23, 1914): 1285.

13. Richard Harding Davis, "When a War Is Not a War," *Scribners* 56 (July 1914): 41-52; Osborn and Phillips, *Richard Harding Davis*, 80-82; and Perry, *Jack London*, 280.

14. Frederick Palmer, "Mexico: The American Spirit in Vera Cruz," *Everybody's Magazine* 30 (June 1914): 814-20, and "Can Mexico Rule Itself?" *Everybody's Magazine* 31 (July 1914): 79-80. For Palmer's earlier experiences in Mexico, see his *Central America and Its Problems* (New York, 1910), 1-43.

15. Palmer, "Mexico: The American Spirit," 808.

16. Ibid., 820. See also Frederick Palmer, "Mexico: Watchful Perspiring in Veracruz," *Everybody's Magazine* 31 (July 1914): 65-78, and "Mexico: Army Housekeeping," *Everybody's Magazine* 31 (Aug. 1914): 198-205.

17. James Creelman, *Díaz: Master of Mexico* (New York, 1911).

18. James Creelman, "Underlying Causes of the Mexican Revolution,"

North American Review 193 (April 1911): 601-2. For other racially slanted interpretations, see William E. Carson, *Mexico: Wonderland of the Sun* (New York, 1907); and Nevin O. Winter, *Mexico and Her People of Today* (Boston, 1909).

19. These commentators soon ceased to write on Mexico. Creelman became associate editor of the *New York Evening Mail* (*Who's Who* [Chicago, 1912]); London returned to California discredited in the eyes of many leftists because of his articles on Mexico (Perry, *Jack London*, 280-82; Davis and Palmer went to Europe in time for World War I (Osborne and Phillips, *Richard Harding Davis*, 83-87; and Palmer, *With My Own Eyes* [Indianapolis, 1932], 278-98).

20. *The Papers of Woodrow Wilson*, ed. Arthur Link (Princeton, N.J., 1966-), 28: 450. for insightful commentary on Wilson's Mobile Address, see Gilderhus, *Pan American Visions*, 16-20.

21. Samuel G. Blythe, "Mexico: The Record of a Conversation with President Wilson," *SEP* 186 (May 1914): 3.

22. Ibid., 4.

23. Ibid.

24. Ibid., 3, 71. On land reform in New Zealand, see Len Richardson, "Parties and Political Change," in *The Oxford History of New Zealand*, ed. W.H. Oliver (London, 1981), 197-241; and Keith Sinclair, *A History of New Zealand* (London, 1980), 172-82, 204-7, 237-38.

25. Gilderhus, *Diplomacy*, 1-52; and Darden Asbury Pyron, "Mexico as an Issue in American Politics" (Ph.D. diss., Univ. of Virginia, 1975), 108-230.

26. Gilderhus, *Diplomacy*, 56-57.

27. Blythe, "Mexico," 3.

28. Gilderhus, *Diplomacy*, 115.

29. Ibid., 53-116, and *Pan American Visions*, 101-12, 124-27, 142-58. See also Smith, *Revolutionary Nationalism*, 71-189; and Lorenzo Meyer, *Los grupos de presión extranjeros en el Mexico revolucionario* (Mexico, 1973).

30. Salvatore Pasco III, *John Barrett, Progressive Era Diplomat: A Study of a Commercial Expansionist, 1887-1920* (University, Ala. 1973); Smith, Revolutionary Nationalism, 130-32; and Henry Bruere, "Mexico Is Righting Herself," *Survey* 47 (Oct. 1921): 16-18.

31. Smith, *Revolutionary Nationalism*, 128-32; and Warren I. Cohen, *Empire without Tears* (New York, 1987), 19-20, 30-33, 65-68.

32. See Chapters 13-14.

33. Herbert J. Doherty, "Alexander McKelway: Preacher to Progressives," *Journal of Southern History* 24 (May 1958): 179-90.

34. McGregor [Alexander McKelway], "Eating Its Children." *Harper's* 59 (Dec. 19, 1914): 596, and "Revolution and Concessions," *Harper's* 58 (Dec. 6, 1913): 7-8. These articles indicated an overriding belief that Mexico should be left to solve its own problems, but McGregor, "President Wilson's Mexican Policy: An Interpretation," *Outlook* 113 (May 3, 1916): 36-39, supported Wilson's policies in Mexico by accepting limited intervention.

35. John Womack, *Zapata and the Mexican Revolution* (New York, 1970), 393-404.

36. Samuel Guy Inman, "A Personal View of Carranza," *Outlook* 111 (Oct. 27, 1915): 470-71. See also Inman, *Intervention in Mexico* (New York, 1919).

37. Justin Kaplan, *Lincoln Steffens* (New York, 1974).

38. Lincoln Steffens, "Making Friends with Mexico," *Collier's* 58 (Nov. 25, 1916): 5-6, 22-23.

39. Steffens, "Into Mexico and—Out," *Everybody's Magazine* 34 (May 1916): 543-44.

40. Ibid., 533-46; Steffens, "Making Friends," 5-6, 22; and Inman, *Intervention*, 80-118.

41. E.V. Niemeyer, *Revolution at Querétaro* (Austin, Tex., 1974); and Linda Hall, *Alvaro Obregón* (College Station, Tex., 1981). For a more favorable view of Carranza, see Richmond, *Venustiano Carranza*.

42. Another liberal statist commentator was Leander de Bekker, who wrote *The Plot against Mexico* (New York, 1919).

43. Harry H. Stein, "Lincoln Steffens and the Mexican Revolution," *American Journal of Economics and Sociology* 34 (April 1975): 199.

44. Robert Rosenstone, *Romantic Revolutionary: A Biography of John Reed* (New York, 1975), 169.

45. Diana Christopulos, "American Radicals and the Mexican Revolution, 1900-1925" (Ph.D. diss., State University of New York at Binghamton, 1980), 195.

46. Rosenstone, *Romantic Revolutionary*, 388. From his contacts in northern Mexico, Reed grasped that Emiliano Zapata was perhaps the most authentic champion of the Mexican people—"the great man of the Revolution" (quoted, 163). Reed's requests for assignment to Zapata's home state of Morelos were denied by editor Carl Hovey of the *Metropolitan*, depriving him of the opportunity to report on one of the revolution's most constant advocates of land reform.

47. Christopulos, "American Radicals," 196.

48. Jim Tuck, *Pancho Villa and John Reed* (Tucson, Ariz., 1984), 108-10.

49. John Reed, *Insurgent Mexico* (1914; New York, 1969), 53, 57, 64-66, 90-91, 115-22, 133, 150-51, 158. Reed noted Villa's vague plans to found military colonies for veterans of the revolution after the fighting ended (133) but made little commentary.

50. John Kenneth Turner, *Barbarous Mexico* (Austin Tex., 1969), 242-58; Ethel Duffy Turner, *Revolution in Baja California: Ricardo Flores Magón's High Noon* (Detroit, Mich., 1981), 4-5; and Raat, *Los Revoltosos*, 240-44.

51. John Kenneth Turner, "Mexico's 'Bandit' Armies," *Collier's* 51 (April 5, 1913): 11, 21.

52. John Kenneth Turner, "Villareal Inspired by Ideals of Socialism, Is Leader of the Revolution in Mexico," *Appeal to Reason*, April 10, 1915, p. 1.

53. Reed, *Insurgent Mexico*, 116.

54. It must be stated that Turner had the advantage of writing in 1916 close to the nadir of Villa's revolutionary career, while Reed saw him near his apogee in 1913. See Turner's three articles in *Appeal to Reason*: "Recall the U.S. Troops from the Mexican Border!", March 25, 1916, p. 1; "The Appeal Breaks Conspiracy of Silence Regarding Military negligence on Border," April 18, 1916, p. 1; and "Villa Has Sold Out to Wall Street," April 3, 1915, p. 1.

55. Granville Hicks, *John Reed: The Making of a Revolutionary* (New York, 1936), 207-8.

56. For a perspective on this elusive character, see Katz, *Secret War*, 260-65, 280-86.

57. Reed, *Insurgent Mexico*, 218.

58. Christopulous, "American Radicals," 220-21; and John Kenneth Turner, "Constitutionalists, Led by Carranza, Are Red Revolutionists of Mexico," *Appeal to Reason*, April 17, 1915, p. 1.

59. Hart, *Anarchism*, 72-73; Colin MacLachlan, *Anarchism and the Mexican Revolution* (Berkeley, Calif., 1991), and Womack, *Zapata*, 393-404.

60. Edward I. Bell, "The Mexican Problem: Restricted Intervention—the True Solution," *Outlook* 111 (Oct. 20, 1915): 421. For the entire series, see Bell, "The Mexican Problem" *Outlook* 111 (Oct. 6, 13, 20, and 27): 320-326, 359-60, 421-27, 467-71. Also see Bell, *The Political Shame of Mexico* (New York, 1914).

61. Clarence Barron, *The Mexican Problem* (Boston, 1917), 13.

62. U.S. Senate, Committee on Foreign Relations, *Investigation of Mexican Affairs* (Washington, D.C., 1920), 829.

63. See, e.g., *New York Times*, Dec. 3, 1919, p. 1; Dec. 5, 1919, p. 2; Dec. 7, 1919, p. 1; and Dec. 9, 1919, p. 2. See also Gilderhus, *Diplomacy*, 96-105; Clifford W. Trow, "Woodrow Wilson and the Mexican Interventionist Movement of 1919," *JAH* 58 (June 1971): 46-72; and Dan La Botz, *Edward L. Doheny: Petroleum, Power, and Politics in the United States and Mexico* (New York, 1991).

64. Thomas Edward Gibbon, *Mexico under Carranza* (New York, 1919), 40; and Gilderhus, *Diplomacy*, 75-76.

65. Jorge Vera Estañol, *Carranza and His Bolshevik Regime* (Los Angeles, 1920), 83.

66. Ibid., 64.

67. Niemeyer, *Revolution at Querétaro*; Berta Ulloa, *La Constitución de 1917* (Mexico, 1983); and Richmond, *Venustiano Carranza.* Doheny financed five studies by academics who were less concerned with Bolshevism than their benefactor but did emphasize the problems that confronted Carranza and his successors. See Walter Flavius McCaleb, *Present and Past Banking in Mexico* (New York, 1920), and *The Public Finances of Mexico* (New York, 1921); Chester Lloyd Jones, *Mexico and Its Reconstruction* (New York, 1921); and Wallace Thompson, *The Mexican Mind* (Boston, 1922), the *The People of Mexico* (New York, 1922).

68. Christopulos, "American Radicals," 378-87, 415-32.

69. Ibid., 378-87.

70. *Gale's Review* (June-July 1920): 5-6, quoted in Christopulos, "American Radicals," 421-22. See also *New York Times*, Dec. 20, 1919, p. 6.

71. Theodore Draper, *The Roots of American Communism* (New York, 1957), 60-64, 106-9, 164-75; and Buhle, *Marxism*, 111-12.

72. Christopulos, "American Radicals," 353-56, 435-37.

73. Ibid., 415-33.

74. Ibid., 436-37; and Draper, *Roots*, 293-302.

75. Christopulos, "American Radicals," 415-539; Manuel Gómez, "From Mexico to Moscow," *Survey* (Oct. 1964): 33-42; Charles Shipman, *It Had to Be Revolution* (Ithaca, N.Y., 1992), 50-91; and *New York Times*, Dec. 26, 1919, p. 6. On Roy as a German agent, see Katz, *Secret War*, 423-24.

76. Carleton Beals, *Glass Houses* (New York, 1938), 50-51.

77. Lawrence Kinnaird, Frederick L. Paxson, and Lesley Byrd Simpson, "Herbert Ingram Priestley" (Berkeley, Calif., 194), Bolton Papers; Woodrow Borah to author, Sept. 10, 1988. On the ideas of historians in the early twentieth century, see Richard Hofstadter, *Three Progressive Historians: Turner, Parrington, and Beard* (New York, 1968); John Higham with Leonard Krieger and Felix Gilbert, *History: The Development of Historical Studies in the United States* (Englewood Cliffs, N.J., 1965); David Noble, *Historians against History* (Minneapolis, 1965); and Ian Tyrell, *The Absent Marx* (New York, 1986).

78. Herbert Ingram Priestley, *José de Gálvez: Visitor General of New Spain* (Berkeley, Calif., 1916).

79. Priestley to E.M. Sait, Nov. 25, 1921, Priestley Papers.

80. Frederick Jackson Turner's publications include *The Significance of Sections in American History* (New York, 1932) and *The Frontier in American History* (New York, 1920). Herbert Eugene Bolton's many works include *The Spanish Borderlands* (New Haven, 1920) and (with Thomas Marshall), *The Colonization of North America* (New York, 1920).

81. Borah to author, Sept. 10, 1988. For example contrast Herbert Ingram

Priestley, *The Mexican Nation: A History* (New York, 1923), 15-43, 72-75, 115-35; with his *José de Gálvez*, 210-33, 267-86.

82. Herbert Ingram Priestley, "On the Outside in Mexico" (Priestley Papers), 30.

83. Priestley, review of three books by Wallace Thompson, *HAHR* 3 (Nov. 1922): 724. See Wallace Thompson, *Trading with Mexico* (New York, 1921), *The People of Mexico* (New York, 1921), and *The Mexican Mind* (Boston, 1922).

84. Priestley, *Mexican Nation*, 428-29.

85. Ibid., 453.

86. Ibid., 428.

87. Robert L. Brunhouse, *Franz Bloom, Maya Explorer* (Albuquerque, N.M., 1976), 40-45, 61-69, 260.

88. William Gates, "Zapata: The Protector of Morelos," *World's Work* (April 1919): 658. This article was the third of five by Gates under the general title "The Four Governments of Mexico" in *World's Work*. The others were "Creole, Mestizo, or Indian," 37 (Feb. 1919): 385-92; "Rehabilitation or Intervention," 37 (March 1919): 570-80; "Yucatan: An Experiment in Syndicalism," 38 (May 1919): 58-68; and "Carranza: 'Constitutionalist,' " 38 (June 1919): 214-24.

89. Gates, "Zapata", 661.

90. Ibid., 662

91. Gates, "Rehabilitation," 570-80; William Gates, "A Solution to the Mexican Imbroglio," *Forum* 62 (Oct. 1919): 415-26, and "Mexico Today" *North American Review* 209 (Jan. 1919): 70-83.

Chapter 3. Revolutionary Enthusiasm

1. Edward Weston, *The Daybooks of Edward Weston*, ed. Nancy Newhall, 2 vols. (Millerton, N.Y., 1961-63), 1:41-44, 60, 71, 129-30, 139, 143.

2. Helen Bowyer, "Why Not Mexico This Summer?" *Nation* 123 (May 23, 1923): 594-95.

3. Henry C. Schmidt, "The American Intellectual Discovery of Mexico in the 1920's," *South Atlantic Quarterly*, 77 (Summer 1978): 335-51.

4. Herbert Corey, "Adventures Down the West Coast of Mexico," *National Geographic* 42 (Nov. 1992): 485. See also Corey, "Along the Old Spanish Road in Mexico," *National Geographic* 43 (March 1923): 225-81, and "The Isthmus of Tehuantepec," *National Geographic* 45 (May 1924): 549-79.

5. Charles E. Chapman. "Travel in Mexico," in *Mexican Yearbook*, ed. R.G. Cleland (Los Angeles, 1922), 154-63.

6. Bowyer, "why Not Mexico?" 595.

7. Weston, *Daybooks*, 1:13-15.

8. Ernest Gruening, *Many Battles* (New York, 1973), 110.

9. Beals, *Glass Houses*, 174-77.

10. Weston, *Daybooks*, 1 : 75-76.

11. Beals, *Glass Houses*, 9-78, 174-282.

12. See Darlene Harbour Unrue, *Truth and Vision in Katherine Anne Porter's Fiction* (Athens, Ga., 1985), 12-26, 71-83, 106-15; Joan Givner, *Katherine Anne Porter: A Life* (New York, 1982), 164-66; Thomas F. Walsh, *Katherine Anne Porter and Mexico: The Illusion of Eden* (Austin, Tex., 1992), 14-94; and Delpar, *Enormous Vogue*, 34, 135, 177-80.

13. Katherine Anne Porter, "That Tree," *Virginia Quarterly Review* 10 (July 1934): 351-61; Unrue, *Truth and Vision*, 131-39. See also John A. Britton, *Carleton Beals: A Radical Journalist in Latin America*, (Albuquerque, N.M., 1987), 31-33.

14. Nancy Newhall, introduction to Weston, *Daybooks*, 1: xviii; and Amy Conger, *Edward Weston in Mexico* (Albuquerque, N.M., 1983), 4-11.

15. Weston, *Daybooks*, 1: 129-30, 134, 139; Carleton Beals, interview with author, June 11, 1973.

16. Beals to Tannenbaum, n.d. (probably 1923), Tannenbaum Papers; Lesley Simpson to Beals, July 18, 1923, and Aug. 22, 1932, CBC.

17. Porter to Beals, Jan. 16, 1926, CBC; Carleton Beals, *Brimstone and Chili* (New York, 1927), 316-18; and Weston, *Daybooks*, 1: 140-41, 152.

18. Givner, *Katherine Anne Porter*, 164-68; Weston, *Daybooks*, 1:129-30, 138-39; and Beals, *Glass Houses*, 174-205, 236-56.

19. Leslie Fishbein, *Rebels in Bohemia* (Chapel Hill, N.C., 1982).

20. Susannah Glusker, interview with author, May 12, 1988; Anita Brenner, "Biographical Information," n.d., Brenner Collection.

21. Anita Brenner, *Idols behind Altars* (Boston, 1970), 171-76; and Weston, *Daybooks*, 1: 16, 32, 174.

22. Mildred Constantine, *Tina Modotti: A Fragile Life* (New York, 1975), 75.

23. Ella Wolfe to Beals, March 25, 1925, CBC; and Bertram Wolfe, *A Life in Two Centuries* (New York, 1981), 350-59.

24. Dos Passos to Beals, Dec. 13, 1926, CBC.

25. Townsend Ludington, *John Dos Passos: A Twentieth Century Odyssey* (New York, 1980), 250.

26. Beals, interview with author, June 13, 1973; Gruening to Beals, Jan. 22 and March 22, 1924, CBC.

27. Weston, *Daybooks*, 1: 137.

28. Ella Wolfe to Beals, June 10, 1925, CBC; and Ella Wolfe to author, July 30, 1984.

29. Ernest Gruening, *Mexico and Its Heritage* (New York, 1928), 383.

30. Gruening, *Many Battles*, 3-106.

31. Harold Ickes, *The Secret Diary of Harold Ickes* (New York, 1954), 1: 304-5, 594, and 2: 6-7, 57, 150, 160-61.

32. Anita Brenner Diary, Dec. 4 and 20 1925, and April 12, 1927, Brenner Collection.

33. Ibid., March 12, 1927.

34. Dewey to Beals, July 22, 1926, CBC; and John Dewey, *John Dewey's Impressions of Soviet Russia and the Revolutionary World: Mexico—China—Turkey* (New York, 1964), 113-60. See also Robert B. Westbrook, *John Dewey and American Democracy* (Ithaca, N.Y., 1991); Charles Howlett, *Troubled Philosopher: John Dewey and the Struggle for World Peace* (Port Washington, N.Y., 1977); and George Dykhuizen, *The Life and Mind of John Dewey* (Carbondale, Ill., 1973).

35. Weston, *Daybooks*, 1: 158.

36. Porter to Ernestine Evans, Oct. 3, 1930, quoted in Unrue, *Truth and Vision*, 84-85.

37. Brenner Diary, Jan. 1, 1929.

38. *Who's Who* (Chicago, 1952), 2384.

39. Memorandum on Frank Tannenbaum, War Department, MID 10516-533, Aug. 1926; Beals, interview with author, June 13, 1973; V.W. Hughes to J. Edgar Hoover, Aug. 8, 1931, FBI Records 61-694-1; and Helen Delpar, "Frank Tannenbaum: The Making of a Mexicanist, 1914-1933," *Americas* 45 (Oct. 1988): 153-71.

40. Frank Tannenbaum, "Mexico—Promise," *Survey Graphic* 52 (May 1924): 129.

41. *Literary Digest* 84 (Jan. 31, 1925): 38-40.

42. John Lloyd Stephens, *Incidents of Travel in Central America, Chapas, and Yucatan*, 2 vols. (1841; rept. New York, 1969).

43. See, e.g., Adolph Bandelier, *On the Social Organization and Mode of Government of the Ancient Mexicans* (Cambridge, Mass., 1879).

44. Frederick Starr, *In Indian Mexico* (Chicago, 1908).

45. Katherine Anne Porter, *Outline of Mexican Popular Arts and Crafts* (Los Angeles, 1922), 33.

46. Ibid., 6.

47. Katherine Anne Porter, "María Concepcíon," *Century* 105 (Dec. 1922): 224-39.

48. Carleton Beals, *Mexico: An Interpretation* (New York, 1923), 3-17, 205-14 (quotation, 205).

49. Frances Toor, "Editor's Foreword," *Mexican Folkways* 1 (June-July 1925): 3-4. See also Toor to Brenner, March 15, 1925, and Toor to Beals, March 15, 1925, Brenner Collection.

50. Robert Redfield, "The Cerahpa and the Castiyohpa in Tepoztlán," *Mexican Folkways* 3 (June-July 1927): 137-43; "An Ancient Art in an Ancient Village," *Mexican Folkways* 4 (Oct.-Dec. 1928): 137-43; and "The Carnival in Tepoztlán, Morelos," *Mexican Folkways* 5 (Jan.-March 1929): 30-34.

51. John Dos Passos, "Paint the Revolution," *New Masses* 2 (March 1927): 15.

52. Ibid.; and Ludington, *John Dos Passos*, 250-51.

53. Dos Passos to Rumsey Martin, Dec. 1926-Jan. 1927, in *The Fourteenth Chronicle*, ed. Townsend Ludington (Boston, 1973), 365-66.

54. Brenner, *Idols*, 206-26.

55. Ibid., 314.

56. See, e.g., ibid., 32, 50-55, 229-39. Brenner's *Idols* also assessed the political crisis of the late 1920s and recognized the limitations of art and culture as forces for beneficial social change within an authoritarian political system. See Chapter 7 for the U.S. leftists' disillusionment with Mexico's leadership.

57. Drewey Wayne Gunn, *American and British Writers in Mexico, 1556-1973* (Austin, Tex., 1974) 123-24. Studies of Lawrence include Tony Slade, *D.H. Lawrence* (New York, 1970); Paul Delaney, *D.H. Lawrence's Nightmare* (New York, 1978); James C. Cowan, *D.H. Lawrence's American Journey* (Cleveland, 1970); Eliot Gilbert Fay, *Lorenzo in Search of the Sun* (London, 1955); Philip Hobsbawm, *A Reader's Guide to D.H. Lawrence* (New York, 1981); and Jeffrey Meyers, *D.H. Lawrence: A Biography* (New York, 1990), 283-325.

58. Katherine Anne Porter, "Quetzalcoatl," in *Collected Essays and Occasional Writings of Katherine Anne Porter* (New York, 1973), 422-23. See also Toor, "Mexico through Frightened Eyes," *Mexican Folkways* 2 (Aug.-Sept. 1926): 45-46; Weston, *Daybooks*, 1: 101-3; and Beals, *Glass Houses*, 186-89.

59. D.H. Lawrence, *Studies in Classic American Literature* (New York, 1964), 131-43 (quotation, 137).

60. D.H. Lawrence, *Mornings in Mexico* (New York, 1927), 21-49, 68-73. See also Gunn, *American and British Writers*, 123-44; Witter Bynner, *Journey with Genius: Recollections concerning D.H. Lawrence* (New York, 1974); Meyers, *D.H. Lawrence*; Keith Sagar, *D.H. Lawrence: Life into Art* (Athens, Ga., 1985); and Ross Parmenter, *Lawrence in Oaxaca* (Salt Lake City, Utah, 1984).

61. Lawrence, *Mornings*, 103.

62. Ibid., 104. See also Pascal Bruckner, *Tears of the White Man* (New York, 1986), discussed in Chapter 15.

63. Lawrence, *Mornings*, 108-11.

64. Ibid., 118-22.

65. Edward Shils, *Center and Periphery: Essays in Microsociology* (Chicago, 1975), 127-34. For a critical assessment of charisma in modern society, see Richard Sennett, *The Fall of Public Man* (New York, 1974), 259-73. My concept of charisma here is similar to that of Enrique Krauze in his analysis of leading

cultural figures in Mexico, *Caudillos culturales en la revolución Mexicana* (Mexico, 1976).

66. Dos Passos, "Paint the Revolution," 15. For an assessment of Rivera's ideas and personality, see "Entrevista con Raoul Fournier" (1977), Archivo de la Palabra, Instituto Nacional de Antropología e Historia.

67. Gruening, *Mexico*, 640.

68. Brenner, *Idols*, 277-87.

69. Ibid., 287.

70. On the influence of Vasconcelos among the young intellectuals of the "Generation of 1915," see Krauze, *Caudillos*, 66-67, 104-5, 186-90, 266-68. The historical context for his education reforms is covered in Mary Kay Vaughan, *The State, Education, and Social Class in Mexico, 1880-1928* (DeKalb, Ill., 1982).

71. Ernest Gruening "Up in Arms against Ignorance," *Collier's* 72 (Dec. 1, 1923): 8, 32-33.

72. Frank Tannenbaum, "The Miracle School," *Century* 106 (Aug. 1923): 499-506.

73. Katherine Anne Porter, "Where Presidents Have No Friends," *Century* 106 (July 1922): 410-13; and Beals, *Mexico*, 78-85.

74. Tannenbaum, "Mexico—a Promise," 130.

75. Ernest Gruening, "The Assassination of Mexico's Ablest Stateman," *Current History* 17 (Feb. 1924): 739, and "Felipe Carrillo," *Nation* 118 (Jan. 16, 1924): 61-62. for a historical assessment of Carrillo, see Gilbert Joseph, *Revolution from Without: Yucatán, Mexico, and the United States* (Cambridge, England, 1982), 185-287.

76. José Vasconcelos, *El Desastre* (Mexico, 1968), 68-86, 106.

77. Gruening to Beals, Jan. 22, 1924, CBC.

Chapter 4. The Limits of the Techniques of Hospitality

1. Schulzinger, *Diplomatic Mind*; James Prothro, *Dollar Decade* (Baton Rouge, La., 1954); Beals, *Glass Houses*, 362-65; James Sheffield, "Mexico" (memoir of his ambassadorship), Sheffield Papers; and Memorandum, Division of Mexican Affairs, Feb. 15, 1926, D.S. 711.12/695.

2. Paul Hollander, *Political Pilgrims* (New York, 1981).

3. Ibid., 3-39. Mexico's qualifications for the third criterion were of short duration: its adoption in the 1930s of socialist education as official doctrine in the nation's schools, the hyperactivity of outspoken Marxist labor leader Vicente Lombardo Toledano, and the presence of collectivism in its land reform program. See Chapters 9-12.

4. Gruening, *Many Battles*, 109-10.

5. Gruening, "The Man Who Brought Mexico Back," *Collier's* 72 (Sept. 29, 1923): 7, 26-27, and "Up in Arms," 8, 32-33.

6. James J. Horn, "Diplomacy by Ultimatum: Ambassador Sheffield and Mexican-American Relations, 1924-1927" (Ph.D. diss., State University of New York at Buffalo, 1969), 91-94.

7. Jesús Silva Herzog to Tannenbaum, Oct. 19, 1926; Tannenbaum to Silva Herzog. Sept. 29 and Nov. 3, 1926, and July 27, 1927; Angel Batiz to Tannenbaum, Sept. 22, 1926; Tannenbaum to Batiz, Sept. 29, 1926; Batiz to Tannenbaum, Oct. 7, 1926; Tannenbaum to Batiz, Oct. 8, 1926; Batiz to Tannenbaum, June 22, 1927; Tannenbaum to Juan de Dios Bojórquez, April 13, 1926, and May 26, 1972—all in Tannenbaum Papers.

8. Delpar, "Frank Tannenbaum," 161.

9. Beals, *Glass Houses*, 177-79, and *Mexico*, pref. and 197-98. See also Britton, *Carleton Beals*, 18-19.

10. Frank Tannenbaum, "The Stakes In Mexico," *Survey* 51 (Jan. 1, 1924): 318-21, and "Mexico—a Promise," 131.

11. Beals, *Mexico*, 137-41. The Calles government took a strong interest in its image and often followed the work of U.S. journalists who had close contacts with the administration. See Aarón Sáenz to Manuel Téllez, Feb. 4, 1926; and Téllez to Sáenz, Feb. 4, 1926, AREM III 628 (010)/1 LE 552-2.

12. Frank Tannenbaum, "Mr. Gompers' Last Convention," *Survey* 53 (Jan. 1, 1925): 391.

13. Ibid., 393.

14. Gruening, *Many Battles*, 124-29.

15. Ernest Gruening, "Emerging Mexico III: Land and Labor," *Nation* 120 (June 24, 1925): 713-15. Socialist William English Walling also experienced Calles's hospitality and produced a book praising his regime's moderation: *The Mexican Question* (New York, 1927).

16. Minister of Foreign Relations Aarón Sáenz, Ambassador Manuel Téllez, and other officials monitored the U.S. press in these years. Téllez was encouraged by Gruening's articles in the mid-1920s: Téllez to Soledad González (Calles's secretary), Dec. 1, 1925, AGN Ramo Obregón-Calles 104-A-36. See also Aarón Sáenz to Fernando Torreblanca, June 24, 1925, AGN Ramo Obregón-Calles 121-R-G-9; John A. Britton, "Propaganda, Politics, and the Image of Stability: The Mexican Government and the U.S. Print Media, 1921-1929" *Annals of the Southeastern Council on Latin American Studies* 9 (march 1988): 5-28.

17. Gruening, *Mexico*, ix.

18. Ibid., 355-90.

19. Carleton Beals, "The Revolution in Mexico," *New Republic* 52 (Oct. 25, 1927): 255-56.

20. The Mexican Press Agency surveyed Washington and New York newspapers for the Calles government; see Francisco Benavides to Calles, Oct. 28, 1927, and the agency's "Boletines," AGN, Ramo Obregón-Calles 721-I-6. See also Britton, "Propaganda."

21. Quoted in Delpar, *Enormous Vogue*, 47-49, 73-74.

22. John A. Britton, "In Defense of Revolution: American Journalists in Mexico, 1920-1929," *Journalism History* 5 (Winter 1978-79): 124-30, 136, and "Propaganda."

23. Christopher Jay McMullen, "Calles and the Diplomacy of Revolution: Mexican-American Relations, 1924-1928" (Ph.D. diss., Georgetown University, 1980) 65, 165-68; and Bryce Wood, *The Making of the Good Neighbor Policy* (New York, 1961), 18-23.

24. Gruening, *Mexico.*, ix-xiii.

25. Ibid., 98-109, 596-611.

26. Ibid., 387.

27. Ibid., 335-90, 497-550, 635-53.

28. Ibid., 151-56, 164 (quotations, 151-52, 156). Gruening found support from George McCutchen McBride, who favored a unified, national system of land redistribution to increase midsized farms or ranchos. See McBride, *The Land Systems of Mexico* (New York, 1923), 157-81.

29. Gruening, *Mexico*, 519-21, 660-61.

30. Ibid., 371-74.

31. Ibid., 662.

32. Frank Tannenbaum, "Viva Mexico," *New Republic* 57 (Dec. 12, 1928): 108-9.

33. Frank Tannenbaum, *The Mexican Agrarian Revolution* (New York, 1929), 393-426.

34. Frank Tannenbaum, "Making Mexico Over," *New Republic* 56 (July 18, 1928): 218.

35. Carleton Beals, "Dwight Morrow," *Nation* 126 (Jan. 25, 1928): 91-93.

36. Britton, *Carleton Beals*, 64-67, 141-52.

37. Bertram Wolfe, "Art and Revolution," *Nation* 119 (Aug. 27, 1924): 207-8.

38. Brenner, *Idols*, 265.

Chapter 5. Reactions on the Left and the Right

1. Wolfe, *A Life*, 304-5.

2. Wolfe recalled the machinations in the Mexican Communist Party in a letter to Charles Shipman (Manuel Gómez), Jan. 21, 1966, Wolfe Collection, Hoover Institution. See also Wolfe, *A Life*, 302-4; Shipman, *It Had to Be Revolution*; and Barry Carr, "Marxism and Anarchism in the Formation of the Mexican Communist Party" *HAHR* 63 (May 1983): 277-305.

3. Bertram Wolfe, "Report on the Mexican Communist Party," n.d. (1924?), typescript, Wolfe Collection, New York Public Library.

4. Wolfe, "Art and Revolution," 207-8.

5. Bertram Wolfe to Ella Wolfe, July 13, 1924. Wolfe Collection, Hoover Institution.

6. Quoted in Horn, "Diplomacy by Ultimatum," 136-38.

7. Hugh Seton-Watson, *From Lenin to Khrushchev* (New York, 1960), 104-5; and Manuel Caballero, *Latin America and the Comintern* (Cambridge, England, 1986), 39-42, 124-25.

8. *El Machete*, Nov. 6-13, 1924, p. 4, and Nov. 13-20, 1924, p. 4.

9. Wolfe, *A Life*, 345-50.

10. *El Libertador* 1 (March 1925): 7; and Wolfe, *A Life*, 345-50.

11. *El Machete*, Oct. 2-9, 1924, p. 4; Oct. 23-30, 1924, p. 3; March 19-26, 1925, p. 3; May 1, 1925, p. 4; and Wolfe, *A Life*, 350-52.

12. Ella Wolfe to Beals, June 10, 1925, CBC. For an excellent account of the activities of Haberman, see Gregg Andrews, *Shoulder to Shoulder? The American Federation of Labor, the United States, and the Mexican Revolution, 1920-1924* (Berkeley, Calif., 1991), esp. 140-68.

13. *El Libertador* 1 (July 1925): 2.

14. Victor Raúl Haya de la Torre to Ella Wolfe, August 16, 1925, Wolfe Collection, Hoover Institution.

15. Bertram Wolfe, *Revolution in Latin America* (New York, 1928), 14.

16. Ibid., 8-15. Wolfe's emphasis on the peasantry was not widely accepted within the Comintern; see Caballero, *Latin America*, 76-106.

17. Horn, "Diplomacy by Ultimatum," 18-19.

18. José Rivera Castro, *La clase obrera en la historia de México en la presidencia de Plutarco Elías Calles* (Mexico, 1983), 112-79; and Jean Meyer, Enrique Krauze, and Cayetano Reyes, *Estado y sociedad con Calles* (Mexico, 1977), 45-51, 151-74.

19. Horn, "Diplomacy by Ultimatum," 33-35.

20. Ibid., 144, 181-83.

21. Tannenbaum to Kellogg, Feb. 18, 1926, D.S. 711.12/732.

22. Sheffield to Kellogg, March 26, 1926, D.S. 711.12/732.

23. Horn, "Diplomacy by Ultimatum," 91-94.

24. Thomas McEnelley to Secretary of State, Nov. 3, 1925, D.S. 812.52/1344; and Joseph Grew to Alexander Weddell, Oct. 9, 1926, D.S. 812.20211/39.

25. Weddell to Secretary of State, Sept. 14, 1926, D.S. 812.20211/39.

26. Untitled report enclosed with Grew to Weddell, Oct. 9, 1926, D.S. 812.20211/39.

27. Weddell to Arthur (Schoenfeld), Dec. 30, 1926, D.S. 812.20211/51.

28. Britton, "Propaganda," 5-28.
29. Dudley C. Dwyre to Secretary of State, Jan. 11, 1927, D.S. 812.20211/52.
30. See *Literary Digest* 84 (Jan. 31, 1925): 37-40.
31. Ella Wolfe Phonotapes—3, Wolfe Collection, Hoover Institution; Ella Wolfe interview with author, July 24, 1984.
32. Lorenzo Meyer, *Los grupos*, and *Mexico and the United States in the Oil Controversy, 1917-1942* (Austin, Tex., 1972), 58, 92-138.
33. Guy Stevens, *Current Controversies with Mexico* (New York, 1926), 14.
34. I.F. Marcosson, "Calles," *SEP* 199 (Feb. 26, 1927): 3-5; "Mexican Complex," *SEP* 199 (March 5, 1927): 8-9; "American Stake in Mexico," *SEP* 199 (March 12, 1927): 25; "Mexico for the Mexicans" *SEP* 199 (March 26, 1927): 22-23; "Mexican Land Problems," *SEP* 199 (April 2, 1927): 30-31; "Radicalism in Mexico," *SEP* 199 (April 9, 1927): 26-27; and "Mexico of the Future," *SEP* 199 (April 16, 1927): 41-42.
35. Thomas Lamont, "Three Examples of International Cooperation," *Atlantic Monthly* 132 (Oct. 1923): 537-46; and Smith, *Revolutionary Nationalism*, 204-28.
36. Dwight Morrow, "Who Buys Foreign Bonds?" *Foreign Affairs* 5 (Jan. 1927): 219-32.

Chapter 6. The Liberal Mainstream and Radical Undercurrents

1. Alan Knight, *U.S.-Mexican Relations, 1910-1940: An Interpretation* (San Diego, 1987) 14-20.
2. Edward Alsworth Ross, *Social Control* (New York, 1901), and *South of Panama* (London, 1915), vii-viii, 208-99, 331-85.
3. Edward Alsworth Ross, *Mexico and Its Social Revolution* (New York, 1923), 3-34, 150-76.
4. Ibid., 98.
5. Ibid., 133.
6. Ibid., 51.
7. Louis Filler, *Progressivism and Muckraking* (New York, 1976), 97.
8. George Seldes, *You Can't Print That* (New York, 1929), 11.
9. Ibid., 354-91.
10. Ibid., 366.
11. Walter Lippmann, "Vested Rights and Nationalism," *Foreign Affairs* (April 1927): 363.
12. Ronald Steel, *Walter Lippmann and the American Century* (Boston, 1980), 235-40; and Richard Melzer, "Dwight Morrow's Role in the Mexican Revolution: Good Neighbor or Meddling Yankee?" (Ph.D. diss., University of New Mexico, 1979), 158-253.
13. On Croly's disillusionment, see Kloppenberg, *Uncertain Victory*, 349-94; and David W. Levy, *Herbert Croly of "The New Republic"* (Princeton, N.J., 1985), 263-300. On Croly in Mexico, see Britton, *Carleton Beals*, 34-36, 44-47.
14. Herbert Croly. "The Imperialist as Snob," *New Republic* 49 (Feb. 9, 1927): 314-16.
15. Herbert Croly, "Mexico and the United States," *New Republic*, 50 (March 30, 1927): 161.
16. Ibid., 164.
17. On Dewey's influence in Mexican education, see Secretaría de Educación Pública, *Memoria que indica el estado que guarda el ramo de educación pública el 31 de augusto de 1926* (Mexico City, 1926), 225; Isidro Castillo, *Mexico y su revolución educativa* (Mexico City 1966), pt. 1, 288-96; and Vaughan, *The State*.

18. John Dewey, "Church and State in Mexico," *New Republic* 48 (Aug. 25, 1926): 9-10; "Mexico's Educational Renaissance," *New Republic* 48 (Sept. 22, 1926): 116-118; and "From a Mexican Notebook," *New Republic* 48 (Oct. 20, 1926): 239-41. See also Moisés Séenz and Herbert I. Priestley, *Some Mexican Problems* (Chicago, 1926).

19. Dewey, "Mexican Notebook," 239-41. Dewey's discussion of Mexico contained tentative liberal statist confidence in the national government. His commitment to the "Great Community" was tied closely to neighborhood democracy, an ideal that placed him on the left wing of the liberal statists, not far from Tannenbaum and the other independent leftists. A thorough exploration of Dewey's thought is Westbrook, *John Dewey*.

20. Gruening, *Mexico*, 151-55.

21. Ibid., 381-90.

22. Ibid., 393-493 (quotation, 393). Gruening relied on Anita Brenner to research state politics in the Ministry of Government (Gobernación) Archives. The sensitivity of the material led ministry officials to close these archives to Brenner, but not before she had taken notes on a large body of material and turned them over to Gruening—contrary to the wishes of government officials. See Brenner Diary, March 6, 1927.

23. Gruening, *Mexico*, 289-331.

24. Ibid., 657-64.

25. Jean Meyer, *La Cristiada* (Mexico, 1973-74), 3 vol.; Robert Quirk, *The Mexican Revolution and the Catholic Church* (Bloomington, Ind., 1973); David Bailey, *Viva Cristo Rey: The Cristero Rebellion and the Church-State Conflict in Mexico* (Austin, Tex., 1974); and José Díaz and Román Rodríguez. *El movimiento cristero: Sociedad y conflicto en los altos de Jalisco* (Mexico, 1979).

26. Steel, *Walter Lippmann*, 241-44.

27. Walter Lippmann, "Church and State in Mexico," *Foreign Affairs* 8 (Jan., 1930): 182-208.

28. Beals, *Mexico*, 162-178.

29. Croly to Beals, March 18 and March 30, 1927, CBC; Carleton Beals, "Civil War in Mexico," *New Republic* 51 (July 6, 1927): 166-69; and Britton, *Carleton Beals*, 44-48.

30. Gruening, *Mexico*, 281; for analysis, see 171-86.

31. Tannenbaum, "Viva Mexico," 108-9.

32. Tannenbaum, *Peace by Revolution*, 66.

33. Meyer, *La Cristiada*; and Quirk, *Mexican Revolution*, 215-47.

34. Brenner Diary, Feb. 16, 1927.

35. Carleton Beals, *Mexican Maze* (New York, 1931), 38-54 (quotation, 137).

36. Tannenbaum, *Mexican Agrarian Revolution* 335-92, and *Peace by Revolution*, 115-46.

37. See W.W. Rostow, *The Stages of Economic Growth* (London 1960); S.N. Eisenstadt, *Modernization: Protest and Change* (Englewood Cliffs, NJ., 1965); Robert Heilbroner, *The Great Ascent* (New York, 1963); and Seymor Martin Lipset, *The First New Nation* (New York, 1963).

38. See Albert O. Hirschman, *Getting Ahead Collectively* (New York, 1984); Ivan Illich, *Deschooling Scoiety* (New York, 1970); E.F. Schumacher, *Small Is Beautiful* (New York, 1973); and Kirkpatrick Sale, *Human Scale* (New York, 1980). Robert Packenham discusses the rise of uncertainty among U.S. policymakers in the 1960s in *Liberal America and the Third World* (Princeton, NJ, 1973), esp. 313-60.

39. Edwards, *Natural History of Revolution*.

40. Dewey, *Impressions* 64.

41. Ross, *Mexico*, 51-52, 120-33.
42. Nor did George Seldes attempt any direct comparisons. His emphasis on the ideal of a free press led him to a severe criticism of the Soviet Union and qualified praise of the Calles government (*You Can't Print That* 215-25, 362-91).
43. Wolfe, *Revolution in Latin America*.

Chapter 7. Two Errant Pilgrims and an Anthropologist

1. Hollander, *Political Pilgrims*. On the role of utopianism in modern thought, see Karl Mannheim, *Ideology and Utopia* (1936; rpt. New York, n.d.).
2. John Crowe Ransom, Alan Tate, et al., *I'll Take My Stand*. (New York, 1930); and Pells, *Radical Visisons*, 43-193.
3. Stuart Chase, *Mexico: A Study of Two Americas* (New York, 1931), 275-303 (quotation, 301). See also R. Alan Lawson, *The Failure of Independent Liberalism, 1930-1941* (New York, 1971), 75-87; Richard N. Chapman, "A Critique of Advertising: Stuart Chase on the 'Godfather of Waste,' " in *Advertising and Popular Culture*, ed. Sammy R. Danna (Bowling Green, Ohio, 1992), 23-28; Chapman, "Ambiguities of Technology: Stuart Chase on Men and Machines," paper presented to the Society for the History of Technology, Nov. 3, 1984; and "Stuart Chase," *Current Biography* (New York, 1940): 162-64.
4. Lorenzo Meyer, Rafael Segovia, and Alejandro Lajous, *Los inicios de la institucionalización* (Mexico, 1978); and Rafael Loyola Díaz, *La crisis Obregón-Calles y el estado mexicano* (Mexico, 1980).
5. Weston, *Daybooks*, 1:188-202; and Constantine, *Tina Modotti*, 99-176.
6. Britton, *Carleton Beals*, 87-134.
7. *Mexican Life*, Feb. 1931, p. 41.
8. Ibid., May 1931, pp. 60-63.
9. Meyer, *El conflicto social*, 9-98; and Arnaldo Córdova, *La clase obrera en la historia de México en una epoca de crisis* (Mexico, 1980), 81-88.
10. Krauze, *Caudillos*, 300-330; and Meyer, *El conflicto social*, 120-21, 166-71.
11. Heather Fowler Salamini, *Agrarian Radicalism in Veracruz, 1920-1938* (Lincoln, Neb., 1978); and Lorenzo Meyer, *El conflicto social*, 260-86.
12. Chase, *Mexico*, 185.
13. Ibid., 168-207, 275-327.
14. Ibid., 224-27.
15. Ibid., 222-27.
16. Ibid., 269-70.
17. Ibid., 251-74.
18. Waldo Frank, *Our America* (New York, 1919), and *The Rediscovery of America* (New York, 1929).
19. For a fairly succinct statement of this position, see Waldo Frank, *America Hispana* (New York, 1931), 317-54.
20. Ibid., 359-60. On Waldo Frank's search for community within the framework of U.S. culture, see Blake, *Beloved Community*, esp. 266-78.
21. Frank, *America Hispana*, 362. Frank did not exclude the Indian component of Spanish American history, although his view of the conquest of the Aztecs posited a "tragic . . . graceful" harmonious logic in Cortes's victory and Spain's consequent domination (220). Frank saw in Peru's José Carlos Mariátegui a synthesis of Incan and Spanish virtues that had no parallel in Mexican history as of 1931 (159-77).
22. Ibid., 248-59.
23. Ibid., 255-58.
24. Ibid., 357-69.
25. Ibid., 368-72.

26. See Frederick B. Luquiens, review of Chase's *Mexico* and Frank's *America Hispana, Yale Review* 21 (Winter 1932): 406-8.

27. Michael C. Meyer and William L. Sherman, *The Course of Mexican History* (New York, 1987), 582-95; and Meyer, Segovia, and Lajous, *Los inicios.*

28. Howard Phillips, "Providing the Arcadia," *Mexican Life*, July 1932, p. 30.

29. Howard Phillips, "Spreading Englightenment on Mexico," *Mexican Life*, April 1932, p. 30.

30. Ernest Gruening to Anita Brenner, June 29, 191, Brenner Collection.

31. See Ernest Gruening, review of Frank's *America Hispana, Saturday Review of Literature* 8 (Oct. 3, 1931): 165.

32. See Ernest Gruening, review of Chase's *Mexico, Saturday Review of Literature* 8 (Aug. 8, 1931), 35. See also comments by Carleton Beals in *Nation* 133 (Aug. 26, 1931): 209; by William MacDonald in *Bookman* 74 (Sept. 1931): 101; and Frances Toor, "Mexican Folkways," *Mexican Folkways*, Oct.-Dec. 1932, pp. 205-11.

33. Robert Redfield, review of Chase's *Mexico, International Journal of Ethics* 42 (1931-32): 354. See also Redfield, *Tepoztlán: A Mexican Village* (Chicago, 1930), 205-23.

34. Redfield, *Tepoztlán*, 199.

35. Ibid., 209. For an account of Tepoztlán's historical circumstances at the time, see Peter Coy, "A Watershed in Mexico's Rural History: Some Thoughts on the Reconciliation of Conflicting Interpretations," *JLAS* 3 (1971): 39-57.

36. Redfield, *Tepoztlán*, 215-16.

37. Ibid., 217-23.

Chapter 8. Pilgrims without a Shrine

1. Quoted in Unrue, *Truth and Vision*, 112. For another reading of Porter's fiction, see Walsh, *Katherine Anne Porter and Mexico*. See also Porter, "The Martyr," *Century* 106 (July 1923): 410-13.

2. Quoted in Unrue, *Truth and Vision*, 81.

3. Ibid., 76-82.

4. Porter, "Hacienda," in *Flowering Judas and Other Stories* (New York, 1958), 242-43. Eisenstein himself never completed the film. Eventually released as *Que Viva Mexico!* it gained more attention as a source of leftist squabbling than as a serious work of art. See Harry Geduld and Ronald Gottesman, eds., *Sergei Eisenstein and Upton Sinclar: The Making of "Que Viva Mexico!"* (Bloomington Ind., 1970); Gunn, *American and British Writers, 115-19.*

5. Marjorie Ruth Clark, *Organized Labor in Mexico* (Chapel Hill, N.C., 1934), and *A History of the French Labor Movement, 1910-1928* (Berkeley, Calif., 1930). Clark's letters to her former mentor, Herbert Eugene Bolton at the University of California at Berkeley, suggested her personal and ideological interests: Clark to Bolton, Nov. 21, 1929; Sept. 10, 1930; and esp. Jan. 4, 1935, all in Bolton Papers.

6. Clark, *Labor in Mexico*, 214-60, 275-78.

7. Freeman, "Mexico, Notes, 1929" (notebook), 110, Freeman Papers.

8. Ibid., 110-14.

9. Meyer, *El conflicto social* 126-30; and Bertram Wolfe, *The Fabulous Life of Diego Rivera* (New York, 1963), 225-39, 253-75.

10. Joseph Freeman, "The Well-Paid Art of Lying," *New Masses* 7 (Oct. 1931): 1011.

11. Daniel Aaron, *Writers on the Left* (New York, 1961), 284-87; and Michael A. Ogorzaly, "Waldo Frank: Prophet of Hispanic Regeneration" (Ph.D. diss., University of Notre Dame, 1983), 173-294.

12. Robert Evans [Joseph Freeman], "Painting and Politics," *New Masses,* Feb. 1932, pp. 22-25.

13. Edmund Wilson, "Detroit Paradoxes," *New Republic* 75 (July 12, 1933): 230-32. Also Freeman to Wilson, July 10, 1933; Freeman to Toor, June 19, 1933; and Toor to Freeman, July 31, 1933, Freeman Papers.

14. Tannenbaum to Bassols, Jan. 28, 1933; also Bassols to Tannenbaum, Oct. 17, 1932, and Tannenbaum to Bassols, Aug. 21, 1933, Tannenbaum Papers.

15. Tannenbaum, *Peace by Revolution,* 125.

16. Ibid., 127.

17. Ibid., 246-47.

18. Beals, who agreed with many of Tannenbaum's basic premises about corruption in high political office, wrote a scathing review of *Peace by Revolution* in which he rebuked his colleague for failing to condemn Morones and other agents of misgovernment in Mexico; see "Peace by Default," *Nation* 138 (Jan. 1935): 50-51.

19. Tannenbaum, *Peace by Revolution,* 161-74, 225-62.

20. Ibid., 87-112, 187-222.

21. Tannenbaum, *Mexican Agrarian Revolution,* 42-90.

22. Ibid., 323-33 and 399-426.

23. Tannenbaum, *Peace by Revolution,* 305.

24. Gruening, *Mexico,* 393-493, 528.

25. Ibid., 159-66.

26. Redfield, *Tepoztlán,* 185-204, 217-23. Redfield saw profound changes in Yucatan in the early 1930s but did not fully analyze these findings in print until several years later. See his three books *Chan Kom: A Maya Village,* (Washington, D.C., 1934); *The Folk Culture of Yucatán* (Chicago, 1941); and *A Village That Chose Progress: Chan Kom Revisited* (Chicago, 1950).

27. Beals, *Mexican Maze,* 34.

28. Ibid., 70-93, 139-150, 205-10.

29. Ibid., 149-50. Beals, Tannenbaum, and the others apparently did not notice the spontaneous radical agrarian movement in Veracruz, led by Adalberto Tejada, at its height from 1929 to 1932. For an excellent study of that movement, see Salamini, *Agrarian Radicalism.*

30. Beals, *Mexican Maze,* 187.

31. See Carleton Beals, "Mexico and the Communists," *New Republic* 62 (Feb. 17, 1930): 10-12; "Mexico Turns to Fascist Tactics," *Nation* 132 (Jan. 28, 1931): 110-12; and "Has Mexico Betrayed Her Revolution?" *New Republic* 67 (July 22, 1931): 249-50. On Beals's arrest and the continuing interest of the Mexican government in its media image, see the Embajada de Mexico (Report) to the Secretaría de Relaciones Exteriores, Feb. 17, 1930, AREM 73-534.2/1; Consulado General de México (New York) to Secretaría de Relaciones Exteriores, Dec. 10, 1932, AREM A/510 (72)/10; and Isidro Fabela to President Emilio Portes Gil, Feb. 15, 1929, Fondo Portes Gil AGN 315/104. For an account of Beals's arrest, see Britton, *Carleton Beals,* 94-99.

Chapter 9. Mexico under Cárdenas

1. Although he was not a dynamic speaker, Cárdenas manifested a certain charisma for U.S. observers, and in his spontaneous visits to rural villages he achieved immediate rapport with the local people. See, e.g., Waldo Frank, "Mexico Today: President Cárdenas and His People," *Nation* 149 (Aug. 12, 1939): 171-73; and Frank Tannenbaum, "Mexico's Man of the People," *Readers' Digest* 31 (oct. 1937): 43-44 (condensed from *Survey Graphic* 26 [Aug. 1937]: 425-27). See also Hugh Joseph Morgan, "The United States Press Coverage of

Mexico during the Presidency of Lázaro Cárdenas, 1934-1940" (Ph.D. diss., Southern Illinois University 1985), for a valuable overview. On charisma, see Arthur Schweitzer, "Theory and Political Charisma," *Comparative Studies in Society and History* 16 (1974): 150-81; and Ann Ruth Willner, *The Spellbinders: Charismatic Political Leadership* (New Haven, Conn., 1984).

2. Verna Carleton Millan, *Mexico Reborn* (Boston, 1939), 198-99. For the background of the expropriation, see Meyer, *Mexico and the United States;* Joe C. Ashby, *Organized Labor and the Mexican Revolution under Lázaro Cárdenas* (Chapel Hill, N.C., 1963); Josefina Vázquez and Lorenzo Meyer, *The United States and Mexico* (Chicago, 1985), 116-52; Luis González, *Los días del presidente Cárdenas* (Mexico, 1981), 167-92; and Jonathan Brown and Alan Knight, eds., *The Mexican Petroleum Industry in the Twentieth Century* (Austin, Tex., 1992).

3. Laurance P. Hurlburt, *The Mexican Muralists in the United States* (Albuquerque, N.M., 1989).

4. Ramón Beteta to Lázaro Cárdenas, April 27, 1938, and Francisco J. Múgica to Lázaro Cárdenas, May 9, 1938, Fondo Lázaro Cárdenas, AGN 432.2/253-8. This issue concerned Mexican officials for years. E.g., in 1940, diplomat Luis Quintanilla sent clippings of a particularly virulent anti-Mexican series in the *New York Daily News* directly to the office of President Cárdenas (Quintanilla to the office of the President, May 30, 1940, Fondo Lázaro Cárdenas, AGN 704.1/124).

5. The publications in English by the Mexican government included *The True Facts about the Expropriations of the Oil Company Properties in Mexico* (Mexico City, 1940); and *Oil: Mexico's Position* (Mexico City 1942).

6. William Cameron Townsend to Lázaro Cárdenas, Jan. 30, 1939, Townsend Papers; James and Marti Hefly, *Uncle Cam* (Milford, Mich., 1981), 75-111; Townsend, *The Truth about Mexico* (Los Angeles, 1942), 15-16; and Townsend, *Lázaro Cárdenas: Mexican Democrat* (Waxhaw, N.C., 1979), 243-80. For examples of Herring's work, see "Cárdenas Triumphs in Mexico," *Current History* 42 (Sept. 1935): 636-38, and "Cárdenas of Mexico," *Harper's* 177 (Oct. 1938).

7. Millan, *Mexico Reborn*, 218-19. For views of liberal statists and an independent leftist, see Herring, "Cárdenas of Mexico," 498-99; Betty Kirk, *Covering the Mexican Front* (Norman, Okla., 1942), 156-65; Townsend, *Truth*, 3-15; and Anita Brenner, *The Wind That Swept Mexico* (New York, 1942), 95-97.

8. Wood, *Good Neighbor Policy*, 217; and *Foreign Relations of the United States, 1938: The American Republics* (Washington, D.C., 1956), 702-7.

9. Clayton R. Koppes, "The Good Neighbor Policy and the Nationalization of Mexican Oil: A Reinterpretation," *Journal of American History* 69 (June 19820: 69.

10. *New York Times*, Aug. 26, 1938, pp. 1, 5.

11. E. David Cronon, *Josephus Daniels in Mexico*, (Madison, Wis., 1962), 112-54.

12. Ibid., 189-90, 203-4.

13. Quoted in ibid., 217; see also 201.

14. Koppes, "Good Neighbor Policy," 63-81.

15. Owen White, "Next Door to Communism," *Collier's* 98 (Oct. 3, 1936): 12-13, 53, and "Your Money in Red Mexico," *Collier's* 99 (Feb. 13, 1937): 15, 59-60.

16. *Newsweek* 12 (July 18, 1938): 40, and 12 (Aug. 15, 1938): 40.

17. Henry F. Allen, "Mexico's Kilowatt Crooks," *Reader's Digest* 33 (Nov. 1938): 58; and Burt McConnell, *Mexico at the Bar of Public Opinion* (New York, 1939), 236-37.

18. *The Atlantic Presents: Trouble below the Border,* special issue of *Atlantic*

Monthly, July 1938; for an analysis, see Morgan, "United States Press Coverage," 532-42. See also McConnell, *Mexico.*

19. Roscoe Gaither, *Expropriation in Mexico* (New York, 1940). See also William E. McMahon, *Two Strikes and Out* (Garden City, N.Y., 1939).

20. One notable exception was British novelist Evelyn Waugh, who wrote provocative criticisms of the Mexican government in the 1930s; see *Mexico: An Object Lesson* (Boston, 1939). Waugh is discussed in Gunn, *American and British Writers,* 181-94.

21. Mexican Consulate General, San Antonio, Tex., n.d., Fondo Lázaro Cárdenas, AGN 111/1721. Many of the circumstances surrounding Kluck-hohn's expulsion remain unclear. For his own account, see Frank Kluckhohn, *The Mexican Challenge* (New York, 1939), 260-65. Virginia Prewett's version is in *Reportage on Mexico* (New York, 1941), 138.

22. Ernest Gruening, review of Kluckhohn's *Mexican Challenge, Saturday Review of Literature* 20 (Aug. 12, 1939): 6. A more radical critique is Virginia Minshun's review in *Nation* 149 (Sept. 2, 1939): 250.

23. Kluckhohn, *Mexican Challenge,* 93-139, 67-193, 250-68; and Prewett, *Reportage,* 131-52, 166-68.

24. Kluckhohn, *Mexican Challenge,* 280.

25. Ibid., 27.

26. Prewett, *Reportage,* 177; for her overview see 155-254.

27. Kluckhohn, *Mexican Challenge,* 238.

28. Ibid., 15-57, 250-68, 280-96; and Prewett, *Reportage,* 131-52, 205-10.

29. For leftists' reviews of Kluckhohn's *Mexican Challenge,* see Waldo Frank *New Republic* 100 (Sept. 20, 1939): 193; Virginia Minshun, *Nation,* 149 (Sept. 2, 1939): 250. Prewett's analysis of the shift to the right under Avila Camacho conflicted with the view of Kirk (*Mexican Front,* 329-48), who saw the new regime as a caretaker for the consolidation of the reforms that Cárdenas had initiated.

30. Bertram Wolfe, "Back to Mexico," April 16, 1936, Wolfe Collection, Hoover Institution.

31. Wolfe to Diego Rivera, Nov. 5, 1936, Wolfe Collection, Hoover Institution. See also Wolfe, *A Life,* 616-48.

32. Bertram Wolfe, *Portrait of Mexico* (New York, 1937), 190-211.

33. Lázaro Cárdenas to Townsend, June 4, 1937, Townsend Papers.

34. Maurice Halperin, "Mexico the Incredible," *Current History* 45 (Nov. 1936): 52. See also Halperin, "Under the Lid in Mexico," *Current History* 41 (Nov. 1934): 166-71; "Inside Mexico," *Current History* 47 (Feb. 1937): 83-87; "What About Mexico?" *New Republic* 93 (Jan. 12, 1938): 270-73; and the *New York Times,* Feb. 28, 1937, p. VII.4. On Halperin and the Communist Party, see Earl Latham, *The Communist Controversy in Washington* (Cambridge, Mass., 1966), 201-7.

35. Cárdenas to Frank, March 18, 1938, Cárdenas Papers, CERM.

36. Waldo Frank, *Memoirs of Waldo Frank,* ed. Alan Trachtenberg (Amherst, Mass., 1973), 194-95; Ogorzaly, "Waldo Frank," 180-81; Cárdenas to Frank, n.d. (probably June 1938), Fondo Lázaro Cárdenas, AGN 151-3/720; and Frank to Cárdenas, April 12, 1940, Fondo Lazardo Cárdenas, AGN 553-4/1.

37. Frank's "Mexico Today" appeared in the *Nation* in four parts: "The Heart of the Revolution," 149 (Aug. 5, 1939): 140-44; "President Cárdenas and His People," 149 (Aug. 12, 1939): 171-73; "Danger on the Right," 149 (Sept. 9, 1939): 265-69; and "The Deepest Danger," 149 (Sept. 16, 1939): 288-90. See also Waldo Frank, "Cárdenas of Mexico," *Foreign Affairs* 18 (Oct. 1939): 91-101.

38. *New Masses,* March 29, 1938, p. 4, and April 12, 1938, p. 9. See also Marc Frank, "Standard Oil vs. Mexico," *New Masses,* April 5, 1938, pp. 3-5.

39. For commentary on the economic problems of the late 1930s see Nathaniel and Sylvia Weyl, *The Reconquest of Mexico* (New York, 1939), 186-97, 253-78, 312-14; and Kirk, *Mexican Front*, 106-23, 156-86.

40. On U.S. leftist ideas and values in the 1930s, see Pells, *Radical Visions; Robert S. McElvaine, The Great Depression* (New York, 1984); Alan Dawley, *Struggles for Justice* (Cambridge,Mass., 1991), esp. 334-417.

41. John Gunther, *Inside Latin America* (New York, 1941), 37, 64.

42. Ibid., 69-75.

43. Kirk, *Mexican Front*, 78.

44. Carleton Beals, review of Kirk, *Mexican Front, Saturday Review of Literature*, 26 (Jan. 9, 1943): 18.

45. Kirk, *Mexican Front*, 36.

46. Ibid., 208.

47. J.H. Plenn, *Mexico Marches* (Indianapolis, Ind., 1939), 166-90, George I. Sánchez, *Mexico: A Revolution by Education* (New York, 1936); and George Booth, *Mexico's School Made Society* (Stanford, Calif., 1941). For historical studies of socialist education, see David Raby, *Educación y revolución social en México* (Mexico City, 1974), 66-99; Victoria Lerner, *La educación socialista* (Mexico City, 1979); and John A. Britton, *Educación y radicalismo*, 2 vols. (Mexico City, 1976).

48. *Life* 1 (Sept. 20, 1937): 37; and Kirk, *Mexican Front*, 40.

49. *Time* 32 (Aug. 29, 1938): 19.

Chapter 10. The Revolution beneath the Revolutionary Image

1. Knight, "Mexican Revolution," 1-37, and "Revolutionary Project, Recalcitrant People" in *The Revolutionary Process in Mexico*, ed. Jaime E. Rodríquez O (Los Angeles, 1990), 227-64; Salamini, *Agrarian Radicalism*; and Paul Friedrich, *The Princes of Naranja* (Austin, Tex. 1986). For arguments that the revolution was much more limited, see Walter Goldfrank, "Theories of Revolution and Revolution without Theory: The Case of Mexico," *Theory and Society* 7 (1979): 135-65; Arnaldo Córdova, *La ideología de la Revolución Mexicana* (Mexico, 1973), and *La politica de masas del cardenismo* (Mexico, 1976); Hamilton, *Limits of State Autonomy*; Ruíz, *Great Rebellion*; Krauze and Reyes, *Estado y sociedad*; and John Hart, *The Coming and Process of the Mexican Revolution* (Berkeley, Calif., 1987).

2. Simpson, *Ejido*, 529-82; Carleton Beals, *House in Mexico* (New York, 1958), 120-77; Henry Allen Moe to Anita Brenner, Dec. 23, 1930, Brenner Collection; and Eyler Simpson obituary, *New York Times*, July 2, 1938, p. 13.

3. Simpson, *Ejido*, 335-42. (quotation, 342).

4. Ibid., 351-52, 440-61. For a revisionist view of the struggle between *veteranos*, and *agraristas*, see Meyer, *el conflicto social*, 173-253.

5. Simpson, *Ejido*, 452-55.

6. Ibid., 456-61.

7. Ibid., 462.

8. Ibid., 482-83.

9. Ibid., 450.

10. For historical studies somewhat at odds with contemporary commentary on the land reform policy of the Cárdenas administration, see Luis González, *Los días del presidente Cárdenas* (Mexico, 1981), 89-163, 195-213; Barry Carr, "The Mexican Communist Party and Agrarian Mobilization in the Laguna," *HAHR* 67 (Aug. 1987): 371-404; and Alan Knight, "Cardenismo: Juggernaut or Jalopy?" *JLAS* 26 (Feb. 1994): 73-107.

11. Carleton Beals, "Cárdenas Organizes Capitalism," *Current History* 46 (May 1937): 47-54 (quotation, 53-54). See also Beals, "Socialism on a Platter,"

Nation 140 (April 10, 1935): 416. Hubert Herring expressed similar views in "The Unconquerable Mexican," *Harper's* 175 (June 1937): 48, and *Good Neighbors* (New Haven Conn., 1941), 319.

12. Aaron, *Writers on the Left*, 439-42; and Anita Brenner, "Class War in Republican Spain," *Modern Monthly* 10 (Sept. 1937): 4-17.

13. Brenner typescript, Nov. 1938, intended for the *New York Times Magazine*; Brenner to Lester Markel, Nov. 22, 1938, Brenner Collection. Also Brenner to Lázaro Cárdenas, AGN 432.2/253-8.

14. Brenner, *Wind*, 75-77.

15. Weyl and Weyl, *Reconquest*, 381.

16. "Contestación al cuestionario presentado al Senor General Francisco J. Múgica por la Senorita Sylvia y Nataniel Weyl" trans. Sylvia Weyl, March 24, 1939, Múgica papers, CERM, vol. 68, docs. 57 and 58.

17. Weyl and Weyl, *Reconquest*, 379-80. This passage was indicative of Nathaniel Weyl's disenchantment with the Communist Party and Soviet Russia. By 1939 he had left the party. See Latham, *Communist Controversy*, 119-20.

18. Weyl and Weyl, *Reconquest*, 344.

19. Ibid., 171-227 (quotation, 227).

20. Ibid., 348

21. Ibid., 351-53.

22. Ibid., 368-69.

23. Simpson, *Ejido*, 553-76 (quotation, 575). See also Lewis Mumford, *Tecnics and Civilization* (New York, 1934); and Howard P. Segal, *Technological Utopianism in American Culture* (Chicago, 1985).

24. Weyl and Weyl, *Reconquest*, 370-71; see also 253-314, 370-84.

25. Anita Brenner, "Mexico Shatters the Mold of Centuries," *New York Times Magazine*, Aug. 28, 1938, p. 19.

26. Bertram Wolfe and Diego Rivera, *Portrait of Mexico* (New York, 1937), 27-45; and Weyl and Weyl, *Reconquest*, 370-84. Liberal statists also tended to see this aspect of the Cárdenas administration in a favorable light. See, e.g., Townsend, *Truth*, and *Lázaro Cárdenas*, 243-304; Hubert Herring, *Mexico: The Making of a Nation* (New York, 1942), 67-77, and *A History of Latin America* (New York, 1955), 376-83.

27. Ogorzaly, "Waldo Frank," 132; and Blake, *Beloved Community*, esp. 143-49, 268-78.

28. "Mexico Today: The Heart of the Revolution," 143.

29. Ibid.

30. McElvaine, *The Great Depression*, 196-263. See also Susman, *Culture as History*, 156-229; and Pells, *Radical Visions*.

31. Irwin Gellman, *Good Neighbor Diplomacy* (Baltimore, Md., 1979), 51-59.

32. Wood, *Good Neighbor Policy*, 247-59.

Chapter 11. Friendly Dissenters

1. Pells, *Radical Visions*, 330-64; William L. O'Neill, *A Better World: The Great Schism—Stalinism and American Intellectuals* (New York, 1982), 13-42.

2. Weyl and Weyl, *Reconquest*, 218-20; Millan, *Mexico Reborn*, 125-32; Maurice Halperin, "Model Farms in Mexico," *Current History* 48 (Feb. 1938): 39-41; and Clarence Senior, *Democracy Comes to a Cotton Kingdom* (Mexico City, 1940). On the history of the Laguna expropriations, see Barry Carr, "The Communist Party and Agrarian Mobilization in the Laguna, 1920-1940: A Worker-Peasant Alliance?" *HAHR* 67 (Aug. 1987): 371-404.

3. Carleton Beals, *The Great Circle* (New York, 1940), 308.

4. Max Miller, *I Cover the Waterfront* (New York, 1932), and *The Great Trek* (Garden City, N.Y., 1935).

5. Max Miller, *Mexico around Me* (New York, 1937), 51-60, 89-90.

6. Ibid., 56.

7. Ibid., 294.

8. Frank Tannenbaum, *Whither Latin America?* (New York, 1934).

9. Austin Evans to Tannenbaum, Dec. 19, 1934, Tannenbaum Papers.

10. Simpson, *Ejido*, 555-58.

11. Tannenbaum to Lázaro Cárdenas, Nov. 8, 1937, Tannenbaum Papers.

12. Tannenbaum to Cárdenas, Dec. 16, 1936, Tannenbaum Papers.

13. Lawrence Duggan to Tannenbaum, March 28, 1938, and Tannenbaum to Duggan, March 30, 1938. See also Tannenbaum to Sumner Welles, Jan. 16 and Oct. 26, 1939, and Sept. 9, 1940; Welles To Tannenbaum, Jan. 17, 1939, Aug. 7 and Sept. 13, 1940; Tannenbaum to Duggan, Oct. 13, 1938; and Duggan to Tannenbaum, Nov. 1938, all in Tannenbaum Papers.

14. For a sampling, see Ignacio García Téllez, *Socialización de la cultura: Seis meses de acción educativa* (Mexico, 1935); Luis Sánchez Pontón, *Hacia la escuela socialista* (Mexico, 1935); and Luis Monzón, *Detalles de la educación socialista implantables en México* (Mexico, 1936).

15. Tannenbaum to Narciso Bassols, Nov. 1937, Tannenbaum Papers.

16. Bassols to Tannenbaum, Dec. 6, 1937, Tannenbaum Papers.

17. Millan, *Mexico Reborn*, 80-87, 238; Plenn, *Mexico Marches*, 262-69; and Weyl and Weyl, *Reconquest*, 235-40.

18. Tannenbaum to Carter Goodrich, Oct. 9, 1939, Tannenbaum Papers.

19. See Tannenbaum, "The Balance of Power in Society," *Political Science Quarterly* 61 (Dec. 1946): 481-504, and "A Note on the Economic Interpretation of History," *Political Science Quarterly* 61 (June 1946): 247-53. Both essays are reprinted in Frank Tannenbaum, *The Balance of Power in Society*, intro. John Herman Randall (New York, 1969).

20. Tannenbaum, Foreword in Townsend, *Lázaro Cárdenas*, v-viii.

21. Norman Sherry, *The Life of Graham Greene* (New York, 1989), 1:656-725; Maria Couto, *Graham Greene: On the Frontier* (New York, 1988), 1-90; and Gunn, *American and British Writers*, 181-94.

22. Sherry, *Life of Graham Greene*, 662.

23. Graham Greene, *Another Mexico* (1939; New York, 1960), 208.

24. Graham Greene, *The Power and the Glory* (New York, 1940), 299.

25. Greene, *Another Mexico*, 81. See also George Orwell, *1984* (1949; New York, 1961); and Rebecca West, *The New Meaning of Treason* (London, 1947).

26. Green, *The Power and the Glory*, 301.

27. Lesley Simpson to Beals, Sept. 1939, CBC. Woodrow W. Borah, interview with author, July 23-24, 1988, and Borah to author, Sept. 10, 1988.

28. Lesley Simpson, *Many Mexicos* (Berkeley, Calif. 1941), x.

29. Ibid., 292-93. The sixteenth-century Spanish *encomendero* was in charge of an Indian community. He could profit from Indian labor but, in theory, had to provide for the workers' spiritual and material needs. See Lesley Simpson, *The Encomienda in New Spain* (1929; Berkeley, Calif., 1960).

30. Simpson, *Many Mexicos*, 319.

31. See Henry Bamford Parkes, *Jonathan Edwards, the Fiery Puritan* (New York, 1930).

32. Henry Bamford Parkes, *A History of Mexico* (Boston, 1938), v.

33. Henry Bamford Parkes, *Marxism: An Autopsy* (Boston 1939); and *Time* 34 (Oct. 23, 1939): 82-84.

34. Parkes, *History of Mexico*, 277-82.

35. Ibid., 360-62.
36. Ibid., 402.
37. Ibid., 404-8 (quotation, 408).
38. Ibid, 397.
39. Ibid., 410.
40. Herbert I. Priestley to Charles B. Lipman, April 14, 1937; Feb. 4, 1938; and Sept. 23, 1941, Priestley Papers.
41. Herbert I. Priestley, review of Parkes's *History of Mexico, HAHR* 19 (Aug. 1939): 334-37.
42. Priestley, "Mexico Moves Left," n.d. (apparently 1936), MS, Priestley Papers.
43. Ibid.
44. Priestley, "Contemporary Program of Nationalization in Mexico," (1938), and"Mexico and the Good Neighbor Policy" (1940), MSS, Priestley Papers.
45. Susman, *Culture as History*, 150-83; and Pells, *Radical Visions*, 292-327.

Chapter 12. The Changing Image

1. Franklin W. Dixon, *The Mark on the Door* (New York, 1934).
2. John Steinbeck, *The Grapes of Wrath* (New York, 1939); and James Agee, *Let Us Now Praise Famous Men*, photographs by Walker Evans (New York, 1941).
3. Frank Tannenbaum, "Cárdenas: That Is the Way He Is," *Survey Graphic* 26 (Aug. 1937): 425-27 (condensed in *Reader's Digest* 31 [Oct., 1937]: 42-44).
4. Roger Dooley, *From Scarface to Scarlett: American Films in the 1930s* (New York, 1981), 205-16; and Andrew Bergman, *We're in the Money: Depression America and Its Films* (New York, 1972).
5. Allen Woll, *The Latin Image in American Film* (Los Angeles, 1980), 6-28; and Carlos E. Cortés, "To View a Neighbor: The Hollywood Textbook on Mexico," in *Images of Mexico in the United States*, ed. John Coatsworth and Carlos Rico (San Diego, Calif., 1989), 91-118.
6. *New York Times Film Reviews, 1913-1968* (New York, 1970), p. 21 (Sept. 27, 1930).
7. Ibid., April 11, 1934, p. 25; and Wool, *Latin Image*, 45-49.
8. Woll, *Latin Image*, 35-38.
9. Ibid., 60-62; and Jerome Lawrence, *The Life and Times of Paul Muni* (New York, 1974), 241-45.
10. *New York Times*, April 26, 1939, p. 27, and April 30, 1939, XI.5; Dooly, *From Scarface to Scarlett*, 158.
11. Woll, *Latin Image*, 61; and Emanuel Eisenberg, "Juárez Conquers Mexico," *New York Times*, July 2, 1939, X.4. For serious analyses of the place of Juárez in the ideology of nineteenth-century Mexico, see Richard Sinkin, *The Mexican Reform: A Study in Liberal Nation Building* (Austin, Tex., 1979); and Charles Hale, *The Transformation of Liberalism in Late Nineteenth Century Mexico* (Princeton, N.J., 1989). See John Huston's account of the writing of the script in *An Open Book* (New York, 1980), 72-74.
12. Published correspondence in *Steinbeck: A Life in Letters*, ed. Elaine Steinbeck and Robert Wallsten (New York, 1975), reflects on this film. See, e.g., Steinbeck to Max Wagner, Nov. 1, 1940 (200-201); Steinbeck to Louis Pond, Monday ?, 1941 (208-9); Steinbeck to Elizabeth Otis, Feb. 7, 1941 (210-12); and Steinbeck to Eleanor Roosevelt, Oct. 1941 (220).
13. John Steinbeck, *The Forgotten Village* (New York, 1941), 134-36. Instead of a screenplay, *The Forgotten Village* used spontaneous acting in a series of prearranged situations. The book contains Steinbeck's narrative written to ac-

company the edited version of the film. For broad studies on Steinbeck's ideas, see Warren French, *John Steinbeck* (Boston, 1975); Peter Lisca, *The Wide World of John Steinbeck* (New York, 1981); David P. Peeler, *Hope among Us Yet* (Athens, Ga., 1987), 149-91; and Jackson J. Benson, *The True Adventures of John Steinbeck, Writer* (New York, 1990), esp. 452-90. For a different view of this film, see Joseph Millichap, *Steinbeck and Film* (New York, 1983), 50-57.

14. Paul Fussell, *Abroad: British Literary Traveling between the Wars,* (New York, 1980), 37-50.

15. Harry Franck, *Trailing Cortéz Through Mexico* (New York, 1935), 338.

16. See Meyer, Segovia, and Lajous, *Los inicios*, 271; *Mexican Life* 9 (July 1933): 29; A.L. Moats, *Off to Mexico* (New York, 1935); and *Literary Digest* 118 (June 1, 1935): 47.

17. Travel guides published in these years included France Toor, *Guide to Mexico* (Mexico City, 1933); T. Philip Terry, *Terry's Guide to Mexico* (New York, 1933); Anita Brenner, *Your Mexican Holiday* (New York, 1932); and Jean Austin, *Mexico in Your Pocket* (Garden City, N.Y., 1937).

18. Eduardo Villaseñor to Emilio Portes Gil, Feb. 11, 1935, Múgica Papers, CERM, vol. 53, doc. 389.

19. Austin, *Mexico*, 7-11.

20. Erna Fergusson, *Fiesta in Mexico* (New York, 1934), 262.

21. Womack, *Zapata*, 422; Edgcumb Pinchon, *Viva Villa* (New York, 1933), and *Zapata, the Unconquerable* (New York, 1941); and H.H. Dunn, *The Crimson Jester* (New York, 1934).

22. Pinchon, *Zapata*, 317-32.

23. J. Frank Dobie, *Tongues of the Monte* (Boston, 1935), 115.

24. Ibid., 250.

25. Michael I. Baumann. *B. Traven: Una introducción* (Mexico, 1970), 81-153. For other comentaries, see Judy Stone, *The Mystery of B. Traven* (Los Altos, Calif. 1977); Ernst Schurer and Philip Jenkins, eds., *B. Traven: His Life and Works* (University Park, Pa., 1987); Donald Chankin, *Anonymity and Death: The Fiction of B. Traven* (University Park, Pa., 1975); Gunn, *American and British Writers*, 93-100; and William Weber Johnson, "Trying to Solve the Enigma of the Sierra Madre," *Smithsonian* 13 (March 1983): 156-75. Heidi Zogbaum, *B. Traven: A Vision of Mexico* (Wilmington, Del., 1992), is unequaled in its depiction of Traven's life in Mexico and the relationship between his personal experiences and the evolution of the ideas expressed in his novels.

26. B. Traven, *The Treasure of the Sierra Madre* (New York, 1935), 117.

27. B. Traven, *Government* (New York, 1935), 175-77. See also Zogbaum, *B. Traven*, 116-33.

Chapter 13. From Selective Amnesia to New Liberal Orthodoxy

1. Vázquez and Meyer, *United States and Mexico*, 153-72; and Howard Cline, *The United States and Mexico* (New York, 1953), 239-305.

2. Frank Tannenbaum, *The Struggle for Peace and Bread* (New York, 1950), xi.

3. Cline, *United States and Mexico*, 6.

4. Walter LaFeber, *Inevitable Revolutions* (New York, 1984), 85-110; Stephen G. Rabe, *Eisenhower and Latin America,* (Chapel Hill, N.C., 1988); and Bryce Wood, *The Dismantling of the Good Neighbor Policy* (Austin, Tex., 1985).

5. Rabe, *Eisenhower*, 77-87; Cole Blaiser, *The Hovering Giant: US Responses to Revolutionary Change in Latin America* (Pittsburgh, Pa., 1976), 101-50; Samuel Baily, *The United States and the Development of South America, 1945-1975* (New

York, 1976), 51-81; James Malloy, *Bolivia: The Uncomplete Revolution* (Pittsburgh, Pa., 1976); and James Wilkie, *The Bolivian Revolution and US Aid since 1952* (Los Angeles, 1969).

6. Wood, *Dismantling*.

7. Dwight D. Eisenhower, *The White House Years* (Garden City, N.Y., 1963), 1:239.

8. Ibid., 421.

9. Ibid.

10. Piero Gleijeses, *Shattered Hope* (Princeton N.J., 1991); Richard Immerman, *The CIA in Guatemala* (Austin, Tex., 1982); Stephen Schlesinger and Stephen Kinzer, *Bitter Fruit* (Garden City, N.Y., 1982); Rabe, *Eisenhower*, 42-63; and Blanche Wiesen Cook, *The Declassified Eisenhower* (Garden City, N.Y., 1981), 217-92.

11. Rabe, *Eisenhower*, 57.

12. Quoted in ibid., 52.

13. Immerman, *CIA in Guatemala*, 61-67; Jim Handy, *Gift of the Devil: A History of Guatemala* (Boston, 1984), 103-47, and " 'The Most Precious Fruit of the Revolution': The Guatemalan Agrarian Reform, 1952-1954," *HAHR* 68 (Nov. 1988): 675-705.

14. Samuel Guy Inman, *A New Day in Guatemala: A Study of the Present Social Revolution* (Wilton, Conn., 1951); Beals to Inman, June 15, 1954, and Inman to Beals, June 27, 1594, CBC; and John A. Britton, "Carleton Beals and Central America after Sandino: Struggle to Publish," *Journalism Quarterly* 60 (Summer 1983): 240-45.

15. Nathan Whetten, "Land Reform in the Modern World," *Rural Sociology* 19 (Dec. 1954), 329-36, and *Guatemala: The Land and the People* (New Haven, Conn., 1961), 165-66. See also Ronald Schneider, *Communism in Guatemala* (New York, 1959); Kalmon Silvert, Guatemala: *A Study in Government* (New Orleans, La., 1954); John Gillin and Kalmon Silvert, "Ambiguities in Guatemala," *Foreign Affairs* 34 April 1956: 469-482; and Richard N. Adams, ed., *Political Changes in Guatemalan Indian Communities: A Symposium* (New Orleans, La., 1957). For an anthropologist's synthesis of the impact of the 1954 coup, see Richard N. Adams, *Crucifixion by Power* (Austin, Tex., 1970).

16. Tad Szulc, *Fidel: A Critical Portrait* (New York, 1986), 329-33, 356, 363.

17. Frank Tannenbaum, *Ten Keys to Latin America* (New York, 1960), 144.

18. Ibid., 170.

19. Ibid., 169-70.

20. Because land reform in both Mexico and Cuba are subjects of some controversy, an evaluation of Tannenbaum's comparison is difficult. For additional perspectives, see Alain de Janvry, *The Agrarian Question and Reformism in Latin America* (Baltimore, Md., 1981); Jeffery M. Paige, *Agrarian Revolution* (New York, 1975); and Eric Wolfe, *Peasant Wars of the Twentieth Century* (New York, 1969). On land reform in Mexico, see François Chevalier, "The Ejido and Political Stability in Mexico," in *The Politics of Conformity in Latin America*, ed. Claudio Veliz (New York, 1967), 158-91; de Janvry, *Agrarian Question*, 123-31; David Barkin, *Regional Economic Development: The River Basin Approach in Mexico* (Cambridge, England, 1970); and Roger D. Hansen, *The Politics of Mexican Development* (Baltimore, Md., 1971). On Cuba in the early Castro years, see James Petras and Robert La Porte Jr., *Cultivating Revolution* (New York, 1971), 331-71; James O'Connor *The Origins of Socialism in Cuba* (Ithaca, N.Y., 1970); René Dumont, *Cuba: Socialism and Development* (New York, 1970); and Jorge I. Domínguez, *Cuba: Order and Revolution* (Cambridge, Mass., 1978), 423-63.

21. Donald Hodges and Ross Gandy, *Mexico 1910-1976: Reform or Revolution?* (London, 1979), 130-73.

22. Richard E. Welch Jr., *Response to Revolution: The United States and the Cuban Revolution, 1959-1961* (Chapel Hill, N.C., 1985); and Jules Benjamin, *The United States and the Origins of the Cuban Revolution* (Princeton, N.J., 1990).

23. David Hackett Fischer, *Historians' Fallacies* (New York, 1970), 243-59; and Ernest R. May, *"Lessons" of the Past* (New York, 1973), 172-82.

24. Robert Packenham, *Liberal America and the Third World* (Princeton, N.J., 1972); Michael Hunt, *Ideology and US Foreign Policy* (New Haven, Conn., 1987); Walter LaFeber, *The American Age* (New York, 1989); and Emily Rosenberg, *Spreading the American Dream* (New York, 1981).

25. Daniel Bell, *The End of Ideology* (New York, 1960), 406; on the Russian Revolution, see 315-92.

26. "Y" [Louis Halle], "On a Certain Impatience with Latin America," *Foreign Affairs* 27 (July 1950): 571, 579.

27. Packenham, *Liberal America*, 34.

28. Ibid., 111-21.

29. Ibid., 129-50.

30. Tannenbaum and Beals, however, saw violence as sometimes necessary, particularly against the oppressive actions of a national government. See Tannenbaum, *Peace by Revolution*, 115-83; and Beals, *Mexican Maze*, 9-54.

31. Packenham, *Liberal America*, 151-60.

32. Theodore H. Von Laue, *The World Revolution of Westernization: The Twentieth Century in Global Perspective* (New York, 1987), 149-96.

33. Richard Pells, *The Liberal Mind in a Conservative Age* (New York, 1985), 335-61; Steel, *Walter Lippman*, 34-35; and Lipset, *First New Nation*.

34. On conservative trends in Mexican politics in the 1940s, see Luis Medina, *Del cardenismo al avilacamachismo* (Mexico, 1978), and *Civilismo y modernización del autoritarismo* (Mexico, 1979); Blanca Torres, *México en la segunda guerra mundial* (Mexico, 1979), and *Hacia la utopía industrial* (Mexico, 1984); Donald J. Mabry, *Mexico's Acción Nacional: A Catholic Alternative to Revolution* (Syracuse, N.Y., 1973); and Hansen, *Politics of Mexican Development*.

35. Pells, *Liberal Mind*, 117-82.

36. Robert Scott, *Mexican Government in Transition* (Urbana, Ill., 1959), 144.

37. Ibid., 295

38. Ibid., 300.

39. Ibid., 293.

40. Ibid., 126. A leading proponent of this view was John J. Johnson, *Political Change in Latin America* (Stanford, Calif., 1958).

41. Fischer, *Historians' Fallacies*, 135-40.

42. Cline, *United States and Mexico*, 371-86.

43. Ibid., 382.

44. Ibid.

45. Ibid., 333-37.

46. Ibid., 360. For somewhat less sanguine discussions of Mexico's industrialization, see Sanford Mosk, *The Industrial Revolution in Mexico* (Berkeley, Calif., 1950); and Raymond Vernon, *The Dilemma of Mexico's Development* (Cambridge, Mass., 1963).

47. Cline, *United States and Mexico*, 360.

48. Ibid.

Chapter 14. The Persistence of Doubt

1. Herring, *History of Latin America*, 384-93 (quotation, 393).

2. Townsend, *Lázaro Cárdenas*, 371-72.

3. Parkes, *History of Mexico*, 421-40.

4. Simpson, *Many Mexicos* (1946 ed.), 17. The book went through four editions and several revisions—especially of the sections on contemporary Mexico. The University of California Press published editions in 1941, 1946, 1952, 1964 (third edition revised and enlarged), and 1966.

5. Carleton Beals, *Latin America: World in Revolution* (New York, 1963), 55-71, 304-9 (quotation, 71).

6. Tannenbaum, *Struggle*, 193-246.

7. Ibid., 244.

8. Tannenbaum did write a private letter to Cárdenas, warning of the possible consequence of too much emphasis on industry at the expense of agriculture. See Tannenbaum to Cárdenas, Nov. 8, 1937, Tannenbaum Papers.

9. Tannenbaum, *Struggle*, 71-101.

10. Ibid., 49-55.

11. Ibid., 179-80.

12. Ibid., 242.

13. Nathaniel Whetten, *Rural Mexico* (Chicago 1948), vii-ix.

14. Ibid., 182-281, 401-53, 523-72.

15. Ralph Beals, *Cheran: A Tarascan Village* (Washington, D.C., 1945), 212-13; and Redfield, *Village That Chose Progress*.

16. Redfield, *Village That Chose Progress*, 176.

17. Ibid., 178.

18. Oscar Lewis, *Life in a Mexican Village: Tepoztlán Restudied* (Urbana,Ill., 1951), 428, 435.

19. Redfield, review of Chase's *Mexico, International Journal of Ethics* 42 (1931-32): 354.

20. Lewis, *Life in a Mexican Village*, 447-8.

21. Oscar Lewis, *Five Families* (New York, 1959), and *The Children of Sánchez* (New York, 1961). For Lewis's 1940-60 overview of broader trends in Mexican society, see his "Mexico since Cárdenas" in *Social Change in Latin America Today: Its Implications for United States Policy*, ed. Richard N. Adams, John P. Gillin, et al. (New York, 1960), 285-345. See also Ralph Beals, review of Lewis's *Life in a Mexican Village*, in *American Sociological Review* 16 (Dec. 1951): 895-96; and the Oscar Lewis obituary, *New York Times*, Dec. 18, 1970, p. 42. On the controversy generated by Lewis's concept of a universal "culture of poverty," see Eleanor Burk Leacock, ed., *The Culture of Poverty: A Critique* (New York, 1971); and Susan Rigdon, *The Culture Facade: Art, Science, and Politics in the Work of Oscar Lewis* (Urbana , Ill., 1988).

22. Lewis, *Children of Sánchez*, xxx-xxxi.

23. Robert Redfield, *Peasant Society and Culture* (Chicago, 1956), 137-38. Ralph Beals reached similar unsettling conclusions in discussing cultural change: *An Introduction to Anthropology* (New York, 1965), 735-54.

24. Mosk, *Industrial Revolution in Mexico*, 21-52 (quotation, 52). for more recent studies of Mexico's economic development in this period, see Stephen Haber, *Industry and Underdevelopment: The Industrialization of Mexico, 1890-1940* (Stanford, Calif., 1989); and Enrique Cárdenas, "The Great Depression and Industrialization: The Case of Mexico," in *Latin America in the 1930s: The Role of the Periphery in World Crises*, ed. Rosemary Thorp (London, 1984), 222-41.

25. Cárdenas, "Great Depression," 222. For a more extensive treatment of agricultural trends, see Whetten, *Rural Mexico*.

26. Vernon, *Dilemma of Mexico's Development*, 176-93.

27. Herring, *History of Latin America*, 376-77.

28. Ibid., 387.

29. Charles Cumberland, *Mexican Revolution: Genesis under Madero* (Austin, Tex., 1952), 253.

30. Ibid., 208-28, 244-59; and Stanley Ross, *Francisco I. Madero: Apostle of Mexican Democracy* (New York, 1955), esp 80-130, 330-40.

31. Charles Cumberland, *Mexico: The Struggle for Modernity* (New York, 1968), 322.

32. Stanley Ross, "Mexico: The Preferred Revolution," in *Politics of Change in Latin America*, ed. Joseph Maier and Richard Weatherhead (New York, 1964), 140-51 (quotation, 151).

33. Elia Kazan, *A Life* (New York, 1988), 395.

34. Robert E. Morsberger, "Steinbeck's Zapata: Rebel versus Revolutionary," in John Steinbeck, *Viva Zapata!* ed. Robert E. Morsberger (New York, 1975), xxix-xxx. For insightful commentary on this film, see Paul J. Vanderwood, "An American Cold Warrior: Viva Zapata!" in *American History/American Film*, ed. John E. O'Connor and Martin A. Jackson (New York, 1979), 183-201; and Woll, *Latin Image*, 95-99.

35. Steinbeck, *Viva Zapata!* 102.

36. Ibid., 104-5.

Chapter 15. A Relevant Legacy

1. On the competition among ideological and cultural systems, see Jackson Lears, "The Concept of Cultural Hegemony"; Hunt, *Ideology*; Michael Hunt, "Ideology," and Michael J. Hogan, "Corporatism," both in Hogan and Paterson, *Explaining the History*, 193-201, 226-236.

2. Bruckner, *Tears of the White Man*; and Hollander, *Political Pilgrims*, 35-39.

3. Bruckner, *Tears of the White Man*, 100-101.

4. Ibid., 172.

5. Ibid., 171.

6. Simpson to Beals, Sept. 14, 1939, CBC.

7. Ibid.

8. See Hale, *Transformation of Liberalism*; Peter Smith, *Labyrinths of Power* (Princeton, N.J., 1979); Kalmon Silvert, *Man's Power* (New York, 1970); William B. Taylor, "Between Global Process and Local Knowledge: An Inquiry into Early Latin American Social History, 1500-1900," in *Reliving the Past: The Worlds of Social History*, ed. Oliver Zunz (Chapel Hill, N.C., 1985), 115-90; Glen Dealy, *The Public Man* (Amherst, Mass., 1977); Roderic Camp, *Intellectuals and the State in Twentieth Century Mexico* (Austin, Tex., 1985).

9. Skocpol, *States and Social Revolutions*, 173. See also Hamilton, *Limits of State Autonomy*.

10. Dana G. Munro, *The Latin American Republics: A History* New York, 1960), esp. 371-85; Samuel Flagg Bemis, *The Latin American Policy of the United States* (1943; New York, 1971); Graham Stuart, *Latin America and the United States* (New York, 1955), esp. 150-85, 448-61; Jeane Kirkpatrick, *Dictatorships and Double-Standards* (New York, 1982); and Mark Falcoff, *Modern Chile, 1970-1989: A Critical History* (New Brunswick, N.J., 1989).

11. Rosenberg, "Walking the Borders," 30-31.

Bibliography

Unpublished Sources

Personal Papers

Beals, Carleton. Collection. Mugar Library, Boston University, Boston, Mass.

Bolton, Herbert Eugene. Papers. Bancroft Library, University of California, Berkeley.

Brenner, Anita. Collection in the possession of Susannah Glusker. Mexico City.

Cárdenas, Lázaro. Papers. Fondo Lázaro Cárdenas, Centro de Estudios de la Revolución Mexicana Lázaro Cárdenas, Jiquilpan, Michoacán, Mexico.

Egerton, John. Newspaper Clipping Files (on Virginia Prewett), Nashville, Tenn.

Freeman, Joseph. Papers. Hoover Institution, Stanford University, Palo Alto, Calif.

Gates, William. Papers. Howard Tilton Library, Tulane University, New Orleans, La.

Gruening, Ernest. Papers. Elmer E. Rasmuson Library, University of Alaska, Fairbanks.

Inman, Samuel Guy. Papers. Library of Congress, Washington, D.C.

Morrow, Dwight. Papers. Amherst College, Amherst, Mass.

Múgica, Francisco J. Papers. Fondo Francisco J. Múgica, Centró de Estudios de la Revolución Mexicana Lázaro Cárdenas, Jiquilpan, Michoacán, Mexico.

Priestley, Herbert Ingram. Papers. Bancroft Library, University of
    California, Berkeley.
Sheffield, James. Papers, Manuscripts, and Archives. Yale University
    Library, New Haven, Conn.
Tannenbaum, Frank. Papers. Rare Books and Manuscripts Library,
    Columbia University, New York.
Townsend, William Cameron. Papers. Summer Institute of Linguistics,
    JAARS Center, Waxhaw, N.C.
Wolfe, Bertram. Collection. Hoover Institution, Stanford University,
    Palo Alto, Calif.
Wolfe, Bertram. Collection. New York Public Library, New York.

Government Archives

Archivo General de la Nación (Mexican National Archives), Mexico
    City: Presidential Papers of Alvaro Obregón and Plutarco Elías
    Calles, Ramo Obregón-Calles; Emilio Portes Gil, Fondo Portes Gil;
    Lázaro Cárdenas, Fondo Lázaro Cárdenas.
Archivo de Relaciones Exteriores de México (Archive of the Mexican
    Ministry of Foreign Relations), Mexico City.
Archivo de la Palabra (Oral History Archive), Instituto Nacional de
    Antropología e Historia, Mexico City.
U.S. Department of State. Records. National Archives, Washington, D.C.
U.S. War Department. Records. National Archives, Washington, D.C.

Author's Interviews and Correspondence

Beals, Carleton. Interviews with author, January 7-8, June 4-8 and, 11-15,
    July 1-2, 1973, Killingworth, Conn.
Beals, Ralph. Interview with author, July 6, 1975, Los Angeles.
Borah, Woodrow. Letter to author, Sept. 10, 1988; telephone interviews
    with author, July 23-24, 1988, Berkeley and Dublin, Calif.
Couturier, Edith. Letter to author, July 22, 1991.
Glusker, Susannah. Interview with author, May 12, 1988, Mexico City.
Gruening, Ernest. Interview with author, March 20, 1974, Washington,
    D.C.; letters to author, Sept. 20 and Oct. 11, 1973.
Hale, Charles. Letter to author, May 21, 1990.
Porter, Katherine Anne. Letter to author, Jan. 28, 1976.
Wolfe, Ella. Interview with author, July 24, 1984, Palo Alto, Calif.; letter
    to author, July 30, 1984.

Dissertations

Beelen, George D. "Harding and Mexico: Diplomacy by Economic Per-
    suasion." Kent State University, 1971.
Christopulos, Diane. "American Radicals and the Mexican Revolu-
    tion, 1900-1925." State University of New York at Binghamton,
    1980.

Horn, James J. "Diplomacy by Ultimatum: Ambassador Sheffield and Mexican-American Relations, 1924-1927." State University of New York at Buffalo, 1969.

Ignacias, C. Dennis. "Reluctant Recognition: The United States and the Recognition of Alvaro Obregón of Mexico, 1920-1924." Michigan State University, 1967.

McMullen, Christopher Jay. "Calles and the Diplomacy of Revolution: Mexican-American Diplomatic Relations, 1924-1928." Georgetown University, 1980.

Morgan, Hugh Joseph. "The United States Press Coverage of Mexico during the Presidency of Lázaro Cárdenas, 1934-1940." Southern Illinois University, 1985.

Orgorzaly, Michael A. "Waldo Frank: Prophet of Hispanic Regeneration." University of Notre Dame, 1983.

Pyron, Darden Asbury. "Mexico as an Issue in American Politics." University of Virginia, 1975.

Wood, Kenneth F. "Samuel Guy Inman—His Role in the Evolution of Inter-American Relations." American University, 1962.

Zelman, Donald L. "American Intellectual Attitudes toward Mexico, 1908-1940." Ohio State University, 1969.

Published Sources

Representative Contemporary Works

My purpose here is to provide an annotated list of salient titles on the Mexican revolution in each of the seven ideological categories used in this book. Many of these authors initiated discussions that are relevant to the continuing effort to understand the revolution, and the commentary may give the reader some direction in following this multisided debate.

The most articulate expression of the independent leftist position is Frank Tannenbaum, *Peace by Revolution* (New York, 1933). Although his assessment of the ability of local community to exert influence on the central government and its policies is overly optimistic, Tannenbaum's analysis of the internal dynamics of the revolution is impressive— especially of the generally ambiguous and often noxious effects of the nation-state and national politics on local communities and on their *campesino* leaders who made the perilous journey to Mexico City.

John Kenneth Turner, *Barbarous Mexico* (Chicago, 1910; rpt. Austin, Tex., 1969, with an introduction by Sinclair Snow), condemned the autocratic rule of Porfirio Díaz as an exercise in cruelty, hypocrisy, and deception with the purpose of preserving the regime at the expense of the ordinary people of Mexico. Turner claimed that they were capable of governing themselves and of improving their material existence if they could remove the burden of the dictatorship. His book was a call for the overthrow of the Díaz system, and his condemnation of its political excesses was consistent with his position in the independent left in the 1910s.

Bertram Wolfe's intermittent work as a Communist in Mexico spanned the 1920s and 1930s, but his interest in that nation continued into the last years of his life, even after his commitment to Communism ended in the 1940s. His most influential book, *Three Who Made a Revolution* (New York, 1964), was a study of Lenin, Trotsky, and Stalin which revealed his disillusionment with Russian Communism. Wolfe's interest in Mexico tended to focus on one person, Diego Rivera. Wolfe greatly revised his biography of the Mexican artist, *Diego Rivera: His Life and Times* (New York, 1939), in *The Fabulous Life of Diego Rivera* (New York, 1963). The reader who compares Wolfe's writing on Mexico in the 1920s and 1930s with the second biography of Rivera will quickly notice the more subdued ideological orientation; though obviously no longer Marxist, it is difficult to pinpoint. Wolfe had become an anti-Communist Cold Warrior, but his retrospective writing on Rivera and the Mexico of the 1920s and 1930s has not only an affection for the artist but a low-keyed appreciation for the Mexican revolution as a populist and nationalist movement, far different from the ideological and politico-bureaucratic excesses of Soviet Communism.

The socialists had little to say about the Mexican revolution until the 1930s. Although Eyler Simpson, *The Ejido: Mexico's Way Out* (Chapel Hill, N.C., 1937), contained a sharply worded socialist prescription for the revolution, it was a relatively small part of a 582-page text replete with extensive and detailed descriptions of social and economic conditions, supported by charts and statistics. Simpson's call for a system of ejidal agriculture designed and supported by the nation-state bore considerable resemblance to the policies proposed and generally implemented by Lázaro Cárdenas, whose regime came under the close scrutiny of Nathaniel and Sylvia Weyl in *The Reconquest of Mexico* (New York, 1939). The Weyls, although sympathetic to Cárdenas's efforts and Simpson's prescriptions, wrote a penetrating and sometimes critical evaluation of the government's efforts to implant socialism in Mexico. Verna Carleton Millan's *Mexico Reborn* (Boston, 1939), though not as analytical and ideologically explicit as the Simpson and Weyl works, nonetheless assembled a collection of portraits of radical activists of the middle and late 1930s. These books focus on radical experiments of the 1930s, but Clarence Senior, *Land Reform and Democracy* (Gainesville, Fla., 1958), carries the story into the 1950s. Senior tracks the local and national efforts to build an ejidal operation in the cottonfields of La Laguna in north central Mexico. He studied Laguna from 1937 to 1952, his travels there including summer trips with college students who helped construct rural schools, irrigation systems, and a cotton gin. His sympathy for the *ejido* community is obvious but he employs the methodology of the social sciences to include failures as well as more positive aspects. His study is of particular interest because it covers the intersection of grassroots initiatives and the programs of the national government from the Cárdenas era into the more conservative 1950s.

Henry Bamford Parkes's influence as a liberal statist was extensive largely because of the publication of successive editions of his college textbook, *A History of Mexico* (Boston, 1938, 1950, 1960, 1970). His skepticism about the government's economic policies in land reform and its operation of the oil monopoly PEMEX led him to the judgement in 1960 that, on balance, the revolution had been a failure in its material aspects but that its political and cultural benefits for the peasantry and workers were of lasting importance. Lingering doubts about economic development and democracy in Mexico kept Parkes out of the third world liberalism camp.

For about two decades after the publication of Frank Kluckhohn, *The Mexican Challenge* (New York, 1939), and Virginia Prewett, *Reportage on Mexico* (New York, 1941), liberal capitalist commentary on Mexican affairs was rare. One of the first studies of private-sector business institutions and doctrines was Robert J. Shafer, *Mexican Business Organizations: History and Analysis* (Syracuse, N.Y., 1973). Though Shafer was not himself a polemicist for liberal capitalism, his interviews with practicing business people and his survey of the publications of the Mexican Chamber of Commerce and private-sector corporate reports constitute a sympathetic study of the struggles, problems, and accomplishments of entrepreneurs from the 1940s to the 1960s.

Journalist I.F. Marcosson provided one of the most extensive conservative analyses of the revolution in the 1920s. Marcosson saw a sharp dichotomy in the Calles years. On one side was Calles, the "radical" leader who challenged U.S. capital in Mexico and, by example, U.S. investments throughout Latin America. Marcosson quoted Calles's boast that as First Chief he had implemented "my bolshevism" in his agrarian reform program. Against this alleged radicalism, Marcosson posed the examples of U.S. entrepreneurs: William Greene, who had risen from "cowboy" and "simple prospector" to become head of one of the continent's largest mining corporations; and Edward Doheny, who rose from failure as a gold prospector to organize a large multinational petroleum enterprise. The activities of Greene and Doheny, along with the spread of U.S. culture and values through institutions such as the American Chamber of Commerce in Mexico and the YMCA, provided competition for the "radicalism" of Calles. Marcosson exaggerated Calles's leftist commitments and ignored the unseemly activities of U.S. entrepreneurs in Mexico, but he did produce a defense of unregulated (from either side of the border) business operations and the thrust of U.S. cultural influences. See his seven-part series in the *Saturday Evening*

Post 199 (Feb. 26; March 5, 12, 26; April 2, 9., 16, 1927); his survey of the international oil business in *The Black Golconda* (New York, 1924); and his reminiscences in *Turbulent Years* (1938; rpt. Freeport, N.Y., 1969), 179-99, for an account of his 1926 trip to Mexico.

Very few serious writers continued to use racist terminology like that employed by Richard Harding Davis and Jack London in the early decades of the twentieth century, but more subtle forms of stereotyping and cultural presumptions began to appear in public speeches and on the printed page especially from the likes of Henry Stimson and Adolph Berle. A sophisticated examination of this type of thinking can be found in Frederick Pike, *The United States and Latin America: Myths and Stereotypes of Civilization and Nature* (Austin, Tex., 1992), esp. 221-365. The book's broad purview is based on Pike's remarkably wide range of reading, and the footnotes contain a treasure trove of contemporary sources and historical analysis for further study.

Third world liberalism—the amalgamation of liberal statism and liberal capitalism—found an articulate voice in Frank Brandenburg, whose synthesis of a half-century of Mexican history appeared as *The Making of Modern Mexico* (New York, 1964). Brandenburg stressed Mexico's impressive record of economic growth in the 1950s and the capacity of the elite-controlled Party of the Institutional Revolution (PRI) to work with the nation's business leaders. Although sometimes critical of the business-government tandem, Brandenburg concluded that Mexico's immediate future was promising. Veteran independent leftist Frank Tannenbaum, by 1964 the dean of Mexicanists in the United States, wrote an introduction to Brandenburg's volume that invited the reader to take the work seriously but, at the same time, cast a time-worn leftist stone at centralized authority in Mexico. Tannenbaum agreed that the PRI system "was an improvement upon the politics of Díaz, but it is not a durable political system for a large and growing nation. Political leadership cannot be manufactured. Dr. Brandenburg is kinder to the political machinery than he need be" (Introduction to *The Making of Modern Mexico*, viii).

Selected General Words

On the slippery but important subjects of ideas and ideology, I have relied heavily on Michael Hunt, *Ideology and U.S. Foreign Policy* (New Haven, Conn. 1987), which establishes a firm structure for dealing with an international context; and also Paul Hollander, *Political Pilgrims* (New York, 1981), which provides a provocative analysis of the shortcomings of radical and liberal observers. Other valuable studies include Steven Biel, *Independent Intellectuals in the United States, 1910-1945* (New York, 1992); and John P. Diggins, *The Rise and Fall of the American Left* (New York, 1992). An important work on the left in Latin America in the 1980s and 1990s is Jorge Castañeda's *Utopia Unarmed: The Latin American Left after the Cold War* (New York, 1993).

Richard Neustadt and Ernest R. May, *Thinking in Time* (New York, 1986), is a stimulating discussion of the role of perceptions of history in the process of governmental decision making. Lloyd S. Etheredge uses a similar approach in *Can Governments Learn? American Foreign Policy and the Central American Revolutions* (New York, 1985). David Hackett Fischer, *Historians' Fallacies* (New York, 19790), a classic study of the pitfalls in historical thinking, has application to the analytical efforts of observers in other fields as well.

A balanced overview of many of the leading approaches to the study of revolution is Michael S. Kimmel, *Revolution: A Sociological Interpretation* (Philadelphia, 1990). Among other useful general works, Theda Skocpol, *States and Social Revolutions* (Cambridge, Mass., 1979), emphasizes the role of governments; Immanuel Wallerstein, *The Modern World System*, 3 vol. (New York, 1974, 1980; San Diego, 1989), emphasizes economic factors. James H. Billington, *Fire in the Minds of Men: Origins of Revolutionary Faith* (New York, 1980), concentrates on ideas, religiosity, and personal idiosyncrasies in movements from the French Revolution to the Russian Revolution. Another perspective emphasizes local and regional bases of revolution among peasants and workers. In this area, see James C. Scott, *The Moral Economy of the Peasant* (New Haven, Conn., 1976); Eric Wolfe, *Peasant Wars of the Twentieth Century* (New York, 1969); Michael Adas, *Prophets of Rebellion: Millenarian Protest Movements against the European Colonial Order*, (Chapel Hill, N.C., 1979); and Craig Calhoun. *The Question of Class Struggle* (Chicago, 1982). The moral economy school has much in common with the independent leftists analyzed here.

The Mexican revolution and its aftermath continue to spawn controversy, scholarship, and, with some frequency, scholarly controversy. In the 1970s and 1980s some historians pointed to the shortcomings of Mexico's leaders of the 1920 and 1930s as indications that the movement itself was a failure, a mere revolt rather than a massive change in the nation's basic institutions. Their revisionist studies often saw more naiveté than skepticism in the publications of those who wrote about Mexico in the 1920s and 1930s. Among them are Ramón Eduardo Ruíz, *The Great Rebellion: Mexico 1905-1924* (New York, 1980); Jean Meyer, *La Cristiada* (Mexico, 1973-74); and the series Historia de la Revolución Mexicana, especially Jean Meyer, Enrique Krauze, and Cayetano Reyes, *Estado y sociedad con Calles* (Mexico, 1977). John Hart, *Anarchism and the Mexican Working Class, 1860-1931* (Austin, Tex., 1987), stresses the defeat of the anarchist movement by the Callista state in the 1920s.

Counterrevisionists responded to these revisionist views particularly Alan Knight in *The Mexican Revolution,* 2 vols. (Cambridge, England, 1986); "The Mexican Revolution: 'Bourgeois'? 'Nationalist'? Or Just a 'Great Rebellion'?" *Bulletin of Latin American Research* 4, no. 2 (1985): 1-37; and "Land and Society in Revolutionary Mexico: The Destruction of the Great Hacienda," *Mexican Studies/Estudios Mexicanos* 7 (Winter 1991): 73-104. Knight developed an argument for a broadly based social revolution in which the nation-state was important but only one of many factors.

Historical studies of the U.S. observers and their interpretations of the Mexican revolution began with Eugenia Meyer, *Conciencia histórica norteamericana sobre la Revolución de 1910* (Mexico, 1970); Drewey Wayne Gunn, *American and British Writers in Mexico, 1556-1973* (Austin, Tex., 1974); Donald C. Hodges and Ross Gandy, *Mexico 1910-1976: Reform or Revolution?* (London, 19779); and Henry C. Schmidt, "The American Intellectual Discovery of Mexico in the 1920's," *South Atlantic Quarterly* 77 (Summer 1978): 335-51. More recent works in history and biography include Helen Delpar, *The Enormous Vogue of Things Mexican: Cultural Relations between the United States and Mexico, 1920-1935* (Tuscaloosa, Ala., 1992), and "Frank Tannenbaum: The Making of a Mexicanist, 1914-1933," *Americas* 45 (Oct. 1988): 153-71; Margaret Hooks, *Tina Modotti: Photographer as Revolutionary* (San Francisco, 1993); Ross Parmenter,*Lawrence in Oaxaca* (Salt Lake City, Utah, 1984); John A. Britton, *Carleton Beals: A Radical Journalist in Latin America* (Albuquerque, N.M., 1987); Darlene Harbour Unrue, *Truth and Vision in Katherine Anne Porter's Fiction* (Athens, Ga., 1985); Thomas F. Walsh, *Katherine Anne Porter and Mexico: The Illusion of Eden* (Austin, Tex., 1992); and Heidi Zogbaum, *B. Traven: A Vision of Mexico* (Wilmington, Del., 1992).

Index